By Richard M. Ketchum

The Winter Soldiers

The Battles for Trenton
and Princeton

RICHARD M. KETCHUM

A John Macrae / Owl Book
Henry Holt and Company   New York

for Liza, Casey, and Tom

Henry Holt and Company, LLC
Publishers since 1866
115 West 18th Street
New York, New York 10011

Henry Holt® is a registered trademark
of Henry Holt and Company, LLC.

Library of Congress Cataloging-in-Publication Data
Ketchum, Richard M.
The winter soldiers: the battles for Trenton and Princeton /
Richard M. Ketchum.—1st Owl books ed.
p. cm.
"A John Macrae / Owl book."
Originally published: New York: Doubleday, 1973.
Includes bibliographical references and index.
ISBN 0-8050-6098-7
1. United States. Continental Army. 2. United States—History—
Revolution, 1775–1783—Campaigns. 3. Trenton, Battle of, 1776.
4. Princeton, Battle of, 1777. I. Title.
E259.K47 1999   98-55352
973.3'32—dc21   CIP

Henry Holt books are available for special promotions and
premiums. For details contact: Director, Special Markets.

First published in hardcover in 1973 by Doubleday

First Owl Books Edition 1999

A John Macrae / Owl Book

Maps by Raphael Palacios

Printed in the United States of America

6 8 10 9 7

CONTENTS

THE WINTER SOLDIERS

CHAPTER ONE

1. A Gentleman from England with Genius in His Eyes

In the raw, unsightly camps west of the Hudson the American army was in trouble. Early in October 1776 a New York militia colonel who suffered with the name of Ann Hawkes Hay poured out his problem to Peter Livingston, the president of the New York Convention in Fishkill. Almost half of his regiment at Haverstraw, Hay reported, lacked weapons and he wondered what in the world he should do or where he could look for reinforcements if the enemy attempted a landing there. He was short of money to pay his men and a few days earlier he had been unable to collect more than thirty-eight of them together, even after repeated summons to duty. Several British cutters had sailed upriver and fired at the shore, damaging Hay's own house and taking away a piece of the hat he was wearing, but despite this real and present danger his soldiers complained that if they left their farms their families would starve; there had been no opportunity to harvest corn or buckwheat and they had been so busy all summer with what Hay called the "publick troubles" that there had not been time to sow winter grain. Worse yet, some of them felt that the Congress in Philadelphia had done the country no favor by rejecting the British government's overtures for reconciliation; all his men cared about, Hay said, was "peace, liberty, and safety," and if they could only have that, they would be content.

When Hay took his griefs to Major General Nathanael Greene, who commanded Fort Lee on the crest of the New Jersey Palisades, Greene considered them worrisome enough to bring to the attention of the commander in chief, George Washington, even though he intended to settle the matter himself. Greene was an independence man through and through, and he made it clear to Hay that he had no patience with the men's grousing. If they didn't follow orders, Hay should send them down to Fort Lee, where Greene would see that they did.

Actually, Greene had a morale problem too. The number of men stationed near the fort varied anywhere from 200 to 2,000, and the presence of that many additional people in a farm community was bound to create friction. When Lieutenant Joseph Hodgkins of the Massachusetts Line wrote to his wife on September 30, he said that he had been in the area for ten days and would be glad to stay longer: "I have been at the trouble of building a log house with a stone chimney," he told her. "I got it fit to live in three days ago, before which I had not lodged on anything but the ground." The difficulty was that those logs, like many others that had gone into soldiers' huts, came from one of the nearby farms. In this neighborhood the fences were laid up French style, five rails high, one on top of another, and nothing could be handier for building. A farmer named Peter Bourdet, whose rocky, wooded land had been cleared for the construction of Fort Lee during the summer, complained that the fences around 125 acres of his pasture had been torn down by the troops and that he had lost three acres of corn and four of flax and oats as well. A lot of the soldiers were sick and so many more were deserting that Hugh Mercer, who was in charge of a mobile reserve known as the Flying Camp, near Perth Amboy, doubted if Washington could muster five thousand dependable troops. He feared the worst if the poorly armed, badly disciplined militiamen he had seen, who were "perpetually fluctuating between the camp and their farms," had to face General William Howe's British veterans.

Yet, as George Washington assured his old friend Mercer, it was not entirely the men's fault; after all, "Men who have been free, and subject to no control, cannot be reduced to order in an instant." All this confusion was the natural result of inexperience, and inexperience was what the Continental Army seemed to have most of in the fall of 1776. It had been in existence for little more than a year and as yet few soldiers had any real training or knowledge of military matters, and their officers were not much better off. Mercer, who was now a brigadier general, had been a physician in Fredericksburg, Virginia, until a year before. Nathanael Greene, who had served in a Providence, Rhode Island, militia company, had seen no active service until May of 1775. And eighteen months later, as he tried to cope with the never-ending series of problems involving the troops, Greene began to wonder if there would ever be any leisure time in which to reflect upon matters of great importance when he had to devote so many hours to paper work. It was this that "confines my thoughts as well as engrosses my time," he grumbled. "It is like a merchandise of small wares." Fortunately, within the past month Greene had found someone to help him with letters and reports, and a highly unusual aide-de-camp he was. The Rhode Island officer's reputation for impulsiveness didn't fully explain his choice of an Englishman who had been in the colonies for less than two years, who was also a civilian with no military experience. But Greene was desperate for help and he was undoubtedly pleased to acquire a staff member who was one of the most celebrated figures in America.

The new arrival had spent some time in Philadelphia, where he had impressed a number of people, including one of the Massachusetts delegates to the Continental Congress, John Adams. "His name is Paine," Adams wrote to a friend, "a gentleman about two years from England—a man who, General Lee says, has genius in his eyes." Genius might be there, but what was more quickly apparent behind the dark, penetrating eyes, beaked nose, and a sensuous mouth that threatened to break into a grin at any moment was an impression that the fellow was looking through you, probing to see what was there. It was not easy to be comfortable in the presence of this Paine.

If ever there was a case of an individual and an idea that came together at the right moment, Thomas Paine was it. He had been driven to the New World by a succession of personal failures and a festering hatred for the society which had brought them about. The son of a poor Thetford corset maker, he had picked up a rudimentary education before going to work for his father as an apprentice staymaker—an occupation he disliked so intensely that he ran away from home at sixteen, went to sea, and served aboard a privateer in the Seven Years' War. Sick of that, he jumped ship and turned up in London, to work at various jobs—staymaker, cobbler, cabinetmaker, tax collector, along with brief sallies into other fields, always skating on the thin edge of defeat, barely avoiding debtors' prison. His first marriage, to a servant girl, ended with his wife's death a year later; a second ended in separation. Like so many other Englishmen, Paine was a victim of enclosure laws enacted two centuries earlier which had remorselessly forced thousands of small farmers off the land

and into the cities. There the luckier, more adaptable ones formed the nucleus of a working class for the industries beginning to spring up in English towns. The less fortunate turned to begging or thieving or worse: in the streets of London Tom Paine witnessed every form of human degradation—murder, drunkenness, brutality, starvation. Not a day passed, he said, but that he saw "ragged and hungry children, and persons of seventy and eighty years of age, begging in the streets." Workers were reduced to serfs, a rigid, inequitable class system marked men for life, and the lower classes were brutalized by a savage criminal code that would hang a ten-year-old boy for stealing a penknife or permit women to be stoned to death in the pillory. Epidemics of disease were a commonplace in the vile, stinking slums; infant mortality was unbelievably high; and with death its handmaiden, life was cheap. Somehow or other, Paine managed to stay afloat in the murky cesspool of lower-class London; somehow he wangled an introduction to the famous Benjamin Franklin and obtained a letter of recommendation from the American ambassador extraordinary; and somehow he left England in October 1774, bound for a new land and a new tomorrow.

Writing to his son-in-law, Richard Bache, Franklin described the Englishman as "an ingenious worthy young man" who might make "a clerk, or assistant tutor in a school, or assistant surveyor." Through Bache's efforts Paine found employment with Robert Aitken, a Philadelphia printer and bookseller who had started a publication called *The Pennsylvania Magazine*. By the time Paine got around to writing his thanks to Franklin three months after his arrival in America, he was able to inform his benefactor that he was the editor of the publication and that circulation had risen from 600 to 1,500 under his stewardship. Paine, it was clear, had a keen ear for what was going on around him; the Philadelphians he met treated him as a sounding board, for he was a recently arrived Englishman to whom they could pour out their grievances over government policy, a man eager to discuss ideas and to sop up the best of them like a sponge.

The London years had left an abiding mark on Paine, a nagging conscience that would make him speak out again and again for the oppressed, and one of the first articles he wrote for the magazine was an attack on the institution that was already beginning to trouble thoughtful Americans. Called "African Slavery in America," it brought him to the attention of Dr. Benjamin Rush, the prominent young physician and reformer. Soon

John Wesley Jarvis' portrait of Thomas Paine caught the intensity of the man whose writings possessed such concentrated fury, but there is little here to support the description of the pamphleteer in later years as "loathsome in his appearance." John Adams thought him a genius, but distrusted him and called *Common Sense* too "democratical." *(National Gallery of Art, Washington, D.C.)*

Rush was urging Paine to turn his mind to the matter of independence from Britain (even in 1775 the doctor's profession and connections prevented him from coming forward personally as a spokesman in that controversy), but Paine hesitated to use the pages of the magazine in this way; for one thing, Aitken was too timid to risk offending his conservative subscribers; for another, Paine himself—like most native Americans —believed that the differences between the colonies and the mother country could still be reconciled. Or so he thought until events outside Boston on April 19, 1775, persuaded him that "all plans, proposals, etc." to patch up the quarrel were "like the almanacks of the last year; which though proper then, are superceded and useless now." In the months following the battles at Lexington, Concord, and Bunker Hill, when George Washington of Virginia was appointed commander in chief of the colonial army and the British forces sat sullenly in Boston besieged by a ragtag mob of New England farmers and tradesmen, Paine found it increasingly difficult to understand how a war could be going on in Massachusetts while Pennsylvania and the other colonies were so little affected.

When Tom Paine had landed in America on November 30, 1774, the long-simmering dispute between England and her possessions in North America was coming to a head—a situation made to order for a passionate, articulate man who was also an uncompromising zealot. Sensing that the country was already "set on fire about my ears," he decided "it was time to stir." Even if Americans did not realize that the moment for action was nigh, the expatriate Englishman did, for as he perceived the situation, "Those who had been long settled had something to defend; those who had just come had something to pursue." Here he found few of the class distinctions that so divided England; here the abundance of land had produced a class of independent farmers; here merchants and planters— men of some wealth—who had felt themselves exploited and excluded by Britain's colonial policies, were aligning themselves politically with the farmers and tradesmen. And, as it happened, Paine's arrival coincided with a period of almost unbearable tension: five months after he began work in Philadelphia fighting broke out between the colonists and the king's troops. Into this tinderbox Tom Paine tossed a spark that turned a disorganized rebellion into the overthrow of an entire social and political system. Through the summer and early fall of 1775, Paine turned his mind increasingly to the idea of independence, and on October 18 he published an article called "A Serious Thought," in which he spoke out boldly for separation from England. In December he asked Benjamin Rush to read a draft of a pamphlet he had written, and Rush urged him to show it to Franklin, Samuel Adams, and David Rittenhouse, three staunch "friends to American independence." Paine's employer, Robert Aitken, refused to publish the manuscript, which was too incendiary for his taste, but a small printer named Robert Bell was persuaded to do so, and on January 10, 1776, the fifty-page pamphlet appeared. Rush had suggested that Paine call it "Common Sense."

The argument between government and the governed had gone on for so long and with such increasing vehemence that it is hard to realize how few Americans had reached the stage of advocating separation from England. Yet in March 1775 Benjamin Franklin—who probably knew as much about the attitudes of his countrymen as anyone—could assure William Pitt, now Earl of Chatham, that "he had never heard in any conversation from any person drunk or sober the least expression of a wish for separation or hint that such a thing would be advantageous to America." With the exception of a few radicals in the colonies (who knew better than to risk losing moderate support by advocating independence), no one took the idea very seriously. Even after blood was shed at Lexington and Concord; even after the grisly business at Bunker Hill, which made it virtually certain that a war of some kind would be fought; even after the Continental Congress had created an army and appointed a commanding general, there was still no real ground swell for separation. In August 1775 Thomas Jefferson stated that he was "looking with fondness towards a reconciliation with Great Britain," adding that he "would rather be in dependence on Great Britain, properly limited, than on any nation on earth, or on no nation." And the following January the Maryland Convention took a firm stand against independence, citing the "experience we and our ancestors have had of the mildness and equity of the English Constitution, under which we have grown up to and enjoyed a state of felicity not exceeded by any people we know of." Americans on the whole were not thinking seriously of independence; they were also loyal to their king, whom they considered a benevolent man who would do right by America if it were not for his advisers. Colonial wrath took the form of animosity to George III's ministers, those "enemies to the freedom of the human race, like so many Master devils in the infernal regions."

What altered the situation so drastically was the sudden, widespread acceptance of the ideas put forward in *Common Sense*. Paine was not the first man to call for independence, but he did so at the critical moment, in words that precisely suited the passions of the hour. *Common Sense* gave tongue to the innermost thoughts of men in every colony—merchant and farmer, lawyer, soldier, delegate to the Continental Congress. Shockingly and with unheard-of daring, Paine attacked King George as a "hardened, sullen-tempered Pharaoh" and "the Royal Brute of Great Britain." He assailed the very principle of hereditary monarchy, proclaimed the need for separation of mother country and colonies, denounced the British ruling group for exploiting the lower classes in America and England alike, and urged the colonists to declare their independence and make their land a refuge for Europe's downtrodden. Not only did Paine appeal to the American liberal; realizing that he must attract conservatives to the cause, he argued that independence would make it possible for the colonies to remain aloof from Europe's wars, take advantage of its beckoning markets, and obtain foreign aid. Since the founding of Jamestown there had been fifteen conflicts in which—with few exceptions—the great powers had participated, an average of one war every generation, and the American colonists had been drawn willy-nilly into these European struggles for trade and empire. "Europe is too thickly planted with kingdoms to be long at peace," Paine warned his readers, "and whenever a war breaks out between England and any foreign power, the trade of America goes to ruin, *because of her connection with Britain* . . . Everything that is right or reasonable pleads for separation. The blood of the slain, the weeping voice of nature cries, *'Tis time to part.*"

Offering his adopted countrymen a vision of what the future might hold, Paine assured them that "the sun never shined on a cause of greater worth. 'Tis not the affair of a city, a county, a province, or a kingdom; but of a continent—of at least one-eighth part of the habitable globe. 'Tis not the concern of a day, a year, or an age; posterity are virtually involved in the contest, and will be more or less affected even to the end of time by the proceedings now. Now is the seedtime of continental union, faith, and honor." Considering the relatively primitive state of communications, there was something almost magical about the speed with which the revolutionary call to arms flew across the colonies. Paine, who gave the money due him as the author's share to charity and even printed 6,000 at his own expense, said the pamphlet sold 120,000 copies within three months; others estimated that half a million were printed. Since there were no copyright laws, pirated editions appeared everywhere; there were even translations into German, French, and Dutch. In terms of the proportionate population it reached, *Common Sense* was the greatest best seller ever published in America—a book exactly appropriate for its particular moment in time. Where others had set men to thinking in abstract terms about freedom, Tom Paine called them to action, urging them to fight for liberty. His arguments were simple, impassioned, and cast in the homely terms every American could understand. Quoting extensively from the Old Testament, Paine reminded men of the words that had thundered down from colonial pulpits; he preached logic and common sense while appealing to the passions and to prejudice.

From Cambridge, Massachusetts, where the army was encamped at the time, George Washington wrote to his friend Joseph Reed, predicting that "the sound doctrine and unanswerable reasoning of 'Common Sense' will not leave numbers at a loss to decide upon the propriety of a separation." Two months later he informed Reed that letters from Virginia indicated that Paine's message was "working a powerful change there in the minds of men." There were, as expected, heated attacks on the pamphlet by those who remained loyal to king and Parliament; but by late spring of 1776 the effects of *Common Sense* were evident everywhere, in the swelling tide of public feeling that moved inexorably toward independence.

2. *The River Is Passed, and the Bridge Cut Away*

With pomp and solemn pageant, Parliament had opened at Westminster on October 26, 1775. His Majesty George III, seated on the throne in his crown and regal ornaments, addressed the members of both Houses in words that left no doubt as to his intentions. The harsh, uncompromising tone of the speech was set in his opening remarks, in an angry attack on those Americans who had inflamed his colonial subjects by "gross misrepresentations" and by infusing in their minds "a system of opinions repugnant to the true constitution of the Colonies," so that they now "openly avow their revolt, hostility, and rebellion." As the M.P. William Innes declared after hearing the king speak, the ringleaders of this mischief in North America were few in number, and if they could only be got hold of they deserved no mercy. Once they were out of the way it should be a simple matter to convince "the lower class" in America that the liberty those people were so fond of talking about could not compare with what they already enjoyed under the British Constitution.

What neither the king nor the M.P. comprehended was that not all of the dissidents in America were of the same stripe. In fact, the reverse was true: George III might lump them together and call them rash, violent demagogues, but with the exception of a few men like Samuel Adams of Boston and Patrick Henry of Virginia, the emerging political leaders in America were prudent, judicious, and sincerely concerned about where their actions might lead. Had the king been more attentive, he might have seen that the radical movement, between 1770 and 1773, was in danger of being ignored to death by the vast majority of colonists; only after the Boston Tea Party did the radicals succeed in persuading the major colonies to send representatives to an assembly known as the First Continental Congress, where their mutual grievances were discussed.

Before *Common Sense* crystallized a large segment of public opinion, representatives to the Second Continental Congress had declared the necessity of taking up arms and had created an army and navy, yet at the same time they were continuing to petition London for reconciliation. This apparent ambiguity reflected to some extent the general fear of what democratic ideas might produce once they were unleashed. The word "democracy" had a different connotation in those days—it suggested civil disorder and mob rule, the kind of rowdiness so evident in annual celebrations of the Boston "massacre," to men like the Reverend Andrew Eliot, who fretted about the "many inconveniences which would attend frequent popular elections." John Dickinson, who had studied law in England, felt the same way. And what worried him was that reforms were unlikely to be achieved through moderation. Beyond such vague fears, however, what most troubled thoughtful men in the colonies was the very nature of the imperial relationship with Britain, especially as it concerned the peculiar nature of America's political structure.

At the time the colonies were founded, British institutions of government had been imported and reproduced in miniature; but whereas in the mother country those institutions had been modified and expanded to meet the needs of changing times, in the colonies they had tended to move in the opposite direction—to contract and be simplified, to drift toward a more medieval form of local representation. Town and county governing bodies had little reason to identify with the embracing imperial structure; representatives serving in them voiced local concerns rather than the problems of empire. Local agencies maintained order, local courts administered justice, local governments made the laws that circumscribed daily life. And most important, the colonial assemblies exercised the power of taxation and had done so for as long as men could recall with no interference or competition from Parliament. So government in the American possessions had come to be a highly decentralized, parochial arrangement, functioning within a loose framework known as the empire with a kind of mystical attachment to it based on loyalty to a distant regal authority.

The attitude of the First Continental Congress had been clearly expressed by John Dickinson, a polite, advertent lawyer from Philadelphia. Dickinson maintained that British sovereignty over the colonies must be limited, that a line must be drawn to distinguish parliamentary authority from that of the colonial assemblies. In this view, London would control the colonies' commercial and foreign affairs, while jurisdiction over internal matters—including, most especially, taxation—remained the "exclusive right" of provincial legislatures. (The king and his ministers, as might be expected, agreed with Dr. Samuel Johnson's pronouncement that "in sovereignty there are no gradations.") For a decade and more, along the sparsely settled coast of British North America, farmers, artisans, scholars, merchants, and professional men had been wrestling conscientiously with this fundamental issue of sovereignty, a word whose meaning was shaded by questions relating to proper representation, the consent of the governed, the inherent rights of individuals, and the nature of compacts between men. These Americans were acutely aware of the role that power played in human affairs; the location and use of power in government, they realized, lay behind all political issues. What gave it such overriding importance in their view was that the natural victims of power gone wrong were liberty and law—in short, the rights of man. Power in itself was not evil; indeed, it was a condition of the contracts mutually agreed to by subject and sovereign for men's governance. The trouble was that men in authority tend to accumulate more power and to misuse it to the point where liberty, as John Adams phrased it, might only be found at last "skulking about in corners . . . hunted and persecuted." And liberty, Adams wrote, "can no more exist without virtue and independence than the body can live and move without a soul." This was an attitude that had convinced many political thinkers that there was something quite special about America. What was at stake here, they believed, was far more than the cause of a mob or a faction—it was the cause of the liberties of mankind.

Take, for instance, the question of slavery.

At first, these colonial philosophers had talked much of slavery—by which they meant the plight of men tyrannized by government, as when they were taxed without their own consent. Slavery was the ultimate political degradation, and a man was better off to dine on a turnip and be a free man, a Massachusetts pamphleteer declared, than to live in luxury and be a slave. But inevitably this kind of discussion led to another set of considerations altogether—to the realities of the enslaved black population in their midst and to the contradictions thus made manifest between principles of freedom professed theoretically on the one hand and the harsh facts of life on the other. As the Virginian Patrick Henry saw it, the "general inconvenience of living here without them" made the freeing of slaves impractical in the southern colonies, yet it was impossible to ignore the contradiction implicit in maintaining the peculiar institution "at a time when the rights of humanity are defined and understood with precision in a country above all others fond of liberty." And the fiery James Otis asked, "Does it follow that 'tis right to enslave a man because he is black? Will short curled hair like wool instead of Christian hair . . . help the argument?" The slave trade was a shocking violation of the law of nature, he stated, which diminished the value of liberty and "makes every dealer in it a tyrant." So those local governing bodies, the colonial assemblies, had begun to take matters into their own hands on this, along with other vital questions. The Massachusetts assembly in 1774 had voted to abolish the slave trade (a decision negated by veto of the royal governor); Rhode Island, declaring that "those who are desirous of enjoying all the advantages of liberty themselves should be willing to extend personal liberty to others," ruled that any slaves imported into the colony would be freed; Connecticut did likewise; Delaware prohibited importation; and Pennsylvania taxed the slave trade out of existence.

If there was seeming agreement on certain issues in the thirteen colonies, it had been a long time coming. For more than a century the British dominions in North America had been divided into a number of small, detached jurisdictions. Individual colonies were isolated from each other by an administrative system controlled from England and by differences of background, economic interest, and social and religious persuasion as well. Southerners regarded New Englanders as rascally sharpers; northern farmers and traders considered the planters loose-living infidels; boundary disputes set one region against another; while their separate trade with England drew each closer to the mother country than to its immediate neighbors. An English visitor to the colonies at the time of George III's accession to the throne found that "fire and water are not more heterogeneous than the different colonies in North America . . . In short, such is the difference of character, of manners, of religion, of interest [that] were they left to themselves, there would soon be a civil war from one end of the continent to the other; while the Indians and negroes would, with better reason, impatiently watch the opportunity of exterminating them all together." Peopled by prickly dissenters, the colonies were jealous of each other and seemed quite incapable of uniting for any common purpose. Indeed, even when their lives and homes were threatened, as they had been in the French and Indian War, the governor of Pennsylvania observed that, to their shame, they refused at the time of General Braddock's defeat to contribute to the defense of their country by establishing a militia or furnishing men, money, or provisions.

Despite all their differences, circumstances had begun to unite a growing number of colonists who found that they had similar views about many things. In part this was the result of improving communications: the postal system (established by the mother country) had made them more aware of each other's existence when like-minded men in different parts of the country began corresponding; merchant vessels coasting along the Atlantic seaboard from one port to another established friendly connections; newspapers and pamphlets circulated from one colony to the next; stages rattling over a growing network of roads bore ideas along with their passengers. And at the same time, the policies of George III and his ministers had succeeded in fraying the fragile strands that tied the separate colonies to the government in London. Affection for the mother country deteriorated with each new restrictive measure that was enacted, while provincial isolation and sectional differences began to be submerged in a growing concern over larger matters.

In the spring of 1776, while Paine's little pamphlet circulated through America spreading the contagion of independence, it began to appear that there was little hope of ever reconciling colonial views with those of the government. The ministry in London had closed off New England's fisheries, colonial trade came to a standstill, American ships were seized by the Royal Navy, and there were ugly, recurring reports that George III was seeking military assistance in the form of Russian and German mercenaries to suppress the uprising in the colonies. It was said that Lord Dunmore, the royal governor of Virginia, was intriguing with Indians to attack the frontier and was holding secret meetings with Negro slaves urging them to cut their masters' throats. Suspicion and rumor fed on the growing distrust of government, while the rush of events was putting independence men in the saddle locally. For although conservatives in the Continental Congress might continue to oppose independence, the fact was that the colonies were fighting an undeclared war with England. Canada had been invaded by troops under Richard Montgomery and Benedict Arnold, George Washington's motley army had forced the British troops to evacuate Boston, and Congress had issued letters of marque to privateers. In May Congress suggested that the colonial assemblies decide whether they should establish governments whose authority derived from the people rather than the king. (This step was thought necessary since George III had excluded the colonists from the protection of his crown, had given them no answer to petitions for redress of their grievances, and had made known his intention of exerting "the whole force of his Kingdom, aided by foreign mercenaries . . . for the destruction of the good people of these Colonies.") A secret committee of Congress had sent out feelers for a French alliance, dispatching Silas Deane* to ferret

* Deane, the son of a Connecticut blacksmith, graduated from Yale in 1758 and rapidly improved his financial and social lot by means of two successful marriages. He became a delegate to the First and Second Continental Congresses, but as a consequence of neglecting his political fences at home, he was not reappointed by the Connecticut Assembly for 1776. Congress, not wishing to waste his talents, decided to send him to France as the representative of two secret committees, to sound out the possibilities of military assistance. The convoluted story of his mission does not belong here, beyond

out the attitude of the Comte de Vergennes, France's foreign minister. Yet for some reason, despite all this unbridled activity, Congress continued to drag its feet on the central issue of separation from England.

It was increasingly apparent that the militants who controlled most colonial assemblies had run out of patience with irresolution in Philadelphia and that they were going to force the move toward independence if Congress did not. As Joseph Hawley wrote to the Boston delegate, Sam Adams, "The People are now ahead of you and the only way to prevent discord and dissension is to strike while the iron is hot. The Peoples blood is too Hot to admit of delays— All will be in confusion if independence is not declared immediately. The Tories take courage and Many Whiggs begin to be chagrined . . ." What is our Congress about? Hawley wished to know; it seemed to be on dead center, dozing and dreaming and waiting for commissioners to arrive from England to discuss an accommodation. Charles Lee, a former British officer who had embraced the rebel cause, told Richard Henry Lee, a Virginia delegate, "If you do not declare immediately for positive independence, we are all ruined. There is a poorness of spirit and languor in the late proceedings of Congress, that I confess frightens me so much that at times I regret having embarked my all, my fortune, life, and reputation, in their bottom. I sometimes wish I had settled in some country of slaves, where the most lenient master governs."

Typical of what was happening in the back country were the deliberations of a group of citizens from Buckingham County, Virginia. A state convention had been summoned to discuss this problem of establishing new governments, and representatives of the county had come together to determine how they would instruct their delegates. The conclusions they reached indicated how far the Virginians had moved toward the idea of separation from England. Enumerating their grievances, they stated flatly that the root of the trouble was lack of confidence in the government; it had been "annihilated," they said, and there was no prospect of restoring it. What these Buckingham County men found so distressing was that the

---

mention of the fact that shipments of arms by the dummy firm of Hortalez & Cie. (see page 43) were in large measure the fruit of his efforts. An ambitious man with strong commercial instincts and a notable streak of cupidity, Deane was subsequently accused of profiteering, incompetence, and treason as a result of his dealings abroad. In 1778 he was recalled to explain his financial transactions, returned to Europe two years later, and finally lost confidence in the American cause. He lived on as a bankrupt exile in France and England and died in 1789 a thoroughly embittered man.

loyalty they once felt toward their king (a loyalty admittedly washed with wishful thinking) had been destroyed by George III's own speeches; clearly he was not the dupe of ministers or Parliament, as they had formerly believed. So the delegates, Charles Patteson and John Cabell, were advised to keep their minds firmly fixed on the primary object of independence and not lose themselves in hankering after reconciliation. "As far as your voices will contribute," they were told, use them to "cause a total and final separation from Great Britain, to take place as soon as possible." What Buckingham County wanted was "a free and happy constitution . . . with a renunciation of the old, and so much thereof as has been found inconvenient and oppressive." Then, voicing a hope that was in the minds of so many Americans, their instructions touched on the matter of foreign assistance. No other nation was likely to intercede as long as the quarrel remained in the family, between subject and subject, but if the idea of reconciliation were abandoned and the colonies "bid the last adieu" to England, then "some foreign powers may, for their own interest, lend an assisting hand, settle a trade, and enable us to discharge the great burdens of the war, which otherwise may become intolerable." On May 15, 1776, at Williamsburg, Patteson, Cabell, and other spokesmen for the most powerful and populous colony passed a unanimous resolution in favor of independence.

The capital, accustomed to the presence of a royal governor and the trappings of empire, was capable of laying on a highly acceptable pageant when occasion warranted, and this was clearly one of those times. A week after the historic vote, independence sympathizers in Williamsburg turned out to celebrate. The train of artillery rumbled onto a field beyond the powder magazine, where gun crews put on a smart display of loading and firing a proper salute; militia companies stepped out on parade to a brisk rattle of drums and tootle of fifes; and a "Continental union" flag was hoisted over the austere capitol—thirteen red and white stripes, with the crosses of St. George and St. Andrew on a blue canton, shimmering in the May breeze. At day's end, in the deepening twilight, the windows of houses all over town suddenly glowed with light—first one, then another, then two or three more—until the sides of the streets were bathed with soft yellow candlelight. It was the housewives' own offering to the brave new world.

While their fellow Virginians were congratulating themselves, two delegates to the Continental Congress—Richard Henry Lee and Thomas Jefferson—were doing their utmost to force Congress to act. What stood in the way was the middle colonies—Maryland, New Jersey, and Pennsylvania, particularly—which, as Lee grumbled, "certainly obstruct and perplex the American Machine." Despite mounting evidence that substantial numbers of people were leaning toward a break ("Every Post and every Day rolls in upon Us Independence like a Torrent," John Adams exclaimed), the cautious members from the middle colonies procrastinated and temporized, arguing that the time was not ripe for severing the British connection. But in the early summer of 1776 their backs were to the wall. Led by John Dickinson of Maryland and James Wilson of Pennsylvania, and James Duane and John Jay of New York, the moderates were forced to make a stand when Lee introduced a resolution on June 7 at the urging of Virginia's state convention that the "united Colonies are, and of right ought to be, free and independent States." Conservatives called for postponement of the vote on this critical matter; they had no authority to decide on such a resolution, they said, and—in what proved a final show of strength—won a delay until July 1. As it turned out, postponement was fatal; on June 14, Connecticut and Delaware instructed their delegates to vote for independence; New Hampshire and New Jersey followed; and on June 28, Maryland had a change of heart.

After Lee's resolution was put off, and before the five other colonies came into line, Congress appointed a committee of five to draft a declaration of independence, naming John Adams, Benjamin Franklin, Thomas Jefferson, Robert Livingston, and Roger Sherman as members. The committee decided to give the job of writing the statement to Jefferson, one of the youngest and newest members of Congress, who was already well known for his views on colonial rights. He also had a reputation, a fellow delegate wrote, "for literature, science, and a happy talent for composition," and his "peculiar felicity of expression" was thought suited to the task at hand. Tom Paine's friend, Dr. Benjamin Rush, regarded Jefferson as a genius of the first order, knowledgeable about many subjects, and "not only the friend of his country, but of all nations and religions." By rights, since Richard Henry Lee was the ranking member of the Virginia delegation and had introduced the resolution calling for independence, he should have been assigned to the drafting committee. But Lee was not popular among the congressmen; some of them regarded him as self-seeking and vain (it was rumored that he practiced gestures in front of a mirror before giving the speeches for which he was famous), and in any case, Lee wanted to return home on personal business, so Jefferson was named in his stead. John Adams liked to tell why the Virginian, and not he, had been appointed to draft the document. As he explained it to Jefferson, "Reason first—You are a Virginian, and a Virginian ought to appear at the head of this business. Reason second—I am obnoxious, suspected, and unpopular. You are very much otherwise. Reason third—You can write ten times better than I can."

Jefferson was now thirty-three, well over six feet tall, slim and erect, with reddish hair and a tendency to freckle. He had inherited a considerable estate from his father and had increased it through marriage. Insatiably curious, he had taken a classical education at William and Mary and for five years studied law with the most notable legal mind in Virginia, George Wythe. In 1775, when he was sent to Congress as a substitute for Peyton Randolph, the members noticed a certain shyness about him, for he seldom spoke in debate.

In the growing heat of summer, Jefferson spent his days in the house of a young bricklayer named Graff, at the corner of Market and Seventh streets. There were few other buildings in the neighborhood, which led Jefferson to think he might benefit from the freely circulating air there. The lodger had the second floor to himself—bedroom, parlor, and connecting passage—and at times he evidently broke his routine of writing by playing with Graff's infant son, who was told years afterward that he had been dandled on the great man's knee. Working in the parlor at a little portable writing desk he had designed for his own use, Jefferson seems not to have been bothered by the lack of a library; he said that he turned to no book or pamphlet in preparing his draft. He did not regard it as part of his charge to invent new ideas or to offer sentiments that had not been heard before, only "to place before mankind the common sense of the subject, in terms so plain and firm as to command their assent, and to justify ourselves in the independent stand we are compelled to make." This was to be "an expression of the American mind."

Earlier in the month Jefferson had set down his ideas for a desirable government for Virginia and had sent these to his old teacher, George Wythe. In a preamble to that paper he had compiled a list of charges against George III, and he drew upon them now in the second-floor parlor of Graff's house. Before June 28 he copied a four-page rough draft from notes he had been making, showed it to Adams and Franklin, who gave him a few suggestions, and then presented it to the full committee. On July 1 Congress returned to the resolution submitted by Lee and the familiar arguments went on for hours in the sultry chamber, with Dickinson speaking carefully and at length for delay, Adams and others urging action. South Carolina and Pennsylvania, when the roll was called, opposed independence; Delaware's delegation was split; New York abstained. During the long summer evening and into the night the radicals worked feverishly to persuade the hesitant and the moderate, and the next day, when Congress reassembled, they were cheered by the sudden arrival of Caesar Rodney of Delaware. Rodney—whom John Adams declared the oddest-looking man in the world, tall and slender as a reed— had ridden eighty miles from his home in Dover through the thunderous, rainy night to swing Delaware's vote for independence. South Carolina's members changed their minds and Pennsylvania's Robert Morris and John Dickinson absented themselves, making it possible for that colony to vote in the affirmative. When New York abstained once again, Congress voted unanimously for independence on July 2—a day the ecstatic John Adams said ought to be commemorated as the moment of deliverance, "solemnized with pomp and parade, with shows, games, sports, guns, bells, bonfires and illuminations, from one end of this continent to the other, from this time forward, forevermore." But the declaration itself was yet to be approved, and the members—to Jefferson's dismay—began to take a hand in rewording it. As they went over every phrase, deleting unnecessary words here and there and eliminating—at the insistence of South Carolina and Georgia—one of the most eloquent passages, an attack on the slave trade, Jefferson writhed silently, comforted only partially by John Adams' stout defense of the document on the floor and by Benjamin Franklin's quiet relation of a homely anecdote. The wise old Pennsylvanian told Jefferson, in an aside, about a hatter who was opening a shop and wanted a signboard for it. What the new proprietor had in mind was a message reading, "John Thompson, Hatter, makes and sells hats for ready money," but one of his friends suggested that the word "hatter" was superfluous. Another told him that no buyer would care who made the hats, so the word "makes" was omitted. Someone else advised him to leave out "ready money," since nobody expected to buy on credit, and yet another man said that since Thompson did not propose to give the hats away the word "sells" should go. When the sign was finally erected, Franklin smiled, all that remained was the name "John Thompson" and the picture of a hat.

When the delegates were at last satisfied with the phrasing of the declaration, on July 4, President John Hancock and the secretary of Congress, Charles Thomson, signed it and it was ordered to be printed and sent to colonial assemblies, committees of safety, and the Continental Army. During the night, copies were run off in John Dunlap's printing shop and on the fifth postriders set out from Philadelphia to carry the momentous proclamation to various parts of those "united States of America" which were now declared free and independent states, absolved from all allegiance to the British crown. In support of this Declaration, the delegates had sworn, they would rely on the protection of divine providence and would pledge to each other their lives, their fortunes, and their sacred honor.

"The river is passed, and the bridge cut away," John Adams exulted as he described to a friend how the Declaration had been proclaimed to the crowd gathered round an "awful stage" in the State House yard. There had been cheers, a salute by a battalion paraded on the commons ("notwithstanding the scarcity of powder"), and the bells, he wrote, rang joyously all day and almost all night. From Boston, where there was an epidemic of smallpox, James Warren wrote his friend Adams that "Your Declaration of Independence came on Saturday and diffused a general joy. Every one of us feels more important than ever; we now congratulate each other as Freemen." Adams's wife, Abigail, reported that a crowd had collected in front of the State House to hear it read from the balcony, and that the king's arms were torn down afterward and burned in King Street. In New York, George Washington had the army regiments paraded in the early evening of July 9 to attend the reading and informed them solemnly in orders that the peace and safety of the new nation would now depend "(under God) solely on the success of our Arms." As well they would.

Opinions varied as to the reaction of men in the ranks. Samuel Webb noted in his journal that the Declaration was received with three cheers— "everyone seeming highly pleased that we were separated from a King who was endeavoring to enslave his once loyal subjects." But Alexander

The Declaration of Independence

Originally, Pennsylvania's small legislative assembly met in private houses, rented by the year. In the 1730s work was begun on a permanent capitol, but the brick State House was not completed until 1748. In 1753 the tower was finished and a bell cast in London, bearing the words from Leviticus, "Proclaim liberty throughout the land unto all the inhabitants thereof," was raised into place. To everyone's dismay, the new bell was cracked while being hoisted into position, but it was successfully recast by two local artisans. In 1775 John Hancock called the Second Continental Congress to order here; that June George Washington was given command of the Continental Army in the hall; and on July 4, 1776, the Declaration of Independence was signed here by Hancock and Secretary Charles Thomson. For many years after the Revolution the State House was neglected, and in 1816 it was nearly torn down. But when the aged Lafayette paid a visit to it in 1824 the public awoke to the old building's significance, and about that time people began calling it "Independence Hall" and its bell "The Liberty Bell." *(The Historical Society of Pennsylvania)*

These are the five men assigned to draft the Declaration of Independence. From left to right are John Adams of Massachusetts, Roger Sherman of Connecticut, Robert Livingston of New York, Thomas Jefferson of Virginia, and Benjamin Franklin of Pennsylvania.

A superb and meticulous craftsman, John Trumbull went to almost any lengths to ensure the accuracy of his paintings. The idea for his most ambitious work, "The Declaration of Independence," was given him in 1789 by his friend Thomas Jefferson, who sketched from memory a floor plan of the Pennsylvania State House for the artist. To obtain portraits of the signers, Trumbull painted Jefferson in Paris, John Adams in London, and most of the others at home in the United States, between 1789 and 1794. Eventually he depicted thirty-six of them from life, nine from portraits by other artists, and two from memory. (One man, Benjamin Harrison, had died, leaving no likeness, so Trumbull substituted a painting of Harrison's son, who was said to look exactly like his father.) The full picture (left), which includes forty-eight figures, is only 31⅛" in width, and the detail shown above, taken from a section about 6" wide, reveals the extraordinary delicacy of Trumbull's work. *(Yale University Art Gallery)*

Thomas Jefferson's rough draft of the Declaration, which he retained throughout his life, consisted of four pages in his own handwriting. A section of the first page, shown above, indicates how the various changes suggested by Franklin, Adams, Jefferson himself, and by other members of Congress were entered on this master copy. Altogether, more than eighty alterations were made before the document was approved. The second paragraph (above), which originally began "We hold these truths to be sacred & undeniable; that all men are created equal & independent ...," was revised to read "We hold these truths to be self-evident; that all men are created equal ..." On the night of July 4 the document was printed and the following day a typeset copy was entered in the Rough Journal of Congress, secured by a wafer. Two weeks later the Declaration was engrossed on parchment and early in August it was finally signed. Late in 1776, when Congress feared for the safety of Philadelphia and decided to move to Baltimore, the Declaration, along with other important papers, was removed to that city.

(Courtesy of the Library of Congress)

Graydon, a Pennsylvania officer whose men were erecting a fortification at the northern end of Manhattan Island, thought otherwise. "If it was not embraced with all the enthusiasm that has been ascribed to the event," he remarked later, "it was at least hailed with acclamations, as no doubt any other act of Congress, not flagrantly improper, would at that time have been." Graydon fancied himself a cut above the average man and was pleased that a "predilection for republicanism" had not pervaded the Pennsylvania troops. Had George III been present in person, he felt, he would have been in no danger of injury from the army, which was only beginning to resent him; the soldiers, he believed, "had not yet acquired the true taste for cutting throats." Perhaps he was right; yet there were, in Congress's indictment of the royal person, the seeds of an attitude that would come uncomfortably close to throat-cutting. Up to now, what had been going on in America might be described as rebellion, or the defiance of authority.

But the momentous proclamation of July 4, 1776, meant that events would take a different course altogether, becoming in the final analysis a revolution, whose purpose was the actual casting off of the system of government by which America had been ruled. And if a symbolic act was needed to substantiate this new mood, it was there for all to see on July 9, on New York's Bowling Green, following the reading of the Declaration.

There, on a grassy plot surrounded by a high fence of open ironwork, stood a heroic statue of George III, garbed as a Roman emperor and mounted on a horse. As the evening hours wore on, a crowd gathered to stare at the figure of their monarch, and suddenly some agile Sons of Liberty scaled the fence, swarmed onto the marble pedestal, attached ropes to the statue, and tugged and hauled until the gilded horse and rider crashed to the ground. In a gesture of pure hatred, the figure of the king was decapitated—an act of violence that provoked Washington to issue a stiff reprimand against this "appearance of a riot and a want of order in the army"—after which the lead statue was carted off to Connecticut to be made into musket balls for the Continental Army.

3. A Business of Necessity

Although Tom Paine had become the hero of the hour to independence men, Congress's action on July 2 put a period to his political activities for a time. As the summer of 1776 wore on, he seems to have regarded his business in Philadelphia as finished and signed up with a militia outfit known as the Pennsylvania Associators, to serve as volunteer secretary to Brigadier General Daniel Roberdeau. By the time they reached Perth Amboy, New Jersey, what discipline and organization the Associators possessed began to unravel, and when the unit was temporarily disbanded in September, Paine sought out Nathanael Greene as a man more likely to be involved in what was going on than Roberdeau was.

Greene was an odd combination of talents and beliefs. Raised a Quaker, he retained the piety of his faith but was unable to go along with the doctrine of pacifism, which he regarded as impracticable under certain circumstances—among them the "business of necessity" in which the colonies found themselves. He had become a general officer as a result of ambition and hard work, and what faults he had were largely those of temperament and inexperience; worst of all was his inclination to be headstrong and impetuous, which meant that he sometimes made important decisions too hastily. In conversation, Greene's manner could be deceptive; when the talk was general, his handsome face lit up frequently with flashes of lighthearted humor, but when there was a job to do he was all seriousness.

Men who noticed the strength of his upper body that came from years at the forge found it hard to believe that Greene was bothered with poor health, yet asthma plagued him, inoculation for smallpox had left a spot in his right eye that pained him frequently, and he suffered with a stiff right knee that caused him to limp.

None of these afflictions had kept him from being something of a ladies' man in his younger days, but the gimpy leg had frustrated his first attempt to become an officer. In 1774, when the men of the Rhode Island Kentish

Guards—one of the best volunteer organizations in New England—were choosing their officers, they refused to have Greene even though he was the best qualified; what kind of volunteer company, the men asked, wanted a captain who limped across the parade ground? The word that he was "a blemish to the company" had mortified Greene, who was sensitive about his leg anyway and now had to worry about how it would seem for a thirty-two-year-old, successful ironmaster to serve as a private. But he swallowed his pride and let his fellow volunteers know that he would gladly carry a musket in the ranks. During the fall and winter of 1774 Greene went frequently to Boston, where he stayed at the Bunch of Grapes Tavern—a favorite hangout of the revolutionaries—inspected the fort the British were building on Boston Neck, intently watched the red-coats drilling on Boston Common, and spent hours at the London Book-Store in Cornhill, which was owned by a fat young man, eight years Greene's junior, named Henry Knox. Both were intensely interested in military affairs, read everything they could put their hands on concerned with the subject, and their long talks formed the basis of an enduring friendship that was to blossom after they became comrades in arms.

The news of Lexington and Concord had reached Rhode Island the night after the battles, and at daybreak the next morning the Kentish Guards were on the march toward Massachusetts (one bystander identified Greene in the ranks by his limp and by the way the musket swayed on his shoulder). Somewhere near Pawtucket they were called back; a postrider brought word that the British troops had been driven back into Boston and there were enough men to keep them from coming out again. Nonetheless, the Rhode Island Assembly voted to raise a 1,500-man brigade known as the Army of Observation, whose mission was to preserve the "Liberties of America"—a task that was to be performed somewhat ironically "in the name of His Majesty, George the Third." When the time came to select a commander, someone in the assembly recalled Greene's willingness to serve in the ranks if necessary, and since no one else appeared to be better qualified, he was given command of Rhode Island's "army" with the rank of brigadier general.

Greene immediately lent his considerable energies and talent to the gigantic task of shaping an army from the confused, disorderly mass of men in the makeshift camps surrounding Boston. While trenches were dug and earthworks erected, the troops drilled and officers fretted over supplies and discipline and the lack of virtually everything required by soldiers in the field. In June the Second Continental Congress decided to adopt the force besieging Boston, making it an American army instead of separate militia outfits from several New England colonies, and on July 2 the forty-three-year-old Virginian who had been named to command this body of men rode into Cambridge. (It was a sleepy Sunday afternoon, and George Washington's first appearance made little impression on a bored soldier named James Stevens, who noted in his diary, "Nothing heppeng extroderly.") When Washington assumed command of the army the next day—the twenty-first anniversary of his surrender, as a young militia officer, to the French at Fort Necessity—the colonies were not officially at war, even though blood in plenty had been spilled, and Americans were still referring to the British regulars in Boston as "the ministerial troops," as if that exempted King George from responsibility for them and their actions. Washington soon discovered that the 16,000 men he was to lead were a long way from being an effective fighting force, and as the months passed, letter after letter from him testified to the chaotic conditions. The army was "a mixed multitude of people . . . under very little discipline, order, or government"; there was no unified command, no money with which to pay the men, no provision for supplying them. Troops from one colony were jealous or suspicious of soldiers from the others; sanitary facilities were almost non-existent; the men lacked blankets, tents, muskets, bayonets; short-term enlistments meant that they could go home when their time was up. At one point the general learned to his dismay that there were but thirty-five barrels of powder on hand—enough for only nine rounds per man; there was a surplus, it seemed, only of incompetent officers. Yet somehow all these difficulties "must be borne with," Washington wrote. "The cause we are engaged in is so just and righteous, that we must try to rise superior to every obstacle in its support."

The man to whom this unbearably difficult and precious mission had been entrusted was a reserved, somewhat distant Southerner who seems to have been held as much in awe by his contemporaries as he was by succeeding generations. No one ever got very close to George Washington; no one made jokes about him; no one gave him a nickname. And he comes down to us across the years as if he had been hewn from marble and then draped in the familiar blue and buff uniform. A man six feet two

Numerous portraits of Washington were painted during his lifetime, but none reproduces so faithfully the lines and form of his features as the life mask made by Jean Antoine Houdon in 1785. As the sculptor claimed, it is the "most perfect reproduction of Washington's own face." *(The Pierpont Morgan Library)*

inches tall in a day when a six-footer was a rarity, Washington stood a good head taller than most of his contemporaries, and despite his rather narrow chest and shoulders, he gave the impression of great physical strength. Weighing over two hundred pounds, he was heavy through the waist and thighs and was large-boned, with big hands and feet; yet despite his frame he moved with astonishing grace, and at a time when nearly everyone rode horseback, he was described by Thomas Jefferson as "the best horseman of his age and the most graceful figure that could be seen on horseback."

Gilbert Stuart, the painter, was struck by the features of Washington's face, which were "totally different from what I had observed in any other human being. The sockets of the eyes, for instance, were larger than what I had ever met before, and the upper part of the nose broader." The nose itself was prominent and somewhat accentuated by high cheekbones; his hair was reddish-brown, his eyes gray-blue, and his face slightly scarred from the smallpox he had had in 1751.

People seeing Washington for the first time were usually impressed less by any individual characteristic, however, than by his commanding presence. As one young French volunteer remarked, he seemed "intended for a great position—his appearance alone gave confidence to the timid and imposed respect on the bold." It was curious, this feeling that he stood above his compatriots in an abstract as well as a physical way. Almost from the beginning his subordinate officers called him "Excellency" or "The General" (the article making it quite clear which of the generals they meant), and some years after the war, when the question of a title for the head of the new republic came up for discussion, someone seriously proposed that Washington be referred to as "His High Mightiness." To modern ears it is a pompous, ludicrous-sounding phrase, yet it suggests what some men of his time thought of him. (There were also those—like Alexander Hamilton, who served on his staff during the war—who thought him honest and well-intentioned, but dull, and certainly no demigod.) An English traveler named Nicholas Cresswell, who was no friend to republicanism or the rebellion, had visited widely in Virginia, where he heard a lot about Washington. As a member of the House of Burgesses, he was told, Washington was always regarded as too bashful and timid to make an orator. As a country gentleman at his Mount Vernon estate, he was noted for his excellent table and hospitality, his knowledge of agriculture, and his "industry in carrying his various manufactories of Linen and Woollen to greater perfection than any man in the Colony." Friends and acquaintances, Cresswell found, reckoned him a just man and an honest one, but not very generous; and the Englishman concluded that there was a tinge of envy in the latter judgment, because Washington managed his plantation so carefully and "seldom enters into those foolish, giddy and expensive frolics natural to a Virginian." Cresswell saw what others had perceived—that the man seemed by nature made for the post of commander in chief, with a manner and bearing uniquely suited to his rank. And, putting his finger on that strange, distant quality, Cresswell said he had heard that Washington "never had an intimate, particular bosom friend, or an open, professed enemy in his life." This was a fine thing in a general, the Englishman thought: if a man would not tolerate factions or cliques, there was bound to be harmony in his official family and his officers would have no way to advance themselves except by merit. "I believed him to be a worthy honest man, guilty of no bad vice, except we reckon ambition amongst the number," he said.

Ambition there certainly was, and pride alongside it. By the time he was twenty-two years old his name, after all, was a household word in the colonies† and—like a boy whose mother tells him that he is better than other little boys and should behave differently—he seems to have fretted constantly about his reputation. Take the remark he made to his fellow Virginian Patrick Henry not long after he was made commander of the Continental forces: with tears in his eyes, he said, "Remember, Mr.

---

† A laudatory and very bad poem appeared in newspapers in 1754, suggesting how young Washington's activities in the Ohio Valley had aroused public interest:

Since first the Sparks of this dire War begun, In this new World, which into Europe run.	1749
Since the perfidious French in hostile Ranks The English drove from smooth Ohio's Banks.	1751
Since Washington entered the List of Fame, And by a journey to Lake Erie came.	October, 1753
Since he defeats a French detached Band, Under the brave Jumonville's command.	May 24, 1754
Since Contrecoeur took hold of English Claim, His Fortress builds and calls it Fort Du Quesne.	June 13, 1754
Since Beau Se Jour yielded to British Fame, And Cumberland adorns its present name.	June 20, 1754
Since Fortune turned to Washington adverse, Who makes good Terms with a superior Force.	July 3, 1754

Henry, what I now tell you. From the day I enter upon the command of the American armies, I date my fall and the ruin of my reputation." Certainly a curious prophecy to be made by a man who had just been given an exceptional vote of confidence; yet throughout his military service he was pursued by the specter that he might be found wanting in the eyes of other men. To a point, in fact, where it is tempting to think that the reserve and remoteness was worn like a suit of protective armor, a steel sheath that presented an unchanging image to an inquisitive, hostile world while concealing, behind the visor, the secret hopes and fears of the inner man.

God knows he had every right to be troubled—at this time and at every stage of the war—for Congress had set him a seemingly impossible task, and it was little wonder if he was haunted by feelings of inadequacy or bothered by his lack of command experience. The job, as he admitted candidly, was "too boundless for my abilities and far, very far beyond my experience," and one of the most touching episodes in his career was the moment when a group of friends from Congress realized for the first time what they had done when they named him to lead the colonial army. Just after his appointment, about twenty of them got together and gave Washington a dinner at Peg Mullen's Beefsteak House in Philadelphia. When the meal ended and the first toast was proposed (a hearty "To the Commander in Chief of the American Armies!"), Washington slowly rose to respond and everyone at the table noticed that he did so almost reluctantly—"with some confusion," one of them said. And all of a sudden the jovial, stag-party mood vanished and was transformed into a profoundly solemn moment, followed by total silence. Not until that instant were those men fully cognizant of the terrifying responsibility they had thrust upon their fellow delegate and friend, who now had to assume a role unlike anything he had ever imagined.

To a great many colonists it appeared that George Washington had almost been created to lead them in their hour of supreme need, and indeed it would be difficult to say what other man possessed the same combination of skills, the strength of character or the stamina, or who else commanded such respect. The last quality was essential to his ultimate success, for thousands of once-loyal British subjects who had respected and honored their king simply transferred that regard to Washington. And because of his exploits against the French and his gallantry with the ill-fated Braddock expedition, he was one of the very few native-born men to have acquired any genuine military reputation. Although events would show that he was less than a brilliant strategist, he had a real gift for improvisation when a situation appeared to be hopeless. He proved above all to be a fighter, aggressive in battle and exceptionally courageous under fire, while as a commander he was tenacious, dogged, and realistic enough to know that he had to survive in order to triumph. Throughout the long war his goal would be a simple one: to win. And his method can only be described as persistence.

In private letters to his brothers he is revealed as a vital, exasperated, often irascible human being, a man of passion, always concerned with his reputation and with how others might think of him. His success, in the end, was to outlast the British commanders, for he could never get together in one place at one time enough troops or adequate resources to beat them in a stand-up fight. Indeed, most of his days were spent not in fighting, but in dealing with an unending series of administrative crises— the crises of insufficiency—not enough clothing, food, ammunition, weapons, blankets, money, transport, troops. Along with everything else he conducted an immense correspondence that kept several secretaries busy constantly (in the Fitzpatrick edition of his writings, the war years alone occupy ten thousand pages), and a high percentage of those letters consisted of efforts to cajole or wheedle or plead with Congress for more necessities. When he accepted command of the army in June 1775, he wrote to his wife, Martha, to tell her that he would "return safe to you in the fall." But his safe return was to be postponed for eight and a half years.

In Cambridge, George Washington approached his nearly insurmountable problems with enormous energy, determination, and a patience that was rubbed thin again and again, and he was aided immeasurably by the fact that the British had been too bloodied by their costly victory at Bunker Hill to take the offensive. To assist Washington, Congress appointed four major generals—Artemas Ward, who had commanded the New England army before the new commander in chief arrived; Charles Lee, a gaunt, eccentric veteran of the British and Polish armies; Philip Schuyler, the large landholder and patriot from New York; and the aging hero of the French and Indian War, Israel Putnam of Connecticut. Eight brigadiers were named, among them Nathanael Greene. As summer turned to fall and fall to winter, Washington saw more and more of Greene and liked what he saw; the Rhode Island troops, he noted, "Though raw, irregular, and undisciplined, are under much better government than any around Boston." Already in December 1775, what John Adams had called the "Grand American Army" was in real danger of disintegration. The men who considered themselves veterans had got to calling the short-term militiamen "Long-Faced People," for the obvious reason, and as winter approached the Long Faces were beginning to leave camp in droves. On December 10 the Connecticut troops' enlistments expired and they left for home. They marched off bag and baggage, Charles Lee snarled, "but in passing through the lines of other Regiments they were so horribly hissed, groaned at and pelted that I believe they wished their aunts, grandmothers and even sweethearts to whom the day before they were so much attached, at the Devil's own palace." Greene said his homesick Rhode Islanders would probably leave at the end of the month. By mid-December only 5,000 men had enlisted for service in 1776, and since all of the original "Eight Months men" would be gone by year's end, Washington ordered that muskets be taken from those who were leaving to arm those who remained. Fortunately, enough men in the ranks and enough of their New England neighbors had a change of heart, realizing that if everyone went home it would be the end of all they had fought and bled for. Some of the Connecticut troops drifted back into camp. Nathanael Greene learned that "the people upon the Roads exprest so much abhorrence at their conduct for quitting the Army that it was with difficulty they got Provisions," so back they came, shamefaced, to sign on for another hitch. By the middle of January over 8,000 men were on the rolls; by March the number was twice that.

During these dark days Greene wrote his friend Samuel Ward, a member of the Congress from Rhode Island, about a matter that was much on his mind. Having seen the dire needs confronting the army—not least of which was the problem of persuading enough men that their ideals were worth fighting for—Greene strongly urged an alliance with France and Spain, along with a declaration of independence which would "call upon the world, and the great God who governs it, to witness the necessity, propriety and rectitude thereof." This was more than a week before Thomas Paine's *Common Sense* appeared.

Fortunately for the situation, help had come to the army from another direction. During January, Greene's 280-pound friend Henry Knox had struggled eastward through the deep snows of western Massachusetts, having commandeered horses, oxen, sleds, wagons, and all the manpower he could find to transport fifty-nine pieces of artillery from Fort Ticonderoga, on Lake Champlain, to Cambridge. Bringing this "noble train" across 300 miles of mountains, streams, and sometimes bottomless roads was one of the heroic feats of the war and was accomplished, Knox said with pride, only "after having climbed mountains from which we might almost have seen all the Kingdoms of the Earth." When the former bookseller and his caravan of big guns arrived in Framingham for delivery to Washington, the fate of the British in Boston was settled. On March 2 the guns began bombarding Boston and for two nights the barrage continued; during darkness on the fourth, while the cannon boomed incessantly, some 1,200 rebels erected fortifications on Dorchester Heights commanding the harbor where the British fleet rode at anchor, Castle William, and the town of Boston itself. When daylight came, the British could see the predicament they were in, and someone heard General William Howe, the commander, say, "The rebels have done more in one night than my whole army could have done in months." As a matter of honor, Howe prepared to drive them off the heights, but he was dissuaded from this bloody plan either by mature second thought or by a towering windstorm that blew in from the south; whatever the reason, Howe and all the other British—officers and rank and file alike—knew that a frontal assault would have been suicidal. So on March 6, 1776, the inevitable began: the British started packing up to abandon Boston. And with the 9,000-man British garrison would go nearly 1,100 Americans who had remained loyal to their king—crammed like herring with their pitifully few belongings into eighty transports in the harbor. Benjamin Hallowell, the former customs commissioner who had suffered every kind of indignity, including a stoning, at the hands of Boston's Liberty Boys, was put in a cabin with thirty-six others—"men, women, and children; parents, masters, and mistresses, obliged to pig together on the floor, there being no berths." For many of the people on this sad hegira—some of them old and sick—it was their last glimpse of a land they had loved as well as any rebel did.

In return for a British promise not to burn the town, Washington agreed not to fire upon the enemy fleet as it left the harbor, and the transports, accompanied by sixteen warships, moved out of range of American cannon and dropped anchor between Castle William and Boston Light. On March 17 the Americans moved into Boston (500 soldiers with small-pox scars went in first, since an epidemic of the disease had broken out in November and December and there were still some cases of it), and the following day Nathanael Greene began making an inventory of the stores, cannon, and other paraphernalia left behind by the British and was pleased to report that less damage than expected had been done to the city. Not until March 27, when a fresh wind from the northwest was whipping up whitecaps in Massachusetts Bay, did the British armada stand out to sea, and as the sails fell from sight off to the east the rebels congratulated themselves with a mixture of joy and relief; their eleven-month siege of Boston was over at last.

For all he may have speculated on this success, Washington allowed himself little time for celebration. He knew the enemy would return in force to strike again, and he could be almost certain of their ultimate desti-nation. New York, he said, "secures the free and only communication be-tween the Northern and Southern Colonies, which will be entirely cut off by their possessing it, and give them the command of Hudson's River and an easy pass into Canada . . ." For this reason, it was "absolutely and in-dispensably necessary" that the army march to New York at once. And on March 20, while the British ships still rode at anchor in Boston harbor, the first rebel units—some riflemen from Virginia and Pennsylvania and Brigadier General William Heath's brigade—headed off toward New York. By early April the commander in chief and the balance of the army were under way.

For days there was consternation up and down the New England coast for fear of what Howe might do, but as it turned out the British com-mander had given the rebels a breathing spell by sailing off to Halifax, Nova Scotia, that "cursed, cold, wintry place," as one of his officers called it. There he planned to rid himself of the encumbering civilian refugees, the hapless loyalists he had spirited out of Boston, while he waited for reinforcements and exercised his troops. There is no record that any American perceived this maneuver of Howe's as a missed opportunity, but it was the first of many such episodes that would give the rebel army just enough relief from pressure so that they could regroup and fight again. By going to New York at once, Howe might have struck a quick blow from which the Americans could not have recovered; there, too, he would have found a host of receptive loyalists, plentiful supplies, and the strategic base Washington wished to deny him. But to Halifax Howe went and there he stayed—stayed, in fact, until June, thus missing several months of campaigning weather. From the British point of view, what had happened in America presented a bleak picture. A year of war had succeeded only in creating a situation completely inimical to the empire's interests: the army now occupied not a single acre of territory in the thirteen colonies; and the army and the government had managed to alienate most neutral opinion in America, creating a reservoir of resentment against the mother country that could never be erased.

CHAPTER TWO

1. *We Must Tax Them*

It was a long, tortuous road that had brought Britain and her American colonies to such a pass—a road that began in the jubilant aftermath of George III's coronation, in an England exuberant with victory in the Seven Years' War, the most recent installment in her century-old struggle with France. In those days Britain's darling was William Pitt, a pale genius with gleaming eyes and long, threatening beak, crippled with gout, a man strangely ignorant of people and politics but possessed of a vision of grandeur and power that men could understand and follow. Agreeing with Daniel Defoe that "Trade is the Wealth of the World," Pitt had no difficulty persuading the commercial interests of London that trade was intricately entwined with national destiny: "When Trade is at stake," he told them, "you must defend it, or perish." Victory brought an enormous upsurge in commerce and prosperity; British ships ruled the seas; and suddenly—almost unexpectedly to many Englishmen—the world lay at their feet, revealing the immense wealth and power to be enjoyed for the plucking. But Pitt's ambitions had outrun those of his more timorous countrymen—including the young king, who had determined that the war must end—and the Peace of Paris that was signed in 1763 was not William Pitt's peace; he had been forced out of the ministry and the terms were dictated by men who dared not seize the spoils his war had yielded. Fearful that a harsh settlement would provoke a vengeful France and Spain to retaliate, they settled for far less than Pitt and the merchants of London had anticipated. The disappointed Pitt, desperately ill and racked with pain, unable to walk without assistance or to speak without stimulants, railed for three hours against the treaty in the House of Commons, but to no avail. (And now, George III's mother rejoiced, "my son is King of England.") Britain might have taken all Pitt wanted, for what good a set of softened terms accomplished; the victor's reduced demands neither mollified nor deceived the vanquished. What France and Spain and all the other continental powers could see was that their enemy had become the greatest, richest empire since Rome. In 1763 she stood alone in glorious but hazardous eminence, having smashed her foes and lost her allies.

The immediate aftermath of the Seven Years' War was that France and Spain, weakened by war and humiliated by peace, could do little but lick their wounds and lie low, waiting for the inevitable opportunity that would bring revenge. It would take a decade and more to come, but when it did, Charles Gravier, Comte de Vergennes, foreign minister of France, recognized it at once in the restiveness of England's increasingly cantankerous colonies. Vergennes and his colleagues had to weigh several hazards in this game: there was the considerable risk that Spain, understandably nervous about holding onto her own extensive colonies, might pull back from an alliance with France; there was the potential danger that the English might retaliate with an attack on the continental powers; and, of course, there was the possibility that George III might call back William Pitt, the architect of victory and one of the few men in public life capable of effecting a reconciliation between mother country and colonies. But the promise vastly outweighed the gamble, Vergennes believed, and he sent the talented Caron de Beaumarchais to London to sample the atmosphere there.

In 1775 Beaumarchais reported what his superior most wanted to hear: "All sensible people in England are convinced that the English colonies are lost to the mother country, and this is my opinion too." Gingerly, Vergennes opened negotiations with Grimaldi, the Spanish foreign minister, to explore the possibility of some kind of joint effort against the British; Spain was willing, and the two continental powers agreed to pool their fleets in the event of war (France's sixty sail of the line and Spain's fifty balanced the strength of the English navy). Of equal portent, Vergennes and Grimaldi had decided by May 1776 to form a curious, nongovernmental trading company: headed by Beaumarchais, the firm of Hortalez & Cie. would conduct a sub rosa arms and munitions business with the Americans without embarrassment to the governments of France and Spain, supplying them, eventually, with 80 per cent of the powder used by rebel troops—the product of the brilliant scientist Antoine Laurent Lavoisier.

This resolve for revenge by France and Spain was to have profound effects on the outcome of the American Revolution, but long before hostilities began in 1775 quite another aftermath of the Peace of Paris was altering the fragile relationship between mother country and colony. For years, Prime Minister Robert Walpole had pursued his policy of "salutary neglect" toward the colonies, which left practical matters largely in the hands of American and British merchants. While this suited most colonists very well indeed, it meant that the relationship between London and the provinces had been allowed to drift until the connective tissue was stretched dangerously thin. In America the years of neglect had produced a state of mind that no longer viewed dependence on the mother country as a fact of life. To a farmer in the Deerfield valley who seldom, if ever, had any contact with a royal official and whose days were crowded with the business of land and livestock, a government located 3,000 miles across the Atlantic was a very remote entity indeed. There was, throughout the colonies, a growing habit of avoiding unwelcome authority from abroad, an increasing maturity and self-sufficiency. Economically, the colonists had prospered by exploiting their bountiful natural resources; politically, they dominated their own assemblies, which in turn controlled the sources of revenue; and militarily, the Seven Years' War had removed the threat of the French and the Indian from their immediate borders. By and large, the Americans viewed British political and economic domination as obstacles to their expanding foreign trade with the West Indies and Europe. They resented their forced dependence on English currency and regarded as a form of exploitation the credit they received from London bankers. The American had precious little hard money, and he was well aware that mercantilism and British protection gave the London merchant an unfair advantage over him.

But if this was the point of view of the colonist, the Englishman had quite another outlook on American affairs. Along with victory in the Seven Years' War had come the realization, agonizing to many of England's country gentlemen who were paying a land tax of four shillings in the pound, that the nation's debt had risen from £55,000,000 to £133,000,000. And there was a determination on the part of these men— not to mention the king himself—that the provincials should pay their share of this huge burden. The average Englishman felt with some justice that the Americans depended upon the mother country for security and financial backing and ought to show their gratitude by sharing in the obligation which their own defense had been partially repsonsible for creating. Without aid from the mother country, it was argued, the colonies would be quickly overrun by other European powers, and the rising complaints from America were not looked upon with much sympathy. "The payment of their just portion to defray the charges of their own defence, is all the oppression under which [they] groan," observed the *Gazetteer and New Daily Advertiser*, and that was a fair summary of how most Britons viewed the matter.

George Grenville, who succeeded Lord Bute in 1763 as prime minister, began by paring government spending drastically, but for all his economies the country gentlemen were still laying out more than 15 per cent of their income in taxes. Grenville extended his policy to the colonies: he would reduce their expenses and make them pay for their own defense and administration. As a means of limiting expense, he took action to prevent further wars with the Indians on the frontier: he forbade westward migration by the colonists and, in effect, set aside everything beyond the Appalachians for the red man. He reorganized the colonial customs system, set in motion a program to stop smuggling, and put through a number of revenue bills—a tax on sugar, new duties on coffee, indigo, wines, and other commodities, and, in 1765, a stamp duty on legal transactions. It was all very reasonable from the vantage point of the Englishman; but to certain Americans it was unjust and smelled of tyranny. No one in a position of authority in Great Britain had any conception that the reaction would be so violent. Nor did anyone conceive that a measure like Grenville's Stamp Act would unify the colonists in opposition to government.

Having observed those jealousies that divided the provincials, the English concluded that there was little to fear from an American union; after all, it was hardly likely that people who were unable to combine against their common foe, the French and Indians, would join in opposition to the mother country. What the Grenville ministry had not reckoned on was the depth of feeling provoked by its measures. Benjamin Franklin had once warned the British: "When I say . . . an union of the colonies is impossible I mean without the most grievous tyranny and oppression." And it was plain, from the way they responded, that a substantial number of Americans regarded Grenville's program as tyrannical and oppressive. In retrospect, the rebellion might be said to have begun in 1765, the year in which delegates from nine colonies gathered in New York ("an Assembly," Caesar Rodney thought, "of the Greatest Ability I ever Yet saw") to protest the Stamp Act and to issue a Declaration of Rights and Grievances, stating firmly that only the colonies could levy taxes on the colonists.

England backed down, Grenville left office, and Rockingham's "lutestring ministry" repealed the Stamp Act. But it was too much to expect that Parliament would allow the challenge to its authority to go unanswered, and in 1766 a Declaratory Act was passed, asserting its sovereign *right* to control the colonies through legislation in all matters. This heated up the quarrel and had the added effect of creating a good deal of liberal sympathy for the colonists in England. Then the situation was made worse by the series of new "external" duties imposed on the colonies by Charles Townshend in 1767—taxes on glass, lead, paper, paint, and tea—which made crystal clear the government's intention of raising a revenue in America.

The issue distilled in the phrase "No taxation without representation" was not a simple one, but what most colonists meant by it was that there should be no taxation except by their own assemblies. Few Americans seriously expected active representation in the British Parliament; on the contrary, they wanted their own representatives in their own assemblies tending to their own ffairs. But at the same time, taxation of the colonists had become, for many members of Parliament, a matter of honor and "the favorite measure" of George III's reign. The Townshend duties led to violence: in 1768 British troops arrived in Boston, there were riots, the Boston "massacre" of 1770, non-importation agreements, and—perhaps most significant—a widening pattern of revolutionary organization. Again the government backed down, and for two years there was a *detente* of sorts, brought about by repeal of all the duties imposed by Townshend except, for form's sake, the tax on tea. When Samuel Adams's Liberty Boys, thinly disguised as Indians, boarded the *Dartmouth*, the *Eleanor*, and the *Beaver* in Boston Harbor on the night of December 16, 1773, and threw 342 chests of tea into the black waters, they did more to set the course of events than anything that had occurred before; for the reservoir of good will in England toward Americans was sharply reduced by this wanton act of destruction and by now the government had had its fill of backing down. Punitive measures were taken, and by the so-called "Intolerable

Acts" the charter of Massachusetts was virtually annulled and the Boston customs house was closed down, thus effectively shutting the port. The immediate effect was to rally the sympathies of the other colonies to Massachusetts, but of larger importance was the assemblage of fifty-six Americans—some of the most distinguished names in the colonies—at Carpenters' Hall in Philadelphia on September 5, 1774. Among the men in this First Continental Congress were Samuel and John Adams from Massachusetts; John Dickinson and Joseph Galloway of Pennsylvania; John Jay and James Duane from New York; Patrick Henry, Richard Henry Lee, and George Washington from Virginia; Christopher Gadsden and Edward and John Rutledge of South Carolina. As William Pitt foresaw, these were men well qualified to rule, and most of them would have ample opportunity to do so as time passed.

There is a temptation to regard the causes of the rebellion as largely economic, and certainly the course of events from 1763 to 1775 provides ample justification for doing so. (Indeed, four years after the war began, George III wrote to his prime minister Lord North, assigning the cause of the war to "laying a tax" and wondering, in hindsight, if it could possibly have been worth what had resulted.) So much of the legislation to which the colonists took exception was enacted to produce revenue, such a proportion of the debate, both in Parliament and in America, centered on taxation—it seems to have dominated the time to the exclusion of other factors. Feelings in England at times ran as high as they did in America against the right of Parliament to tax the colonies: "You sought a revenue," General Henry Conway declared in Commons in November 1775, "to which you had not a single pretension . . ." And Charles James Fox the following spring mocked the North ministry's program when, reminding the members of Parliament that both they and the king had pledged that no future tax was to be levied on the colonies, he described what had happened to that "sacred promise." The country gentlemen, he said, "are promised a revenue. The tea duty—the only tax you have—makes no revenue. Yet a revenue must be had from America; and if the Americans will not of themselves give a revenue, we must tax them . . . The object, therefore, of the war is the tea tax, which neither does nor ever will raise any revenue. But it is a tax, and therefore, according to the noble Lord's [i.e., North's] logick, we tax them. But it is no new tax, and therefore we keep our word . . . And upon this curious bead-roll of syllogisms, we are to prosecute a ruinous war, or to make a shameful peace."

But economic factors were not the only burs on the bush. Exacerbating the situation was a feeling of disdain or contempt many Englishmen had for their provincial cousins, along with a tendency to lump all colonials into one category—a mistake that was to have important consequences after hostilities began. If the average Briton gave any thought to the inhabitants of North America, it was probably to regard them as a rather unappealing lot who lived in trading posts, backwoods settlements, or plantations. By and large, Crèvecoeur's observation that "the rich stay in Europe; it is only the middling and the poor that emigrate" held true. It was estimated that as many as 40,000 convicts had been shipped to America during the eighteenth century (at a time when the population of the colonies was rising from 200,000 to 2,000,000—which presumably meant that almost one man in fifty was a former prisoner), giving rise to Samuel Johnson's celebrated remark about Americans: "Sir, they are a parcel of convicts, and if they get anything short of hanging they ought to be content." There was a pronounced feeling in England that the colonial was, at best, a second-class Englishman, definitely inferior to the true Briton. As one newspaper remarked about John Hancock, "Mr. Hancock may be a very good Englishman among Bostonians, but he is no more an Englishman amongst Englishmen, than General Gage is a King amongst Sovereigns!" A comparative study of the natives of British India and those of British America, made at the time, showed that the latter were a rum lot indeed: the Indians were observed to be docile and submissive; the Americans haughty, insolent, "impatient of rule, disdaining subjection, and by all means affecting independence."

For all the tensions involving questions of taxation and the differences between two widely separated peoples, there was an underlying issue so fundamental as to dwarf everything else that surfaced in the years of mounting trouble: that central question of sovereignty on which the colonists had such decided views. Thanks in no small measure to the years of "salutary neglect," after 1763 British policies had run head on into a refusal by the colonial assemblies to accept the premise that they were subordinate. In Britain there could be no real discussion of whether the assemblies were separate and sovereign: most Englishmen found it inconceivable that the Americans regarded them as autonomous. And as Governor Thomas Hutchinson put it in an address to the Massachusetts Assembly in January of 1773: "I know no line that can be drawn between the supreme authority of Parliament and the total independence of the Colonies. It is impossible that there should be two independent legislatures in one and the same state, for although there may be but one head, the King, yet two legislative bodies will make two Governments as distinct as the kingdoms of England and Scotland before the Union." The Massachusetts legislature thought otherwise, of course, and their view was given violent expression when the tea was dumped into Boston Harbor. Outrageous as that act seemed to most Englishmen and many Americans at the time, the unlawful destruction to which they objected was only a superficial wound; the deadly sickness implicit in the event was the premise that a sizable number of colonists no longer regarded the supremacy of Parliament as acceptable.

So long as that attitude persisted in the colonies, there could be little question of what Britain must do; the king and his ministers saw that they had no alternative but to take up the challenge to constitutional authority. George III, who began to enjoy real popularity in England for the first time as a result of his increasingly tough policy, recognized that the die was cast and that there could be no turning back. Action met with reaction; British determination stiffened; and the colonists, refusing to be coerced, were provoked into organized resistance. Finally and inevitably, Great Britain was forced to a test of strength which began when General Thomas Gage was ordered to seize colonial stores of arms and ammunition in the towns outside Boston.

2. *America Will Be Brought to Submission*

On May 26, 1775, Parliament rose for the summer and the members headed for home. At almost the same time, the schooner *Quero* of Salem, Massachusetts, Captain John Derby commanding, sailed up a stream at the Isle of Wight unnoticed by British authorities. Captain Derby disembarked, took public transportation to Southampton, made his way to London, and delivered a packet of papers to Arthur Lee, the agent of the Massachusetts Bay Colony. In the package were copies of the Essex *Gazette* dated April 25, which contained a detailed account of a battle between the king's troops and armed Americans at Lexington and Concord. "A BLOODY BUTCHERY, by the BRITISH TROOPS: or, the RUNAWAY FIGHT OF THE REGULARS," the headlines screamed, below a double row of heavy black coffins symbolizing the colonials who had fallen in the action.

Derby had been commissioned by the Massachusetts Committee of Safety to "hasten to London" so that the provincial version of the fighting would arrive there first. He had made the crossing in four weeks and in doing so made possible the first propaganda victory of the war, for the day after he arrived the news was all over England. The London *Evening Post* printed an extra, carrying the account as it had appeared in the Essex *Gazette* and reprinting some depositions from Americans which had been forwarded with Derby by Dr. Joseph Warren, president of the Massachusetts Provincial Congress. Thomas Hutchinson, lately royal governor of the Bay Colony, took the distressing news to the Earl of Dartmouth, secretary of state for the American Department, who was, Hutchinson noted in a classic of understatement, "much struck with it."

Members of government were surprised by the news but not so alarmed as they might have been, since what they read was an American version and as such almost certainly unreliable. The king remarked to Dartmouth after reading the account, "It is not improbable but some detachment sent by Lieut. General Gage may have not been strong enough to disperse the provincials assembled at Concord; but no great reliance can be given to the manner in which it will understandably be exaggerated in American newspapers, or when related by an American trader." Hutchinson assured Dartmouth that the account must be biased since Captain Derby belonged "to one of the most incendiary families" in New England. Although there may have been private forebodings (the historian Edward Gibbon, who was a member of Parliament at the time, wrote to a friend that "this looks serious and is indeed so"), nearly everyone in government assumed that this first report was erroneous or deliberately falsified and awaited General Thomas Gage's official report. On June 1, when no word had yet come in from Gage, Dartmouth wrote him, commenting upon the newspaper accounts brought by Derby, which were "plainly made up for the purpose of conveying every possible prejudice and misrepresentation of the truth." But concern and irritation showed through Dartmouth's expression of regret "that we have not heard some account from you of the transaction." Still, by the time the "American trader" had slipped away as mysteriously as he had come (agents sent by Dartmouth failed to find him or his ship in Southampton), a sense of relaxation and complacency began to take over. One Londoner observed that ". . . people are returned to that happy tranquility of mind, which cannot, I fancy, be much interrupted, unless the Regatta day should prove wet and cold."

Gage had, of course, sent a full report of the action at Lexington and Concord to Dartmouth (it began, remarkably, "I have now nothing to trouble your lordship with, but of an affair that happened here on the 19th instant . . ."). He had dispatched it on April 24—five days after the fight took place and four days before the fast little *Quero* sailed—but the heavily laden packet on which it was sent arrived two weeks after Derby got to Southampton and not until June 10 was Gage's report made public. When members of government had a chance to scan it, they realized at once that the tidings were somber indeed, for they agreed in every respect save one with the news brought by Captain Derby: Gage maintained that the rebels had fired first. Somewhat ponderously, the British commander in Boston informed his superiors that a state of hostilities existed and that his troops had suffered 244 casualties at the hands of the rebels.

Those few ministers who were in town when Gage's document arrived viewed the situation with concern, but the king reassured them: ". . . with firmness and perseverance America will be brought to submission." There was no doubt in his mind but that "old England" would make her "rebellious children rue the hour they cast off obedience." And then he revealed the determination that was to rule his attitude toward America throughout the entire war—a harsh, unbending line that would be followed no matter what the consequences: "America," he stated, "must be a colony of England or be treated as an enemy. Distant possessions standing upon an equality with the superior state is more ruinous than being deprived of such connections."

It was June 15 by the time all members of the cabinet returned from the country so that a full meeting could be held at the prime minister's residence, and the men who assembled in Lord North's drawing room to discuss recent events in Massachusetts realized that they were now members of a war cabinet and that the first order of business was how to raise the armed forces needed to subdue the insurrection. On July 1 Lord Dartmouth wrote to Governor William Tryon, who had recently returned to New York, giving him the British view: ". . . however desirable a reconciliation with America may be, it must not be sought for on the ground of a submission of the authority of Great Britain to their pretensions, but can only be found in their submission to that authority." Obedience, Dartmouth went on, "is, and must be, that bond of peace and unity upon which the dignity and security of the Empire are to depend."

During that summer of uncertainty, many reasonable men who had endeavored to stave off a final confrontation were taking sides in anger. Benjamin Franklin, who had spent the winter and spring of 1775 in London, trying to influence George III favorably on behalf of the colonists, had finally left England under threat of arrest. Even so, he still believed that there were no real reasons why solutions to the outstanding problems could not be found. A resolution of the dispute, Franklin thought, was "rather a matter of punctilio, which two or three sensible people might settle in half an hour." The difficulty then and, increasingly, as the weeks wore on, was that there were fewer and fewer people whom Franklin would call sensible. In the first week of July he was so upset by the course of events that he wrote what was to become a famous letter to his old friend William Strahan, the London printer and a member of Parliament. By then Franklin knew—as, of course, Strahan could not—of the tumultuous events in Boston that meant war.

Philad. July 5, 1775

Mr. Strahan,

You are a member of Parliament and one of that Majority which has doomed my Country to Destruction. You have begun to burn our Towns and murder our People. Look upon your Hands! They are stained with the Blood of your Relations! You and I were long Friends: You are now my Enemy,

and

I am

Yours,

B. Franklin

During the last days of August, when word reached London that the Americans had captured Fort Ticonderoga on Lake Champlain and Crown Point farther down the lake, Lord North wrote his sovereign, ". . . the war has now grown to such a height, that it must be treated as a foreign war, and . . . every expedient which would be used in the latter case should be applied in the former." That degree of consternation resulted less from the taking of the forts than from earlier, gloomy tidings out of Boston: on July 20 rumors of a major battle began circulating in London and five days later were confirmed when Gage's report of the June 17 fight for Bunker Hill was published. (Once again Gage had delayed writing to England; after the engagement he apparently thought it might be possible to seize Dorchester Heights on the other side of Boston and thus be able to include some good news along with the horrifying casualty list, but the Dorchester Heights movement was called off at the last minute because of the substantial risk involved.) London was aghast at the extent of the slaughter: casualties totaled nearly 50 per cent of the king's troops engaged, and it was at once clear that although the British may have won the battlefield, they had won no victory. (Members of the Opposition and the press had perceived earlier that Lexington and Concord were no British triumphs either: "A most vigorous retreat," Edmund Burke had called that affair, "twenty miles in three hours—scarce to be paralleled in history; the feeble Americans, who pelted them all the way, could scarce keep up with them.") One sarcastic letter to Lord North suggested that if there were eight more such "victories" as Bunker Hill no one would be left to report them, and Gage's grudging praise of the Americans' valor and determination was of little consolation: they had displayed, he wrote, "a conduct and spirit against us, they never showed against the French, and everybody has judged them from their former appearance and behavior." At the moment only the king seemed to possess the confidence and energy required to pursue what promised to be a bloody, tragic war. "We must persist and not be dismayed," he wrote North, bucking him up. As a scapegoat for Bunker Hill, the king and his ministry had no trouble focusing on Gage—who, for his part, had already fixed the blame on the government. Three days after his report on Bunker Hill reached London it was decided to call him home for "consultation" and to replace him as commander in chief of His Majesty's forces in North America with General William Howe, who had led the redcoats up the slopes of Charlestown Heights toward Bunker Hill on June 17. In October Thomas Gage, whose career in the colonies had spanned two decades and had ironically begun and ended with the two worst disasters of British arms on the North American continent—Braddock's defeat and the battle for Bunker Hill—sailed for England, his career ruined by the very people he had tried his best to serve.

In that summer and autumn of 1775 numerous Englishmen had an opinion on whether there should be war or no war, and if so, how it should be fought, but as a practical matter nothing would be done until King George III and his first minister, Frederick, Lord North, had determined the policy to be followed. And since the amiable, deeply loyal North was in many respects merely the creature of his sovereign, the basic guidelines would in fact be formulated in the small, stubborn, unstable mind of George III—a man who was just beginning to come into his own as the ruler of Great Britain.

3. Everyone Who Does Not Agree with Me Is a Traitor

His Most Gracious Majesty George William Frederick, King of Great Britain and Ireland and Elector of Hanover, who would reign throughout the American Revolution and for thirty-seven years afterward until he was blind, deaf, and hopelessly mad, was thirty-seven years old in 1775 and in the fifteenth year of his sovereignty. The first of his line to care deeply about England, he had succeeded to the throne because his great-grandfather, George I, had been selected by Parliament as a Protestant successor to the childless Queen Anne. That first George, who was born in Hanover, a small, independent German kingdom, in 1660, one hundred years before the coronation of his great-grandson, found the English people not to his liking, never bothered to learn their language, did not trouble to attend cabinet meetings, and spent most of his time in dalliance with a mistress, the Duchess of Kendal, who was described by a contemporary as "very little above an idiot." Because of George I's almost total lack of interest in his kingship, Robert Walpole assumed immense powers as first minister, with profound political results for Great Britain. George II, who succeeded his father to the throne, resembled him in most respects except for the fact that he spoke some English. He was not fond of his subjects, his heart was in Hanover, and he was a stingy, avaricious man without friends, who liked to count his money coin by coin and sought solace in the company of women—every evening at nine it was his custom to join his mistress, Lady Suffolk. His strong-willed wife, Caroline Wilhelmina of Anspach, produced a son, Frederick Louis, in 1707, a young man destined to be outlived by his father, who hated him and quarreled with him incessantly (when Frederick died in 1751, his father remarked, "I am glad of it").

The third Hanoverian king to be named George was born prematurely in 1738, and the most important inheritance he received from his father was a set of "Instructions for my son George," which had a lasting effect on the young man. His father urged him to "Employ all your hands, all your power, to live with economy . . . If you can be without war, let not your ambition draw you into it . . . At the same time never give up your honour nor that of the nation." And, to avoid the practice of his two predecessors: "Convince this nation that you are an Englishman born and bred, but that you are also this by inclination." In conclusion, the prince known as "Poor Fred," who never became king, remarked, "I shall have no regret never to have worn the Crown if you do but fill it worthily."

Young George's mother was bitterly disappointed when her husband's death deprived her of the right to become Queen of England, but she determined to compensate for that loss through her son. He was tutored constantly, isolated from the outside world, but he was eleven before he could read with any degree of skill. By the time he reached his teens he was still shy and backward, and because of the animosity that existed between his mother, father, and grandfather, his boyhood was filled with mistrust and confusion. The young man had a good physique, with the long nose and small chin typical of the Hanoverians, prominent blue eyes and full lips, but he was lethargic, slow-witted, and lived in terror of his grandsire.

The unhappy George, seeking a substitute father, found one in his mother's favorite counselor, the Scotsman John Stuart, third Earl of Bute. George always referred to the dour, intelligent Scot as his "Dearest Friend," and would make no move—personal or official—without consulting him. The domination of the young man by Bute and the queen mother became the subject of public discussion, and the general feeling was that the two conspired to use the innocent prince for their own greedy ends, while George's pathetic attachment to his mother became an ugly joke. Once, riding through the London streets, he was accosted with cries of "Are you going [home] to suck?" Having led a life of abnormal isolation before his coronation, George followed simple country ways, gardening and tinkering with machines. Stubborn and unimaginative, he held to childlike ideals, and as he came closer to the throne he was determined to follow his father's counsel, to restore the majesty and power of the crown, which had fallen through neglect into the hands of England's great families. When George succeeded his grandfather in 1760 he was twenty-two years old; he wanted not only to rule but to be father and friend to his subjects. And faithfully remembering his father's "Instructions," he made his first declaration as king: "Born and educated in this country, I glory in the name of Briton." But instead of acclaim, his credo was greeted with cynicism; his audience was offended because of their assumption that Bute, the Scotsman, had persuaded George to use the term "Briton" instead of "Englishman." And to the superstitious, there was something ominous in the fact that a large, costly jewel fell out of George's crown at his coronation, an augury memorialized in verse:

> When first, portentous, it was known
> Great George had jostled from his crown
> The brightest diamond there,
> The omen-mongers one and all
> Foretold some mischief must befall;
> Some loss beyond compare.

A year later his betrothal to Princess Charlotte of Mecklenburg-Strelitz was announced (Horace Walpole observed that there were "not six men in England who knew that such a princess existed"). The obscure young lady was seventeen and homely, with a turned-up nose, wide mouth, and yellowish complexion, and the queen mother and Bute left nothing to chance as far as the wedding was concerned: Charlotte arrived in London at 3 P.M. on September 22, 1761, and was married that same day. Dutifully she bore George fifteen children before she was forty, seemingly enjoying with him the simplest possible home life in the most uncomfortable surroundings. In contrast with the gay, frequently wanton high life that characterized upper class Britain in the eighteenth century, that of the royal family was pedestrian and insular; George not only lacked the common touch but was totally out of sympathy with the age. By comparison with the glittering courts of Europe, the near-empty drawing rooms of Britain's royal couple were as different as chalk from cheese—Horace Walpole wrote scornfully of the "recluse life" of the monarchs, and the six bored princesses referred to their home as "The Nunnery."

The king did not really enjoy people. Awkward, self-conscious, and shy, in private he spoke very rapidly, punctuating his remarks with frequent interjections of "What? What? What?" spoken in quick succession (this appeared to be more a nervous habit than a request for information, since he seldom waited for an answer). Shortly after his marriage he had what was thought to be a temporary attack of insanity; then he remained sane until 1788, when he stepped from his coach in Windsor Park and greeted an oak tree as Frederick the Great.* He was nervous, brusque, and tactless, and could be heartlessly cruel to servants. Often inarticulate, he had neither the imagination nor flair for interesting conversation, and he was frequently oblivious to the needs or problems of others. Once Chatham, suffering terribly with gout, called on him and the king kept

---

* Recent studies by two physicians interested in the king's malady indicate that he was suffering from a rare hereditary disease known as porphyria, which apparently afflicted members of the royal houses of Hanover and Stuart (from Mary Queen of Scots onward). Porphyria has a bewildering variety of symptoms, many of them agonizingly painful to the victim, including temporary paralysis, difficulty in swallowing and breathing, a racing pulse, violent stomach cramps, hyperagitation, irritability, sleeplessness, confusion, delirium, convulsions, and severe and widespread disorder of the entire nervous system. It was little wonder if the mental agitation that accompanied and followed this physical distress caused George's physicians to think that his mind was deranged.

Not surprisingly, the king's doctors—understandably alarmed by the apparent manifestations of mental disorder—completely neglected the physical ailment which had caused them, since the symptoms did not jibe with those of any illness with which eighteenth-century medical men were familiar (porphyria is so rare that it was not clinically defined until the 1930s). There is no evidence that George's mind was affected by the first attack, which occurred in 1765 when he was twenty-six years old, but in 1788, when he lost his reason for a period of time, the attending physicians argued inconclusively for months over whether he was insane or merely delirious. The interesting byways of medical research on a historical personage are set forth in detail by Drs. Ida Macalpine and Richard Hunter in *George III and the Mad-Business.*

him standing for two hours. By nature a fearful, sensitive introvert who worried about his capacity to rule, George tended to overcompensate or overreact when confronted with a problem and to become stubborn and intractable. He seldom forgot; he never forgave.

Early in the reign George III realized that his immediate task was to break the power of the powerful Whig families that had dominated England since the death of Queen Anne at the same time he undid the importance of the ministry, or cabinet, in order to shift the balance of power in both cases to the crown. For the first decade of his rule there was a succession of short-lived ministries and no real stability while the young king groped toward a workable arrangement. Much as he disliked having to do so, he became a politician of sorts, dispensing patronage and making and unmaking ministers. As Chatham's illness deepened into madness that removed him from the scene, George moved steadily toward his goal of personal rule, using a system of court favorites to push his own policies and to weaken those governments in which he had little or no confidence.

By the time he called Lord North to head the cabinet in 1770, the king had a tight personal grip on the House of Commons. He knew how firmly a man was entrenched with his constituency, he knew his price to become one of the "king's friends," he knew who could be bullied or bribed with one of his "golden pills."

His copious correspondence was a measure of the microscopic attention he gave to affairs of state. Having a strong point of view on every question, no matter how insignificant, he inundated his ministers with memoranda and letters giving them his opinions. Although he dominated the North administration, he did not actually lead it: he regarded his role as a moral one—to see that the ministers persevered and to prod them to do their duty by bucking up the fainthearted and shoving the slothful. "If others will not be active, I must drive," he once remarked, and with a firm spirit of determined confidence he backed resolute measures as the only effective means to solve the colonial problem. "When once these rebels have felt a smart blow," he said, "they will submit; and no situation can ever change my fixed resolution, either to bring the colonies to a due obedience to the legislature of the mother country, or to cast them off." For a ruler whose attitude toward certain of his subjects was so inflexible, he had remarkably little knowledge of them. He seemed to feel that all that was required was firmness, in the manner of the traditional parent-child relationship, after which the Americans would submit dutifully. "No one," he wrote, "must suppose the Americans poor mild persons who after unheard of grievances had no choice . . . the truth is that the too great leniency of this country increased their pride and encouraged them." In all he did, George was motivated by the conviction that he must exert every ounce of his strength to prevent the dissolution of the empire that had been entrusted to him. And he distrusted everyone who disagreed with this single-minded goal: "I wish nothing but good," he once observed, "therefore everyone who does not agree with me is a traitor and a scoundrel." It was easy to see how a man who felt that way about his personal convictions would not change his mind readily. "I know I am doing my Duty," he wrote to North on July 26, 1775, referring to the policy of coercion he had determined to follow with the colonies, "and I can never wish to retract." No doubts intruded on that stubborn mind.

There was, furthermore, agreement by the king's ministers as to the broad lines of policy to be pursued; the trouble lay in the degree of determination likely to be applied to the task. It was a moot question if the king's resolve could be transmitted to Lord North, the leader of government, who had little stomach for the war (certainly none of the ardor characteristic of a successful war minister) and who was not optimistic of victory. Despite the king's influence on governmental policy, its effective execution depended in the final analysis on how well crown and Parliament worked together, and the single most important factor in this equation was the man selected by the king to be his first minister. In 1770, when George was forced to call for a general election, he had sought a man who would follow his policies and pull the government together and turned to the chancellor of the exchequer, Frederick, Lord North, eldest son of the first Earl of Guilford. "If you don't accept, I have no one else," he was obliged to tell him, and for all the king's determination to have things his own way, the management of events for the next twelve, destiny-laden years was largely in North's hands.

North bore a startling physical resemblance to the king. He was already round-shouldered, corpulent, with a bloated, sleepy, piglike face, and an oversize tongue which thickened his speech. As Horace Walpole wrote of him, "Nothing could be more coarse, or clumsy, or ungracious than his outside. Two large prominent eyes that rolled about to no purpose—for he was utterly short-sighted—a wide mouth, thick lips, and inflated visage, gave him the air of a blind trumpeter." But inside, to follow Walpole's figure of speech, was quite a different man. Cultured, personally charming, quick-witted, shrewd, and honest, North had patience and tolerance to deal with the dull-witted and a sense of humor that neither wounded nor offended. His even temper and ability to provoke a laugh—often at his own expense—infuriated his opponents. (Once when a member attacked him, shouting that he was slumbering over the ruin of the country, North yawned and replied, "I wish to heaven I was.") In fact, he owed high office to this conciliatory disposition, for he had never headed any political faction and had never developed any important political enemies. Once in office, his mastery of the art of politics and his command of the House of Commons gave him a longevity no other man was capable of at that time and under those circumstances.

There were three general categories of representatives in Commons: politicians, "Court and Treasury" men, and independent members. Politicians, typically, were men whose ambition for office outweighed most other considerations; so long as they and their friends were in power, they would resort to almost any means to retain it; out of favor, their basic policy was opposition to the "ins." A second group, which comprised perhaps a third of the House in 1775, were the Court and Treasury supporters—generally military men or lawyers or civil servants who supported the ministry of the king's choice because of the patronage they obtained for doing so. By all odds the largest bloc in Commons consisted of independents—most of them country gentlemen obliged to no man for their seats or for their sources of income. They were suspicious of the professional politicians who usually dominated the debates and thus inclined to side against them, but in the normal course of events were too unpredictable to be thought of as a voting bloc. These were not, however, normal times.

The curious mix of politics and prejudices that motivated these three groups was one reason why colonial problems had been so little heeded during the years of mounting trouble. Because of the way government functioned, an eighteenth-century administration, in order to survive in office and achieve real political stability, had to be led by a politician who commanded the confidence of the king and had the support of Commons. The latter qualification meant that he had to be able to count on the Court and Treasury members while not alienating too many of the independents. If, in addition to this support, the prime minister was himself also a member of Commons, he had an excellent chance of survival. Walpole and Pelham, before North, had met all the conditions, but for the first decade of George III's reign no other minister had: Grenville was in Commons, but lacked the king's confidence; Bute, Rockingham, Chatham, and Grafton were all isolated in the House of Lords. And the consequence was a succession of unstable ministries and a colonial policy that vacillated like the English weather.

Although North had shortcomings that frequently exasperated the determined king, George insisted on retaining him because he provided both political equilibrium and stability, which meant—despite all·the outcries of the Opposition—some years of almost unquestioned support for the royal policies vis-à-vis the American colonies. Edmund Burke, on so many occasions an opponent of North and his program, saw both his good qualities and his shortcomings. He was, Burke thought, "a man of admirable parts, of general knowledge, of a versatile understanding, fitted for every sort of business, of infinite wit and pleasantry, of a delightful temper, and with a mind most perfectly disinterested." But the fatal flaw was that "he wanted something of the vigilance and spirit of command that the time required." North himself recognized the deficiency, more than once owning up to an "indolence of temper." But the king, knowing he had no alternatives, clung to North through thick and thin, preferring lethargy and indecisiveness and a man he could drive to the difficulty of supplanting him. (As late as 1779 George III was still wistfully hoping that North might "cast off his indecision and bear up, or no plan can succeed; he must be more exact in answering letters or let others do it for him; and he must let measures be thoroughly canvassed before undertaken, and when adopted must not quit them.")

Burdened with enormous responsibilities and temperamentally unsuited for war, North became more despondent and exhausted by his duties as the conflict wore on. He kept saying that he wished to retire, but his friends could never decide if he meant it or not, for even when he complained that he had been "forced into the post that he now held," he was likely to add that loyalty to his monarch and a sense of obligation would prevent him from abandoning it "till the storm had subsided." As the years passed and as he began to lose hope that something—a victory, a chance for settlement—would turn up, North retired more and more into the routine of departmental work, gloomy, inaccessible, conducting his affairs out of sight in order to avoid the problems and crises that exposure might bring. Attacked during the first year of the war by Charles James Fox as a "blundering pilot," he responded with a pathetic, sniveling description of his predicament "under the weight of Government." Isaac Barré commented that if North found his office "so burdensome, so thorny, and so wretched," his countrymen would willingly release him of his charge, for it was obviously one "for which nature had never formed his talents." North, he said, "had given the world the most perfect demonstration that he could neither make war, nor establish peace." For either of those tasks, North could rely on a large following in both Houses, based upon his position at the Treasury and the patronage he controlled, but with all the help he could normally muster he had no absolute majority and had to rely on the independents to give him another sixty votes or so on any key issue. How they would vote remained to be seen, and here lay the heart of the matter, which was not resolved until the first major legislative test was put before Parliament when it sat, after the king's speech from the throne, late in October 1775.

As a practical matter the cabinet—which consisted of eight or nine principal ministers—made or approved policy. North presided at the meetings, which were conducted weekly over the dinner table unless some emergency demanded that the several ministers most concerned with a problem be quickly assembled. With him, among others, sat three secretaries of state. The Earl of Suffolk headed the Northern Department, or the department of Northern Europe; Viscount Weymouth ran the Southern Department; and, after November 1775, Lord George Germain was secretary for the American Department. When the cabinet reached a decision, which was then written up in memorandum form, the appropriate secretary of state carried it to the king and saw that it was transmitted into the proper channels and carried out. So the efficiency of the system inherited by North depended on the ability and talents of the secretaries of state, since they bore the responsibility for administering cabinet directives. In practice, few decisions of consequence were taken without cabinet approval—a technique that spread the responsibility and provided the protection of group decision for an individual.

Through seven years of an immensely trying, costly, foreign war,

North was obliged to hold his own against an extraordinary array of talent that spoke almost continuously in opposition to the policies and proposals he brought before Parliament, supported by countless letter-writers and pamphleteers who attacked the government with vehemence and venom on almost any occasion. That he was able to do so is partly a measure of the man's parliamentary skill, but also an indication of the support he had in both Houses of Parliament. First among the voices of opposition was Edmund Burke, Dublin-born and gifted in tongue as only an Irishman can be. Now in his late forties, Burke had a full, cultured mind, a vivid imagination, and a broad interest in human affairs that combined to make his the most eloquent voice for the colonial cause. In March 1775, in a brilliant speech lasting three hours, he had offered a plan for reconciling the differences between England and America, and when he finished, his brother wrote, he received "the loudest, the most unanimous and highest strains of applause," for "such a performance even from him was never before heard in that house."

Inseparable from Burke as a spokesman for liberty was gross, dissolute Charles James Fox, twenty years Burke's junior, whose passions were women, gambling, and politics, in that order. A man who "never formed a creditable connection with a woman in his life," the stumpy Fox liked to hold morning court for his admirers, dressed in a rumpled nightgown, and was cordially despised by George III for his gaming, his liaisons with women, and his brilliance. But where Burke as a speaker lacked self-control (some of his orations ran to 30,000 words) and was prone to use fulsome rhetoric, Fox came more easily to the heart of the matter. As a member wrote after hearing Burke's stirring speech on conciliation, "He is always brilliant in an uncommon degree, and yet I believe it would be better if he were less so." By contrast, Fox, "by stating crabbedly two or three of those ideas which Burke has buried under flowers . . . is thought almost always to have had more argument." Unlike Burke, Fox had money; his father, Henry, had married Caroline Lennox, daughter of the Duke of Richmond and great-granddaughter of Charles II, and had done exceedingly well for himself as paymaster general in the Seven Years' War. It was estimated that some £50,000,000 had passed through his hands during that time and much of it had rubbed off in the process.

If Fox was anathema to the king, he was nothing as compared to "that devil Wilkes." Ugly, squint-eyed, with bad teeth and a nose that looked as if it had been smashed by a fist, John Wilkes possessed a sharp, pene-trating wit which he used to considerable effect against North and his coa-lition. By this time, Wilkes had already had a remarkable career by any lights. He had married an older woman and squandered her fortune, been elected an M.P., and become publisher of the *North Briton*, a paper that dealt in scandal and personalities. The government had proceeded against him for treason following his paper's vicious attack on one of the king's speeches, had ransacked his house and arrested him, but Wilkes, sup-ported by the mob that championed him, got off. Once the government seized a parody Wilkes had written, an "Essay on Woman," and tried to convict him on charges of blasphemy and libel. When the Earl of Sand-wich, who had read the parody to the House of Lords, bumped into Wilkes at a club and asked whether he expected his career to end by the pox or a hangman's noose, Wilkes replied, "My Lord, that might depend upon whether I embraced your lordship's mistress or your principles."

Finding himself in jeopardy, Wilkes fled to France and was expelled from the House of Commons and later convicted by the Court of the King's Bench of seditious libel and blasphemy. Wilkes *in absentia* became a symbol of oppression, and huge crowds gathered in his behalf shouting "Wilkes and liberty!" In 1768, when he returned to England and a hero's welcome, he was seized and imprisoned, but the mob converged on the jail, forced the king's ministers to leave London, and then marched on the royal residence; troops rushed to the scene and opened fire on the rioters, killing six and wounding fourteen. Wilkes was sentenced to two years and a £1,000 fine; he was re-elected from Middlesex, whereupon the House declared him ineligible and called for another election. Again he was elected, rejected, and renominated. A public subscription of £20,000 (some of it from America) was raised to pay his debts and towns were named for him in the colonies—the fate of Wilkes, American dissidents came to believe, was involved with their own. When Wilkes was released from prison, he was elected an alderman of London, then lord mayor of the city, and was at last re-admitted to the House of Commons.

This thorny triumvirate and their colleagues—who realized that the liberty of the king's subject was as much an issue in Britain as it was in America—was capable of making life miserable for the North ministry, but despite all their talents and arguments, the tally of votes followed nei-ther eloquence nor logic. George III and North had behind them a solid, silent, indifferent majority that would support their policies almost unquestioningly; again and again the forces of opposition were smothered by the North steam roller. For all of Burke's eloquence, the first resolution on his plan for reconciliation was beaten by a vote of 270 to 78, and others met a similar fate.

Liberal and moderate voices were raised repeatedly in Parliament, but they were voices that went largely unheeded because they were both out of power and out of public favor. The great majority of the middle classes in England were revolted by the disorder and violence they saw across the Atlantic and, having smarted for years under what they regarded as unfairly burdensome taxes compared to what the colonials paid, they fell in comfortably with the policies of their king and his ministers. With the result, Edward Gibbon wrote, that "the executive power was driven by the national clamor into the most vigorous and repressive measures." As the summer of 1775 turned to autumn, all signs pointed to the fact that the lines were drawn and the administration increasingly confident.

By August, George III had given his reply to Lexington, Concord, and Bunker Hill. After removing Gage, "the mild general" responsible for those disgraces, he issued a proclamation, saying: "I am clear as to one point, that we must persist and not be dismayed by any difficulties that may arise on either side of the Atlantick; I know I am doing my duty . . ." Entitled "A Proclamation for Suppressing Rebellion and Sedition," it was issued on August 23, 1775, from St. James's Palace and printed by Benjamin Franklin's old friend, William Strahan. The burden of the message was that many of the king's subjects in North America, "misled by dangerous and ill-designing men," had forgotten the allegiance they owed the mother country and had engaged in rebellion. Reminding his subjects of their duty, the king called upon them to aid him in suppressing the revolt, bring the traitors to justice, and disclose all conspiracies against the realm. This was Great Britain's blunt declaration of war, an edict that ended all possibility of reconciliation. (In Paris the Comte de Vergennes recognized it for what it was and began to feel his way toward some form of active support for the rebels. In September one of his agents sailed for America to undertake discussions, and that same month Beaumarchais returned from a visit to the colonies to urge active aid for the revolution.)

Another action by the king that revealed not only how the wind was blowing but also that it was gathering gale force was his response to a petition submitted by the colonial Congress in Philadelphia. This document, which had originated in the mind of John Dickinson, spokesman for Pennsylvania's proprietary interests and the Quakers, besought the king in obsequious terms to bring about a settlement between the opposing views by repealing the statutes to which Americans had so long objected.

Signed on July 8, 1775, by virtually all members of Congress—almost one year to the day before many of the same men put their signatures to a far more important document—it was, it turned out, the last attempt on their part to settle the differences with England amicably. Written by Dickinson after the battles in Massachusetts, it represented a moderate's sincere effort to bring about reconciliation. From the standpoint of radicals in Congress, signing it was a calculated risk, done in the belief that it would be rejected and that rejection would swing the moderates into line behind a declaration of independence. Carried to England by William Penn's grandson Richard Penn, it provoked a minor tempest there and led eventually to a debate in the House of Lords on whether Penn should be called to appear before that body. Finally the peers agreed to examine Penn concerning his views on independence, the colonial capacity for resistance, and other matters; this was followed by further angry debate, centering on the argument that recognition of the petition was tantamount to recognition of the authority of the rebel Congress. But by that time it was mid-November 1775, and the rush of events had passed by the House of Lords. What was significant was that the king had refused even to receive Penn and his "Olive Branch Petition" after he and Arthur Lee presented it to Lord Dartmouth. "We thought it our duty," they wrote to Congress, "to press his Lordship to obtain an answer; but we were told, as His Majesty did not receive it on the throne, no answer would be given." In other words, George III would heed no appeal from the moderates in America, and when that message reached the New World, no one much cared what luck Penn might have with the House of Lords. On November 2 Samuel Ward of Rhode Island wrote that two ships had just arrived from England, bearing news of the Proclamation of Rebellion and of the king's rejection of the Olive Branch Petition. Ward saw immediately that both decisions would be of "immense service" to independence men, whose "councils have hitherto been too fluctuating; one day, measures for carrying on the war were adopted; the next, nothing must be done that

would widen the unhappy breach between Great Britain and the colonies
. . . Thank God, the happy day which I have long wished for has at
length arrived . . . One [southern] gentleman, who has been most sanguine for pacific measures, and very jealous of the New England colonies,
addressing me in the style of *Brother Rebel*, told me he was now ready to
join us heartily. 'We have got,' says he, 'a sufficient answer to our petition; I want nothing more, but am ready to declare ourselves independent.'"

The king's refusal to answer the petition was read in Congress on November 9 and within weeks was published by newspapers everywhere,
carrying the news to Americans of all political persuasions that there was
now no turning back. Years afterward, John Jay recalled that he had
never—"until after the second Petition of Congress"—heard any American "express a wish for the Independence of the colonies." Thomas
Jefferson wrote to John Randolph at the end of November that the colonies now had only one step to take, which was to "declare and assert a
separation. It is will alone which is wanting, and that is growing apace,
under the fostering hand of our King." And Jeremy Belknap, a chaplain
with the rebel army outside Boston, observed that independence was becoming "a favorite point" with the troops, who now found it offensive to
pray for the king.

4. It Was the War of the People

If evidence were needed of the support George III commanded in England, it was made abundantly clear when Parliament, after hearing the
king denounce the leaders of rebellion and announce his plans to increase
the size of the armed forces by hiring foreign troops, began to debate
these measures. Following his speech of October 26, 1775, a resolution
was introduced in each House, paraphrasing the royal message, and immediately debate commenced. For weeks it went on, and through all the
speeches ran a feeling of mounting rancor and frustration on the part of

the Opposition. There were constant references to the rights of British citizens, to the peril resulting if certain despotic steps taken against the colonists were in turn introduced in England. Again and again, the "unjustness of the cause" was cited, and the points made in Parliament were taken up across the land. Universities took sides, as did clergymen and merchants; even military men expressed their antipathy to the war.

Sir Jeffrey Amherst rejected offers of an active command, as did Lord Frederick Cavendish, another hero of the Seven Years' War, and General Henry Conway spoke out vigorously against crown policies. In the House of Lords the Marquis of Rockingham condemned the North ministry and called the king's program "big with the most portentous and ruinous consequences." The Earl of Coventry termed the coercive measures "madness and absurdity," saying that even if the colonists were defeated, it would require a standing army to keep them in subjection. The Duke of Grafton proposed the repeal of every bill passed since 1763 relative to America, in order to remove all points at issue; condemning the use of foreign troops, he stated that if his health did not otherwise permit, he meant "to come down to this House in a litter, in order to express my full and hearty disapprobation" of the king's proposals. The Bishop of Peterborough stated that if it was not liberty itself the colonials were contending for, "it is at least the *opinion* of liberty, which operates no less forcibly on the passions of mankind." There were references to the courage and determination of the rebels at Bunker Hill and outcries against the intended use of foreign mercenaries, but when the vote was taken there were sixty-six peers in favor of the crown's recommendations and only thirty-three opposed.

In the House of Commons the same pattern emerged—a few voices speaking for the measures, a preponderance of eloquent argument opposed, but the votes supporting the crown overwhelmingly—278 to 108. The ministry's margin of confidence clearly indicated how the independents—the country gentlemen—were voting, reassuring North and his colleagues that their policies were acceptable to the average Englishman whose opinion counted and who believed that the Americans had to be put in their place and taught a lesson. So if vindictiveness and short-sightedness often substituted for magnanimity and vision, it could not be blamed entirely on George III and his ministers. A substantial majority of their countrymen were behind them. (Years later, after the treaty of peace had been signed, North looked back on the whole disastrous affair and reminded the members of Commons that he had had the support of the country: "The American war," he noted, "has been suggested to have been the war of the Crown, contrary to the wishes of the people. I deny it. It was the war of Parliament. There was not a step taken in it that had not the sanction of Parliament. It was the war of the people, for it was undertaken for the express purpose of maintaining the just rights of Parliament, or, in other words, of the people of Great Britain over the dependencies of the empire. For this reason, it was popular at its commencement, and eagerly embraced by the people and Parliament.")

Many of those in opposition were convinced that the ministry had closed its ears to the possibility of a negotiated settlement. "Why," Sir James Lowther cried after reading the Olive Branch Petition, "have we not peace with a people who, it is evident, desire peace with us?" To which North replied that all the colonists need do was admit to Great Britain's legislative supremacy or—if they could not bring themselves to that—contribute their fair share to the support of the government.

The Opposition warned that Britain's trade would suffer from a war with the colonies. Members were reminded that America was the lifeblood of England; Mr. Bayley asserted that Britain's exports to the colonies before this "fatal war" began amounted to £3,500,000, of which 75 per cent was goods manufactured at home. But the fact of the matter was that by 1774, after the Boston Tea Party, the alliance between London's mercantile interests and the provinces had eroded badly, and British merchants were now looking to other markets. Extremism had alienated the commercial groups that had defended the provincials in earlier years, and while it was true that a war would have an adverse effect on some of them, others would profit by it. Before closing the port of Boston and taking steps to close down American trade, North had shrewdly taken soundings to assure himself that those Englishmen likely to be affected by such a move were not numerous enough to upset his plans. As for the Opposition's hopes for a more conciliatory attitude on the government's part, the debates of winter finally convinced them that there was little hope. As David Hartley put it poignantly at the end of a long debate, "Every proposition for reconciliation has so constantly and uniformly been crushed by Administration, that I think they seem not even to wish for the appearance of justice. The law of force is that which they appeal to. . . ."

But the law of force required something more than talk by the ministry: it demanded the means of applying force. Bunker Hill had convinced George III and his advisers that there could be no turning back, but when North and the cabinet began taking stock of their situation, it was evident that the military problem was formidable. Both the adjutant general of the army and the secretary-at-war were on record as saying that any conquest of America was hopeless. Even before the reports came in from Bunker Hill, the adjutant general had declared that a plan to defeat the colonies militarily was "as wild an idea as ever controverted common sense," and Lord Barrington, secretary-at-war, had equally strong opinions on the subject. He thought the Americans might be reduced by the fleet, but never by the army. John Wilkes, taunting North on the matter of military conquest, suggested that the prime minister, even if he were to ride at the head of the entire British cavalry, could not venture ten miles into the American countryside. Reminding him of the vastness of America, Wilkes observed that the sole result of the Boston campaign was the capture of "one hill of less than a mile's circumference"; as for the rest of the country, he predicted, "The Americans will dispute every inch of territory with you, every narrow pass, every strong defile, every Thermopylae, every Bunker Hill."

From his friends North could get all the advice he needed, and then some. William Innes, rising in the House of Commons to outline a pet scheme, urged that the army be shifted to one of the southern colonies where the troops could fortify themselves in impregnable positions and let the provincials attack if they pleased, while the British sallied forth as opportunity arose. In this manner, Innes reasoned, the British "success against one half of North America will pave the way to the conquest of the whole, and it is more than probable you may find men to recruit your army in America . . ." There it was: the will-o'-the-wisp that would light so many dreams of British victory, the hope that there would be a massive uprising of the loyalists, brave men and true who would rally behind the forces of the crown and put down the rebellion of their fellow countrymen so that British troops could be spared. As dissension spread throughout the rebel ranks, Innes argued, they would retreat to the interior and simply die on the vine, perishing for lack of the food, clothing, and manufactured goods which would be denied them by a naval blockade.

Speaking of the loyalists, General William Howe had given his opinion, early in 1775, that "the insurgents are very few, in comparison with the whole of the people." Estimates were made that the loyal Americans might make up as much as half the total population of the colonies. So there came into currency a half-formed notion, tucked away for the time being in the back of the official mind, that there was a large and potentially useful body of Tories over there in the colonies which might be called upon one of these days. They would be useful while fighting was going on, and more so once it was over, since the recovery of the colonies would require that they be governed by local administrations, with loyal militia preserving the reconciliation that would eventually be effected. As Lord George Germain, the American secretary perceived, the leadership of the rebellion was essentially a small, highly vocal minority, whereas loyalist sentiment was much more numerous and would certainly prevail in the long run.

Where British policymakers failed disastrously in this matter of the loyalists was in their almost total miscalculation of its effectiveness and how they could capitalize on it. Although Germain was correct in his estimate of loyalist strength, he went wrong in assuming that a considerable number of Americans *could* remain loyal or side actively with the mother country if unsupported and unsustained by the crown. The problem the loyalists on the other side of the Atlantic faced was that while they were numerous enough, they were neither organized nor evenly distributed; and where they were weak or outnumbered—as their fate in Boston had demonstrated—they were harassed and intimidated by mobs of rebellious townsmen who had the advantages of both organization and leadership.

It was an easy matter to lump all the colonial people together and to assume that all were cut from the same cloth. Between this tendency and the demands of the moment, consideration of the loyalists was virtually ignored, along with the political and military assets they represented. No effort was made in the first critically important year to cement attachments that already existed or to win over the minds of the waverers. It was a mistake so grave, some men believed, as to risk losing the colonies and perhaps even the war. But just then official Britain had its collective mind on the manpower, materiel, and logistics that would be needed to put down the insurrection.

There was, for anyone who cared to think about it, some irony in the fact that the mighty empire had a terrifying deficiency of fighting men. It had been determined that an army of 20,000 would be required to strike in the spring of 1776, since no large-scale effort could possibly be made before then. Meantime, the Irish establishment, which was supposed to consist of 13,500 troops, was down to 7,000. In England and Scotland there were 11,000 infantrymen on paper, of whom 1,500 or more were invalids, leaving no more than 9,500 soldiers with which to defend the home islands and reinforce the troops in America. Armed forces were scattered about on garrison duty—7,700 of them in Gibraltar, Minorca, the West Indies, and elsewhere. And there were 10,000 in North America or en route there, but the regiments shattered at Bunker Hill had been ordered home to begin recruiting while those remaining in Boston were still surrounded by rebels. Apart from these men, their weapons and equipment, and some stores of gunpowder, there was very little of the British presence evident on the other side of the ocean. In fact, as John Pownal wrote to General Henry Clinton in the fall of 1775, "Unless it rains men in red coats I know not where we are to get all we shall want."

Even estimating what was wanted was a formidable task, because the enemy's potential strength was almost impossible to assess. Germain's American Department figured the population of the colonies at approximately 2,500,000 souls, of whom half a million or more were Negro slaves. If one fourth of the white population could bear arms, the strategists might conjecture, the rebels could theoretically raise an army of some four- to five-hundred thousand men. But there were all those loyalists to be deducted from this figure—perhaps half?—and there was known to be a substantial body of pacifists in the colonies—individuals of strong religious conviction who would not fight no matter what their politics.

Another factor was the immense size of the country and its political division into thirteen colonies, which meant that the rebels could, under the best of circumstances, mobilize only a small fraction of the total military potential at a given moment. Still another unknown was the caliber of the American fighting man, although on this particular point a good deal of opinion was available. The British had had a close look at the colonial soldier less than twenty years earlier, when they fought side by side against the French and Indians, and at that time General James Wolfe had called the American Rangers "the worst soldiers in the universe." Wolfe's successor in North America, General James Murray, who was now governor of Minorca, assumed that George Washington's best troops must be recent immigrants to the colonies, since "the native American is a very effeminate thing, very unfit for and very impatient of war." Two months before Lexington and Concord the Earl of Sandwich had rebuked a member of Opposition on the question of numbers. "Suppose the Colonies do abound in men?" Sandwich had asked, "What does that signify? They are raw, undisciplined, cowardly men. I wish instead of forty or fifty thousand of these *brave* fellows they would produce in the field at least two hundred thousand; the more the better, the easier would be the conquest; if they did not run away, they would starve themselves into compliance with our measures . . . ."

In military circles it was almost universally believed that a war would be a quick one. As Major John Pitcairn, writing home from Boston on March 4, 1775, said, "I am satisfied that one active campaign, a smart action, and burning two or three of their towns, will set everything to rights." Reports in the wake of Lexington and Concord had tended also to confirm the low opinion of the rebels: there, when they had every advantage and should have overwhelmed the retreating, beleaguered redcoats, their lack of discipline and poor marksmanship had allowed most of the British troops to escape. Even Bunker Hill failed to convince many Englishmen that the rebels would fight; it was argued that they had finally retreated when they ran out of ammunition and were unable to withstand the bayonet charge of the regulars. (Actually, many Americans had a low regard for their own military prowess. As part of their English inheritance, they had a passionate dislike of a standing army, which was likely to be a forerunner of the loss of liberty, and they had, moreover, very little patience with any form of discipline. Although they were accustomed to handling weapons, the Americans had scant training and virtually no discipline, knew nothing of maneuvering in battle, were reluctant to serve for any length of time or at any distance from home, and—if they had to fight—preferred doing so from a concealed strongpoint or in the woods.)

A few British officers who had served in the opening campaign were skeptical, however. Lord Rawdon, writing from Boston in December 1775, predicted that future operations would be carried on "with an inveteracy unparalleled in the histories of modern wars," and that same month Charles Stuart wrote that "every circumstance seems to promise a most bloody civil war." But that was not the sort of opinion that counted for much in the England of 1775–76; events were moving too fast for the voices of caution or reason to be heard.

Contemptuous the British might be about the rebel militiamen, but few of them, no matter how eager they were for war, would deny the fantastic difficulty of fighting the Americans in their own country. Speaking in the House of Lords, the Duke of Richmond begged the peers to consult their geography books, to observe that the enormous country abounded "in forests and underwoods, intersected by deep and broad rivers . . . where every bush would conceal an enemy" and where the invading army "would be obliged to draw all its provisions from Europe, and all its fresh meat from Smithfield market."

No matter. After a summer of uncertainty and an autumn of debate, the die was cast. A policy of coercion would be followed, and preparations were already under way to reinforce the army in America. In September Lord North began discussions with a merchant-shipping agency to handle the regular movement of provisions in convoys, and in October the last regular monthly mail packet sailed for New York. As so often happens when people are not wise enough to settle their differences peaceably, war may have seemed to the ministry a simpler solution than all those that had been attempted with such signal lack of success during the past decade.

5. A Full Exertion of Great Force

Recruiting was going badly, especially in England and in Ireland, and it became clear that unless the nation were to abandon the effort to suppress the rebellion it would have to hire foreign troops, for the British army was simply not large enough to prosecute the war along with all its other commitments. The king and his advisers had been investigating several possible sources of assistance. Among the earliest considerations, which seems to have dated back to the time of a cabinet meeting in mid-June, 1775, was the employment of 20,000 Russians, and the English ambassador at St. Petersburg had been requested to sound out Catherine the Great. The Earl of Suffolk all but licked his chops in anticipation of what these mercenaries would do to the Americans: "I have been thinking about these 20,000 Russians," he said. "They will be charming visitors at New York and civilise that part of America wonderfully." It was late in the fall when George III received Catherine's refusal to lend her soldiers. "A clear refusal," he called it angrily, "and not in so genteel a manner as I should have thought might have been expected from Her; She has not had the Civility to answer in her own hand and has thrown out some expressions that may be civil to a Russian Ear but certainly not to more civilized ones."

Meantime, another plan had been entertained: the king was the Elector of Hanover, and he could rent out certain of his German regiments, freeing British garrison troops at Gibraltar and Minorca for colonial service. ("I do not mean to make one Sixpence by this," wrote the honest king.) But the lion's share of the men needed had been offered to George III in the summer of 1775 by several petty princes of Germany. These rapacious princelings customarily had difficulties meeting the expense of running their courts (Frederick, Landgrave of Hesse-Cassel, was said to have 100 children and maintained at court a French theater, an opera company, and a corps de ballet; his son William, the ruler of Hesse-Hanau, had 74 illegitimate offspring to support in addition to his other obligations). They were accustomed to renting out their subjects as a source of revenue, and when they heard of the English monarch's plight, they "snuffed the cadaverous taint of lucrative war," in Burke's wonderful phrase and wrote him volunteering the services of their men. The princes of Brunswick, Hesse-Cassel, and Waldeck, and the Margrave of Anspach-Bayreuth generously offered their troops—for a price—fully equipped and ready for duty. Offers from Bavaria and Würtemberg came in, too, but were refused because of the poor quality of the men and equipment.

No debate that had gone on before in Parliament produced an acrimony comparable to that aroused by the business of hiring mercenaries. Lord North, in introducing the proposal, stated that the only possible objection to treating with the German princes could be on the bases of whether the troops were needed, whether the terms were advantageous, and whether the force they would add was adequate to reduce America, as he put it gracefully, "to a proper constitutional state of obedience." Lord Barrington, explaining the necessity for hiring them, pointed disparagingly to the "luxury of the times," which had increased employment of the "lower orders of the people" in Britain, enabling them to go into industrial factories and thus avoid the recruiting officer. The reaction of the Opposition was immediate and about what was to be expected. Britain, said Lord John Cavendish, was "disgraced in the eyes of all Europe" by this appeal to "petty German states in the most mortifying and humiliating manner." To proceed with the treaties was to "submit to indignities never before prescribed to a crowned head presiding over a powerful and opulent kingdom." On the basis of what Lord North was asking, there would be some 12,000 foreigners in the dominions of the British crown— none of them under the control of either king or Parliament. Captain James Luttrell gave his opinion that the hiring of Hessians would cause five times their number to enlist in Washington's army and predicted that the Germans would soon desert, settle in America, and then turn about and fight the English. After Colonel Isaac Barré condemned the proposed treaties, he moved that an appeal be made to His Majesty asking him to use his best efforts to see that the foreign troops "be clothed with the manufactures of Great Britain," and this appeal to commercialism was one of the few opposition motions to pass. Chatham, warming to the subject in Lords, attacked the use of "mercenary sons of rapine and plunder, devoting them and their possessions to the rapacity of hireling cruelty! If I were an American, as I am an Englishman, while there was a foreign troop in my country, I would never lay down my arms, never! never! never!" And from Europe, Frederick the Great chimed in on the debate, stating that he would make all the Hessian troops marching through his dominions to America pay the usual cattle tax, because they had been sold as beasts.

As the Christmas holidays approached and 1775 drew to an end, the North ministry rolled up its biggest majorities on a bill that was the last significant act passed by Parliament aimed at exercising authority over the colonies. The Prohibitory Act seemed, on the surface, an ambivalent measure. On the one hand, it repealed the Boston Port Act, the Fisheries Act, and the Restraining Act—three important causes of friction. But on the other, it prohibited all trade and intercourse with the colonies during

the course of the present rebellion. North, defending the bill, also defended the use of force by saying that since the colonists had appealed to
arms, the government was bound to pursue the matter in that manner,
too. And unless the king dismissed him or unless a majority in the House
of Commons asked for his resignation, he would "not give up the conduct
of this business to anybody else."

In reply to North, Fox stated that the Prohibitory Bill was nothing less
than a declaration of war, an act of despotism that punished the loyal and
disloyal alike. On the Thursday before Christmas, just before the bill
came to a vote, David Hartley arose and delivered a wistful speech bidding farewell to the colonies. The Opposition, he realized, was "overpow-
ered by numbers, and all our entreaties and remonstrances are in vain. An
inflexible majority in Parliament have now declared all America to be an
independent hostile State." But Parliament would rue this day, he went
on, for the fate of America was clear for all to see. "You may bruise its
heel, but you cannot crush its head. It will revive again. The New World
is before them. Liberty is theirs. They have possession of a free Government, their birthright and inheritance, derived to them from their parent
State, which the hand of violence cannot wrest from them. If you will cast
them off, my last wish is to them, may they go and prosper!" But the Prohibitory Act passed by an overwhelming majority and Burke, in despair,
said "it was almost in vain to contend, for the country gentlemen had
abandoned their duty, and placed an implicit confidence in the Minister."

The following March, when John Adams learned of the measure, there
was a kind of fierce joy in the way he condemned it in a letter to Horatio
Gates: "I know not whether you have seen the Act of Parliament call'd
the restraining Act, or prohibitory Act, or piratical Act, or plundering
Act, or Act of Independency, for by all these titles is it called. I think the
most apposite is the Act of Independency, for King Lords and Commons
have united in sundering this country from that I think forever. It is a
compleat Dismemberment of the British Empire. It throws thirteen Colonies out of the Royal Protection, levels all distinctions, and makes us independent in spight of our supplications and entreaties."

Another significant development of the fall of 1775—one more indication of the government's toughening attitude—had come about after the
Duke of Grafton declared in the House of Lords that although he was ill
he would attend the debates in a litter if necessary, in order to protest the

actions being taken against America. That kind of statement was more or less to be expected from members of the Opposition, but Grafton was also a member of the cabinet and the king was incensed. When George III demanded his resignation Grafton gave it in person, using the occasion to speak bluntly about the errors of government and telling the king, apropos his decision to hire foreign troops, that "his Majesty would find too late that twice that number would only increase the disgrace, and never effect his purpose." In truth, Grafton's departure, which created an opening in the cabinet, suited the king's purposes admirably, because he and North had been trying for some time to ease Dartmouth out and replace him with a man who would press the war more vigorously. Dartmouth, the secretary of the American Department, was a close friend and relation by marriage of North, but he viewed the coming struggle with unmitigated dread. It was clear that someone of stronger fiber was needed and the king and his prime minister had fixed upon Lord George Germain. At first Germain was offered the gentle Dartmouth's position, but Dartmouth would have none of that; then, after much behind-scenes maneuvering and payoffs to certain recalcitrant ministers and fears that the ministry would fall, important administrative changes were made. Dartmouth was given the Privy Seal and his former post was taken by Germain, a controversial, stormy petrel who, with the king and North, was to become closely identified with the course and continuation of the war.

Born a Sackville, he was the favorite son of the first Duke of Dorset and had gained a certain recognition as a soldier at the battle of Fontenoy, where he was wounded leading his regiment in action. During the Seven Years' War he was lieutenant colonel of ordnance and later colonel of the regiment commanded by Wolfe. But in Germany, at the battle of Minden, his actions cost him an obloquy that plagued him for the rest of his life. Serving as commander of the British contingent under Prince Ferdinand of Brunswick, he either ignored or refused Ferdinand's orders to attack and was scathingly reprimanded in general orders. Subsequently he demanded a court martial, which found him guilty of disobedience (though not cowardice). Seven of the court's fifteen members nevertheless voted in favor of the death penalty, but a two-thirds majority was necessary and Sackville was punished by being declared "unfit to serve His Majesty in any military capacity." George II, who supported his kinsman Ferdinand against Sackville and was infuriated by the leniency shown the latter, struck out Sackville's name from the list of privy councillors with his own hand, and bitterly ordered that the court martial sentence be read to every regiment in the army. (As a final indignity, the king removed the name of Sackville's mother from the list of those customarily invited to evening parties at the court.) After George III succeeded his grandfather, Sackville was restored to the Privy Council and in 1770, in order to inherit a fortune through the will of Lady Betty Germain, he changed his name.

A tall, athletic-looking, vigorous man, Germain was melancholy, lonely, and usually dined at home alone, and although he seems to have enjoyed a happy family life, there were hints that he was a homosexual. Whatever else he may have been, he was a man of obstinacy and immense pride who had, a friend said, no ability "to attract the heart." Germain's attitude toward the war first recommended him to George III, for he was known to believe that the only solution to the American problem was a policy of firmness (he made no secret of his belief that earlier ministries had played into the Americans' hands by their cowardly repeal of the Stamp Act and by the passage of other half-hearted, ineffective measures). When he heard the news of the battle for Bunker Hill, Germain wrote a friend that "one decisive blow is absolutely necessary. After that the whole will depend upon the diligence and activity of the officers of the navy." (One characteristic that did little to endear Germain to his fellow minister the Earl of Sandwich, First Lord of the Admiralty, was that Germain never lost an opportunity to criticize the navy's weakness in America or to show his contempt for that arm.) He had neither friends nor personal following in Commons, where his numerous enemies frequently referred to his court martial and played upon his readiness to debate, where he might be exasperated into revealing a piece of information that North had managed to obscure. In the ministry itself, beside the active hatred of Sandwich, he was cordially disliked by the Earl of Bathurst, the lord chancellor, and by Barrington, who had been responsible years earlier for arranging his court martial. Happily, subordinates generally liked and respected him; as an undersecretary wrote, he had "no trash in his mind" and was both punctual and precise, customarily using language that had not a superfluous word.

Convinced that the rebellion consisted of a seditious minority that could be smashed by a quick blow, Germain favored the use of a large army and an overwhelming strike from which the Americans could not recover. "As there is not common sense in protracting a war of this sort," he wrote, "I should be for exerting the utmost force of this Kingdom to finish the rebellion in one campaign." That and a crippling commercial blockade, he believed, were the type of actions that would ultimately destroy support for the American Congress, forcing the people to turn for direction to those loyalists who had remained faithful to their king. For the herculean task before him, Germain would need every iota of his considerable energy, since he was the individual who controlled the machinery of war in the colonies, and the system's efficiency would depend in large measure upon his ability. As the pace of preparations was stepped up, he had to co-ordinate military activities in the several theaters of war, see that the lines of communication were clear there and in England, arrange for transports for men and equipment and horses, supervise the embarkation of convoys and storeships, oversee recruiting and the purchase of tents and camp gear, ordnance, and other stores, find escorts for the convoys, and solve a myriad of problems relative to the war effort.

By the middle of February 1776 Lord North was able to report to both Houses of Parliament on three treaties that had been signed with the German princes. The Reigning Duke of Brunswick had agreed to furnish a corps of infantry of 3,964 men and 336 light infantry—the corps to consist of five regiments and two battalions, furnished with tents and other necessary equipage, and commanded by "expert persons." They would all be ready for service by the last week in March. It was strictly a business arrangement: King George III would grant the corps the same pay, forage, and other perquisites as those enjoyed by his own troops and would take care of the sick and wounded in hospitals, transporting them back to Brunswick when they were no longer able to serve. Their pay was to be known as "Levy Money" and a rather complex equation had been worked out by which His Most Serene Highness the duke would be reimbursed for the soldiers furnished. Each foot soldier and trooper was to be worth thirty crowns banco (the crown was pegged at four shillings, ninepence, three farthings), and the money was to be paid the duke one third upon signature of the treaty and two thirds two months later. Thirty crowns banco would be deducted for each soldier missing without leave on the day of review by George III's commissary; three wounded men were to count as one man killed in action; "a man killed shall be paid for at the rate of levy money"; and so on. Looked at another way, His Most Serene Highness had determined that each of his subjects' lives was worth £7 4s. 4½d. to him in English money (the dead soldiers' widows and orphans would receive not one penny). In the event of extraordinary loss by battle, siege, disease, or the loss of a transport vessel, the King of England would not only make good the loss of each soldier but would also pay for recruits to replace them. And in return for the corps's oath of allegiance to His Britannic Majesty—which would be taken "without prejudice to the oath which they have taken to their Sovereign" the duke—Britain would also pay Brunswick an annual subsidy of 64,500 German crowns as long as the troops were in British hire, and twice that when their pay ceased, for a period of two years after the mercenaries returned home.

Although there were minor differences in the other treaties, the terms accepted by the Duke of Brunswick were more or less standard. The Landgrave of Hesse-Cassel agreed to provide 12,000 men—four battalions of infantry of five companies each; two companies of chasseurs; and a "General and other necessary officers." The Prince of Hesse-Cassel, Reigning Count of Hanau, was to supply 660 infantrymen; the Prince of Waldeck eventually found 670 infantrymen, two pieces of field artillery, two bombardiers, and twelve gunners; and by terms of an "Ulterior Convention" with Hesse-Cassel, signed late in April 1776, more artillery was found—a detachment of 128 men, with six fieldpieces. Eventually, counting additional levies and some troops from Anhalt-Zerbst, 29,166 Germans would serve George III in America and Canada.

As the ramifications of these arrangements became clear, it began to dawn on many Englishmen that the American war was going to be a very costly business indeed. The Duke of Richmond asked his colleagues to consider what a single American scalp would cost, computed on the basis of an estimated payment of £1,500,000 per annum for the foreign troops. Speaking for the Opposition on April 1, 1776, Hartley conjectured that the war that year alone would cost £17,000,000, and Lord North had to admit that "he could not divine what the expense of the campaign would amount to." Early in May George III called in the outstanding gold coin to help defray certain extraordinary items, while the Earl of Shelburne rose in the House of Lords to state that "this country, already burdened much beyond its abilities, is now on the eve of groaning under new taxes, for the purpose of carrying on this cruel and destructive war."

It was not only the ordinary price of waging a war that would have to be met but, as in all wars, the cost of waste and inefficiency. Already, in the autumn of 1775, storms had delayed provision ships so that the cattle they were carrying died and had to be thrown overboard; and greedy contractors were hard at work bilking the government at every opportunity. Adding to the waste was the cumbersome nature of supply operations: the navy's provisions, for instance, were purchased by its own Victualling Board, while the army's were bought by the Treasury; troopships were furnished by the Navy Board, ordnance transports by the Board of Ordnance; and so on. Naval operations were hideously complex. The service had as many men as there were in the British army, plus a huge network of dockyards and storage depots all over the world and its own recruiting and purchasing operations. Nor was its efficiency improved by the fact that John Montagu, Earl of Sandwich, First Lord of the Admiralty, was unprincipled, corrupt, and inept.

A wealthy man with political influence, the closest Sandwich came to knowledge of nautical matters was that his brother was a sailor; he seldom put in an appearance at the navy yards, knew almost nothing of ships, and when an official complained of desertions, the terrible state of discipline, and dockyards which were in "a wretched disabled state," Sandwich replied that he had "neither leisure nor inclination to enter into a discussion upon the subject." On the strength of his character alone, Sandwich would have disappeared from history. As a contemporary described him, he was "Too infamous to have a friend, Too bad for bad men to commend." But his name has gone down to posterity in the English-speaking world because he hated to be interrupted at cards: to avoid having to leave the gaming table in order to eat, the earl hit on the idea of putting some meat between two slices of bread and the resulting confection was named for him. But the story of his administration was the story of fraudulent contractors, ships in no condition for combat, stores that were bad or missing altogether, and delays real or fabricated. As Germain once complained to North, "I never could understand the real state of the fleet." Sandwich was notoriously nonchalant about everything, and when challenged that the navy was unprepared for war, he only called the Americans cowards, as if that were enough to insure British victory. The Duke of Richmond, writing to Admiral Keppel about the first lord, said, "I would determine not to trust Lord Sandwich for a piece of ropeyarn."

Unhappily for the prosecution of the war, the first lord was as autonomous as he was cavalier and had less interference from the cabinet than did most other department heads.

But even had a bigger man than Sandwich been in charge of the fleet, nothing could be done about the size of the Atlantic Ocean. It had taken nearly six weeks for London to get the news of Lexington and Concord and to realize that England was at war with her colonies. The minimum time for an Atlantic crossing was four weeks, and westbound ships took longer even under optimum conditions—a fact that had made it practically impossible before the war for officials in London to consult with royal appointees in the colonies on matters of high policy. The result had been that the government was always in the position of waiting for news or being forced to act in ignorance of the effect of earlier decisions. As Edmund Burke described the situation in his final, magnificent plea for conciliation, "Three thousand miles of ocean lie between you and them. No contrivance can prevent the effect of this distance in weakening government. Seas roll, and months pass, between the order and the execution; and the want of a speedy explanation of a single point is enough to defeat a whole system." Sometimes the westerly passage took two months, and during the war it was not unheard of for an important dispatch to reach its ultimate destination in the colonies three or four months after leaving London. One cause of delays, as the war continued, was the activity of American cruisers, but the shortage of dispatch vessels and the North Atlantic storms also took their toll (Admiral Keppel warned in November 1775 that "no vessels could keep the sea upon the coast of North America in the winter season"). All of which left British battlefield strategy largely in the hands of the commander in the field. If at times he was confused, the fault lay partly in the time lag, but even more in the ambivalence of the North administration's policy that the long months of rancorous debate had made so evident.

Again and again, defending his program, Lord North would remark that "we are prepared to punish, but we are nevertheless ready to forgive." There was a curious duality of purpose implicit in such a statement, a picture of a war leader bearing in one hand the club of coercion and in the other the carrot of conciliation, as if he were never entirely sure which one to employ. Where the American objective of absolute independence, once proclaimed, was clear-cut, Britain's turned out to be diffuse and limited: it was the overthrow of the revolutionary government and the punishment of all rebels, but only as a preliminary step toward the final harmonious restoration of the colonies to the mother country. As long as a political accommodation would be sought, it meant that there would be no scorched-earth policy, no extensive destruction of enemy property in villages or towns. It would be a limited war.

The ambiguity extended even to the character of the enemy, who was, after all, of the same race—a fellow countryman, in fact—and whose loyalty to the crown might be extremely difficult to determine. Some of this dilemma was to be detected in the words of George III, who had far fewer doubts than most of his subjects; after General Howe's victories in New York in 1776, the king wrote him that "Notes of triumph would not have been proper when the successes are against subjects, not a foreign foe." Behind this confusion of objectives lurked a far more serious problem, of continuous concern to thoughtful men: while England concentrated her military and naval resources in North America, there was the risk that Europe's major maritime powers—vengeful and adventurous and undistracted by war on the Continent—would form a coalition against her. It was the dread of such an eventuality that had guided British foreign policy for centuries, and the American war made such a possibility all the more likely.

As a direct result of the somewhat contradictory government attitudes, the expeditionary force bound for North America in the spring of 1776 was to be commanded by the Howe brothers, an admiral and a general, who were simultaneously charged—along with their military duties—with negotiating a peace with the American rebels. The logic behind this split role was that the army would teach the insurgents obedience by the example of overwhelming force; the navy would show them the economic consequences of rebellion by a blockade of their coast; and in the resulting chaos, a political solution would be found. In the king's October speech, he had proposed sending commissioners to the colonies to treat with any of them that might wish to renew allegiance to the crown. It was generally accepted that the king had little faith in this maneuver, since he had long since concluded that force was the only way to solve the problem, but he may have acquiesced in it as a sop to those who still believed that conciliation must be tried. "I have always feared a commission as not likely to meet with success," he told North, "yet I think it right to be attempted, whilst every act of vigour is unremittingly carried on." Two months later he was more certain than ever that he was right and was convinced that a conciliatory attitude would enrage the majority of Englishmen. Nevertheless, in the early months of 1776 the choice of commissioners had narrowed down to Richard, Lord Howe, the admiral, and his younger brother, General William Howe. A number of factors had influenced their appointment, but in each case a certain logic, combined with political expediency, reassured the government in its choice.

General Howe was already in America, of course. He had arrived in Boston late in May 1775, in time to lead the attack three weeks later against the rebel defenses around Bunker Hill. A big man for that day, he was six feet tall and, like his older brother, "Black Dick," had a swarthy complexion and dark hair. The two men were so taciturn that they were considered inscrutable by contemporaries (Horace Walpole referred to William as "one of those brave silent brothers [who] was reckoned sensible, though so silent that nobody knew whether he was or not." And a soldier who knew the general remarked that the two brothers had in common "the sullen family gloom. In one thing they differed, Sir William hated business and never did any.") Yet both were generally regarded as capable military officers. William had served in the army in Europe and first came to America in 1759 to command the British light infantry. He led the "forlorn hope" under Wolfe that stormed the Heights of Abraham, served in Havana, and as a major general was selected to train the light companies of army regiments. Politically, he was opposed to the war: as a member of Parliament from Nottingham, he assured his constituents in the 1774 election campaign that if he were appointed to command in an American war he would refuse.

There had been another brother—George Augustus, third Viscount Howe—who was one of the most popular men in the colonies at the time of his death in Abercromby's hopeless frontal attack on Fort Ticonderoga in July 1758. Afterward, some of the New Englanders who had served with him and loved him erected a monument in Westminster Abbey in memory of "the affection their officers and soldiers bore to his command," and in America a legacy of glamour still attached to the name Howe. It was thought that this was one reason behind William's appointment to command, but another factor that may have been involved was the brothers' illegitimate descent from George I.

In both the Howes could be seen the same curious ambivalence that characterized so much of what was happening in England in 1776. On the one hand there was the general's extraordinary personal courage in battle, demonstrated at Bunker Hill; yet there was his imprudent remark to his Nottingham constituents and a remarkable letter he had written to a Mr. Kirk of his home district in February 1775 in reply to Kirk's question if Howe remembered his pledge not to serve in America: "My going [to America] was not of my seeking," he said. "I was ordered, and could not refuse, without incurring the odious name of backwardness to serve my country in distress . . . Every man's private feelings ought to give way to the service of the public at all times; but particularly when of that delicate nature in which our affairs stand at the present." In somewhat similar fashion, Admiral Howe had hemmed and hawed about fighting the colonists. In a Commons debate, in his plodding, almost inarticulate way, he had "lamented the struggle which every British officer must feel whose lot it was to serve in such critical situations." Professing himself—like all British military men—animated by glory of his country, he nevertheless had to admit that in the present circumstances an "alacrity for battle" was missing. But on the other hand, should his sovereign command him to go he would consider it his duty to obey. Like his brother, Lord Howe was favorably disposed to the Americans, but the truth of the matter was that both of them were seeking employment at the beginning of the war and found it prudent to rationalize acceptance of a command. How prudent in the admiral's case might be seen from the fact that while it was said he had not spoken to Lord George Germain since the St. Malo expedition of 1758 and "both hates and despises Lord Sandwich," those were the two men through whom he would have to conduct all his business from America.

When the curious mission of the Howe brothers was debated in the House of Commons, they were much praised as officers, but a number of members questioned their qualifications as peace negotiators. "They have now got a character which they are entire strangers to," Lord John Cavendish objected, "the filling of which, even if the nature of the business would permit, I much doubt they are equal to." In reply, North indicated that the Howes' instructions did not give them enough leeway to embarrass the government. They had the power only to grant "general and also special pardons" and to "confer with any of his Majesty's subjects, without exception." (General Thomas Gage had been given much the same authority when, on June 12, 1775, he had issued a general pardon, excepting from it only John Hancock and Samuel Adams. Anyone refusing the pardon was to be treated as a rebel and a traitor.) The Howes were also empowered to inquire into the state and causes of the provincials' complaints—although the hour was rather late for that. The commissioners "cannot offer any terms," North assured the House; "they hold out no ultimatum; they make no concessions"; their mission was strictly to confer and to ascertain what grounds for peace might exist. Meantime, North reminded his audience, the Americans must have "some proof of our resolution and power." Thus the Howes, at the head of an awesome expeditionary force, would hold out an olive branch of sorts—or at least give the impression of doing so. While admitting that their peace mission had slim hopes of succeeding, North was sure it was worth trying if the nation could derive any benefit from it. Furthermore, he concluded unexpectedly, "the business of a General is as much to negotiate as to fight." Such a role might also give him some knowledge of the enemy's strength, some insight into "important secrets" which could serve as a basis for future accommodation. Charles James Fox denounced the plan as a high-level spying maneuver while Lord George Germain disagreed with the conciliatory move for a different set of reasons. He had no desire to delay the inevitable with an ill-conceived peace mission; as William Knox, his undersecretary wrote, "The truth was, Lord George having now collected a vast force, and having a fair prospect of subduing the Colonies, he wished to subdue them before he treated at all."

Similarly, the King of England.

In his speech closing the session of Parliament on May 23, 1776, George III left no doubt as to the royal intentions. There was in his words a perfunctory hint of appeasement, but there was no mistaking the steel behind them. "We are engaged in a great national cause," he said, "the prosecution of which must inevitably be attended with many difficulties, and much expense; but when we consider that the essential rights and interests of the whole empire are deeply concerned in the issue of it, and can have no safety or security but in that constitutional subordination for which we are contending, I am convinced that you will not think any price too high for the preservation of such objects.

"I still maintain a hope that my rebellious subjects may be awakened to a sense of their errors, and that, by a voluntary return to their duty, they will justify me in bringing about the favourite wish of my heart, the restoration of harmony and the re-establishment of order and happiness in every part of my dominions. But if a due submission should not be obtained from such motives and such dispositions on their part, I trust that I shall be able, under the blessings of Providence, to effectuate it by a full exertion of the great force with which you have entrusted me."

CHAPTER THREE

1. A Mere Insidious Maneuvre

One of the agreeable aspects of Colonel Henry Knox's headquarters at the foot of Broadway was the fine view it afforded of New York Harbor. Knox was a native of another seaport town, Boston, where a modest success as the owner of a bookstore had taught him to seize the niceties of life where he found them. Here in New York he had gotten into the habit of eating breakfast on the broad stair landing over the front entrance, where he could look out the window and watch the morning sunlight play on the shimmering water and gleam on sails of small craft plying back and forth across the bay. It was a pleasant prospect: off to the left, beyond the village of Brooklyn, lay farm country and the sandy reaches of Long Island; to the right were the salt marshes of New Jersey; and beyond them the soft green hump of Staten Island. A pleasant prospect, ordinarily, that is— but not on that particular morning in late June 1776, when Knox sighted, off to the south and moving through the Narrows, the topmasts and sails of dozens of ships, which could mean only one thing. The British had arrived at last.

Coming on before a spanking breeze and a fast-moving tide, the vessels were capable of reaching the city in half an hour, and New York was suddenly in a panic—alarm guns firing, troops running to their posts, women packing up belongings and wondering fearfully about the children's safety, while Knox—after furiously scolding his wife Lucy for not having left town earlier for some place of refuge—hustled off to see that his batteries were ready for action. (Lucy, who was almost as fat as her mountainous husband, was hastily packed off to Connecticut, where she lost no time in making known her opinion of the local residents. She was a Flucker of Boston, daughter of Thomas Flucker, the former secretary of the province, who had departed with his wife when the British evacuated the city, and although Lucy had married a plain man who was wedded to the rebel cause, she was apt to put on airs. "Take care, my love," her husband cautioned her, "of permitting your disgust [of] the Connecticut people to escape your lips . . . The want of that refinement which you seem to speak of is, or will be, the salvation of America; for refinement of manners introduces corruption and venality.")

New York's moment of terror was premature. The British fleet sailed in, dropped anchor off Staten Island and for the time being did nothing, but from what Knox and others in New York could judge of the enemy's intentions, it began to look as if John Adams had been right in saying that the talk of peace overtures was like waiting for "a Messiah that will never come." Adams commented acidly that all this nonsense about peace commissioners was "as arrant an illusion as ever was hatched in the brain of an enthusiast, a politician, or a maniack."

Yet the Declaration of Independence was scarcely a week old when a curious episode gave Americans a hint of the schizophrenia that prevailed in London. While thousands of troops were disembarking from those transports anchored in the bay, and cannon, ammunition, and tons of supplies piled up on the shores of Staten Island, Admiral Howe made his first move in the role of peace commissioner. It was on Sunday, July 14, a day of pelting rain which prevented the holding of divine services aboard the flagship, when Lieutenant Philip Brown of the Royal Navy climbed into a waiting barge to be rowed under a flag of truce toward lower Manhattan. Americans in three boats put out to meet him in the middle of the harbor, and when they learned that he carried a letter from Howe to Washington they ordered him to lay to while they returned for instructions. Back they came, shortly, with Knox and Washington's adjutant, Joseph Reed, on board, to ask how the letter was addressed. Brown stood up in the barge, bowed, took off his hat, and informed them it was a letter from Lord Howe to Mr. Washington.

"Sir," Reed replied stiffly, "we have no person in our army with that address."

Brown showed them the outside of the letter, which clearly bore the inscription, "George Washington, Esq., New York." Reed repeated that he could not accept the letter and Brown, mystified, asked what address was required. It should be inscribed with the name of *General* Washington, came the response, a title all the world knew "since the transactions of last summer." There appeared to be little more that Brown could do under the circumstances, so after exchanging a few letters from prisoners to their friends, the officers saluted and the boats started to pull away. But Lieutenant Brown could not resist one last comment: "I am sure my Lord Howe will lament exceedingly this affair," he told them, "as the letter is quite of a civil nature, and not a military one. He laments exceedingly that he was not here a little sooner." (The Americans took this to be a reference to the recent Declaration of Independence.) Then Brown bid them farewell in what Knox described as "the most genteel terms imaginable" and headed back to the flagship to report.

The admiral, who seems to have believed that he could bring about a peace within ten days, was thoroughly annoyed. "So high is the Vanity and Insolence of these Men!" his secretary Ambrose Serle wrote. The truth was that "the Punctilio of an Address" would never have stood in the way of receiving a letter from such an important personage had the rebels been the least disposed to treat with him. "They have uniformly blocked up every Avenue to Peace," Serle complained, so that "there now seems no Alternative but War and Bloodshed, which must lay at the Door of these unhappy People."

The following day the Howe brothers conferred, swallowed their pride, and decided to try again, and on the sixteenth sent another message to "Mr. Washington." Again the little *opera bouffe* was repeated, the letter was refused "for the same idle and insolent reasons," and the next day the commissioners tried another tack, inquiring if His Excellency General Washington, would be willing to receive General Howe's adjutant general. Word came back immediately that he would, and an appointment was set for noon on July 20.

Both parties prepared carefully for the interview: Washington, meticulously dressed, came early to Knox's headquarters and had his guard drawn up at attention in front of the house, with orders to open ranks when the British officer arrived. And when Lieutenant Colonel James Patterson appeared, he addressed the American commander in a manner that would have done justice to some royal presence. Every other word, Knox reported, was "May it please your Excellency," or "If your Excellency so pleases." Then he came to the heart of the matter. He explained that Lord Howe and his brother were empowered by His Majesty

George III to settle the unhappy differences with the American colonies and that Patterson's visit should be considered as the first in a series of steps leading toward that goal. Washington replied that as commander in chief of the army he had no authority to discuss the subject and stated bluntly that it was his impression that the commissioners were only authorized to grant written pardons. If this was the case, he went on, there could be little reason for further discussion, since the Americans did not believe they were in the wrong but were only defending what they regarded as their natural rights. This unsettled Patterson, who brought the conversation around to the exchange of prisoners, and finally inquired, "Has your Excellency no particular comments with which you would please to honor me to Lord and General Howe?"

"Nothing, sir," Washington replied, "but my particular compliments to both."

And there the interview ended. Before the British officer left he was offered a "cold collation" (which Knox regretted that Lucy could not have shared, since the general's servants "did it tolerably well"), but Patterson refused, saying he had had a late breakfast and that the admiral and the general were waiting lunch for him.

So, the carrot having failed, the stick would be used, and the peace commissioners donned the habits of warriors. By now it was apparent to every American family in the vicinity of New York that the big push was coming. As the daughter of Brigadier General John Morin Scott, a New York militia commander, wrote, "We have our coach standing before our door every night, and the horses harnessed ready to make our escape, if we have time. We have hardly any clothes to wear; only a second change." Warned by William Livingston that the British army was about to move, the Scotts fled from their house on the night of a violent thunderstorm. "We were obliged to stop on the road and stay all night," the young lady went on, "and all the lodgings we could get was a dirty bed on the floor. How hard it seems for us, that have always been used to living comfortable! Papa, with his brigade, has gone over to Long Island, which makes us very uneasy. Poor New York! I long to have the battle over, and yet I dread the consequences." As well indeed she might.

A few days before General William Howe's mighty army was ferried across the bay to Long Island, his brother the admiral received a friendly letter from Benjamin Franklin, whom he had known in London. Franklin assured Lord Howe that the sincerity of his countrymen, as expressed in their petitions to the crown, was genuine, but that the contempt with which those proposals had been rejected had completely altered the sentiments of Americans toward the mother country. To suppose that they could now be persuaded to submit to Britain's demands was fruitless—the time for that sort of thing was long since past. The Howes, by then, had reached the same conclusion and decided that a successful invasion of Long Island might persuade the rebels to change their tune.

When the first British warships arrived in New York Harbor, causing Knox and others such consternation, there was no way the Americans could know how large a force the British planned to use against them. But in the days that followed, the immensity of England's effort began to be evident: on June 29 forty-five ships sailed into the bay; on June 30 eighty-two more arrived, and from these vessels over 9,000 British regulars debarked onto Staten Island. Nor did there seem any end to it: in July another fleet came in from England; thirty transports, escorted by nine men-of-war under Admiral Peter Parker, sailed into port from Charleston, South Carolina, where they had been turned back by the guns of Fort Sullivan; and on August 12, twenty-eight transports and more warships hove into sight. An American rifleman named Daniel McCurtin had been one of the first to see the vast force that began to arrive in June: "I was upstairs in an outhouse," he said, "and spied as I peeped out the Bay something resembling a wood of pine trees trimmed. I declare, at my noticing this, that I could not believe my eyes, but keeping my eyes fixed at the very spot, judge you of my surprise when in about ten minutes, the whole Bay was full of shipping as ever it could be. I declare that I thought all London was afloat." With an almost audible sigh of relief, McCurtin's journal continued: "Just about five minutes before I see this sight, I got my discharge."

It was, all told, an army of 32,000 well-disciplined, trained, thoroughly professional soldiers, all of them well-armed and equipped, and supported by ten ships of the line, twenty frigates, hundreds of transport vessels, and possibly 10,000 seamen—the greatest expeditionary force Britain had ever sent out from its shores. More ominous, this huge array of armed might was only one part of a strategic movement that called for General William Howe to seize Manhattan and march northward up the Hudson Valley, while General Guy Carleton, with another army, pushed south from

Canada through the Champlain Valley to join him in Albany. Once in control of the Hudson, the British could isolate New England from the other colonies and deal with the two regions separately. As an English general was to put it, ". . . as long as a British army held the passes of that noble river and her cruisers swept their coasts, the colonists would have found it almost impossible to have joined or fed their respective quotas of troops."

To oppose this formidable host, George Washington had less than 20,000 men under arms, led by amateur officers, none of them adequately trained or equipped, all poorly supplied and paid in paper dollars whose value was diminishing with each passing day. As one of Washington's aides predicted, "A warm and bloody campaign is the least we may expect," and at dawn on August 22, after a violent storm had lashed the bay, the Americans saw the awesome British fighting machine go into action. While half a dozen naval vessels took station in Gravesend Bay to cover the movement, more than eighty flatboats and galleys began transporting enemy infantry from Staten Island to Long Island. Boatload after boatload moved across the water, carrying light infantry and grenadiers of the British army; then the watching Americans caught their first glimpse of the German mercenaries, the so-called "Hessians," whose arrival they had dreaded ever since they learned that King George III had hired them to bring the British army to full strength.* Some 8,000 soldiers from Brunswick, Hesse-Cassel, Hesse-Hanau, and Waldeck were heading into combat for the first time in America. They had set foot in the New World for the first time on Staten Island, under circumstances that neither they nor the British had found congenial, sleeping at night on the sand, with nothing to cover them but a few bushes "that harbour millions of moschitoes—a greater plague than there can be in Hell itself," as one Scots soldier complained. And there had been an incident that deeply troubled the German soldiers. On a hot August night, just before they went into action, hundreds of British and Germans had sat around an enormous bonfire, laughing and cheering while four rebel leaders were

---

* As early as May 9, 1776, Washington wrote to Artemas Ward reporting a rumor that the German troops were en route to America and, by coincidence, that same day Ward sent a letter to the commander in chief stating that the captain of a vessel which left Cork on April 1 had brought word that "Hessians and Hanoverians were coming to America." Later in the summer, Congress voted a reward of fifty acres of land to any Hessian who would desert and become an American citizen.

burned in effigy. The figures of John Witherspoon, president of the college at Princeton, and Generals Washington, Israel Putnam, and Charles Lee had just been set afire when a wild thunderstorm suddenly interrupted the fun. The soldiers dashed for whatever shelter they could find, and after the rain had passed, some of the men returned to the vicinity of the bonfire to discover that three of the dummies had been consumed by the flames, but the effigy of George Washington remained intact, as good as it ever was. The symbolism was not lost on the foreigners; as a British deserter relayed the story, the incident "caused a great deal of fear among the Hessian troops, most of whom are very superstitious."

Once the enemy made his move, Washington was going to need all the help he could get, supernatural or otherwise. While waiting to see what William Howe would do, he had divided his army, leaving most of the men on Manhattan to cover a stroke there, while ferrying others over to Long Island. It was a risky maneuver with the British navy at hand, but until he could be certain of Howe's plans, Washington had no choice but to have troops ready to defend both places. Even when he saw the enemy barges heading for Long Island he thought it was a feint; he was sure the blow would fall on Manhattan. The result of this indecision, a Hessian officer noted gleefully, was that "not a soul opposed our landing."

What followed is quickly told. Washington's outnumbered, outgeneraled troops were badly beaten on Long Island, although by a minor miracle the survivors escaped when they were ferried across to Manhattan under cover of rain and a providential fog. Routed again when the British landed at Kip's Bay, they lost New York City and fled to the upper reaches of Manhattan Island where they were licking their wounds when Howe sprang another surprise. This time it was an amphibious turning movement, a landing in Westchester designed to cut off Washington's supplies and his line of retreat. To counter it, the rebel commander left about 1,500 men in the stronghold known as Fort Washington, at the northern end of Manhattan Island, and fell back to White Plains where, on October 28, a rough but inconclusive skirmish was followed by another American retreat.

In ten weeks, Washington had lost Long Island, New York City, and much of Westchester. On the whole of Manhattan Island, the rebels held only one isolated fort. And to the British, so far, it all seemed like a glorious, laughable lark. As Francis, Lord Rawdon, described it to Francis

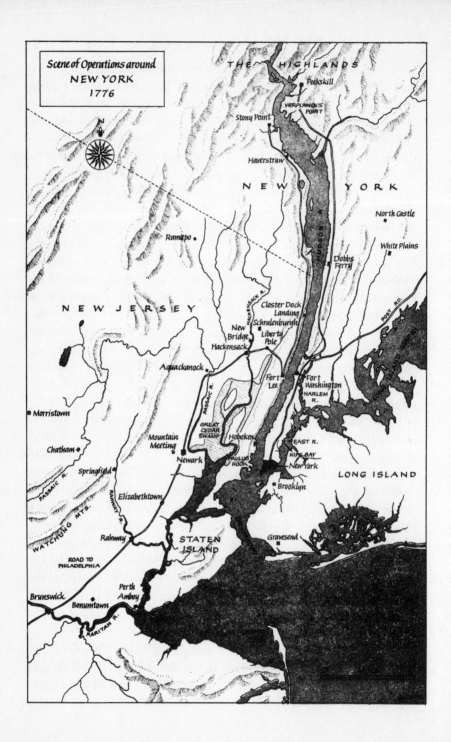

Scene of Operations around
NEW YORK
1776

Hastings, tenth Earl of Huntingdon, "the fair nymphs" of the American countryside "are in wonderful tribulation, as the fresh meat our men have got here has made them as riotous as satyrs. A girl cannot step into the bushes to pluck a rose without running the most imminent risk of being ravished, and they are so little accustomed to these vigorous methods that they don't bear them with the proper resignation, and of consequence we have most entertaining courts-martial every day." In good health and fine spirits, the English troops could scarcely wait to get at the "first corps of psalm-singers" they could find, although Rawdon confessed that his grandmother might change sides if she knew that the Hessians "sing hymns as loud as the Yankees, though it must be owned they have not the godly twang through the nose which distinguishes the faithful." Noting that Carleton's recent success in Canada had thoroughly dispirited the rebels—who now had his victorious army in their rear and Howe's before them—Rawdon stated flatly that Washington's rabble "cannot bear the frown of adversity." The Americans had pulled together all the troops they could muster, but these soldiers and all the earthworks they might put up would only be trifling obstacles to "a body of men so keen for service as ours are."

A major change of heart on the part of British planners rather than a desire to give the troops an outing was behind this New York campaign. Now that a major war was contemplated, Boston, which had loomed so large in 1775, was all but forgotten, since New York—which dominated all land and water communications—was the *only* essential city in America from a military standpoint. Beyond all other strategic considerations, it was the gateway to the mighty Hudson River, a huge arm of the sea that was navigable for 150 miles to a point beyond Albany. The planners in London, studying their maps, could draw a line from there to Lake George, which looked to be a stone's throw from Lake Champlain, which flowed into the Richelieu River, which emptied into the St. Lawrence, and see that by holding this long, arterial chain of water they could split the former colonies in two, neatly severing New England from the middle and southern provinces. And the beauty of the Hudson was that it was an estuary; ocean tides ran all the way to Albany and except during the spring runoff the lower river had scarcely any downstream current to hinder the fleet. With the navy at Howe's disposal, New York would be a British bastion, guarded almost literally by sea power alone. Its control gave the British an interior position, shoving Washington's communications northward some thirty miles beyond the British lines to the Hudson crossing between Stony Point and Verplanck's Point, as a result of which, any rebel troops moving between New Jersey and Connecticut had to make a long, time-consuming detour. Because the British fleet might sail up the Hudson, Washington was compelled to keep his main supply depots at Fishkill, behind the looming wall of the Highlands, and the forts and batteries protecting them suddenly became critically important.

Soon after the Long Island debacle, Admiral Howe sent another letter to Franklin in Philadelphia, expressing again his hope of bringing about peace. As the admiral knew, the British victory had not only demoralized the rebel army and put faint-hearted civilians in a mood to accept an easy way out of the war; it had also given the peace commissioners a useful face card to play in the tricky game of negotiation.

This particular face belonged to Major General John Sullivan, a swarthy, arrogant man from New Hampshire who seemed destined to travel under some unlucky star. Sullivan was one of a number of American prisoners taken on Long Island, and since captured officers of high rank were treated in the eighteenth century rather like guests, it was natural that there should be a good deal of conversation between Lord Howe and his captive over dinner and wine, much of it having to do with the issues underlying the conflict. The British seemed to have high hopes that in Sullivan they had the proper agent for their purposes, for he was, Captain Frederick Mackenzie remarked, "bred to the law, and is said to be one of their best officers," while a Hessian colonel pronounced him a "man of genius." Sullivan was neither, and unfortunately he was impressed with his own importance and was something of a fool and fell hook, line, and sinker for the bait served up by the admiral and his secretary Serle. England wished only for a peaceful settlement, Howe told him repeatedly, but if he as peace commissioner were to have any chance of success, he had to converse with Washington or with some members of Congress. The problem of approaching the latter, he said candidly, was that he could not treat with them as officials, since that would be tantamount to recognizing Congress; but, on the other hand, there was no reason he could not meet them as private citizens. The thought of playing an important role in bringing about peace appealed greatly to Sullivan, and on August 30, after giving his parole, he was allowed to pass through the

American lines to request Washington's permission to go to Philadelphia and pass the word of Howe's desire to negotiate. Reluctantly, Washington approved, and Sullivan rode off toward the capital, unaware that he was about to open a real can of worms.

On September 2 he appeared before a session of Congress to announce sweepingly that the Howes had full power to negotiate and that Lord Howe personally believed that Great Britain's taxation policies were unjust and that the government had no right to interfere with the colonies' internal affairs. Sullivan was asked to put all this in writing, which he did the next day, significantly omitting any mention of Howe's putative denial of England's right to control America's internal business. John Adams, who regarded Sullivan as a gullible decoy, told Benjamin Rush sourly that he wished the first ball fired on Long Island had gone through Sullivan's head, for the paroled general had presented Congress with a first-class dilemma. If they made no move to follow up Howe's offer to talk, they would be accused of wishing further bloodshed; on the other hand, if they accepted Howe's invitation to send certain members as private citizens, they forfeited recognition as the legitimate representatives of the new American government. Adams was vexed by the whole matter: he recognized that it must have been highly tempting to Sullivan to undertake this confused errand, but the man had been taken in so thoroughly and had reported the facts of the case so badly that Adams felt nothing but contempt for him. Sullivan should have realized that the times were too critical to indulge in a wild goose chase like this; neither the army nor the Congress nor anyone else could afford to have their attention diverted "by such a poor artifice and confused tale." It was a thoroughly reprehensible business as far as Adams could judge, yet Congress devoted four days to solemn debate on what should be done.

One faction favored the outright rejection of Howe's offer; another was for hearing what he had to say. Dr. Witherspoon argued that since there was not the slightest thought of giving up the independence Congress had just declared, a conference with the Howes would only be a "forerunner of disgrace" that would encourage the Tories and further dishearten independence men and the army. No one had any real hope for the meeting, but it was finally decided that a committee of Congress—not those private citizens Lord Howe had asked for—should go and find out if Howe had any authority to deal with them and what his proposition was. So John

Adams, Benjamin Franklin, and Edward Rutledge were duly appointed to call on Lord Howe on Staten Island and go through what all of them regarded as a charade.

Before leaving Philadelphia, Adams wrote his cousin Sam, who was then in Boston, to reassure him—knowing that the old fire-eater would have a fit if he thought that Congress was planning to kowtow to the British. And on September 14, after the conference with Howe, he sent off another letter reporting that the entire affair, as he had foreseen, had been a waste of time.

The peace commission was "a bubble, an Ambuscade, a mere insidious Maneuvre, calculated only to decoy and deceive," and their conversation had made it clear that Howe had no real authority to accomplish anything of value. He could talk to American rebels, he could listen to their grievances, and he could grant pardons, but beyond that he had to refer matters back to England for action. And what good that might do, anyone could guess. At the meeting Franklin told the admiral that since America would surely not accept British domination again, it was the duty of good men on both sides of the Atlantic to do what they could to promote peace, acknowledge America's independence, and work out a treaty of friendship and alliance between the two sovereign countries. Rutledge added a new wrinkle: he observed that the colonies had submitted for two years "to all the Inconveniences of Anarchy" and had lived virtually without governments, all in hopes that a reconciliation could be achieved. Nothing had come of this effort, the Americans' patience had run out, and now they had their own governments. Surely, Adams cut in, His Lordship did not imagine that they could reverse all that now? And surely, after they had declared their independence, the government of Great Britain would not trust them if they agreed to revert to the old form of government? (Adams took some pride in the fact that he was not as awed by Lord Howe as he had expected to be. He told his wife Abigail that Howe was a well-bred man about fifty years old, but with a manner "not so irresistable as it has been represented. I could name you many Americans in your own Neighbourhood, whose Art, Address and Abilities are greatly superiour.")

Since none of the committee had expected their mission to accomplish anything, the best they could say was that it had been an agreeable excursion—four days' relief from the unending problems facing Congress.

From the British standpoint, the failure of the efforts to deal with Congress meant that there was only one other recourse, which was to try to reach the American people directly, so on September 19 the Howes issued a proclamation warning of the consequences of risking their lives for an "unjust and precarious cause" and urging them to return to allegiance to the king. But they received so little evidence of willingness on the rebels' part to accept their offer to restore "public tranquillity," that the overtures were dropped, to await a more propitious moment. Their military expectations gave the brothers Howe good reason to suppose that such a moment might be coming soon.

2. The Troops Were in High Spirits

Five miles inland from the Hudson, the village dozed in the warm sun of Indian summer, the most glorious autumn in memory. Although it was the county seat, Hackensack was less a town than a string of individual houses, mills, and other buildings clustered for convenience' sake along the post road; the pulse of the settlement beat in the rich countryside surrounding it—in the well-watered pastures, fertile meadows, and farmsteads as prosperous as the Dutch who owned them. The Hackensack Valley was dotted with solid, comfortable, sandstone houses, with high-peaked roofs and curved, overhanging eaves; beyond them were fat red barns, well-fed, sleek horses, and the big, heavy Dutch wagons that were a symbol of prosperity throughout the middle colonies. Not without reason had a governor of New York called his New Jersey neighbors "the most Easie and happy people of any collony in America."

There was little to suggest that a war was as nearby as the Paulus Hook ferry operated by Fatty Van Vorst. Fatty's landing was just ten miles from Hackensack—an afternoon's trip by water or road—yet anyone making the three-quarter-mile ferry ride from the New Jersey shore to the foot of Cortlandt Street in lower Manhattan now passed under the guns of British warships and landed in a city occupied by British and Hessian soldiers. There were signs—more and more of them every day—that the fighting which had erupted in New England and New York would come before long to New Jersey. Already the serene valley had become a meeting place for deserters, spies, and the other shadowy characters who move in and out of the periphery of war; the more prudent families in the neighborhood had packed up and moved elsewhere, to wait until danger passed by; and nearly every Whig house in the region sheltered a refugee from New York. By day and night, anxious men and women hurried along the road, driven by knowledge that Indian summer was ideal campaigning weather for the British army.

Where the village green faced the road leading to Philadelphia, there was a white-steepled church, a stone courthouse, an inn, and—at the head of the green—an imposing house built of dressed stone three feet thick, which was the home of Hackensack's leading citizen, Peter Zabriskie. Zabriskie, whose surname came from a Polish ancestor who had migrated to America by way of Holland in 1662, was related by blood or marriage to a number of Dutch families in the area. A deeply religious man, he was equally intense about his politics, and in 1774 he had gone as a delegate to New Brunswick to elect representatives to the First Continental Congress; the following year he was a member of the local Committee of Correspondence. In a region sharply divided by the dispute with the mother country, no one had to ask where Peter Zabriskie stood, and it was almost inevitable, when—in mid-November 1776—General George Washington, the commander in chief of the American army, sought a headquarters in Hackensack, that his staff would select the three-story Zabriskie house as the right place.

Washington was bone tired. Behind him were two and a half months of desperate campaigning and a succession of humiliating, heartbreaking defeats, and it was a measure of his helplessness that just now, in order to ride from White Plains to Hackensack, he had had to make a sixty-five-mile detour to avoid the British pickets and the warships patrolling the lower Hudson. Ordinarily the soul of patience and tact, it was all the commander in chief could do to conceal the scars of the past months, the agonies of frustration and disillusionment, while trying to make plans to meet the dangers that threatened from every side. What now confronted him was the specter of total disaster, for after running away from the enemy since the end of August, he was now running out of men and time. It appeared that only the onset of winter might save him—weather that would drive the enemy into barracks and give the Americans time to draw breath and replace their losses; but the beautiful autumn days held, and the enemy could be expected to make the most of them.

Since there was no way to confront the British on anything like equal terms in a stand-up fight, Washington and his officers decided at a council of war on November 6 to split the army into four parts, on the theory that Howe must be prevented from overrunning the countryside and that there must be a force to slow him down, wherever he went, until additional help could be found. Of the 14,500 men still present and fit for duty after the disasters on Long Island and Manhattan, some 7,000—mostly New England and New York regiments—were assigned to eccentric, ill-tempered Major General Charles Lee, who had just joined Washington after the victory at Charleston. He would remain at North Castle, above White Plains, for the present, guarding the approaches to New England. About 4,000 men under Major General William Heath would be stationed in the Highlands, thirty miles upriver from New York, as an outer line of defense for the vital Hudson waterway. The lower end of the river was the responsibility of Nathanael Greene, now a major general, who had 3,500 men in two strong points—Fort Washington on the Manhattan side and Fort Lee (formerly Fort Constitution) opposite it on the New Jersey bank. For his own command, Washington planned to take over the regiments that had been recruited west of the Hudson, which proved to be about 2,000 effectives, supplementing them with New Jersey militiamen and some 5,000 other soldiers from what was called the Flying Camp, or mobile reserve, west of the Hudson. The numbing fact was, however, that no appreciable numbers of militiamen appeared, while the troops in the Flying Camp seemed to have vanished. One of the commander's aides observed that everywhere the roads were jammed with soldiers "returning to their homes in the most scandalous and infamous manner," while those who were not deserting were simply waiting for their enlistments to expire. All the militiamen from Massachusetts would complete their terms of service on November 17, while nearly all the regiments which had been raised by the Continental Congress were scheduled to disband on November 30 or December 31.

On the fourteenth of November the Board of War in Philadelphia, reflecting a rising tide of alarm in Congress, informed Washington that a large part of the British fleet had sailed from Sandy Hook; it was the board's nervous supposition that those ships might be carrying troops toward Philadelphia. Actually, Washington had long since anticipated such a move on Howe's part and, assuming that the British would head for the colonial capital, had sent instructions to the New Jersey Committees of Safety advising "all those who live near the water, to be ready to move their stock, grain, carriages, and other effects back into the country." Since forage was so essential to the enemy, he had urged that "not a blade" of it be left for them. And on the same day the Board of War wrote him, Washington sent a letter to John Hancock, president of the Continental Congress, notifying him that he was in New Jersey, positioning troops against a British attack.

Since the main elements of the British army were camped on the east bank of the Hudson at Dobbs Ferry, about thirteen miles above Manhattan, Washington was guessing that Howe would cross the river there and head southwest across New Jersey; he "must undertake something on account of his reputation," Washington thought. Then a dispatch came in from General Lee, written hastily on the night of November 12, reporting that the enemy was on the move and apparently heading toward New York. Lee was a bit uncertain about this and took the occasion to express dissatisfaction with his scouts, who do not "venture far enough" and "bring back very lame, imperfect accounts." Nevertheless, it was all Washington had to go on, and if true it almost certainly meant that Howe was about to invest Fort Washington, the only place on Manhattan Island still in American hands. Although the likelihood of such an attack had increased almost daily since October, the American commander had had too many other problems on his mind to give this careful attention, and in any case he had confidence in the energetic and intelligent Nathanael Greene, whose responsibility the Hudson forts were. Yet there were warning signals aplenty of what was in store for Fort Washington. One ominous event had occurred on November 5, when the British frigate *Pearl* and two victual ships sailed up the Hudson past the two rebel fortresses, passing over the sunken vessels and other objects that had been placed in the water between them to prevent any such traffic. Although the ships had been 'damaged by gunfire from the shore, it was clear to

Washington that all the effort that had gone into sinking those obstructions in the river had been a waste of time; furthermore, as he wrote Greene, "If we cannot prevent vessels passing up, and the enemy are possessed of the surrounding country, what valuable purpose can it answer to attempt to hold a post from which the expected benefit cannot be had?" He was inclined "to think it will not be prudent to hazard the men and stores at Mount Washington, but, as you are on the spot, leave it to you to give such orders as to evacuating Mount Washington as you judge best." All very gentlemanly and polite, but the meaning should have been clear to Greene.

Washington also expected that Greene would remove most of the stores from Fort Lee, which was used as a supply depot and would certainly be overrun by the British if they moved into New Jersey. But Greene, who had a stubborn streak, had his own notions about all this: he argued that the two forts pinned down a disproportionate number of enemy troops and that, even if attacked, the Americans at Fort Washington were in no real danger since they could be evacuated quickly to the other side of the river. The clincher in Greene's mind seems to have been that Congress had ordered the river to be obstructed "at whatever expense"—something that was impossible to do unless the two forts were held. And there matters remained until Washington arrived at Greene's headquarters and discovered to his chagrin that his lieutenant had not removed the stores from Fort Lee and, far from withdrawing troops from Fort Washington, had actually reinforced that garrison.

It was indicative of Washington's fatigue and general despair that, as a staff officer wrote, he "hesitated more than I ever knew him on any other occasion, and more than I thought the public service permitted." Instead of overriding Greene's orders, he acquiesced reluctantly, reasoning that Greene was more familiar with the situation and could be relied on to handle matters effectively. As he wrote his brother John Augustine, Washington intended to let matters stand "till I could get round and see the situation of things," and after spending some time with Greene on the fourteenth, he rode the next day to Hackensack to see what had to be done to defend the river crossings between there and Philadelphia.

Somehow the American commander also found the time that sunny November afternoon to write a curious letter to the Board of War, expressing annoyance that one of his requests had been ignored. Even while war and the killing went on, the niceties were observed in the eighteenth century. "Having given my promise to General Howe," Washington wrote, "that Peter Jack, a servant of Major Stewart, who was sent to Philadelphia with . . . other prisoners, and who has nothing to do in the military line, should be returned to his master, agreeable to the usage of war in such cases, I must take the liberty to request the favor of you to have him conveyed to General Greene by the earliest opportunity, that he may be forwarded to his master in compliance with my promise." Washington and Howe had exchanged punctilious notes on this matter a week earlier, and on the eleventh the American general had even received a formal letter of thanks from British Major Charles Stewart, anticipating his servant's return.

Shortly after five o'clock, not long after Washington had dictated this letter, a messenger galloped up to the Zabriskie house with an urgent message from Greene. It was the worst possible news. With Greene's dispatch was an enclosure from Colonel Robert Magaw, a young Pennsylvanian in command of Fort Washington, stating that the British, under flag of truce, had demanded the garrison's surrender. They had given Magaw two hours to decide between that alternative and having his men put to the sword. In reply, Magaw had scolded General Howe for playing "a part so unworthy of himself and the British nation" and had then defied the enemy: ". . . actuated by the most glorious cause that mankind ever fought in," he wrote, "I am determined to defend this post to the very last extremity."

Washington called for his horse and raced back across the six miles to Fort Lee in the gathering dusk, only to find that Greene was on the other side of the river with General Israel Putnam and Magaw. Since no one in the fort could give him any information beyond the fact that there had been no attack, the commanding officer hurried down a farm road that led to the landing below, ordered a boat, and was rowed out onto the dark river. Part way across the Hudson a black shape loomed ahead, which proved to be a boat with Greene and Putnam aboard, and when they came abreast the oarsmen held the sides of the boats together while the officers talked above the creak of gunwales and the slapping of water. Greene informed Washington that "the troops were in high spirits"—a fact that counted heavily with the commander—and "would make a good defense." Realizing that nothing more could be done until daybreak,

Washington returned with the others to the New Jersey shore. Unbeknownst to any of the American officers, while they were conversing out there on the water some thirty flatboats loaded with British infantrymen were floating quietly upstream on the incoming tide, unnoticed by the rebel sentries on Jeffrey's Hook below Fort Washington, heading for a break in the shoreline where the Harlem River made an island of Manhattan.

Before sun-up the next morning Washington, with Generals Greene, Putnam, and Hugh Mercer, was down at the landing below Fort Lee again, and as Greene told the story, ". . . just at the instant we stepped on board the boat the enemy made their appearance on the hill . . . and began a severe cannonade with several fieldpieces." From the boat they could make out the movement of men, high up on the bank. The attack had commenced far off to their left—along the northern approaches to Fort Washington, just below the King's Bridge over the Harlem River; but almost at the same time a violent barrage from British batteries to the south of the fort indicated that more than one assault was being made. And simultaneously, off to the north, the frigate *Pearl* came about near the entrance to the Harlem River and opened fire on the fort's outer works— "scouring the woods" with cannon fire, as Captain Thomas Wilkinson recorded in his log. About five hundred yards below Jeffrey's Hook, at a point where a little stream tumbled down the hillside back of the fort high above them, the four American generals scrambled ashore and began making their way up the steep bank, to see what they could make of the situation.

3. *A Citadel Within Reach*

The fort which had been named for the American commander in chief stood within half a mile of the highest point on Manhattan Island, a narrow, craggy region of wild beauty. At the northern end of the island a rocky spine almost four miles long and about three quarters of a mile wide had been formed during the glacial period, and this granite hump ran north and south, separating the Hudson River on the west from the Harlem River on the east. At its northern extremity, Spuyten Duyvil Creek connected the two rivers and separated Manhattan Island from the mainland; at its southern tip, a high promontory known as the Point of Rocks jutted into and brooded over the Harlem Plains. From the streams on either side of the long ridge, cliffs rose precipitously to a height 200 feet above water level. For nearly all of its length the rocky spine was strewn with boulders, relics of the ice ages, and in the thin alluvial soil thousands of birch trees had taken root, growing in all the steep crags and crevices so that the area was known locally as "the birch-bark country." For years no white man had laid claim to this inhospitable terrain; the few remaining Indians cultivated maize, fished, and hunted there. Then, inevitably, the white settlers intruded, and when the post road was cut through the wood more of them came, building farmhouses between Breakneck Hill— where the road climbed steeply northward from the plains of Harlem— and the King's Bridge, a toll span operated under the king's license, connecting Manhattan Island to the Westchester mainland. In 1756 a well-to-do British officer named Roger Morris built a handsome dwelling east of Breakneck Hill and the post road on a site commanding a magnificent vista across the Harlem River toward Long Island. (Morris had been Washington's comrade-in-arms at Braddock's defeat in the Pennsylvania wilderness; badly wounded there, he was carried back to Virginia on a litter. When fighting broke out in 1775 he remained loyal to the king and fled north to the Highlands, leaving his home deserted.) By the time of the Revolution there were several other houses in the neighborhood, some inns along the highway, and off to the north, a few farms in the lowlands along the Harlem.

In June 1776, soon after the American army arrived from Boston, a group of officers had surveyed this ground, contemplating placing a fort somewhere on the rocky ridge. Henry Knox, the fat chief of artillery, went over the terrain with Generals Greene, Heath, and Israel Putnam and concluded that the heights, if properly fortified, would be virtually impregnable. Later that month the commander in chief took in the area with his surveyor's eye and decided that this could be the key to the defense of the lower Hudson, since the highest point of land dominated the river at its narrowest place—where the little protuberance called Jeffrey's

Hook reaches out toward the New Jersey shore. From here there was a superb view of the Hudson and a prospect of the Palisades to the west, all of northern Manhattan, and beyond the Harlem River into Westchester and Connecticut.

Some newly arrived Pennsylvania troops began constructing a fort under the supervision of Colonel Rufus Putnam, the army's chief engineer (Putnam denied any real talent for the job—he regarded his appointment by Congress as "wholly unexpected," since he had no "knowledge of the art" beyond what he had read in some books on fortifications after his arrival in New York). The Pennsylvanians' commander, Brigadier General Thomas Mifflin, was a cultivated man "full of activity and fire," who had a rare talent for haranguing his men, but since it was a fiercely hot summer and the work was unusually difficult, the soldiers were not generous in their praise of Mifflin. He had under him some of the best-equipped, best-trained troops in the Continental Army, however, including the battalions of Colonels Shee, St. Clair, Wayne, and Magaw. Shee's men were mostly aristocratic Philadelphians, while Magaw's were rough frontiersmen from the Cumberland Valley.

For more than a month they hauled boulders from the heights down to the river's edge and loaded them into a collection of rotting hulks and cribs made of timber, which had been chained together and stretched across the river from shore to shore. When the stone-filled coffers sank to the bottom, long spars projected to the surface. This line of obstructions was known as a "chevaux de frise" and its purpose, of course, was to prevent British men-of-war from negotiating the river and outflanking the American position on Manhattan Island.† After the chevaux de frise was

† The rebels, fully conscious of the enemy's overwhelming naval superiority, had come up with another defensive weapon which—had it worked as intended—might have altered the situation considerably. In 1771, while he was still a freshman at Yale, an inventive genius named David Bushnell had demonstrated the devastating potential and practicability of underwater explosions, and by 1775 he had designed and built a curious machine, about 7-1/2 feet long and 6 feet deep, known as the Turtle. Propelled by one man, this copper-sheathed capsule could attach a time bomb to the underside of an enemy ship and leave the scene before it exploded. As Alexander Laing describes the Turtle in *American Ships*, "It could surface promptly and reliably from dives to a recorded depth of at least three fathoms. It had the two essential instruments for subsurface navigation by day or night [a compass and depth gauge] . . . It had secondary provisions for all its vital functions: water tanks and pumps supplemented by a vertical screw and by lead ballast that could be jettisoned in a crisis, ventilators with automatic and manual controls, propulsion by hand or foot power, screens to protect the intake orifices for both air and water." It was, in short, the first submarine, and Bushnell had already demonstrated that it worked.

Unhappily, what was lacking when the time came to prove the new weapon in combat was an ex-

completed, early in August, the rough work with shovel, axe, pick, and mattock went on. So little soil covered the rocky surface where the fort and its outer works were laid out that tons of dirt had to be hauled by hand from the low ground around the base of the cliffs; the lack of topsoil also meant that no adequate ditches or trenches could be dug around the perimeter of the fort.

Alexander Graydon, a twenty-four-year-old captain in John Shee's battalion, recalled later that their efforts during the course of that hot, dry summer produced immense mounds of earth, a perpetual cloud of dust, and something that assumed "a pentagonal form . . . finally issuing in a fort of five bastions." Building barracks was another chore that occupied the men from July into September; no one knew if they would winter here, but all summer long the hewing and sawing of timbers, the forging of nails and spikes, and the hasty assembling of buildings and tent platforms had continued. By August all the troops in the immediate area were under the command of Major General William Heath, a bald, tubby, forty-year-old farmer from Roxbury, Massachusetts. Heath had been fascinated with military matters since childhood and had been one of the first to turn out at the Lexington alarm, but it became evident as the war went on that he was better suited to service in camp than in the field, and it was clear from the detailed instructions Washington felt obliged to give him that the commander in chief regarded him as an officer of somewhat limited capacity. By mid-September, Washington had established his own headquarters near Heath's, in the elegant home of his old comrade Roger Morris, where he kept a sharp eye on what was going on in camp. He was annoyed by the "shameful inattention in some of the camps to decency and cleanliness, in providing necessaries and picking up the offal and filth of the camp" and issued orders that the men account for every round of

---

perienced operator: Bushnell was not sturdy enough to run it himself; the man trained to do so—his brother—fell ill with a fever; and the mission was turned over to an intrepid but uninitiated volunteer, Sergeant Ezra Lee. The first attempt, against H.M.S. *Eagle*, sixty-four guns, failed when the screw used to attach the explosive struck an iron plate on the *Eagle's* bottom, and with dawn approaching Lee disengaged and headed for safety. (The charge was cast adrift, exploded, and thoroughly alarmed the British, who quickly shifted their ships to a less exposed berth.) A second attack on another ship fizzled when Lee lost sight of his target, overshot the mark, was prevented from returning by the tide, and took flight when a British lookout spotted his conning tower. To Bushnell's chagrin, the Turtle was aboard a rebel sloop which was sunk by the British in October 1776, and although he recovered the craft, no further effort was made to use the first submarine against enemy surface vessels.

powder and cartridges expended, to keep them from wasteful firing of their weapons.

Since most of these men were new to the business of soldiering, the camps around Mount Washington, as the long ridge on upper Manhattan came to be called, were even sloppier and more makeshift than most. Many troops lacked shelter of any kind; wood was scarce in the vicinity, planks and boards precious, and officers found it necessary to order that boards be used only for tent floors and not for siding. A good many of the men caught cold; Colonel Ewing grumbled that his Maryland battalion was "very sickly, owing to our lying on the cold ground, without straw or plank, which is not to be had, and medicine very scarce." There was a lot of pilferage in camp, especially of clothing, and the surgeons complained constantly that they were short of medical supplies. Discipline was lax at best, for most of the soldiers simply had not had time to absorb the rules of the new game they were playing, nor were they particularly well suited to it. Several ensigns in Webb's Massachusetts regiment were tried for using abusive language to their senior officers and were publicly reprimanded. James McCormick, a private in Sargent's regiment which was stationed at the King's Bridge, tried to desert and was condemned to death by court martial. Sadly, almost as if he were hoping to find some loophole, Washington approved the court's finding, and on October 2 at 11 A.M. the off-duty troops paraded to watch McCormick being hanged.

The chaos of the camp was compounded each morning at eight when a market opened beside the post road on the southeast slope of the hill below the fort. From that hour until sunset, Tory farmers, traders, and hucksters of all kinds drove into camp to sell produce at exorbitant rates (finally the quartermaster general resorted to price control and issued a schedule of authorized charges); off-duty troops, cooks, farmers in their wagons, and women milled around, exchanging gossip, haggling, fighting, and creating a scene that could hardly be described as military. Meanwhile, work on the fort went on, kicking up the huge clouds of dust of which Graydon and others complained. Rufus Putnam had planned an elaborate, sprawling series of outer works in addition to the main fort itself, so that it often seemed to the men as if the whole island was being dug up. The main walls of the fort, which were made of earth, were in the shape of an irregular pentagon and had ravelins, or earthen bastions, with openings for guns, reaching out from each angle. The walls enclosed an area of about three or four acres, while the ravelins protected a fire zone three times that size. In front of the entrance there was a small outwork, or covered way. Since there was no powder to spare for blasting out rock, there was no ditch surrounding the fort—only, as a British officer noted later, "good Abbattis," or sharpened stakes that protruded slightly upward and outward like the quills of a porcupine and served essentially the same purpose. Although the fort was well situated, it had many drawbacks, as Alexander Graydon realized: "There were no barracks, or casemates [for artillery], or fuel, or water within the body of the place." Not only was there no spring or well inside the fort's walls; the nearest water was the Hudson River, about a thousand feet distant, down a steep cliff. And by the middle of November 1776 no magazines had been built for the storage of powder and ammunition.

Extending out beyond this central citadel, like satellites around the sun, were countless earthworks and redoubts, only a few of which deserved to be called forts. Batteries had been placed on Jeffery's Hook, below the fort; on the hill overlooking Spuyten Duyvil Creek; at the north end of the island commanding the King's Bridge and Dyckman's Bridge; and along Laurel Hill above the Harlem River. At the south end of the long ridge were three lines of defense intended to ward off invasion from the direction of New York. On September 15, when Washington's army had been literally run out of town by the British, they retreated to the relative safety of Harlem Heights, behind the Point of Rocks, and there the exhausted, beaten men had been put to work by the commander in chief, digging trenches and earthworks along the lines of a plan that his sure eye for the ground had already perceived. As the British had begun to realize, every time the rebels got a breathing spell they dug like moles; overnight the hillside was pockmarked with trenches and foxholes—an east–west, zigzag series of earthworks that began at the Hudson and ran all the way across the ridge about three quarters of a mile north of the Point of Rocks. This first line of defense was supported later by a second, stronger position, about a third of a mile to the north; and a third line was planned a quarter of a mile north of that, reaching from the Hudson to the Morris house. All in all, this complex network of defensive positions covered nearly ten miles—a lot of territory to defend against a determined, skilled, and powerful enemy who also controlled the water approaches.

The reason the fort had been constructed in the first place was to serve as the eastern anchor for the line of sunken hulks that were to obstruct shipping on the Hudson. So it might have been argued, after the *Pearl* and other vessels sailed across the chevaux-de-frise, that neither Fort Washington nor Fort Lee was any more effective than the underwater obstructions. But the rebels were not yet convinced of this: they knew they had punished the *Pearl* and the two victualers (they had, in fact, killed ten men, wounded as many more, and inflicted some damage on the vessels); and they had been impressed by another incident involving the *Pearl* that occurred on October 27. This persuaded them that Fort Washington could not only be defended but could be a real thorn in the side of the British.

When General Howe suddenly and unexpectedly moved his army by water to Westchester, Washington followed as rapidly as possible, leaving behind a garrison to man Fort Washington. To keep an eye on the rebels there, a small force commanded by Hugh, Earl Percy, remained in the British lines below Harlem Heights. Some of the Americans had already seen Percy in action, when he led a relief force out of Boston and saved the redcoats retreating from Concord, and they respected him; he was a first-class soldier with common sense as well as courage. Although he was a long-nosed aristocrat, from a Northumberland family that traced its lineage to one of William the Conqueror's Norman barons, Percy had opposed the government's policy toward the colonies and had only come to America at the urging of the North ministry. It was thought that the Bostonians would be impressed by the young man's attractive personality, his liberal outlook, and his thoroughly noble background. Percy had charmed Boston, all right, and he had come away from his first fight with the rebels with respect for them. "Whoever looks upon them as an irregular mob," he warned a friend in England, "will find himself much mistaken. They have men amongst them who know very well what they are about . . . They are determined to go thro' with it, nor will the insurrection here turn out so despicable as it is perhaps imagined at home." Percy had fought with distinction at Long Island and was now a lieutenant general commanding one of the three divisions of the British army.

Opposing him, in command of Fort Washington, was the Scotch-Irish colonel from Pennsylvania named Robert Magaw, whose background was about as different from Percy's as it could possibly be. He had practiced law for some years in his home town of Carlisle, on the frontier of Cumberland County, and like many another colonial lawyer had organized local resistance to what he regarded as misgovernment. In 1775 he joined Colonel William Thompson's Pennsylvania regiment as a major and within a year had formed his own regiment, the 5th Pennsylvania, for which he recruited boys from his home county. Magaw was a man of action and evidently a responsible character, for neither Washington nor Greene seems to have hesitated for a moment about leaving him in charge of the important post.

Early in the morning of October 27 Magaw's sentries reported that Percy's troops were launching an attack, supported by two British frigates moving up the Hudson. Magaw ran to the outer defense line to direct things personally, and while the cannon in the redoubt there opened fire on the British infantry, he sent for an eighteen-pounder which could reach the frigates. As soon as the big gun was in position, it opened at short range on the *Pearl* and the *Repulse*, which were close in to shore, and Magaw had his men load with double shot, for he could see that the men-of-war were at a terrible disadvantage: they could neither elevate their guns sufficiently to reach the men on the heights, nor could they weigh anchor, since the tide was coming in and might carry them onto the chevaux-de-frise. Magaw's cannon and the guns of Fort Lee cut up the sails and rigging of the ships, and both vessels had boats out, towing them out of range. Meanwhile, Percy's men and the rebels in the trenches were banging away at each other, but it began to look as if the British troops had only stirred things up in order to draw the Americans' attention away from the frigates. Several of Percy's men were killed or wounded, and the rebels lost a man whose head was carried away by a shell. One British officer observed that the Americans were "continually reinforced from the works" until there were about 3,000 of them in evidence—too many for the British just then. In any event, the artillery duel finally died away and Nathanael Greene, who had come over from Fort Lee to see what was going on, felt confident enough about the situation to leave the scene about 3 P.M. "Our artillery behaved incomparably well," he wrote proudly. "Colonel Magaw is charmed with their conduct in firing at the ship and in the field."

So charmed, in fact, were both Magaw and Greene that they felt a new surge of confidence about the strength of their position. Magaw boasted that he could hold out in Fort Washington until the end of December, while Greene could not "conceive the garrison to be in any great danger." Alexander Graydon, who seems not to have had much affection for Magaw, noted drily that the colonel evidently "had heard of sieges being protracted for months and even years," and since the "place he had to defend was called a Fort and had cannon in it, he thought the deuce was in it, if he could not hold out for a few weeks." Graydon had no faith whatever in all those outworks around the fort nor in the ability of the whole complex to sustain a siege; since no parallels were required to approach it, "the citadel was at once within the reach of assailants."

The past is filled with minor incidents that may or may not have affected the course of history. Whether these seemingly insignificant events actually altered the future direction of things is not easy to judge; yet it is difficult to argue with complete assurance that everything would have remained the same had they not occurred at all. For instance, Colonel Robert Magaw might never have had to make good on his boast of withstanding a siege, and the Americans might not have suffered their most disastrous defeat of the entire war, had not fate intervened in the person of William Demont, an American deserter. Desertion itself was nothing unusual; a lot of it went on, on both sides, particularly in the lines around Fort Washington where the no man's land between British and rebel trenches was so close that sentries could call back and forth to each other. (In the early days of the confrontation there the British got into the habit of lobbing a round or two at the Americans just to provoke the provincials into wasting ammunition, but as time went on the men in the front lines tended to lose their animosity for fellow sufferers a few yards away. On at least one occasion a British sentinel called over to an American private to ask for a chew of tobacco; without hesitating, the rebel pulled a twist from his pocket and threw it across the creek to the redcoat, who bit off a chunk and tossed it back.) So it was not difficult for a determined man to steal across the lines at night, undetected.

The trouble in this particular case was that Demont, the deserter, was Colonel Magaw's own adjutant, a fellow Pennsylvanian thoroughly knowledgeable about every detail of the fort, who had decided for reasons best known to himself to betray the post and its defenders. There are two hints as to his motives—one from Captain Mackenzie, who interviewed him when he came into the British lines and reported that Demont spoke much of the "great dissensions in the Rebel Army, everybody finding fault with the mode of proceeding, and the inferior officers, even Ensigns, insisting that, in such a cause, every man has a right to assist in Council, and to give his opinion . . . The people from the Southern Colonies declare that they will not go into New-England, and the others that they will not march to the southward." If Demont could be believed, Mackenzie thought, the rebels "must soon go to pieces." The second explanation is suggested by Demont himself, in a letter written years later when he made a claim for £182 owed him by the British government. "I sacrificed all I was Worth in the World to the Service of my King & Country," he said, "and joined the then Lord Percy, brought in with me the Plans of Fort Washington . . ." No one will ever know whether it was all that dissension in the ranks that caused him to panic or whether he betrayed the fort in hopes of obtaining some reward (the British made him a commissary of prisoners some time later and ultimately he was awarded £60 for his treachery). But the fact is that Demont—who had access to full information concerning the post and its outworks—slipped through the lines under cover of darkness on November 2 and told the British all he knew, presumably informing them about the number, location, and size of cannon, the number and quality of the defenders, and their supplies of powder, food, and water. Whatever Demont had hoped to achieve, the results came quickly.

By now Howe had almost certainly made up his mind to storm Fort Washington, and yet it is quite possible that the intelligence provided by Demont triggered his decision to move at once. Percy sent the information straightaway to Howe at White Plains, and during the long night hours of November 4 American pickets there heard the unmistakable rumble of heavy wagons that meant the British were breaking camp, and the next morning it was discovered that the enemy had fallen back on Dobbs Ferry. While Washington and his generals decided to split the American army into four parts in order to counter Howe's next move, the British commander, armed with detailed intelligence concerning Fort Washington, knew where and how to strike most effectively, and he had recently welcomed a new ally to whom he decided to give the post of honor in the attack.

Lieutenant General Wilhelm Freiherr von Knyphausen had lately arrived in New York harbor at the head of the second grand division of German mercenaries. Like all Hessian officers, Knyphausen was a nobleman—a grim, silent, sharp-featured one; sixty years old, of medium height, with ramrod-straight carriage, he was known to his tablemates as a man who buttered bread with his thumb. With him had come 3,997 Hessians, 670 Waldeckers, and a company of jägers, and for twenty-one weeks the poor devils had endured the agonies of crossing the Atlantic in eighteenth-century troop transports. Packed like herrings, the tall men were unable to stand up between decks or to sit up between the berths. Six men had been assigned to bunks that normally accommodated four, so that they had to sleep "spoon fashion," which meant that all six had to turn over in bed at once, on signal. The food was terrible—dried peas, old rotten pork, and maggoty biscuits as hard as stone; while the water, so thick with filaments that it had to be strained, stank so the soldiers held their noses while drinking it. After the horrors of that crossing, almost anything would have seemed an improvement, and as soon as his men got their land legs back Knyphausen requested that they be given the honor of making the main attack on Fort Washington.

Howe had determined to storm the fort from three directions simultaneously, with a fourth movement intended as a feint. Knyphausen's forces would come at the fort over the difficult ground at the north. Lord Percy was to lead a brigade of Hessians and several British battalions from the south, while Lord Cornwallis with the 33rd Regiment and Brigadier General Edward Mathew with the light infantry and the Guards, crossed the Harlem River and drove up Laurel Hill to the east, slightly above the fort. Then, to confuse the rebels, a feint would be made by the 42nd Highlanders under Lieutenant Colonel Thomas Sterling, who would land on the west bank of the Harlem River just above the Morris house. By now, of course, the Americans knew something big was coming: for days Knyphausen's men had been working at the northernmost end of the island, just below the King's Bridge, building breastworks, moving cannon into place, and exchanging musket fire with the rebel pickets. At the other end of the American lines Alexander Graydon was on duty one stormy night, posted in an empty house near the Point of Rocks, when a British deserter named Broderick appeared at the door and asked to be taken in. While they talked, he told Graydon that an attack was coming in six or eight days, or as soon as the British got their heavy artillery into position on the east bank of the Harlem.

On November 15, 1776, the day George Washington rode from

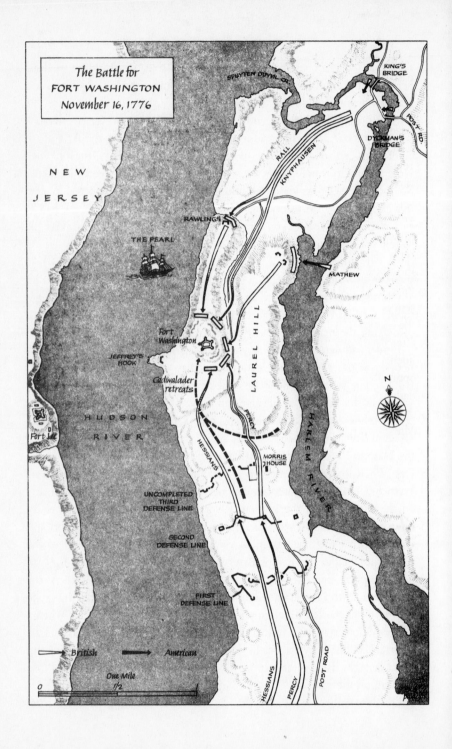

The Battle for
FORT WASHINGTON
November 16, 1776

NEW
JERSEY

SPUYTEN DUYVIL CR.

KING'S
BRIDGE

POST RD.

DYCKMAN'S
BRIDGE

RALL

KNYPHAUSEN

RAWLINGS

THE PEARL

MATHEW

Fort
Washington

LAUREL HILL

JEFFREY'S
HOOK

Cadwalader
retreats

HUDSON

RIVER

PERCY

HESSIANS

MORRIS
HOUSE

N

Fort Lee

HARLEM RIVER

UNCOMPLETED
THIRD
DEFENSE LINE

SECOND
DEFENSE LINE

FIRST
DEFENSE LINE

British   American

HESSIANS

PERCY

POST ROAD

One Mile
1/2
0

White Plains to Fort Lee and on to Hackensack, a boat put out from the east bank of the Harlem under a flag of truce. At 1 P.M. it landed on the opposite shore and from it stepped Lieutenant Colonel James Patterson, the suave adjutant general of the British army who had tried to open the peace discussions with Washington in July. Patterson handed a letter to Lieutenant Colonel Michael Swope, the adjutant appointed by Magaw to replace the recently departed Demont. (Had Swope known what the future held, he might have been tempted to follow his predecessor; he was captured the next day and remained a prisoner of war for over four years.) After a brief conversation, Swope hurried off to the fort with the message, handed it to Magaw, and waited while the colonel wrote his reply, in which he informed the British that he would defend his post "to the very last extremity." Another Pennsylvania officer, Thomas Bull, took a copy of Magaw's letter across the Hudson to Greene, who read it, sent it posthaste to Washington in Hackensack, and immediately crossed the river with Israel Putnam to talk things over with Magaw. It was well after dark when they headed back to Fort Lee with their message of confidence that the defenders were in good spirits. They might have been less optimistic had they realized that somewhere in their wake those thirty flatboats loaded with British infantrymen were floating upstream toward the staging area, just around the bend of the Harlem River at Delancey's Mills.

4. *Ye Should Never Fight Against Yer King*

General William Howe was a commander who liked to have everything in readiness before sending troops into battle. In the eighteenth century an army fought according to the book, and Howe's was no exception, for although he had contributed to the development of the so-called light troops that provided the army with additional flexibility, he was basically an orthodox officer. And what he had to deal with, when all was said and done, was a body of men whose average intelligence was not high, who were in the ranks because they came from the poorest elements of the population and could find no better employment, and who did everything by the numbers. What counted in battle was order, alignment, discipline, and massed firepower—not speed and independent initiative.

Before dawn on November 16 the light infantry, the Guards, and Knyphausen's Germans were stirring. Pulling on their blue and white uniform coats over yellow breeches and waistcoats, the Germans formed into order of march quickly, for Knyphausen was impatient to get moving before daybreak, while they still had a chance of surprising the rebels. In the half light the men looked taller and more ferocious than usual; most of them had blackened mustachios, and over their wigs—coated with tallow and powdered with flour—the privates wore cocked hats and the grenadiers brass-plated bearskins. The right division, commanded by Colonel Johann Rall, formed up under the lee of some woods at the foot of Marble Hill; the left, under Major General Martin Schmidt, in open fields along the road to the King's Bridge. While these men were trotting into position, the Waldeck regiment was ferried across the river by the indefatigable flatboatmen who had brought the troops up the Hudson the night before, and the Waldeckers, under Lieutenant Colonel von Koehler, joined Rall's units. Then the flatboats headed downstream to pick up another load—the light infantry and Grenadier Guards under Brigadier General Edward Mathew. Not until these men had reached Laurel Hill, across the river, was the general attack to begin. But as so often happens in a complicated military maneuver, a small, unforeseen factor threw everything badly off schedule. No one had remembered that the Harlem, like the Hudson, was a tidal river. And at that hour of the sixteenth the tide was low and the flatboats could not get close enough to shore to pick up the light troops and the Guards. Meantime, the advance Hessian units were in position on the hillside where their attack would begin and were starting up through the woods when the order came to turn back. So back they went, to wait in line for hours for the signal to advance again, while their impatient commander fumed at the delay he knew would cost him many men.

At 7 A.M.—just about the time Washington and his generals were crossing the Hudson again—the battery of big guns across the Harlem opened up, raining shells on Laurel Hill and the American battery there; at the same time the German fieldpieces commenced firing, and the frigate *Pearl* tacked into the bay formed by Spuyten Duyvil Creek and started hammering away with round and grapeshot at the rebel entrenchments. A young Irish ensign, George Hart, watching events from the east bank of the Harlem, reported that the *Pearl* and *Repulse* kept up a constant fire, but added sourly that "their shot went mostly over the Fort in amongst our men."

Eleven miles to the south, in New York City, the Reverend Mr. Shewkirk, pastor of the Moravian Church, recorded in his diary that the cannonading was heard from early morning until noon. A practical man of God, Shewkirk was thinking less of the men involved in battle than of something much closer to his heart. He hoped that the result of the fighting would be that "the Jerseys will be open'd, as also with the places up the East River; so that the Inhabitants may come to the city and provisions be brought in; especially wood, which is not to be had, and is extremely dear; a cord of oak wood, bought formerly for 20s. now 4£." Another civilian with a slightly less mercenary attitude toward the battle was Ambrose Serle, who had come to America as Lord Howe's secretary. Serle was a civilized, educated man who did not regard the Americans as either, and he was convinced, after four months in the colonies, that minority rule, backed by a mob, resulted only in madness and sin. What else could it be when men cast off their allegiance to God and to "his substitute, the King?" But Serle was in a good mood this day; early in the morning he sailed up the East River with the admiral ("a most pleasant and agreeable Passage"), his heart set on a fine outing. "As this was to be an important Day," he said, "and the Time of attacking the Enemy in their strongest Works, I was stimulated to be a Spectator above all the Fineness of the Weather, though that was exceedingly delightful. I heard a violent Cannonade all the Way I sailed," he noted, "and had a fine View of the Action, some little Time before the Crisis of the Day, from the hilly Rocks, near Harlem Plains." That was where he and Lord Howe joined Percy, and where they doubtless saw Captain Frederick Mackenzie, who had also caught up with the earl after reporting for orders early in the day and finding Percy already out with his troops. Percy's cannon were busy firing on the rebel earthworks rimming the Point of Rocks and overlooking the post road, trying to blast out Magaw's eighteen-pounder, which had done such damage to the two British ships, and several smaller rebel fieldpieces in the batteries. All morning the barrage continued, ripping limbs out of trees and showering the American defenders with rocks and dirt, but still there was no movement by the British infantry.

Another eyewitness to this was Stephen Kemble, an American who was related to several of the patrician families of New York, the Stuyvesants and Van Cortlandts, and whose father, a member of the governor's council until 1775, had owned huge estates in New Jersey. Kemble joined the British army during the French and Indian War; his sister had married General Thomas Gage, commander in chief of the British forces until Howe replaced him; and Kemble was now in the somewhat awkward position of serving his brother-in-law's successor as deputy adjutant general. Noting that things were not going according to plan, he observed that the landing of the light infantry, about a mile below the King's Bridge, did not take place until noon. The fault, Kemble realized, was the tide which "by some neglect [was] not foreseen before," so most of the morning slipped by before the general attack got under way. The Germans, after the long delay, had formed into two columns again, and as soon as they were set the other movements could begin, seriatim, in a semicircle around the rebel positions: first, the Guards, who crossed the Harlem to form on Knyphausen's left; then the 1st and 2nd Light Infantry; then the 42nd Highlanders; and finally, when all these units had passed over the Harlem, Percy with the 3rd Brigade of British infantry and Stirn's Hessians would attack the Americans from the south. It was, in short, a huge encircling movement aimed at driving the defenders back into their works, where they could be strangled.

Someone in London with intelligence had concluded, months before the British landed in New York, that the key to military action in and around the island of Manhattan was maneuverability of the troops. Naval control of the broad, deep channels surrounding the island was not enough, it was reasoned; the army would have to seize land, and this was to be achieved by enabling them to cross shallow bodies of water and to land on beaches. From the outset, the campaign around New York was planned as an amphibious operation, and the British had brought with them, aboard transports and men-of-war, dozens of flat-bottomed boats to be rowed by seamen from the fleet. The boats had been used first to land troops on Staten Island, then for the attack on Long Island; they ferried

men up the East River, carried Howe's army to Kip's Bay and Throgs
Neck and Pell's Point, and now they were to be the deciding factor in the
attack on Fort Washington, giving Howe's soldiers the mobility they
needed to uproot and overwhelm a determined, entrenched enemy.

As soon as the tide had risen sufficiently, the flatboats moved into shore,
picked up six battalions of Guardsmen and light infantry, and began
ferrying them across the Harlem River to the landing point at the foot of
Laurel Hill, where the soldiers plunged into the marshy area below the
cliffs. The landing was covered by a furious barrage from the opposite
shore, and the rebel gunners were made even more helpless by their ina-
bility to fire their fieldpieces down the cliffside at the attackers. "It was no
disgrace to the militia, that they shrunk" from the British artillery fire,
Alexander Graydon wrote; "such of them at least as were exposed to it
without cover. I question whether the bravest veterans could have stood
it." While General Cornwallis waited with the 33rd Regiment in reserve,
Mathew—who was accompanied by his commander, General William
Howe—jumped off with the first amphibious attack wave of about 2,000
light infantry and grenadiers—big, disciplined veterans, accustomed to
rough going. In that day the light troops and grenadiers constituted an
elite corps and were often used as the spearhead of an attack, since the
men were physically stronger and better trained and the companies usually at or near full strength. Scrambling up the hillside, they had little
difficulty reaching the top; then they ran into some resistance from the
Pennsylvania volunteer companies defending the redoubt at the crest of
Laurel Hill. Most of these fellows were Scotch-Irishmen from Lancaster,
York, and Bucks counties, led by William Baxter and his second-in-com-
mand, Michael Swope. Several of the companies had been in the fighting
on Long Island, where one of them—Gerhart Graeff's—had lost all but
eighteen of its men. Baxter and his militiamen were among the reinforcements sent over from Fort Lee by Greene several days earlier, and right
now these 500 men had no chance against an enemy force four times
larger, supported by massive artillery fire. The fight was short-lived: Baxter himself was one of the first men down, run through by a British
officer's sword; Jacob Dritt's company was roughly handled and Ensign
Jacob Barnitz was savagely wounded in both legs (fifteen months later,
when he was exchanged, he had to be carried home to York County on a
litter). When McAllister's battalion saw their captain fall, it was all over;

those who could ran toward Fort Washington, leaving their redoubt to Mathew's light companies. As soon as Magaw's gunners saw what had happened, they turned their cannon against the redoubt, so the British pulled out quickly and began angling south and west in the direction of the fort.

Off to the north the Hessian right, commanded by Colonel Johann Gottlieb Rall, got under way first, moving up the steep hillside just below Spuyten Duyvil. Rall was a big, noisy, bully of a man, completely reckless in battle, a heavy drinker and barroom brawler off duty. He had fought well at Chatterton's Hill near White Plains, where his brigade decided the day for the British, and it was probably at his own request that he was now leading the right wing of the main attack, where the going would be toughest. With him went the first grenadier battalion under Lieutenant Colonel von Koehler, and the Waldeck regiment, some 1,200 men, preceded by a hundred or more picked feldjägers under Major von Dechow. (These green-uniformed jägers, or chasseurs, were hunters and gamekeepers recruited from the forests of Germany, and they made capable scouts and sharpshooters.) It was 11 o'clock, according to the log kept by Lieutenant William Scott on His Majesty's Ship *Pearl*, when the Germans were seen moving through the woods past the ship's berth toward the rebel outposts. Against almost no initial opposition, the Waldeckers and grenadiers clambered up the steep bank while the soldiers behind them hauled howitzers and other guns around the hillside of Spuyten Duyvil Creek and onto the summit above. The Waldeckers and grenadiers then headed south at the double, along the river's edge, and reached Tubby Hook, whose precipitous banks were tiered with felled trees, brush, boulders, and three abatis filled with Pennsylvania and Virginia riflemen. As George Hart said, this hillside was "so rutted up by Entrenchments that I can't describe it," and at the top of this formidable position were two guns behind a redoubt formed of boulders that stretched entirely across the summit.

Only now did the main body of Hessians—some 4,000 men who had been standing, under arms, for four hours—begin their advance. The left column, commanded by Major General Martin Schmidt, consisted of Rall's own regiment—a rather inferior outfit which had been hastily thrown together in Hesse; the fusilier von Knyphausen Regiment, named for the general; the Wutgenau regiment; and a company of jägers commanded by Captain Wedern. Preceded by their line of scouts and some field artillery pieces, they marched off down the post road, heading for the fort. In the center, between Rall and Schmidt, came the units under Knyphausen: out in front was a skirmish line of 120 jägers and forty grenadiers, commanded by Colonel von Donop; and behind came the Huyne, Bunau, and Alt von Lossberg regiments, the latter led personally by the general. Somewhat hampered by fences and wooded patches in the farm lands and marshes, they swung off on an angle that would intersect with Rall's position in front of the outlying rebel battery and abatis. Along the way they crossed some swampy land where the tall rushes grew head high, and they were approaching the wooded hillside when a shattering fire hit them.

Up on that hill were some of the best soldiers in the rebel army. Nathanael Greene had sent Colonel Moses Rawlings with 250 Maryland and Virginia riflemen from Fort Lee as reinforcements, and these were veterans of frontier fighting as well as the battles of the present war. Rawlings' men, in fact, were the survivors of several outfits that had stood fast on Long Island, enabling the panicky militiamen to escape to the rear, and they had beaten back a British attack on Harlem Heights in mid-September—the nearest thing to a victory Washington's troops had seen since the British arrived in New York. The colonel himself had signed up in June 1775 in Maryland's first contingent of troops, which was commanded by an experienced Indian fighter, Michael Cresap. When Rawlings led his boys into the American camps outside Boston, they had created quite a stir. They were cocky, independent, inured to physical hardship and exposure, and they had brought a new weapon into the war —the so-called Pennsylvania or Kentucky rifle. Five feet long or more, slender, with a rifled barrel made by German immigrants in Pennsylvania, this gun could fire a half-ounce ball with extraordinary accuracy. Whereas a ball from the British Brown Bess or other muskets dropped to the ground after traveling 125 yards and had little likelihood of hitting a man at half that distance, an expert rifleman could put one shot after another into a six-inch target at 250 yards. But the rifle had disadvantages: for one, it took almost twice as long to load as a musket; for another, its small bore and grooved barrel were soon fouled by repeated firing and had to be swabbed out.

Rawlings' present position was ideal: his men could fire from behind huge rocks or trees, dart quickly to another concealed spot to load, and fire again from yet another location. Confronting the terrible tangle of fallen trees and rocks, the withering fire from the riflemen, and the cannon fire from above, the Germans were set back again and again, and Knyphausen was cursing the early morning delay that had deprived him of the element of surprise. His first charge was broken and a second was forced back even though the resolute old general himself scrambled up the hillside at the head of his troops, tearing at piles of brushwood, ignoring the fire from above. Schmidt's men had arrived now from the post road and some of them began moving up along the eastern slope of the hill in an effort to get behind the American riflemen. While the cannonade from the rebel guns, described as "terrible" in their effect by Ensign Wiedeshlat, pounded into them, the marksmen systematically picked off the German officers. The colonel and two other officers of Knyphausen's regiment were dead; Captain Wedern fell, along with one of his lieutenants; and many others were killed. Ensign Thomas Glyn, who was in a Guards regiment under General Mathew, knew what the Hessians faced on the north slope. It was "strong ground very difficult of access," he observed, "with Abbatis of great length placed in every path." (Glyn had also perceived that the rebels had overextended themselves: their works were "too extensive for the number of troops, as was generally the case with the Americans, who were indefatigable in constructing redoubts.")

While this murderous fight was going on north of the fort, Percy had swung into action at the southern end of the rebel lines. Since early morning his guns had been firing at them and he advanced in two columns—Stirn's brigade of Hessians attacking on the height of land above the Hudson River, on the left, and Percy himself (still accompanied by the admiral of the British fleet, Richard Howe) leading the right. They ran into very little opposition, according to Frederick Mackenzie, even when they formed a battle line about 200 yards from the American lines, where they had orders to wait until the sound of gunfire from the direction of the Morris house signaled the arrival of the 42nd Regiment. In other words, Percy was to hold back until the feint had been made by the Highlanders under Sterling; as soon as the latter reached the Morris house, Percy would move again to the attack. While they waited, Mackenzie said, they heard a "very severe fire of Musquetry beyond Fort Washington," where the Hessians were running into such trouble.

On the hillside facing Percy and his waiting legions was Captain Alexander Graydon with his company. He had been in the army for less than a year, and until now things hadn't been at all bad. After recruiting men from the countryside outside Philadelphia (opposition to Britain, he decided, "originated with the better sort," among whom the cause of liberty was "fashionable"), he had attended a round of parties in the city and then had been ordered to deliver some specie to General Schuyler at Lake George—a trip on which he had met the famous Benjamin Franklin and the other American commissioners returning from a fruitless expedition to Canada. And toward the end of June he had brought his company into camp near the King's Bridge, where they soon began wielding pick and shovel in the construction of Fort Washington. Graydon was thoroughly familiar with the lay of the land, but right now, with Percy's assault force inexplicably stopped out there in front of them, he was about to jump out of his skin with suspense.

Graydon and about 800 men served under Lambert Cadwalader, a Pennsylvanian who was Magaw's second in command and who had the responsibility of holding those three defensive lines that crossed the heights from the Hudson to the cliffs on the other side. If Cadwalader was uneasy now, it was not only because of the superior force that faced him; as luck would have it, Generals George Washington, Nathanael Greene, Israel Putnam, and Hugh Mercer had just passed through the rear of his sector bound for the Morris house, to see what was going on, and to make matters worse, the members of the top command had no sooner left than a runner brought word to Cadwalader that there was an attack in force, somewhere in his rear, off toward the Morris house. He sent Captain David Lennox with fifty men on the double to oppose the landing, and one of them brought back a message that what they faced was the entire 42nd Regiment—some 800 men. Although the rebels had no way of knowing it, this was the force Howe had sent across the Harlem as a feint to confuse the Americans. As it happened, the Highlanders under Thomas Sterling landed on the west bank of the river at a point that was easily the weakest in the defense lines. The first landing parties spread out, trying to find a path through the rocks and crags overhanging the marshy wash of the river, worked their way southward, and began climbing a gorge formed by a stream. Lennox and his men, plus another hundred or so sent by Cadwalader when he heard that they were confronted with an entire regiment, began shooting from a hilltop at the men who were still crossing in flatboats, and their fire was murderously effective; out on the river eighty Highlanders were killed or wounded. Furious at having been made sitting ducks out on the water, they charged up the gorge in an effort to get at their enemy and found themselves on a summit overlooking the Morris house.

When Percy heard the shooting in this area he renewed his advance. Graydon and some others were over on the extreme right of the American lines, facing the oncoming Hessians under Stirn, and they were forced to fall back when enemy artillery made the position too hot to hold. As Graydon retreated to the second defense line, the Highlanders were approaching the heights above the Morris house, and there—out in the middle, between these two jaws of the nutcracker—was the commander in chief of the American army, with three of his top generals. "There we all stood in a very awkward position," Nathanael Greene wrote afterward, in a masterpiece of understatement. The officers had seen all they could see of Magaw's troop dispositions; indeed, even if they had not approved, there was little they could do about it at this juncture, and they were in imminent danger of being captured or killed. "We all urged his Excellency to come off," Greene reported. "I offered to stay, General Putnam did the same, and so did General Mercer, but his Excellency thought it best for us all to come off together, which we did about half an hour before the enemy surrounded the fort." It is interesting to speculate how differently the course of the war might have gone had they not left when they did, slipping off down a farmer's track that led to the river and to the waiting boat at Jeffrey's Hook. From there the little party was rowed across to the New Jersey shore and climbed the Palisades to watch the engagement from Fort Lee. (There was, at about the same time and place, an almost exact parallel to this on the British side: Captain Mackenzie was concerned for the safety of Admiral Howe, the general's brother, who was "with Lord Percy's Corps, and close up to Morris's house about the time of the attack there. He was unattended by any Officer or Servant, and myself and another officer assisted in opening a part of a line of Abbatis to make way for him to get forward.")

Magaw, meanwhile, realizing that Cadwalader was going to be trapped between Percy and Sterling, sent Thomas Bull to tell Cadwalader to pull his troops in toward the fort. Word of this withdrawal just barely reached

Graydon, on the extreme end of the line, in time to prevent his company from being caught by the advance of some mounted enemy troops. By now a good part of Cadwalader's force was falling back through the woods, pursued by Hessians and Percy's redcoats, while off to the rebels' left the sound of gunfire from the approaching Highlanders grew louder and nearer. Lennox's outnumbered militiamen had done all they could to hold off the 42nd and now they headed for the protection of the fort.

The Scots took cover behind a line of barrack huts near the Morris house, where they discovered to their surprise that they were in the rear of Cadwalader's second line of trenches. Fortunately for the rebels they hesitated, probably thinking that the entrenchments held troops who were concealed from view, and this pause was long enough for Cadwalader to do what had to be done: he ordered all his men to retire from the lines into the fort as soon as a signal was given. Those out on the left, moving obliquely across the hill toward Fort Washington, had to pass in front of the Highlanders, and somehow they managed to return their fire and hold them off long enough for most of the retreating men to get by. But inevitably some did not. Alexander Graydon was one of the unlucky ones who were still too far out in the lines to avoid being caught as Percy's men and the Highlanders closed ranks and raced across the heights toward the Hudson, to seal off the line of retreat. Graydon and Andrew Forrest, a fellow officer, had managed to send their troops to the relative security of the fort and were reconnoitering on the hill in hopes of locating Cadwalader when they realized that they were surrounded. There was nothing to do but surrender, so the two men clubbed their flintlocks as a signal of capitulation and began walking toward the enemy. Either their gesture was misunderstood or the Highlanders didn't care to observe it, for at least ten rounds were fired at them (as long as he was being shot at, Graydon was thankful that it was "these blunt shooters" and not American riflemen who were doing it). Their weapons were taken by an officer of the 42nd, who put them in charge of a sergeant. (In a broad Scottish brogue he lectured them: "Young men, ye should never fight against yer King.")

A British officer rode up on a horse and, seeing Graydon and Forrest, called out to their captors: "What! Taking prisoners! Kill them, kill every man of them!" Graydon knew that Howe had threatened to put the garrison to the sword if it did not surrender, so he removed his hat, bowed to the officer, and said, "Sir, I put myself under your protection." The plea worked. He and other rebel officers who had been rounded up were taken to the Morris barn where they were insulted and ordered about by men Graydon described as "upstart Cockneys" and "contemptible whipsters," one of whom tried to tear off his cartouche box, which bore the king's device. Eventually about 200 Americans were there, some wounded, some in uniform and some not, and for a while curious British officers stuck their heads into the barn to look at them, as if to see what manner of men they were. The barn grew more and more crowded, the air increasingly oppressive, and the men desperate for water, but as far as Graydon was concerned the ultimate insult came from a British sergeant who sat with pen in hand and paper on his knee, asking each officer for his name and rank. It was not that the sergeant was uncivil, Graydon said, only that he possessed an air of impudence "which belongs to a self-complacent non-commissioned officer of the most arrogant army in the world."

With the collapse of Magaw's outer lines on the south and east, the rebels streamed back toward the fort ("Our men stood laughing at them as they passed, crying out, 'Make room for the soldiers!' " an English officer said), crowding into its exterior and interior walls, getting in the way of the hard-pressed artillerymen, consuming what little water was left, and adding to the confusion and mounting fear. The trouble was that the third defensive line on the south—the one intended to run across the heights to the Morris house—had never been completed, so there was nothing for Cadwalader's men to fall back on except the fort; while on the east, there were no real lines—only isolated redoubts—since the rebels had not anticipated a concentrated attack from that quarter. Off to the north the defense still held, but nearly two hours of desperate fighting had taken its toll of the riflemen. There were fewer of them now, and incessant firing had fouled their weapons so that they were forced to push boulders down the steep hillside against the attackers. Up on the crest the little American battery had taken fearful punishment from the Hessian fieldpieces and from salvos fired from the *Pearl*. (The American battery had gotten in its licks, too: ". . . we received many shot in our Hull, and our Rigging much damaged," the *Pearl*'s commanding officer noted.) The wife of one Pennsylvania gunner, John Corbin, who had come with him to camp on the heights, was with him behind the redoubt, and after several men fell she pitched in, swabbing and loading the gun. During the worst of the fighting her husband was shot dead by a musket, and she took charge of the cannon, loading and firing it herself, until she was terribly wounded by grapeshot. At that, the battery was silenced.

Below the redoubt the riflemen's fire had nearly ceased; the Hessians, sensing that the end was near, began moving up the hill, but even without a spirited defense, it was still tough going. "We were obliged to creep along up the rocks, one falling down alive, another shot dead," said John Reuber of Rall's command. "We were obliged to drag ourselves up by the birch-tree bushes up the height where we could not really stand." There was hand-to-hand fighting as they pushed toward the summit, with the Pennsylvanians and Virginians swinging desperately with clubbed rifles, throwing rocks or anything else they could lay their hands on at the on-rushing Germans. But finally there was no holding back the assault wave, and with a mighty surge the grenadiers and Waldeckers reached the top, swarmed over the walls of the redoubt lunging with bayonets at anything that moved, and as bugles sounded the charge a great roar went up from the Hessians who were so close to the rebels that it seemed all one crowd, pursuers and pursued together, milling, swirling, yelling and cursing and running. This was what Washington and the other generals, watching anxiously from Fort Lee, could see, and the story was told that the commander in chief saw the rout of the riflemen with tears in his eyes. As well he might; they had performed nobly for several hours against the fiercest, most determined opposition, in a fight that had been lost before it began. Washington undoubtedly perceived the ferocity of the assault: not only had the Germans encountered the worst possible obstacles in their attack on the hill; they were still boiling mad as a result of what some of Magaw's men had done to them a week earlier. (On the ninth of November, in a skirmish below the King's Bridge, the Americans had killed thirteen Germans, including an officer, and then—the ultimate indignity—stripped them of their uniforms and left them naked on the field.) Washington, seeing the collapse of the northern lines and observing the bayonet charge of the enraged Germans, scribbled a note to Magaw, asking him to try to hold out until nightfall if he possibly could, when the general (doubtless thinking of the near miracle that had saved the troops on Long Island) would do his utmost to rescue the fort's defenders. He handed the note to an aide, Captain John Gooch, who hurried down to the river and was rowed across to the other side.

In order to reach Magaw, Gooch was going to need a lot of luck, for before he reached the opposite shore, the Waldeckers had worked their way through the wooded bank along the river and reached a point where they were between the walls of the fort and the Hudson. Magaw and his men were almost completely surrounded. Meanwhile, Knyphausen's troops made the summit and paused for breath behind a stone barn off to the north of the fort while Schmidt's regiments halted just below the brow of the hill, where they were covered from the fire from the fort. Knyphausen spoke to Rall, telling him his men had earned the distinction of demanding the surrender, and Rall called to a company commander. "Hohenstein, you speak English and French," he said. "Take a drummer with you, tie a white cloth on a gun barrel, go to the fort, and call for a surrender." Captain Hohenstein went off at once; later he reported that the rebels "kept firing at me and the drummer until we came to the glacis," where the defenders finally realized what was going on and ceased fire. Several soldiers came out to meet the German officer, and after tying a scarf around his eyes, they led him in through the outer works and Cadwalader came to meet him. Hohenstein apparently had been authorized by Rall to make terms with the Americans, for he told Cadwalader that the rebels should march out of the fort and lay down their arms before General Knyphausen. They would be expected to deliver all ammunition and other provisions to the German commander, but, Hohenstein added, "I gave him my word that all, from the commanding officer down, should retain their private property. Finally, a white flag should be immediately hoisted, to put a stop to all hostilities." Hohenstein refused Cadwalader's request for four hours' time in which to consider the ultimatum, allowing him "only half an hour to speak with his officers."

Captain Mackenzie, approaching the fort from the south, heard the roll of rebel drums, beating the parley; Captain John Peebles of the 42nd, over on the east side, heard it, noted that it was about three o'clock, and slowly the firing died away. Just now Captain Gooch, who was traveling under some lucky star this day, clambered up the hillside from the river and made his way into the works to seek out Magaw, arriving there just before the Waldeckers from the north and Stirn's Hessians from the south joined up to encircle the fort. But Magaw's time was almost up when Gooch appeared; the Germans had given him half an hour to make up his mind and he had to decide at once between surrendering or attempting to. carry out Washington's request that he hold out till nightfall. There really was no choice, as Magaw knew. He was surrounded and the fort could not withstand a bayonet charge; besides, the exhausted, desperately thirsty men were so crowded within the earthworks that any resistance could lead only to a slaughter. Howe, who had accompanied Mathew and the light infantry, met Percy near the eleven-mile stone near the fort and dictated terms which were also given to Magaw—"an immediate & categorical Answer to this second Summons of Fort Washington." General Howe, the message stated, was "pleased to allow the Garrison to keep Possession of their Baggage, and the officers to have their Swords." Bidding farewell to Gooch, Magaw walked off to talk with Hohenstein.

"His fate seemed hard to him," the German captain recalled sympathetically. To Magaw's request for easier terms, he suggested that the American commander accompany him to see Knyphausen, who was only a hundred paces from the fort. The American colonel went along on this hopeless errand, fairly certain that the German general would not concede anything to the rebels, but he gave it a try anyway. As George Hart heard later, Magaw "offered to surrender, provided he was allowed to march out with the honours of war and 2 field Pieces. The answer was that if they did not lay down their Arms, and surrender Prisoners in half an hour that he would storm the Fort. They very prudently accepted of the terms in less than 3 minutes. The General put up his watch,—lighted his pipe," and the dejected Magaw returned to the fort to pass the word that he had capitulated.

By some miracle, the intrepid Gooch—who did not regard himself as one of the fort's defenders and therefore not a party to the surrender—ran to the edge of the embankment, leaped over the edge, and slid and tumbled to the bottom, avoiding bayonets and musket fire from the Hessians who tried to stop him, reached his boat, and made his way back across the Hudson to inform Washington of Magaw's decision. At four o'clock the observers in Fort Lee saw the American colors flutter down from the flagstaff. Although they could not know it, it would be seven years before an American banner flew over New York again.

When Koehler's grenadiers marched into the fort, none of the defenders knew quite what to expect, despite Hohenstein's assurances that they would be treated well. Captain von Malmburg was in charge of the detail, and he reported that he was immediately "surrounded with officers with fear and anxiety in their faces. They invited him to their barracks, pressed punch, wine and cold cakes upon him, complimented him on his affability, and told him they had not been led to expect such from a Hessian officer." Southeast of the fort was a meadow that belonged to one Blazius Moore, and here the Americans filed out between a double line of troops from the Rall and Alt von Lossberg regiments. One German, watching them lay down their arms and their "yellow, blue, and white banners," observed that Knyphausen stood silently, looking on with disdain while, to the disgust of the British, the Hessian infantrymen closed in on the rebel prisoners and began robbing them. "To our shame," Stephen Kemble wrote, "tho' [the Americans] capitulated for the Safety of their Baggage, they were stripped of their Wearing Apparel as they Marched out by Hessians, till a Stop was put to it by making them take a different Route." Finally, at about 5 P.M., the demoralized captives tramped off toward the British lines at McGowan's Pass under heavy guard, leaving behind in the cold evening air some 96 wounded and 59 dead comrades. The British and Hessians, between them, had lost 84 killed or missing and 374 wounded, of which the Germans accounted for much the heavier share— 58 dead and 272 wounded.

The American casualties were only a fraction of their total loss, however. Some 230 officers and 2,607 soldiers marched off as prisoners of war, some to a hellish end. Captain Mackenzie saw them all the next day, just before they were moved to New York, and observed that they "were in general very indifferently clothed; few of them appeared to have a Second shirt, nor did they appear to have washed themselves during the Campaign. A great many of them were lads under 15, and old men: and few of them had the appearance of Soldiers. Their odd figures frequently excited the laughter of our Soldiers." When the prisoners arrived in the city they were lined up "near the Jews burying ground," according to an eyewitness, but even among all the British sympathizers "no insult was offered to them when paraded, nor any public huzzaing or rejoicing as was usual on similar and less occasions." The worst was still to come. Many captives were taken to be quartered in churches; because of a fire that had raged through New York on September 21, housing was at a premium, and prisoners of war had the lowest priority on accommodations. Two days after the battle about 400 men were marched to the Moravian Church at Fulton and William Streets, where Pastor Shewkirk—now that the British had won—would presumably be able to obtain the firewood and provender he was so anxious to get. Shewkirk was horrified at the thought of turning any part of his church over to the unfortunate men and immediately hurried off to appeal to higher authority. While he did so, "the prisoners with the guard stood above half an hour in the street before our doors." Then Shewkirk's temporal prayers were answered: the order was cancelled. Thankfully he wrote in his diary, "If these prisoners had come in, how much would our place have been ruined . . . not to mention the painful thought of seeing a place dedicated to our Saviour's praise made a habitation of darkness and uncleanness."

So while Pastor Shewkirk's house of worship remained light and clean, those to whom he had refused refuge went elsewhere. One of them, Oliver Woodruff, spent the winter in Bridewell prison, where he "never saw any fire except what was in the lamps of the city. There was not a pane of glass in the windows, and nothing to keep out the cold but the iron gate." Others were herded into the Sugar House—a stone warehouse with almost no light or ventilation, and no heat in winter or air in summer. Hundreds of them perished and the dead often lay for days before they were removed for burial. Some officers were paroled (Lambert Cadwalader was released in return for a favor his father had once done a British officer), but many remained with the privates and non-coms in the ghastly prisons. One New Yorker who walked by the Sugar House on a hot summer day recalled vividly the sight of "every narrow aperture of those stone walls filled with human heads, face above face, seeking a portion of the external air." And in the city's few prisons, injured and diseased men were pigged together, systematically neglected and starved. Of more than 2,800 men who had marched out of Fort Washington on the afternoon of November 16, 1776, there remained, some eighteen months later when an exchange of prisoners was effected, only 800 survivors.

The loss of materiel was equally staggering, considered in the light of the Americans' needs and their capacity to replace it. Mackenzie noted in his diary that the victors had found, in the fort and the nearby batteries, thirty-four cannon of different sizes, two $5\frac{1}{2}$-inch brass howitzers, a "great quantity of ammunition," several stands of colors, and about two weeks' provisions for the troops. Examining the fort, he concluded that there would have been no difficulty in storming it since there was no outer ditch; in fact, Mackenzie believed, had not Howe given orders only to drive the defenders into the fort, there was no doubt that the troops—

"especially the Hessians, who were extremely irritated at having lost a good many men in the attack"—would have taken it by storm. And, he thought, "The Carnage would have been dreadful, for the Rebels were so numerous they had not room to defend themselves with effect, and so frightened they had not the power." Mackenzie didn't care for the Hessians' shameful conduct; even though the rebels had no right to expect mild treatment, he liked to think that "it is right to treat our Enemies as if they might one day become our friends." He was a solid, plain-speaking, honest man who considered humanitarianism to be the distinguishing characteristic of the British troops.

There was one final act to the tragedy that had to be played out in the waning hours of daylight on November 16. Once the bystanders at Fort Lee had seen their comrades march out of the fort, they loaded their cannon in a kind of blind, frustrated rage and began firing at Fort Washington. As Captain Mackenzie noted in his diary, "They were 32 [pounders] and the shot came quite home. But no person was hurt by them."

That night the German troops in their camp heard that the fort they had fought so hard to take would be renamed Fort Knyphausen, although the fact was not made public until Howe's orders of the twenty-first. Two days afterward, Ambrose Serle went for another outing, riding with Mr. Foxcroft, the postmaster general, to the lines about the captured fort. They were astonished to think how much effort had gone into constructing the works, and a British officer to whom they talked said the rebels must be fools or cowards or both to have fortified such a place—this type of natural stronghold was easy to defend, without having to build any earthworks.

A disquieting thought crossed the mind of Ensign Thomas Glyn as he looked at the abandoned fort. If "regular troops" had been defending the place, he mused, "our Army would probably have failed with great loss."

5. *The Rebels Fled Like Scared Rabbits*

British partisans were not alone in the conviction that the fall of Fort Washington had been the result of mismanagement, cowardice, or worse. Among Americans, there was general agreement that the fault had been largely Nathanael Greene's. The Pennsylvanian Alexander Graydon, who was now locked up in a New York prison, was to maintain for the rest of his life that Greene would never have sacrificed the fort's defenders had they been New England men. James Duane was highly critical of Greene's bungling; in a letter to Philip Schuyler he observed dourly that zeal and ardor were all right as far as they went, but were no substitute for experience. Washington's secretary, Tench Tilghman, was convinced that the fort would have been evacuated in good order had not Greene persuaded the commander in chief that the troops could leave it at a moment's notice, protected by the guns of Fort Lee, and Tilghman was mortified at the thought of the repercussions in Europe. "We were in a fair way of finishing the campaign with credit to ourselves and I think to the disgrace of Mr. Howe," he believed, if Washington had only followed his own good judgment and withdrawn the garrison when Howe moved from Dobbs Ferry. And Joseph Reed, another member of Washington's official family who was normally one of Greene's staunch supporters, told Charles Lee that Greene's tactics had kept Washington "in a State of Suspense till the Stroke was struck. Oh! General," he groaned, "an indecisive Mind is one of the greatest Misfortunes that can befall an Army."

To which Lee, with something less than complete loyalty to his commanding officer, replied, "I lament with you that fatal indecision of mind which in war is a much greater disqualification than stupidity or even want of personal courage." Lee followed this up with a message to Benjamin Rush in Philadelphia, noting that he had foreseen and predicted all that occurred at Fort Washington and suggesting that if only he, Lee, were given the necessary authority, "I could do you much good, might I but dictate one week." Charles Lee had not the slightest doubt that he was a better general than George Washington, and he was no man to let grass grow under his feet where he detected an opportunity. While criticism of Greene mounted, Lee was further encouraged by an unctuous letter from Reed: "I do not mean to flatter nor praise you at the expense of another," it read, "but I confess I do think that it is entirely owing to you that this Army, the Liberties of America, so far as they are dependent on it, are not totally cut off. You have Decision, a Quality often wanting in minds otherwise valuable. . . ." All of which was heady talk to a man of almost unlimited ambition.

Even Washington had lost some of his confidence in Greene. On November 19, when Lee informed the general that he had turned down some of Greene's recommendations of Rhode Island officers, Washington approved the action almost apologetically for having taken Greene's advice. Greene himself was disconsolate about the disaster at Fort Washington. In an agonized letter to his friend Knox he said, "I feel mad, vexed, sick, and sorry,—never did I need the consoling voice of a friend more than now." Privately, he laid some of the blame at Rufus Putnam's door, for not having constructed several redoubts which Knox and Greene had urged him to build, and he was critical of Magaw for permitting the troops to abandon the outer lines and jam together in the fort at the end. But his worst indignation was reserved for the soldiers who had panicked. Although most of them were inexperienced levies from the Flying Camp, that didn't excuse them in Greene's eyes; it was his opinion that a man ought to fight for his country whether he had been trained or not. But none of Greene's efforts to look elsewhere for the blame excused him from what proved to be his own worst blunder of the war. The only good to come out of the painful lesson was that he never repeated the mistake; never again would he rely on raw militiamen to stand off an attack by British regulars.

Four days after the fall of the fort George Washington learned about the final moments of the battle from Colonel Cadwalader, who had been released by the British, and nothing he heard lessened the sickening sense of humiliation he felt. The loss meant that Fort Lee was of no further value to him; in fact, the odds were that it was now a real liability—another trap for its defenders unless they and the stores in the fort were removed at once. Washington ordered Greene to get them out at once—to Bound Brook, Springfield, Princeton—wherever they would be safe in the event the British crossed the Hudson, and Greene reported on the eighteenth that he was moving them off as fast as he could locate wagons. He had sent to Newark for boats to assist in the job, but he was worried: "The stores here are large, and the transportation by land will be almost endless." Nevertheless, he began dispatching loads of powder and ammunition by wagon, not daring to trust them to transportation by water.

On November 17 Washington was advised that the Massachusetts Long Faces in Lee's command were marching home; their enlistments had expired and they were getting out while the getting was good. None of the states had contributed any more men to the Flying Camp and Washington calculated that he would have no more than 2,000 soldiers with whom to oppose Howe should the British attack west of the Hudson. In Hackensack on the nineteenth, the general had his first opportunity to finish a long letter to his brother John Augustine which he had begun at White Plains two weeks earlier. After giving him an account of the recent catastrophe, he was unable to keep the pent-up indignation from spilling out; he had begged Congress again and again for long-term enlistments, he said, a request that had only resulted in delays, quarrels about the appointment of officers, and the nomination of men who "are not fit to be shoe blacks." Finally, in an outburst of pure despair, he added, "I am wearied almost to death with the retrograde motion of things, and I solemnly protest that a pecuniary record of £20,000 a year would not induce me to undergo what I do; and, after all, perhaps, to lose my character, as it is impossible under such a variety of distressing circumstances to conduct matters agreeably to public expectation, or even of those who employ me, as they will not make proper allowances for the difficulties their own errors have occasioned."

Soberly, he followed this up with a letter informing Congress of the army's dilemma. He had approximately 2,000 troops around Hackensack and Fort Lee; there were another thousand under General Stirling‡ at

---

‡ The Revolution was rich in contradictions and surprises, and not the least of them was the man who called himself "Lord Stirling." His father, James Alexander, arrived in New York as a refugee from Scotland and the Rebellion of 1715, became a prominent lawyer, and married the widow of a wealthy merchant. He backed John Peter Zenger's independent newspaper, which opposed the colony's royal governor, and when Zenger was arrested for printing allegedly libelous statements, Alexander and

One of the many sketches and maps made especially for Lord Percy during the war was this wash drawing of Fort Lee, taken from the east side of the Hudson River, somewhere in the general area of Fort Washington.

(Courtesy of His Grace, the Duke of Northumberland)

Rahway and Brunswick; Lee was at White Plains with most of the army; Heath was at Peekskill and his 4,000 men were all that stood between a possible juncture of Howe's army and the British force moving down from Canada. Meanwhile, it was imperative that Lee should join Washington, in case Howe elected to march on Philadelphia. The general was still totting up these problems when an express rider reined up in front of the Zabriskie house with more bad news. During the rainy night, boats had crossed the Hudson below Dobbs Ferry and disgorged a strong enemy force, which was now moving south toward Fort Lee.

A Bergen County Tory named Major John Aldington, who owned a brewery which the American army had commandeered for a storehouse,

---

another attorney undertook to defend him. They were disbarred for questioning the credentials of two of the judges, with the result that Andrew Hamilton of Philadelphia received credit for successfully defending Zenger in a case that was a landmark victory for freedom of the press in the colonies. The son, William, was a fine mathematician and astronomer, a man of social position and substantial wealth, but he evidently felt that something had been denied him. During the French and Indian War he served as an aide to Governor William Shirley of Massachusetts, accompanied him to England, and there, in 1759, the young man lay claim to the earldom of Stirling. He was able to persuade a jury that he was descended from an uncle of the first earl, but the Committee of Privileges of the House of Lords ruled otherwise. Undaunted, Alexander returned to America and his elegant home in Basking Ridge, New Jersey, where he employed the title as long as he lived. None of his republican contemporaries seem to have boggled at it: they called him "Lord Stirling" without blinking an eye, styled his wife "Lady Stirling," and referred to the couple's daughter as "Lady Kitty."

saw his chance for revenge after Fort Washington collapsed. He got word to the British that it was possible to land troops at tiny Closter Dock Landing on the New Jersey shore—a point from which a narrow, concealed, nearly vertical path led to the summit of the Palisades above Fort Lee. So improbable was a landing there that the rebels had not even bothered to guard the place (four years later, in fact, General Anthony Wayne—who was not easily daunted—concluded that the site was entirely unsuitable for any military operation). Under cover of darkness on November 18, the ubiquitous British flatboats made their way silently up the Hudson, hugging the east bank until they reached Spuyten Duyvil Creek and were concealed from view. The next day orders were issued to two chasseur companies, the 1st and 2nd Light Infantry, the 1st and 2nd Grenadiers, two battalions of Guards, the 33rd and 42nd Regiments, three battalions of Hessian grenadiers, a company of loyalists without arms, and three guides—including, in all probability, John Aldington—to be ready with full kit at 9 P.M. under the command of Lord Cornwallis. During the night they marched north to the Philipse house on the west bank of the Hudson and by daybreak the next morning the first troops disembarked on the New Jersey side at Closter Dock Landing. By nine o'clock the entire assault force was ashore, and Cornwallis formed them up in two columns for what Ensign Glyn called "a very rapid march." Luckily for the Americans, a farmer spotted the British columns and hurried off to warn the garrison at Fort Lee, narrowly averting a complete surprise.

Washington had just finished breakfast and was going over some correspondence with his aides, Colonels William Grayson and Robert Harrison, when the express arrived. At precisely ten o'clock, Harrison noted, a "smart firing" was heard near Fort Lee. Harrison assumed incorrectly that the attack was from the south, but he was right in thinking that the enemy "seem determined to push matters, and the weather is most favorable for 'em." For the glorious fall days had ended, and the drenching rain would turn the New Jersey roads to soupy mud, making it impossible to haul more stores from the fort. Equally disturbing was the knowledge that the troops would be at a terrible disadvantage if they had to fight in the rain; their muskets were useless if their powder was wet, and unlike the redcoats, few of them had bayonets and those who did lacked the British zeal for cold steel.

Immediately, Washington called for horses and he and Grayson galloped off to Greene's headquarters in English Neighborhood, where he learned that the British had apparently committed a large force to the attack. After deciding that Lee should cross the Hudson at once near King's Ferry in order to join him, while Heath and Stirling stood by, ready to march at a moment's notice, he and Grayson rode on to the little crossroads at Liberty Pole, where Grayson left for Hackensack to dispatch Lee's orders. The commander in chief headed for New Bridge, where the British were almost certain to come in order to seal off the line of retreat across the Hackensack River. It was going to be a close-run thing, for if Cornwallis made for New Bridge he was likely to get there before the soldiers from Fort Lee did; if not, and if he marched directly to the fort, the retreating Americans would probably meet the British head on near the Liberty Pole crossing. It was sheer luck that neither eventuality took place; the British artillerymen and seamen had had a rough time dragging their fieldpieces up the rocky, narrow ascent from Closter Dock Landing, and the delay was just enough to allow Greene's men to make a headlong dash from the fort toward Liberty Pole and on to New Bridge. Cornwallis must have assumed that the rebels would put up a fight for Fort Lee as they had for Fort Washington; otherwise, there is no explaining his failure to cut off their escape route by seizing New Bridge. But Washington had no intention of repeating the earlier disaster; he had decided to abandon Fort Lee as soon as the stores were removed.

When the British columns climbed the narrow track from Peter Bourdet's house and marched into the fort in perfect order, with their drums rolling, it was one o'clock, and the scene that confronted them was enough to appall the disciplined regulars. The redoubts and outer works were empty, but strewn all over the interior of the fort were blankets, stores of all kinds, cannon, food, and all the paraphernalia of the garrison which Greene had been unable to carry off. Ensign Glyn noticed that breakfast kettles were still boiling on the fires, all the tents were still standing (they were put to use that night by Cornwallis's men), and the sick had been left behind to fall into British hands. The woods nearby were full of stragglers, whom Greene had tried without success to round up, and most of them were swept up by the redcoats and sent off to prison in New York. Another British officer observed contemptuously that the tables were spread for the officers' dinner, and inside the fort twelve men were found, all dead drunk. "There were forty or fifty pieces of cannon found loaded," he added, "with two large iron sea mortars and one brass one with a vast quantity of ammunition, powder, and stores. . . ." The rebels had "fled like scared rabbits," one Englishman wrote, "and in a few moments after we reached the hill near their entrenchments, not a rascal of them could be seen. They have left some poor pork, a few greasy proclamations and some of that scoundrel Common Sense man's letters, which we can read at our leisure, now that we have got one of the 'impregnable redoubts' of Mr. Washington's to quarter in . . . We intend to push on after the long faces in a few days." Between Liberty Pole and the fort the British had seen the road strewn with muskets, knapsacks, and twelve artillery pieces abandoned in the panicky retreat. In the meadows beyond the fort were numerous cattle that had been driven from Pennsylvania and New Jersey to feed the rebels and would now find their way into enemy stomachs.

Although most of the garrison had made a dash for New Bridge, some men fled south and west, waded through marshes to a point opposite a mill in Hackensack, and were ferried across the river by boats. When all those who were coming were safely across New Bridge, the drums beat and Washington rode off at the head of the marching columns along the road to Hackensack, where they would turn west to the Passaic River crossing. "It was about dusk when the head of the troops entered Hackensack," a local man recalled. "The night was dark, cold and rainy, but I had a fair view of Greene's troops from the light of the windows as they passed on our side of the street. They marched two abreast, looked ragged, some without a shoe to their feet and most of them wrapped in their blankets." It did not require much imagination for the residents of Hackensack to see that the army on which the survival of the American cause depended was just about on its last legs.

Washington returned to the Zabriskie house for the night, soaked from a long day in the pouring rain, consoled only by the thought that he had managed to save most of the men, if not the stores. But all in all, the combined loss at Forts Washington and Lee was staggering. Nearly 3,000 men were dead or captured, 150 cannon and 12,000 rounds of shot and shell were gone, along with 2,800 muskets and 400,000 cartridges, plus tents, clothing, food, and other equipment. In terms of men and equipment lost, it was the worst defeat of the Revolutionary War.

CHAPTER FOUR

1. These Things Raise the Heads of the Tories

In that long-ago fall of 1775, when militiamen from Connecticut and other New England colonies left the lines around Boston in droves as their enlistments expired, driving Washington and Greene nearly to distraction, the Continental Congress had cobbled together a solution that seemed to the delegates, at the time, like a good one. They had decided that the Continental Army—originally created in June, when Washington was named to the command—should consist of 20,372 men from the four New England colonies (which were then the only ones actively at war) with regiments of 728 men each, including officers. The soldiers were to be paid every month (Congress settled on a calendar month basis to the disgust of the sharp Massachusetts men, who had figured out that the shorter lunar month meant more paydays), and there were provisions for outfitting them with muskets, clothing, and blankets. On January 1, 1776, twenty-seven regiments were raised—all from Massachusetts, Connecticut, Rhode Island, and New Hampshire except Colonel William Thompson's Pennsylvanians, who made up the First Continental Infantry—and their term of enlistment was one year, until the last day of December 1776. The idea was that this army would form the hard core of resistance to the British, augmented from time to time by various local militia outfits, where and when required, and everyone expected that by the time its year was up, the dispute with Great Britain would be settled. No one really imagined that the war would go on longer than that, but if it did, why then the men serving in the Continental Army could simply be re-enrolled in December of 1776 for another year's hitch. It all promised well enough on paper, but the reality was another matter altogether.

Long after the event it would become the stuff of legend, and little boys would sit at the knees of garrulous old men, listening to heroic tales of the "Grand Army" that put the redcoats to rout. At every Fourth of July celebration white-haired veterans would be shepherded onto platforms draped with flags and bunting, to nod and doze through the long orations while their minds drifted back to that long ago day when the world was young and eager and alive with brave comrades. But General Washington's army, in the late fall of 1776, was a far remove from the legend it would become; it was tired and hungry and ragged, fearful not about the distant future but about what the next twenty-four hours might produce and sullen with the knowledge that it had been badly beaten every time it had gone into battle and forced to retreat after every engagement. It was, in short, inclined to think about the future only in the light of the past, and the immediate past had been all bad.

Along with everything else that had happened to them, these men did not seem to be getting the kind of support they might expect from the government that had requested their services. The Congress had realized, of course, that if you were going to have a large body of men under arms, these people had to be clothed and fed, among other things, and in October they had published a list of articles that were supposed to be issued to each soldier who signed up for the Continental Army. The men were to receive two linen hunting shirts, two pairs of stockings, two pairs of shoes, two pairs of overalls (which had been found to be much more serviceable than trousers), a leather or woolen jacket, a pair of breeches, and one leather cap or hat. This outfit, which was prescribed largely at Washington's insistence, was sometimes known as the "rifle dress" because it was associated—in the minds of the British, at least—with the apparel worn by skilled riflemen. "It is a dress," the commander in chief noted, "which is justly supposed to carry no small terror to the enemy, who think every such person a complete marksman." More to the point, perhaps, it was also a good deal easier to come by than uniforms of bright-colored material, which were less utilitarian as well. It was highly unlikely, however, that anything like a majority of the men with Washington at this time were outfitted in anything like this manner, for there was a long time between the promise and delivery, and there was simply no manufacturing capability in the states for producing clothing in the quantities required.

With the exception of a few outfits like Haslet's Delaware regiment and Smallwood's Marylanders, which had marched into camp fully attired in fancy militia uniforms, the average soldier appeared in whatever he could lay his hands on, and the commonest uniform—if it could be dignified by such a label—was the brown or gray hunting shirt, worn with the hat, trousers, stockings, and shoes a man had brought from home.

The Continental regiments were supposed to consist of eight companies of seventy-six privates each, plus officers, non-coms, and drummers and fifers, and in October Congress had also decided to offer enlistees a bounty of twenty dollars (the promised uniform was said to be worth another twenty, which meant—the recruiting officers would say—that a man actually received a forty dollar bounty for signing up), plus one hundred acres of land "at the end of the War." One general, publishing these tidings to his troops, observed that the "noble Bounty" was such "an ample & generous Gratuity" that no American could hesitate to enlist "to defend his Country and posterity, from every Attempt & Tyranny to enslave it." Yet the fact of the matter, as British Captain Frederick Mackenzie had observed, was that many of the rebels lacked shoes and stockings, wore only a thin linen shirt and trousers, and had no blankets. Taken together with their recent defeats, the inevitable falling morale, and their lack of suitable winter quarters, Mackenzie thought it would be "astonishing if they keep together 'till Christmas."

Except for the men in the rifle companies, the private in the Continental Army carried a smoothbore musket which was, like his uniform, supposedly government issue but which he had more than likely brought from home or picked up somewhere along the way, and this gun theoretically had an eighteen-inch bayonet attached, which very, very few possessed at this stage of the war. Many of these firelocks were the British Brown Bess, others were the product of local gunsmiths, but all functioned in more or less the same somewhat erratic fashion. The Brown Bess was a highly unreliable weapon that was over four and a half feet long, weighed ten pounds, and fired a three-quarter-inch ball. In dry weather a man firing it into the wind was likely to be burned in the face by a backfire or flare from the touchhole; in wet weather it was virtually useless, unless the powder in the pan was protected so that it would fire. Since the man was not expected to be a marksman, the gun did not even have a rear sight. A ball fired horizontally would travel about 125 yards before falling harmlessly to the ground and the maximum effective range was between 80 and 100 yards, which meant that fighting had to be at very close quarters. This put a premium on volley firing, which made up in sheer weight what it lacked in accuracy, and the soldiers were drilled in loading and firing on command—which was by no means as easy as it sounds. First, the soldier bit off the end of a paper cartridge containing black powder and a musket ball, shook some powder into the firing pan, closed the lid, and after resting the butt of the musket on the ground, stuffed the cartridge into the muzzle and rammed it home. When he pulled the trigger, the firing cock fell, striking flint against steel; this spark ignited the powder in the pan, fire flashed from the touchhole and into the charge, and the ball was projected. But there were so many possibilities of a misfire—caused by damp powder, a worn flint, a fouled touchhole—that often there was no explosion. For all these uncertainties, a certain amount of destruction was bound to result from a volley fired at short range almost simultaneously by a large number of men standing in line, and it created considerable confusion in the ranks of the men who had to face it.

For the rebels, the problems went beyond the musket's slowness and limited range; from the beginning of hostilities they were horribly short of the powder required to fire their weapons. So serious was the shortage that Benjamin Franklin in 1776 actually advocated the use of bows and arrows by the army, arguing that a good man could fire four arrows for every bullet, that his vision would not be obscured by smoke, and that an enemy—who could not see a bullet—would have his attention diverted by flying arrows and when stuck through with one would be in no condition to go on fighting. Strenuous efforts were made throughout the war to encourage the manufacture of gunpowder and to have citizens conserve the niter and sulfur used in its fabrication; instructions for making powder were drawn up by various committees of safety and widely circulated; and Congress agreed to purchase all the saltpeter produced by the states.

Lead for musket balls was sought everywhere; roofs were stripped of it, rain spouts and sash weights were melted down into bars to be distributed to the troops, who heated them and molded them into the proper size balls for their muskets (the lead statue of King George III that was pulled down on New York's Bowling Green was said to contain four thousand pounds of metal which was quickly hauled away and made into bullets to fire at the sovereign's troops). Another scarce item required for firing the musket was the flint, and since a good one would last only about sixty rounds before it had to be repaired or replaced, it was essential that the army have plenty on hand. The difficulty was that the supply of good stone was short and workmen capable of shaping them few. Early in the war a good many farmers carried powder horns, often richly decorated with maps, pictures, the names of their owners, and patriotic motifs, but it wasn't long before everyone realized how much more efficient the paper cartridges were; they held a fairly uniform charge, were ready for use in an emergency, and could be made up in advance of any anticipated action.

As in the matter of uniforms and weapons, the Congress was meticulous in prescribing the rations soldiers were to get: a daily allowance of a pound of beef or pork or salt fish, a pound of bread or flour, and a pint of milk and a quart of spruce beer or cider, supplemented with weekly rations of peas, beans, or other vegetables, rice or Indian meal, candles, and soap. But as with everything else, the requirements were almost never met.

One reason the American soldier was so poorly equipped and clothed and fed had to do with his heritage. An overwhelming majority of the former colonists were of British extraction and their ancestors had left England either at the time the Stuart kings were seeking to create a standing army to deprive them of their civil and religious liberty, or when Cromwell—who brought down the house of Stuart—was using his own troops as instruments of another form of tyranny. So the dread of a standing army and all that went with it came naturally, and the very idea of a military force which would be enlisted for the duration of the war was anathema to Congress and the country at large. Never fully resolved, the problem was to plague George Washington throughout the war, and his correspondence with Congress constantly mentions the difficulties of trying to function efficiently when he could not count on an adequate reserve of experienced men. Captain Mackenzie, an acute observer who was fascinated by the dilemma of the American command, came to the conclusion that the only sure, reliable strength of the rebel army consisted of former Europeans—particularly Irishmen. The latter made up a preponderance of many regiments, he believed, and were "much better able to go through the fatigues of a Campaign, and live in the manner they at present do, than the Americans." It all had to do with the fact that the Irish had more spirit than the native American, Mackenzie believed, plus a desire to rise above their traditional state of poverty, and they would fight "for the sake of a present subsistence. Clothing & plunder; and the prospect of acquiring some property, and becoming men of some consequence, in case they are successful." But alas, "Among so many ignorant people" the rebel propaganda carried much weight. To wean them away from the American army, the captain speculated, would require "every means in our power to undeceive them from the cause and support of Rebellion by full promises of pardon to such as surrender within a certain limitted time."

Irishmen there were in plenty, but the rank and file of the American army included such a hodgepodge of different types that it was impossible to categorize them. Dr. James Thacher, an army surgeon, observed that the biggest problem the American command faced was the prejudice that colored all relations between New England and southern soldiers. The latter were "unaccustomed to that equality which prevails in New England," and there were frequent instances of the bad blood between the "Yankee" and "Buck-skin," as they called each other. A Massachusetts colonel permitted his son, who was a shoemaker by trade, to set up shop in the colonel's quarters—a breach of propriety that outraged some sensitive officers from Pennsylvania who were stationed nearby. One of them, a lieutenant colonel, got drunk one night, charged into the colonel's room and broke up the cobbler's bench and then proceeded to assault the Massachusetts officer. This was accompanied by much noise and confusion, a crowd of Pennsylvanians turned out in their man's defense, and before anyone knew what was happening the Massachusetts and Pennsylvania soldiers were firing away at each other there in camp, and several men were severely wounded. The whole thing was settled amicably a few days later when the light colonel sent some of his riflemen off to shoot a bear and treated the Massachusetts boys to steaks, but as Thacher said, the incident never would have occurred had it not been for that Massachusetts colonel's being "more conversant with the economy of domestic life than the etiquette practiced in camp."

The fact that the army was made up of men from thirteen separate, independent colonies meant that the soldiers generally regarded their own homeland as a place quite distinct from—and a good deal better than—any other, and even Washington was guilty of this sectional prejudice.

More than once he referred rather tactlessly to the "levelling" tendencies of the New England regiments, which he deplored. (This just may have been a hangover from French and Indian War days; in 1756 his friend Thomas Gage, then a British major, informed him that the New Englanders were "the greatest boasters and worst soldiers on the continent. We have enlisted soldiers from all the provinces, but I never saw any in my life as infamously bad.") And other officers felt it, too: Colonel Anthony Wayne, writing to Horatio Gates about the commander in chief's woes, said, "My heart bleeds for poor Washington. Had he but Southern troops [Wayne was a "Southerner" from Pennsylvania] he would not be necessitated so often to fly before an enemy, whom, I fear, has lately had but too much reason to hold us cheap."

Of all the personnel problems that afflicted Washington, none nettled him quite so much as the paucity of good officers. Accustomed as he was to the life style of the plantation owner, who expected and demanded respect and prompt obedience from his servants, he and other Southerners found it almost impossible to comprehend the lack of distinction that prevailed between New England officers and their men. In the northern colonies, the small farm was a leveling influence: company officers were usually neighbors of the men they commanded, and the latter were not about to salute or defer to a friend or neighbor just because he had some rank, nor did they observe such amenities as obtaining permission to leave camp to attend to some errand they had in mind. As Washington's aide Joseph Reed told his wife, "Where the principles of democracy so universally prevail, where so great an equality and so thorough a levelling spirit predominates, either no discipline can be established, or he who attempts it must become odious and detestable, a position which no one will choose. You may form some notion of it when I tell you that yesterday morning a captain of horse, who attends the General from Connecticut, was seen shaving one of his men on the parade near the house." New England had fewer of those social distinctions that prevailed in the South and the result frequently was, as Washington regretted, that the privates treated their officers as equals and regarded them "as no more than a broomstick, being mixed together as one common herd" in which neither order nor discipline could be seen. The Yankee officer, elected by the men of his company, might well be a good drill master back home on the village green, but when it came to exercising real leadership, that was something else again. "These N. England men," Charles Lee complained, "are so defective in materials for officers, that it must require time to make a real good army of 'em." And Nathanael Greene, a Rhode Islander himself, admitted, "We want nothing but good officers to constitute as good an army as ever marched into the field. Our men are much better than the officers." He had neither seen nor heard of a single instance of cowardice among seasoned troops where they had good officers to lead them, and was convinced that if the officers were as able as the privates, "we should have nothing to fear from the best troops in the world."

It is worth remembering that the assumption of an officer's responsibility in that war entailed risks far beyond the normal combat duties. Although there are few references to it (Washington did admit later that he and his comrades had fought "with halters about their necks"), a dark specter that hung over many of the rebel leaders was the penalty that might face them if they were unsuccessful or if they were captured by the enemy. The punishment then in force for treason against the king was vividly described by a judge sentencing a group of Irish rebels: "You are to be drawn on hurdles to the place of execution, where you are to be hanged by the neck, but not until you are dead; for, while you are still living your bodies are to be taken down, your bowels torn out and burned before your faces, your heads then cut off, and your bodies divided each into four quarters, and your heads and quarters then to be at the King's disposal; and may the Almighty God have mercy on your souls."

Quite apart from the perils and problems that faced his army in the general sense, Washington was painfully aware of his weakness in two particulars—cavalry and artillery. At the same time that Howe was petitioning Germain for more light horse, because of "the dread the enemy have of them," Washington was requesting that Congress establish one or more corps of cavalry, since he was convinced "there is no carrying on the war without them." A brilliant horseman himself, Washington was also a farmer, and he knew how much forage cavalry mounts would consume and had no desire to burden his army with feed for a lot of hungry animals. What he had in mind was a highly mobile, independent corps of cavalry that would operate on its own—not as part of the regular army—and fight either as dismounted infantry or as true cavalry, for he had begun to realize how vulnerable his skirmishers, the riflemen, were when they were exposed to enemy horsemen. It took them so long to load that they were often ridden down before they could fire another round, and those of his men who had experienced the shattering psychological and physical impact of a cavalry charge had no desire to repeat it. But not until the following year would he have even the makings of an effective cavalry corps.

As for artillery, he informed Congress that as long as the Continentals remained inferior to the British in this arm, it must "carry on the war under infinite disadvantages, and without the smallest probability of success." Until now, he said, rough terrain had favored the Americans, but as soon as the fighting moved out into "a level, champaign country," they could expect the worst, and he urged Congress to take immediate steps to establish a decent train of artillery, equipped with brass guns up to twenty-four pounders, officered by men of proven ability and experience. Happily, he had in Henry Knox an officer capable of making the most of the present limited resources. Knox had about eighteen guns now and a mixed bag they were, including some that had been hauled across the mountains from Fort Ticonderoga to Dorchester Heights in the winter of 1775–76, and two small brass field pieces that had once graced Captain Adino Paddock's train of artillery in Boston. Toward these two, which had been named "Hancock" and "Adams," Knox felt an almost mystical attachment, for they dated back to the days when he had served, as a boy of eighteen, in Paddock's Train, which was made up of mechanics and shopkeepers from the South End of Boston. Captain Paddock was a determined loyalist and he and Knox inevitably fell out politically, after which the former bookseller helped organize another militia troop called the Boston Grenadier Corps, many of whose members found their way into the rebel army. But before that occurred, someone got wind that Paddock intended to turn the guns of the Train over to General Thomas Gage, and one night Billy Dawes—who later rode with Paul Revere to warn the Massachusetts minutemen that the British were on the march—slipped into the armory with some other Liberty Boys, took the guns from their carriages, and hid them in a schoolhouse. Later they spirited the cannon away to a blacksmith shop and concealed them under a pile of coal, and finally took them out of the city by boat to deliver them to Henry Knox on Dorchester Heights. (The guns were fired in seventeen engagements during the war—one was captured and retaken several times—and eventually both were returned for safekeeping to the Ancient & Honorable

Artillery Company in Boston, where they were touched off on ceremonial occasions until 1821.)

For all his hopes, George Washington never did get a full complement of men in the ranks, the promised weapons, ammunition, uniforms, foodstuff, and blankets did not come through in the quantities expected or required, and now, with its year of life nearly up and with enlistments due to expire in a month's time, the army was rapidly falling apart at the seams. (As it turned out, the general was never—throughout the entire course of the war—to have what might be called a veteran army, but only a small cadre of well-trained, experienced men. Now and in the future it was to be a force constantly in flux, with men going or coming as new recruits arrived and the short-term soldiers went home.)

There was also more to his present problems than met the eye: the democratic New Englanders had never fully adjusted to the fact that the commanding general was a Virginian and an aristocrat. Thus far he had done little to justify his earlier reputation as a military man and there was a growing conviction that the direction of the army might be better off in the experienced hands of Major General Charles Lee, the former British officer who was immensely popular with the rank and file and who seemed to have a much clearer idea of what he was about than the tall, remote Virginian. Every private and non-com knew they had been outgeneraled, outmanned, and outgunned each step of the long, dreary way from Long Island to Fort Lee, and it took little imagination to see, as the short November days ran out, that worse was still to come. Cornwallis was hot

This delightful sketch, carved on a Revolutionary soldier's powderhorn, is a rare depiction of a rebel fieldpiece limbered up. The artist has also taken pains to show the Continental uniforms quite accurately.   *(Collection of Harold L. Peterson)*

on their trail; Hessians were combing the countryside for loot; the British cavalry was pounding off in all directions across the New Jersey roads; Howe, with the main body of his army, would doubtless follow Cornwallis into the Jerseys; still another British army was making its way south from Canada; and even then the enemy had so much might to spare that a huge fleet had sailed out through the Narrows carrying 6,000 troops toward God knew what destination along the coast. For the dog-tired, demoralized, footsore Americans, the one thin ray of hope was that Lee would soon be marching to their relief with the largest part of the army.

Washington's retreating soldiers, hunched over against the cold November rain, were the embodiment of a young, totally unsophisticated, naïve nation (despite the critical need for men, soldiers were still being cashiered for profanity and laziness), and their plight reflected only too accurately the confusion and general lack of organization that characterized the recently formed United States of America. It had been Washington's notion from the beginning that the Continental Army would be the linchpin that could hold all the disparate elements of the American states together; Congress was neither strong enough nor well enough regarded to accomplish that, but an army composed of men from an increasing number of states, who had fought and bled together side by side, might be capable of welding the cause together in some semblance of viable unity.

So it might, had not the army virtually ceased to exist as a fighting force. Scattered across the landscape from Westchester to the Hudson Highlands to New Jersey, not one of its divided parts was capable of standing off 5,000 British on its own, and there was considerable reason to doubt that those widely separated parts could be assembled in time to accomplish anything, even in concert. The rate of attrition was such that Lee's return of November 16 indicated 11,000 rank and file; a week later he had 9,200; and by month's end he was down to 7,000. The quartermaster corps, unable to provide for the troops, was forced to send out foraging parties with instructions "to take all" from the Tories, but only "a part" from friends. Not unexpectedly, this practice was rapidly cooling off the number of friends; as the president of the New York Committee of Safety wrote starchily to John Hancock, "The soldier who plunders the country he is employed to protect is no better than a robber, and ought to be treated accordingly." And a loyalist in New York gleefully reported that "the subjects of the new States in the United Colonies are already so harassed, fleeced, and pillaged, by an unremitting extortion and oppression, that they are weary and sick of independency."

In all directions, the search for men went on. Massachusetts induced a few Stockbridge Indians to enlist in the Continental Army, but was obliged to send them by horse and wagon, "as they made some objection to travelling so far on foot." Lee sent off letters to the New England governors, begging them to put a stop to the "rage for privateering" which attracted so many potential soldiers. In Connecticut a group of "aged men" volunteered for duty; there were twenty-four of them, whose combined age was said to be a thousand years, and they left behind wives and 149 children and grandchildren. It was hopeless to count on the militia; Washington informed Congress that they had come into the Flying Camp without muskets, which had to be issued to them. "Many of these threw their arms away, some lost them, whilst others deserted, and took them away." Sadly he concluded that "this will forever be the case, in such a mixed and irregular army as ours has been."

Meanwhile, the immediate effects of his army's disintegration were becoming apparent. It does not require a military expert to recognize a beaten army that is running for its life, and the silent bystanders in those little towns and farmsteads of New Jersey who watched Washington's files slog down the main road through town and out again, heading south and west, realized that the sole means of resistance to the enemy was gone, perhaps for good. It takes a long time for an army—even one of a few thousand men—to pass by a fixed point when the men are marching two or three abreast, strung out across several miles. There was no effort to keep a cadence on this occasion—not even a possibility of it; the artillery and the wagons, creaking and groaning through the mud, cut the road to pieces, forcing the foot soldiers to break ranks and pick their way along outside the rutted tracks on the edge of the fields. Farmers milking their cows in the morning looked out the barn door and saw the van approach, and it was milking time in the afternoon before the rear guard passed by, herding the stragglers along. Night fell as the last sounds of tramping men died away in the distance, and with those departing footsteps went the only force capable of holding the trust of Americans who believed in it or the respect and fear of those who did not. Josiah Bartlett heard from some Tories that "the Regulars drive our Army before them like a parcel of sheep . . . These things raise the heads of the Tories," he told a friend, "and very much depress the spirits of the friends of liberty. If you have any good news to inform us of," he added, "pray send it along as soon as possible to cheer our drooping spirits." As he foresaw, even before the last straggler disappeared down the road, the New Jersey Tories began coming out of the woodwork, smelling defeat and the chance for revenge.

Cornwallis' veterans had spent the night of November 20 under rebel tents and in the blockhouse at Fort Lee, and the next day the general set up headquarters in English Neighborhood after ordering his light troops to secure New Bridge over the Hackensack River. At noon on the twenty-second, after they took possession of Hackensack, a resident wrote that "the church green was covered with Hessians, a horrid frightful sight with their whiskers, brass caps and kettles or brass drums." With the arrival of the British, hundreds of local men appeared almost magically, proclaiming their loyalty to the king, queuing up to receive brand new green uniforms that marked them as loyalist troops; as if by design, Hackensack's leading Tories were named officers of the 4th Battalion of New Jersey Volunteers and spent the day conferring with the British, organizing their men into companies, and making plans to take a long-awaited eye for an eye from Whig neighbors. Abraham Van Buskirk was appointed a lieutenant colonel as a reward for bringing in more than a hundred volunteers from Ramapo and for his active intelligence work prior to the British arrival. Joseph Barton, once known as a Whig sympathizer, led a sizable number of young men from Sussex County into town and was also given a lieutenant colonelcy. And for every active loyalist there was a wavering supporter of the rebel cause who saw the shape of things to come and signed an oath of allegiance to George III. From Ramapo a Continental Army colonel named Jedediah Huntington wrote to Heath that "the greatest part of the people between this and the enemy's camp are friendly to them and will do them all the service in their power." What they had in mind was made abundantly clear the day after the British occupied Hackensack, when they closed in on the house of the young Dutch Reformed minister, Dirck Romeyn, who had made no secret of his belief in America's political liberties. While a crowd of cheering Tories looked on, British and loyalist troops ransacked the house, emptied the barns, drove off the livestock, and left the place a desolate, hollow shell, punctured with broken windows and doors. Fortunately,

Romeyn was away at the time and managed to escape with his sick wife and their eight-year-old child to New Paltz. That same day the Tories and British descended on the home of William Christie in Schraalenburgh, stripped it of everything but the heavy furniture, and carried off his hogs and a horse.

When the British had evacuated Boston in March, over a thousand loyalists went with them, not daring to stay behind without the protection of the king's troops. In New Jersey, eight months later, the tale was reversed; all the fears and pressures to which the loyalists had been subjected vanished with Washington's army. These people were now backed by the presence of Howe's regulars and they intended to make the most of it.

It is all too easy to think of America in 1776 as a nation of revolutionaries, but the reverse of that would be nearer the truth. There were deep, abiding differences of opinion. Many years after the war ended, John Adams estimated that the sentiments of the country had been divided into three equal parts: one third of the people, he said, remained loyal to the crown; another third supported the Revolution; while the rest of his countrymen stayed neutral, taking neither one side nor the other. There is no particular reason to doubt the accuracy of Adams' estimates; but they suggest little more than a state of mind and they depend, in any case, on one's definition of that word "support." If by "support" is meant a willingness to fight and die for a cause, it is worth remembering that a nation which included a free white population of over 2,000,000 never, in all the years of war, put more than 25,000 soldiers into the field at one time, nor did the people who stayed at home ever adequately clothe or support that relative handful of soldiers. On the other hand, nothing like a third of the population was willing to enlist in the ranks of the loyalists, either. Perhaps history is like that, after all—when the chips are really down, maybe there is never more than a handful of citizens who dare to stand up and be counted, while a preponderance wait in the wings to see what will happen.

What seems clear about this matter of loyalties is that there was, in 1776 and later, a substantial segment of the total population which had little taste either for active revolt or for active support of the mother country—there was, in other words, a great, silent, neutral majority that was content to sit on its hands and watch while others bore the immensely difficult burden of supporting one side or the other. No matter which position an individual took, by early winter of 1776 the time had come when the people of New York, New Jersey, and Pennsylvania at least had to face up to the issue and determine where they stood. Practicalities decided it for some, who plotted a course based on how their decision might affect their business, their family, or their relations with friends and neighbors. For others, it was a far more intimate problem, one that required a long, searching look into the conscience before taking a stand that inevitably involved deep personal loyalties and a sense of honor.

Recently the members of the New York Convention had put this central question to their constituents by declaring that "every individual must one day answer for the part he now acts," and they received an eloquent response from young Peter Van Schaack, suggesting the anguish suffered by thoughtful men confronted with this dilemma. Van Schaack had married into an old, prosperous New York family and promptly threw himself into the struggle for American liberty. But when he came up against the thorny, fundamental issue of independence, he drew back, hoping to remain neutral, and he was man enough to give the New York Convention the reasons behind his decision. He had refused to answer their demand for a statement of allegiance, he told them, because whatever response he made would either bring punishment on himself or force him to take an oath that he could not give. Although a majority of New Yorkers might favor independence, he argued, there were men of completely different sentiments who had strong reservations about the desirability of that course: "The question whether a government is dissolved and the people released from their allegiance is, in my opinion, a question of morality as well as religion, in which *every man* must judge, as he must answer for himself . . . No majority, however respectable, can decide for him . . . I hold it that every *individual* has still a right to choose the State of which he will become a member; for before he surrenders any part of his natural liberty, he has a right to know what security he will have for the enjoyment of the residue, and 'men being by nature free, equal and independent,' the subjection of any one to the political power of a State can arise only from 'his own consent' . . . Upon these principles, I hold it that you cannot justly put me to the alternative of choosing to be a subject of Great Britain, or of this State."

If Van Schaack fairly represented one persuasion, there were other shades neither so articulate nor so high-minded, men for whom the Revolution was essentially a class war, a struggle between the haves and the have-nots, or between those in power and those out of it. In the middle states, loyalty had far more adherents than in New England, where there was a deep, long-standing tradition of self-government. And where such powerful feelings of allegiance to Britain existed, the loyalists were likely to be more than a vocal minority—they became active partisans of the Tory cause in spite of the way the mother country largely ignored them and their efforts. They hated the rebels, and for a variety of reasons the rebels loathed them, most of the latter accepting the fact that they would have to fight the British but regarding it as monstrous that their neighbors and fellow countrymen should take up arms against them. And the inevitable result was that on those occasions when two such bodies of men met in combat, there were apt to be more instances of unbridled hatred and passion and cruelty than the two opposing armies of Great Britain and America ever exhibited toward one another. Perhaps it would have been different if the loyalists had been a small minority, but the fact was that they were too strong and numerous to be neglected, and long before the war broke out there had been intensive efforts to intimidate or punish them or eliminate them as an outright threat.

The Provincial Congress of Massachusetts, for example, condemned Tories as "infamous betrayers of their country," while the Continental Congress urged that watchdog committees in every county and town search them out and publicly expose them as "enemies of American liberty." That the so-called committees of safety had done so, often with uncontrolled fury, was clear from the number of whippings, tarrings and featherings, and acts of vandalism that had been perpetrated on outspoken loyalists. Alexander Graydon had witnessed the visit of a group of Philadelphia Liberty Boys to the home of Doctor Kearsley, a hot-tempered, hostile Tory. They seized him at his front door, cut open his hand with a bayonet when he tried to resist, and forced him into a cart that was paraded through the streets "to the tune of the rogue's march," surrounded by dancing, jeering youths and idlers. The cart was brought round to a coffeehouse, where the plucky doctor, "foaming with rage and indignation, without his hat, his wig dishevelled and bloody from his wounded hand, stood up in the cart and called for a bowl of punch." In Charleston, South Carolina, an Englishman told of a man who was tarred and feathered ten or twelve times in as many sections of town for expressing his loyalty; in New York a cooper named Thomas Randolph was stripped naked, coated with tar and feathers, and carted around town in a wagon until he publicly begged pardon and promised to recant his loyalty to the king. These were not isolated incidents; they occurred with harsh regularity up and down the seaboard, poisoning relations between neighbors and increasing the determination of loyal citizens to strike back in vengeance when their time came, as it surely would. The situation was further exacerbated by acts of the various provincial legislatures, which cast the appearance of legality over such procedures. Laws were passed requiring proof of loyalty to the colonial cause, imposing stiff penalties against allegiance to the crown, curtailing the Tories' freedom of speech and movement, and making loyalty to George III punishable by the confiscation of property, banishment, or even—in extreme cases—death.

If the measures were often cruel, the danger represented by the Tories was all too clear. They were numerous and they were everywhere, aiding and trading with the enemy, spying and informing on the rebels, organizing secretly or signing up openly to fight against the revolutionary movement. And there was an arrogance about a lot of them that the American Whig simply could not stomach. Old Judge Samuel Sewall, who had left Boston for London when he could no longer tolerate what was going on in his native country, warned an American friend: ". . . could you form a just idea of the immense wealth and power of the British nation, you would tremble at the foolish audacity of your pigmy states. Another summer will bring you all over to my opinion. I feel for the miseries hastening on my countrymen, but they must thank their own folly." That archrebel Sam Adams, who was about as good a hater as it was possible to be, believed that "much more is to be apprehended from the secret machinations of these rascally people than from the open violence of British and Hessian soldiers, whose success has been in a great measure owing to the aid they have received from them." And another fiery Bostonian, Joseph Hawley, stated unequivocally after independence was proclaimed that it should be accompanied with a "declaration of high treason." Can we exist for long, he asked, "without exterminating traitors?"

It was little wonder that this festering residue of hatred and fear erupted after the flight of Washington's army across New Jersey, causing a chameleonlike shifting of loyalties on the part of those who valued safety above everything and bitter civil war, often conducted by roving, undisciplined bands of rowdies, intent on revenge or plunder or both. "The defection of the people in the lower part of Jersey," Washington perceived, "has been mostly due to the want of an army to look the enemy in the face." Yet it was also, in all fairness, a heritage of old grievances bubbling over the sides of the cauldron now that the lid was off. By comparison with Massachusetts, New Jersey was relatively new to the business of opposing the crown and lacked the homogeneity of background and religion that characterized so much of New England. Bergen and Essex counties were peopled with Dutch farmers, Quaker settlements were scattered through the state, Perth Amboy was mainly Church of England (crown officers and rich merchants, mostly), New England Congregationalists had settled Elizabethtown and what was originally called New Ark. The hills north and west were frontier country where poor miners and smiths worked for a handful of wealthy ironmasters. To the south, in the Great Cedar Swamp, were smugglers and cattle rustlers. Up the Delaware River were colonies of industrious Swedes; while the lush agricultural land around Princeton resembled the plantations of Virginia, both in its gentleman farmers and the number of Negro slaves who toiled in their fields.

Until May 1776 the king's delegate responsible for administering this heterogeneous colony had been an offspring of Benjamin Franklin's considerable sexual appetite. William Franklin, the illegitimate son, was acknowledged and cherished by his father (though not by his father's wife), was raised a gentleman, took part in an expedition against Canada, served as clerk to the Pennsylvania Assembly and comptroller of the post office, went to England with his father and took a degree at Oxford, and in 1762 assumed his place as the new royal governor of New Jersey. The appointment was made at the urging of the Earl of Bute, who seems to have had the idea that the favor might make Benjamin Franklin more tractable. But the old man was a rebel at heart, as his son was not, and by 1774 the ideological gap between them was such that he called William a "thorough courtier" who saw "everything with government eyes." Later old Ben tried to persuade William to give up his office and join in the resistance to government, but his son refused and from that time forward conducted a running battle with the growing opposition in his colony. By the time he and his father broke off all relations, the New Jersey Assembly was trying to reduce William Franklin's salary and made it a condition of paying the rent on his house that he move either to Perth Amboy or to Burlington, where they could keep a watchful eye on him. On February 13, 1775, he prorogued the assembly, complaining irascibly that the members had seized every opportunity of "arraigning my conduct, or fomenting some dispute" and accusing them of being "actuated by unmanly private resentment, or by a conviction that their whole political consequence depends upon a contention with their Governor." The situation went from bad to worse, and by late May, after he dissolved the assembly again, the First Provincial Congress of New Jersey had met and royal government ceased for all practical purposes. A new constitution was adopted the following month and William Livingston, a member of the First Continental Congress, was elected governor.

By and large, most wealthy men in the state sided with William Franklin and the court party, but a few like Richard Stockton of Princeton, Elias Boudinot, and William Alexander—the man who insisted on calling himself Lord Stirling, after a claim to a lapsed Scottish earldom—backed the movement to send delegates to the Second Continental Congress. For a time Franklin stayed on in residence at Perth Amboy, maintaining the fiction of royal government although he had neither an assembly nor soldiers to do his bidding, and in January 1776 he suspended Lord Stirling from his council for abetting the organization of provincial militia. Stirling promptly put the governor under arrest, and although he was released on orders of the chief justice, the assembly voted him "an enemy of the liberties of this country," called him before them to testify, subjected him to a vicious personal attack, and hustled him off to Connecticut as a prisoner.

By midsummer, after representatives of New Jersey's Provincial Congress voted for independence, the lines were pretty well drawn throughout the state. While the newly formed Convention of the State of New Jersey organized militia companies, Tories grew increasingly active—wealthy men secretly raised battalions of loyalist troops who would be ready to fight when the time was ripe, and armed bands of "pine robbers" preyed on isolated militia detachments and kept a steady flow of information moving into British headquarters. So when the king's troops finally landed in New Jersey, making it safe for the Tories to emerge, they were prepared for action and itching for revenge.

General John Morin Scott of the New York militia, who was having the devil's own time persuading his men to stay in camp or re-enlist, wrote acidly that thirty local men had just signed up for service with the enemy. And from Jedediah Huntington, Heath got word that every man and woman in the vicinity of Ramapo was "constantly distressing me with their fears and apprehensions from the enemy and Tories. They are confident the latter have so much knowledge of the country as to guide a body of troops any where among the mountains." Parties of armed men roamed by night through every neighborhood, secret meetings were held to plot forays against the rebel militia and to harass known or suspected Whigs, and all the while timorous British sympathizers flocked to New York seeking sanctuary—so many of them, one Englishman commented, that had it not been for General Howe's foresight in laying in supplies "we might have had a famine."

By November 30 Admiral Richard Howe judged that the moment was right to resuscitate his peace offensive, and he issued a proclamation offering full pardon to all those who had taken up arms against the king provided they took an oath of allegiance to His Majesty within sixty days from that date. Had the admiral been aware of the rhubarb stirred up by his last proclamation, he might have thought twice before plunging ahead again now, but fortunately for his peace of mind news of the controversy it had created had not yet crossed the Atlantic. George III had opened another session of Parliament with a speech condemning the leaders of rebellion who had with "indignity and insult" rejected all efforts at conciliation and affirming the intention of government to prosecute the war vigorously and decisively. The smug confidence of the address was directly traceable to the knowledge of William Howe's initial victories in New York and the recovery of Canada, and although the king suggested that another campaign would be necessary, there was a strong hint that one summer more of fighting would put an end to the troubles in America.

But the session had no sooner begun than Colonel Isaac Barré threw a spanner into the proceedings by reading an American account of Colonel Patterson's unsuccessful effort to get the peace talks under way. Barré was incensed by the ministry's heavy-handed approach to such a delicate matter; if they had sent a trumpeter from camp to camp, prior to every action, it would have been "more effectual than a ridiculous attempt at a treaty, overlaid by absurd forms and idle punctilio." But what really stuck in his craw was the way the ministry had deliberately ignored the Parliament. They had not bothered to inform members about the meeting between

Patterson and Washington; Barré himself had to read about it in the pages of the London *Gazette*. And the blundering commissioners had had the effrontery to issue a proclamation that did not even mention the name or authority of Parliament. The Americans had been offered a pardon, in short, for declaring their allegiance to the *king*—not to the body which made the laws by which the country was governed. Lord John Cavendish declared that "Parliament were rendered cyphers" by this extraordinary declaration by the Howes. He even inquired of North and Germain if the thing was a forgery, which they admitted with some embarrassment that it was not. Charles James Fox, taking up the cry, accused the administration of being "perfectly uniform and consistent" in exhibiting contempt of Parliament; in America, he said, "all was peace, conciliation, and parental tenderness; in England, nothing but subjugation, unconditional submission, and a war of conquest." And he could not help wondering, since the ministry had gone to such pains to suppress the peace commissioners' proclamation, what other matters of a like nature were being similarly concealed? North and Germain offered a lame, awkward explanation of the affair, and it was a measure of the majority that stood solidly behind them that they got out unscathed so that both Houses could return to other business.

Some weeks passed before Lord Howe heard anything of this from home, and he went ahead with his new proclamation, hoping that it—in combination with the military successes of the past weeks—would have the desired effect on the rebels and their morale. By all odds the most attractive bait in the proclamation was the assurance that all Americans who swore loyalty to the crown would receive its protection from molestation by Hessians, Tories, and British regulars, but even so it was largely the weak-kneed and the faint of heart who took advantage of the offer. Whig sympathizers were dismayed by how many did and by the fact that the number included Richard Stockton, a signer of the Declaration of Independence, and Samuel Tucker, who had once presided over the New Jersey Provincial Congress. And not surprisingly, diehard Tories were outraged by the proclamation. Some 3,000 people profited by the pardon in New Jersey and all of them, the Tories reasoned, were to be let off free as birds just when it was finally possible to punish them for treason or resistance to authority. Lord George Germain was disturbed about the effect of the offer when he learned of it; he wanted everyone who did not accept a

I do acknowledge the UNITED STATES of AME-
RICA to be Free, Independent and Sovereign States, and
declare that the people thereof owe no allegiance or obedience to George the Third, King of Great-Britain; and I
renounce, refuse and abjure any allegiance or obedience to
him; and I do   that I will, to the ut-
moft of my power, fupport, maintain and defend the faid
United States againft the faid King George the Third, his
heirs and fucceffors, and his or their abettors, affiftants and
adherents, and will ferve the faid United States in the office of
                                which I now hold, with
fidelity, according to the beft of my fkill and underftanding.

George Washington's answer to the Howes' proclamation of November 30
offering a pardon to those taking an oath of allegiance to His Majesty appears
above. How effective this may have been is difficult to say: it might be supposed
that it worked where the rebel army was clearly in control of the local situation
and people were afraid *not* to sign it; and that it did not in those areas where the
British presence was felt.   *(The Historical Society of Pennsylvania)*

pardon within sixty days to be punished as an example to others, and before long he requested that General Howe send him a list of those who
had submitted. He did not expect the leaders of the rebellion to capitulate
easily, but he appears to have been hopeful that the pardons would eat
away at their popular support as individuals came over to the British side
in substantial numbers.

That same possibility troubled Washington, who retaliated by issuing a
proclamation of his own ("one of the dying Groans of Rebellion," Ambrose Serle called it), demanding that anyone who had received the enemy's pardon either surrender it at American headquarters and swear allegiance to the American cause or else go over to the British at once. It may
not have occurred to him at the time, but the second alternative proved to
be the strongest possible antidote for loyalty to the crown. For many a
man who took the king's pardon and went with high hopes into New
York to wait out what promised to be a short war, the experience was
shattering. They found themselves in a city dominated by British officials
who looked contemptuously on American refugees as second-class citi-

zens and treated them accordingly. They were hard put to find food, clothing, or work, the dream of returning to their New Jersey homes ebbed away as the war dragged on, and they came to curse the decision that had brought them to such a pass.

But in early December there was no denying the success of the government's appealing offer. Governor William Livingston did his halting best to reassure fellow Whigs by saying that the oaths of allegiance would have a salutary effect: they made it possible, he claimed, to distinguish friends from enemies and tell "the persevering patriot from the temporizing politician." But that was whistling in the dark. The effectiveness of the proclamation was one more indication that America's cause no longer had enough appeal to make a majority of men risk their lives, their fortunes, or their sacred honor for it.

2. The Times That Try Men's Souls

Half a century after the American Revolution, long after George Washington had died, the Prussian military theorist Karl von Clausewitz wrote a book, *Vom Kriege*, in which he presented his ideas concerning the principles that govern warfare. The basis of all war, he stated, is combat, and a battle avoided is one that a general knows he will lose. Since "superiority in numbers becomes every day more decisive" as an engagement draws near, the essence of strategy is to make use of time and space in such a way that a general can go into combat with all available forces concentrated against the enemy. In eighteenth-century warfare, Clausewitz realized, the two most important goals were the enemy's principal field army —which embodied the will and the means of resistance, and his capital city—the political center of gravity.

Four years before Clausewitz was born, George Washington was acquiring a knowledge of those same principles in the hardest possible way. Time and space were working against him, so was the British superiority in numbers, and he simply had to avoid coming to grips with the enemy until he could pull together every soldier at his disposal; unless he did so, and quickly, the British were in a fair way of gobbling up both his army *and* the capital city. When Cornwallis came down off the Palisades from Fort Lee, he would find the flat, swampy plains of New Jersey—criss-crossed by rivers and sluggish streams—stretching off to the west almost as far as the eye could see before the land began to rise again. One hundred miles to the southwest lay Philadelphia, and between the British and the capital were four sizable rivers—the Hackensack, Passaic, Raritan, and Delaware—each of which had to be crossed by bridge or boat. Other than those obstacles, only the ghost of an army stood in the invaders' path —that, and the fog, the chilling rain, and roads soggy with water and mud. Washington had to get a head start on Cornwallis; the American general had been caught between two rivers before, on Manhattan Island and again at Fort Lee, and he had no intention of being trapped now on a narrow peninsula. On the route to Philadelphia there were no natural strongholds—the country was "almost a dead flat," he saw—and all the picks and shovels the army possessed had been lost at the two Hudson River forts. With a heavy heart, Washington left the "very fine country" around Hackensack to the enemy and on the morning of November 21 marched to Aquackanock Bridge, crossed the Passaic, and headed due south toward Newark. His army of "half starved, half clothed, half armed, discontented, ungovernable, undisciplined wretches," as Judge Thomas Jones described it, was in full flight across New Jersey.

Meanwhile, the coming of Lee's troops was a matter of life and death. Those 7,000 soldiers included the most experienced and best disciplined men in the Continental Army, and it was imperative that they move quickly from Westchester into New Jersey to join Washington. On the twentieth, the moment he learned that Cornwallis was marching on Fort Lee, the commander in chief had had Grayson alert Lee to his situation, suggesting that he cross over to the west bank of the Hudson at once. Later that day an express rider from Heath encountered Joseph Reed, who told the man to wait while he wrote out an urgent dispatch to Lee. Reed had no pen, ink, or paper, but the messenger pulled a piece of wrapping paper from his pocket and handed it to the adjutant general with a

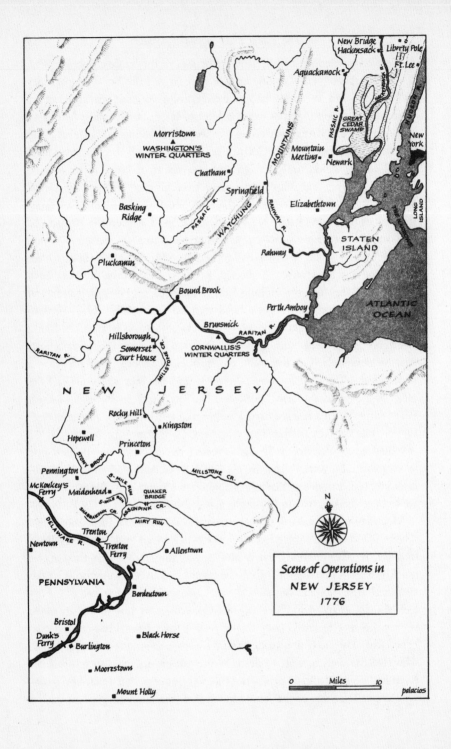

Scene of Operations in
NEW JERSEY
1776

pencil. In agitation, Reed began scribbling, "Dear General, we are flying before the British. I pray . . ."—and there the borrowed pencil had broken. It was nearly dark when the rider returned to Heath's Peekskill headquarters with this scrap of paper and a verbal message from Reed; the man had been galloping across the countryside all day, he was dead tired, and he requested that someone else carry the word on to Lee. No, Heath told him, the message might be garbled if he didn't deliver it personally, and in any case General Lee might have some questions to ask him. So the poor fellow mounted his horse again and rode off through the night and crossed the Hudson to find Lee. Some hours later he was back with a dispatch that Heath found highly perplexing.

"I have just received a recommendation—not a positive order—from the General," Lee wrote, "to move the corps under my command to the other side the river." But Lee saw no possibility of crossing near Dobbs Ferry, King's Ferry was too roundabout a route, so Heath would have to send 2,000 men from *his* command to join the army under Washington. Now Heath was no man to extemporize; he believed in operating by the book, and nothing in his orders from headquarters gave him any authority to go along with Lee's unexpected directive. So he sent off a query to the commander in chief: should he or should he not detach the troops as Lee requested? (It was well for Heath that he did, for Washington was determined not to weaken the puny little force guarding the Highlands and was astonished by Lee's apparent blindness to the possible consequences of doing so.) Under normal circumstances this misunderstanding might have been passed off as one of those inevitable breakdowns in communication between widely separated commands, but as events were to prove, the circumstances were far from normal. For what neither Heath nor Washington could know was that Charles Lee had no intention whatever of going to Washington's aid just now.

By any lights the most controversial general in the Continental Army and in many respects the most intriguing character was Charles Lee, whose personality and career were a strange, complex bundle of paradoxes. There was something of Jekyll and Hyde in Lee: he was a man who saw things black or white; no shades of gray intruded on his turbulent, agile mind. He either loved or hated, and as a result enjoyed warm, lasting friendships or made bitter, enduring enemies; few people who got to know him found it possible to be neutral on the subject of Lee (the famous beauty Lady Sarah Lennox, who married Lee's cousin Charles Bunbury after her romance with George III had been squelched by the queen mother, said that Lee, given the excuse, could be every bit as tyrannical as the king). Vain and ambitious, he was honest enough to admit that he was both; melancholy and cynical, he could be gay, witty, gregarious, and optimistic in the bleakest circumstances. He loved money and what it bought him, yet he was often exceedingly careless of it; and while he made a habit of personal cleanliness, his clothes were habitually unkempt, his appearance unbelievably slovenly. Lee possessed real intellect and had a true gift of phrase; but he was also profane, a heavy drinker, a womanizer, and a man who delighted in dirty stories. He was born a few months before George Washington, in the old fortress town of Chester, England, to a family that had been gentry there since the thirteenth century. Although he was the youngest of seven children, only he and his sister Sidney survived childhood, and Charles himself never really enjoyed robust health. Tall, angular, bony, as thin as a scarecrow, he was a permanent ugly duckling, with tiny hands and feet, a lean, dark, pinched face, and a nose so long he was called "Naso" by one of his friends. A true child of the eighteenth-century Enlightenment, he had a thorough knowledge of history and the classics, was fluent in French and Italian, read Greek and Latin, and even learned to speak an Indian dialect on his first tour of duty in America with the British army. He carried good books with him wherever he went and his library included the works of his favorite, Shakespeare, and the writings of Montaigne, Homer, Vergil, Milton, Xenophon, Seneca, Montesquieu, Thucydides, Horace, and Rousseau, whom he called his "divine and incomparable master."

At the age of fourteen he received a commission as ensign in his father's regiment and at nineteen purchased a lieutenancy in the 44th, where he came to know and admire Thomas Gage, with whom he served in the ill-starred Braddock expedition. During the French and Indian War he struck up a friendship with the famous superintendent of Indian affairs Sir William Johnson, lived among the Mohawks, married a daughter of White Thunder, a Seneca chief, and acquired the name Ounewaterika, which meant "boiling water, or one whose spirits are never asleep." (Ever after, for good reason, he was known to English friends as "Boiling Water.") Wounded in the 1758 attack on Fort Ticonderoga, he openly criticized the commanding officer, General James Abercromby, as a "damn'd beastly poltroon" and "our booby in chief," and later his violent temper got him into a scrape with the law in Philadelphia. Back in England after the war, he unsuccessfully sought an important post, became a member of a notorious group of rakes, and was active in literary, theatrical, and political circles. Lee was basically a liberal, though no republican, and he began writing letters and pamphlets opposing the increasing authority of George III. He served under John Burgoyne in Portugal, where he won a brilliant minor victory and became a colonel in the Portuguese army, and in 1763, after being put on half pay at home, he sailed to the Continent to become aide-de-camp to King Stanislaus of Poland.

Traveling back and forth between Europe and England, he made more enemies in high places with each visit home on account of his political views, and was commissioned a major general in the Polish army. He fought with the Russians against the Turks and had a duel with another officer in Italy (the affair began with swords and was concluded with pistols after Lee lost two fingers; he shot the other man dead and fled Italy for his life). By then he was suffering from gout, rheumatism, increasing moodiness, and irritability. Returning to England, he repeatedly attacked the king and his ministers, calling George III a "despicable, stupid, not innoxious dolt," and was rumored to be the author of the famous *Junius* letters. Finally, he had had enough of the Old World and sailed from London to America, where he arrived in October of 1773.

In New York he quickly made a friend of James Rivington, the printer of the New York *Gazetteer*, who later became an outspoken Tory and Lee's foe; he went to Philadelphia where he met all the important members of Congress; visited Jefferson in Virginia; met Ezra Stiles, Samuel Adams, Joseph Warren, and John Hancock, who lionized him in Boston. Traveling about the country, he spread the word that Britain had no generals who amounted to anything and a regular army totally unequipped to fight under conditions existing here; coming from him, it was a persuasive argument to Americans who had grave doubts about the consequences of war with England. By 1774 British officials in America were concerned by the trouble Lee was stirring up, and that year Rivington began attacking him in print as factious, evil, superficial, and a disappointed placeseeker. Toward the end of 1774 Lee spent five days at Mount Vernon as Washington's guest, and by the time of Lexington and Concord he was so well known in the colonies that he became, with Washington, Hancock, and Artemas Ward, a leading contender for the top post in the American army. He was regarded by some Americans as "the greatest general in the world," and the congressmen he had assiduously cultivated assumed that he certainly knew more about warfare than any American.

In the final analysis Congress could not choose Lee to command the army; they wanted a man from the most important colony, Virginia, and they had to have a native-born American, so Washington received the appointment. Lee was named major general, ranking behind the commander in chief and Artemas Ward of Massachusetts, and immediately went before a committee of Congress to inform them that he had a fortune of £11,000 and wanted assurance that he would be indemnified for its loss should the British confiscate it. The request didn't sit well with some delegates, yet it was true, as Lee said, that he stood to lose a good deal more than other American officers since his decision to fight in the rebel army would probably cost him all he owned in England whether the Americans won or lost, and, in addition, he was giving up a lieutenant colonelcy in the British army which was potentially worth £4,000 a year. On June 22, 1775, Charles Lee wrote Lord Barrington, severing his connection with the British army, renouncing his half pay, and saying that while he would fight for England against her hereditary enemies, he was now "obliged in conscience, as a citizen, *Englishman*, and soldier of a free state" to oppose the king. But even before his letter arrived, his name was stricken from the half-pay list.

With the army outside Boston, Lee set up headquarters in a farmhouse he named Hobgoblin Hall. By then he had grown more slovenly in his habits, more eccentric in manner, and had acquired a curious passion for dogs (which he said he fancied over humans) and always traveled with a pack swarming at his heels. Abigail Adams met him and remarked that he looked like "a careless, hardy veteran . . . The elegance of his pen far exceeds that of his person." (Lee somewhat nonplussed the lady by ordering his favorite dog, Spada, to climb onto a chair and offer her its paw.) Jeremy Belknap found him "a perfect original, a good scholar and soldier, and an odd genius; full of fire and passion, and but little good manners; a great sloven, wretchedly profane, and a great admirer of dogs—of which he had two at dinner with him, one of them a native of Pomerania, which I should have taken for a bear had I seen him in the woods." As early as January 3, 1776, Lee was advocating independence: remarking that the king's speech of the previous October "absolutely destroys all hope of re-union," he asked Robert Morris, "Why are we to eternity whining about a connexion with these depraved people?" He was sent to New York to supervise the building of defenses; he was expected to lead the invasion of Canada (an expedition that was finally put under the command of Rich-ard Montgomery and Benedict Arnold); then he was appointed to head up the Southern Department. He was beginning to be looked on as the indispensable man; as John Adams wrote him, "We want you at N. York—We want you at Cambridge—We want you in Virginia." And as George Washington confided to his brother Jack, "He is the first officer in military knowledge and experience we have in the whole army."

The perceptive Washington also observed that "he is zealously attach'd to the cause, honest and well meaning, but rather fickle and violent I fear in his temper." At the defense of Charleston, William Moultrie sensed that dark temper, saying that Lee was "hasty and rough," but admitting that he "taught us to think lightly of the enemy, and gave a spur to all our actions." Lee, of course, reveled in all of this: after independence was de-clared he wrote enthusiastically to Patrick Henry, "I us'd to regret not being thrown into the world in the glorious third or fourth century of the Romans; but now I am thoroughly reconcil'd to my lot."

Given that restless, insatiable ambition and an immense vanity, Charles Lee needed few spurs like the one he had received from Joseph Reed to begin thinking that George Washington's hour as commander in chief was nearly up after the unbroken chain of disasters between Long Island and Fort Lee. And there were no doubts in Lee's mind as to the man who should and would replace him. Rumors were already running through camp that Lee would soon supersede Washington: Lee was on close or in-timate terms with the important members of Congress, he was well aware of his popularity and reputation with the army, he had more accumulated military experience than the other Continental officers put together, and, thanks to his participation in the victory at Charleston, he was widely ac-knowledged as a winner. (When he passed through Philadelphia on his way back from the South, covered with the borrowed glory of William Moultrie's triumph, Congress passed a special vote of thanks to him for the successful defense of Charleston.) Each new defeat suffered by the army brought Lee closer to the conviction that Washington simply was not up to the task of leadership and that country and cause would be better served with Charles Lee in active command, with Washington perhaps in an administrative role as chief of staff. When word reached him of the catastrophe at the New Jersey fort which had been named for him, Lee almost certainly thought that Washington was through, an attitude bolstered by Joseph Reed's fawning letter in which he expressed the hope that Lee would soon be "removed from a place where I think there will be little call for your judgment and experience, to the place where they are likely to be so necessary." Reed was not alone in this opinion, he assured Lee; "every gentleman of [Washington's] family, the officers and soldiers, generally, have a confidence in you. The enemy constantly inquire where you are, and seem to be less confident when you are present."

So when Lee received Washington's plea to hasten to New Jersey, he replied that too much was at stake in Westchester for him to move; he had a chance to strike a killing blow at the famous Indian fighter Major Robert Rogers and his Tories and considered it unwise to leave the approaches to New England unprotected. On top of that, he complained, his army was desperately short of blankets and shoes. Then he began an ugly quarrel with William Heath, for whom he seems to have had little use. After Heath received Lee's orders to detach 2,000 men for duty with Washington and requested clarification from the commander in chief, he replied to Lee that his men were under orders to stay where they were. Infuriated, Lee hurled off an insulting response, telling Heath, "I perceive that you have formed an opinion to yourself, that should General Washington remove to the Straits of Magellan, the instructions he left with you upon a particular occasion have to all intents and purposes invested you with a command separate from, and independent of, any superiors." If Heath was under the impression that because he and Lee were both major generals they were equal in rank and importance, he had better disabuse himself of that notion promptly. It was not only "prejudicial to yourself, but to the publick." Lee had ordered Heath to send those troops, and by God, Heath would do it or Lee would know why not: "I will and must be obeyed."

Meanwhile, Lee was hatching some curious plans of his own. To James Bowdoin, president of the Massachusetts Council, he addressed a letter noting that Forts Washington and Lee had been lost because no one had listened to his advice and observing that he could now expect little help from Washington, who was somewhere in New Jersey. With emphasis on the first person singular, he said, "I shall look for assistance" to Connecticut and Massachusetts. Describing the urgent need for troops and supplies, he asked Bowdoin to do his utmost to send them at once—not to Washington, but to Lee. The next day, November 22, he went further. Condemning the indecision which "bids fair for tumbling down the goodly fabrick of American freedom," he castigated Congress for its fumbling. He had concluded, he told Bowdoin, that it was no longer necessary in these critical days to wait around for civilians to make up their minds; it was up to energetic, purposeful military men to save the country "in spite of the ordinances of the Legislature. There are times when we must commit treason against the laws of the State for the salvation of the State." Closing on a note of high self-confidence, he assured Bowdoin that if more troops were sent to him, nothing more was to be feared from the enemy; he was determined, with some help from God, to "unnest 'em even in the dead of winter," and if Massachusetts and Connecticut sent reinforcements promptly, "I will answer for their success."

Lee could be glib, he could be acid, and his letters were full of emotion-charged statements and opinions, concealing nothing. It was virtually inevitable that Washington would hear at second or third hand what his chief lieutenant thought about his conduct of affairs, but as it happened, he learned it directly from the horse's mouth, and on two separate occasions.

After writing his obsequious letter to Lee, Joseph Reed visited Governor Livingston to seek help in gathering militia from New Jersey, and during the adjutant general's absence from headquarters a letter addressed to him came in from Lee. Assuming it was business, Washington opened it and read with dismay that Lee was ignoring the request that he cross the Hudson and had, instead, ordered Heath to detach 2,000 troops for Washington's use. Several days later, with Reed still absent in Burlington and Washington desperate for news from Lee, the general opened another communication to his aide. "My dear Reed," it began, "I received your most obliging, flattering letter; lament with you that fatal indecision of mind which in war is a much greater disqualification than stupidity, or even want of personal courage; accident may put a decisive blunderer in the right, but eternal defeat and miscarriage must attend the man of the best parts if cursed with indecision." Repeating his reasons for not following Washington's recommendations, which were put "in so pressing a manner as almost to amount to an order," Lee then summarized his immediate plans to operate independently in Westchester, spoke of the possibility of French intervention, and finished by saying that as soon as he had despatched Rogers and his Tories he would "fly to you; for to confess a truth, I really think our Chief will do better with me than without me."

So there it was, out on the table for the commanding general to see and to ponder—the unvarnished evidence of what his adjutant general and his principal lieutenant thought of him, compounded by the equally shattering news that Lee planned to act on his own hook, crossing over to Jersey only when the spirit moved him. Washington was less surprised by the blunt remarks of a man whose fickleness he had already come to mistrust than he was stunned by the revelation that Reed, the member of his official family on whose friendship he most relied, had turned against him. For Lee's letter, he realized, was "an echo" of one that Reed had sent.

It was characteristic of the gentleman from Virginia that he wrote at once to his aide, politely explaining that Lee's letter had inadvertently come to his eye and apologizing for opening what had proved to be a personal communication, "which neither inclination or intention would have prompted me to." Thanking Reed rather stiffly for his "trouble and fatigue" in going to Burlington, he sent his respects to Mrs. Reed. That was all, and unless Reed wished to discuss the matter further, Washington intended to say no more. He already knew, or had guessed, that Reed was planning to resign as adjutant general, but now he could only wonder if the reason was the press of personal business or disaffection. When Reed received Washington's curt note, he wrote to John Hancock resigning as adjutant general, but four days later—probably at the request of the commander in chief, who had no possible way of replacing him just then—he retracted the resignation and returned to camp. It was undoubtedly a moment of terrible embarrassment for Reed, who fully expected that the unfortunate event would be discussed at length to clear the air. But Washington said nothing: the ugly subject was shoved under the rug and out of sight as if nothing had occurred. Reed never forgave him for this, and it was several years before Washington revealed his feelings, when he told Reed, "I was hurt not because I thought my judgment wronged by the expressions contained in [the letter], but because the same sentiments were not communicated immediately to myself." But the damage was done and never quite repaired, and the easy-going, intimate relationship the two had enjoyed was gone for good.

Quite apart from the breach of loyalty by Reed and Lee, they were accurate in their appraisal of Washington, whose conduct had been indecisive from the time General Howe left White Plains until Fort Lee collapsed. But it is difficult not to sympathize with the man: he was mentally and physically exhausted from the long, disastrous summer, and there had not been a day's respite from acute problems since the day he took command of the army in June of 1775. By now he surely lacked confidence in his own or his army's capacity to accomplish an almost superhuman mission, and he was not unaware of the high regard in which Lee was held nor of his own inadequacies. He was indeed hesitant these days, and he had been grievously wrong in allowing Greene's overconfidence to sway his own intuition and judgment against maintaining the Hudson forts—an error that had led the army close to utter ruin. Polite to a fault, he was beginning to appreciate the perils of letting that habit affect important military decisions, for in failing to give Lee positive orders that were unmistakably clear he was at least partially to blame for his present dilemma. Concerned always with his reputation and what others thought of him, he could see that his star was now in eclipse as a result of that ingrained disposition to be gentlemanly. Yet for all the self-doubt Washington felt, for all the anguish Reed's defection caused him, he yielded to neither of them.

It was unfortunate that these troublesome moments of self-doubt had to come when they did, while the fortunes of the army were at absolute rock bottom; yet in a curious way it was probably fortuitous that they coincided, for Washington was given no time to dwell on his own misfortunes. There may have been a moment when all these problems passed in review before his mind, tempting him to quit or to find some relatively painless way out, but the plight of his army and pressure from the enemy would not permit it, and from some deep inner source he found the determination and the will to go on, seeking the miracle that would save the cause before it was too late. Tom Paine had a chance to observe Washington often during this time, and he remarked, "There is a natural firmness in some minds which cannot be unlocked by trifles, but which, when unlocked, discovers a cabinet of fortitude; and I reckon it among those kind of publick blessings which we do not immediately see, that God hath blest him with uninterrupted health, and given him a mind that can even flourish upon care."

Washington had begun to get his back up. From the Passaic River on

November 21 he informed Lee more explicitly about his situation: ". . . the public interest requires your coming over to this side," he told him bluntly, and "I would have you move over by the easiest and best passage." Nor was Washington the only one concerned about the public interest; that, or something like it, was uppermost in the minds of members of the Pennsylvania Council of Safety, who published an almost frantic broadside the next day. Addressed to the citizens of Philadelphia, it advised them that "our enemies are advancing upon us, and . . . the most vigorous measures alone can save this city from falling into their hands . . . There is not time for delay; and by your conduct the Continent will be influenced. We therefore entreat you, by the most sacred of all bonds —the love of virtue, of liberty, and of your country—to forget every distinction, and unite as one man in this time of extreme danger. Let us defend ourselves like men determined to be free." A mass meeting, to be called by the ringing of bells, was scheduled for the next day; Congress and the city fathers heard one rumor after another about the British plans to march on Philadelphia; a committee was named to visit Washington and learn his plans; another was to find means of reinforcing him and obstructing the enemy's advance.

By the time Washington reached the Passaic, British scouts were not far behind; in a letter to Germain, Howe reported that a detachment of the 16th Dragoons, under Lieutenant Colonel William Harcourt, had scoured the countryside as far as the river and found it abandoned by the rebels. But for some reason neither Howe nor Cornwallis were in a hurry to follow. Washington established headquarters in Newark on the twenty-third, where Cornwallis' continued inactivity permitted him to stay for a few days, and from there he reported to an anxious Congress on the state of the army. Stirling was in Newark with 1,000 men, but they were "broken down and fatigued—some without shoes, some had no shirts," and for several days past most of them had been drunk and brawling among themselves. Including Stirling's troops, Washington calculated that he had 5,410 men—but more than 2,000 of them would leave in a week when their enlistments were up, and there were rumors that other units, whose terms expired on January 1, planned to go over the hill before then. The blackest disappointment of all was the complete failure of the New Jersey militia to come in despite all the appeals made to them and despite the immediate threat to their own state. At no point during the retreat had as many as one hundred men joined up in a single body; from the whole of Newark came only twenty privates and not one officer. As for the future Continental Army, Colonel Huntington told Heath, "I expect to be here the 1st of January without any men, unless something more is done to encourage the new inlistment."

Surprisingly, a shred of optimism still persisted here and there, perhaps because things couldn't possibly get worse. In reply to a letter from Joseph Trumbull, Samuel Webb wrote, "You ask me a true account of our situation: 'tis next to impossible to give it to you; I can only say that no lads ever shew greater activity in retreating than we have since we left you. Our soldiers are the best fellows in the world at this business . . . Our whole body did not amount to 2000 at the time the enemy landed in the Jerseys, of consequence we had it not in our power to make a stand till we arrived at [Newark], where we have collected our force and are not only ready, but willing to meet the lads in blue and red as soon as they think proper . . . If they come on soon we shall, I trust, give a good account to our country. This must be before the 1st of December, as most of the troops on this side are then their own masters." But few officers were even as sanguine as Webb about what lay ahead.

Washington's irritation with Lee was beginning to show; the letters he wrote were scrupulously polite, but there was an edge to what he said now. From Newark he reported crossly that a negligent post rider had permitted all mail from the east to fall into enemy hands at Hackensack on Friday, November 22, and he warned Lee that any important information he had included in that packet would now be known to the British. As for Heath releasing any men, that was out of the question; the posts and passes through the Highlands were far too important to leave unmanned. It was Lee's division he wanted, and he asked for "frequent expresses" concerning the line of march, "that I may know how to direct it." For now, at last, the enemy was stirring.

The 2nd and 4th Brigades of redcoats and a battalion of the 71st had crossed the Hudson to join Cornwallis, who had taken advantage of two soft, warm days to cross the Hackensack at New Bridge; now he was marching south with his army in four long columns. November 26 brought more heavy rain and a letter from Lee, expressing doubt that he would bring along "any considerable number of men, not so much from a want of zeal in the men as from their wretched condition with respect to shoes, stockings &c, which the present bad weather renders more intolerable." And, infuriatingly, Lee was still talking about the opportunity to strike the enemy near White Plains! That afternoon Washington's aide Robert Harrison sent a dispatch to General Philip Schuyler, requesting him to send all the Pennsylvania troops in the Northern Department to Brunswick as soon as possible, advising them to march by a "back and secure route" to avoid the enemy. Schuyler complied promptly, ordering eight regiments to leave Albany on December 2 under the command of Horatio Gates. But Albany was a long way off, and it might be weeks before Washington saw those reinforcements. Meantime, he sent off still another note to Lee, a curt reminder that all of his previous requests had been so explicit that there was nothing more to add. As for the distress of Lee's troops, Washington replied shortly, "I feel much; but what can I do?" He was only too familiar with the pitiful condition of his own men, who were taking advantage of the temporary shelter and campfires that could be kept going day and night in Newark. The cold was as hard to bear as the discouragement; some men had only strips of rawhide on their feet, wrapped under the soles and bound to the ankles, while those who had shoes sometimes kept them on so long that the leather had to be cut from their feet. As one soldier recalled, "fighting happens seldom, but fatigue, hunger, cold & heat" were constant companions on the march, and through the sodden flatlands of New Jersey these men had plodded along roads rutted knee-deep by the artillery, continuously pelted by rain that soaked and chilled to the marrow, huddling together at night because the wood they found was too wet to make a decent fire. Almost to a man, they lacked tents or blankets, and many were without stockings, shirts, or trousers.

In the long history of the human race there are enough instances of triumph over adversity to suggest that a few perverse souls are always capable of doing their best after the chips are gone, when by all that is logical they should call it quits and give in to the inevitable. George Washington, who was frequently at his best when it appeared that things could not possibly get worse, was a good example of the type, and so was that remarkably impassioned man from England Tom Paine.* Paine had left Fort Lee

---

* Paine was also one of those men, of whom American history affords numerous examples, who fitted almost precisely the needs of a particular moment, only to be discarded or traduced in later years when the nation no longer had need of them. It was inevitable that a man of such strong personal be-

with Greene and had endured all the hardships of the retreat. "Both officers and men," he related afterward, "though greatly harassed and fatigued, frequently without rest, covering, or provision . . . bore it with a manly and a martial spirit. All their wishes were one, which was, that the country would turn out and help them to drive the enemy back." Having seen and borne it all himself, Paine sensed that there was in this extraordinary exhibition of valor and fortitude a nobility and a source of inspiration for other Americans, if only they could hear about it, and when the army arrived in Newark and paused to draw breath, Paine sat before the campfire at night, peering into the flames and thinking over what had just happened to all of them, and before long he was setting down on paper what he thought the American people should know.

"These are the times that try men's souls," he began. "The summer soldier and the sunshine patriot will, in this crisis, shrink from the service of his country; but he that stands it *now*, deserves the love and thanks of man and woman. Tyranny, like hell, is not easily conquered; yet we have this consolation with us, that the harder the conflict, the more glorious the

---

liefs would make enemies, especially among conservatives like Gouverneur Morris, who once complained to congressmen that Paine was "a mere adventurer *from England*, without fortune, without family or connexions, ignorant even of grammar." The end of the war found Paine short of funds, and he addressed a memorial to Congress, stating affectingly, "Trade I do not understand. Land I have none . . . I have exiled myself from one country without making a home of another; and I cannot help sometimes asking myself, what am I better off than a refugee." Ultimately, the state of Pennsylvania granted him some cash and New York gave him a farm in New Rochelle which had been confiscated from a loyalist, but by 1787 the restless Paine was on the move, carrying to England the model of an iron bridge he had designed, which he hoped to have built in the land of his birth.

No country welcomes the other's radical, and when he wrote *The Rights of Man*, an attack on critics of the French Revolution and an appeal to Englishmen to overthrow their monarchy, he was outlawed by the British government. Fleeing to Paris, he became a member of the Convention, voted against the death penalty for Louis XVI, and was thrown into jail, where he completed writing a treatise called *The Age of Reason*. Paine was a deist, not an atheist, but this work was unfairly condemned as an "atheist's bible" and regarded as a vicious attack on religion, and in 1796 his steadily diminishing reputation in America suffered further when he denounced George Washington in print. By the time he returned to the United States in 1802 most of his friends had turned against him, but he continued to play a contentious role in politics. Unlike many radicals, Paine remained one with advancing age, and he spent his last years in New Rochelle and New York City, slandered as a drunkard and an adulterer, ostracized from society, impoverished and despised when he died in 1809.

Not even death brought peace to this stateless, wandering soul. Denied a burial in consecrated soil, he was interred in a corner of his farm, where curiosity seekers desecrated his tombstone before William Cobbett, the English reformer, stole his remains and shipped them to England. But when Cobbett died, Paine's bones were still unburied, and eventually passed with Cobbett's effects into the hands of a furniture dealer and vanished.

triumph. What we obtain too cheap, we esteem too lightly; 'tis dearness only that gives every thing its value. Heaven knows how to put a proper price upon its goods; and it would be strange indeed, if so celestial an article as *Freedom* should not be highly rated."

Having seen his companions rise above the agony and fears that had dogged every step they took, he found it immensely reassuring. " 'Tis surprising to see how rapidly a panick will sometimes run through a country. All nations and ages have been subject to them. . . . Yet panicks, in some cases, have their uses. They produce as much good as hurt. Their duration is always short; the mind soon grows through them, and acquires a firmer habit than before."

Judging from the contents of what Paine decided to call "The American Crisis—Number One," it appears that he must have written the first, and perhaps other portions, of his eloquent message while he was still at Newark, adding to it a few days later an account of the events that had transpired from the fall of Fort Lee until the army left Newark. As soon as he was done, he rushed to Philadelphia and arranged to have the manuscript published in the *Pennsylvania Journal*, where it appeared on December 19, 1776. By that time the army and the country would need his inspiring message more than ever, for the sands of resistance were running out now and they grew thinner with every passing day.

3. The Campaign Having Closed

On the same day the proclamation of amnesty was issued, General William Howe dictated two long reports to his superior, Lord George Germain. A commanding officer who has just racked up an unbroken string of victories is entitled to blow his own horn, but Howe's summary of the army's activities since the twelfth of October was all modesty, mixed with warranted pride in his men and some handsome compliments for subordinates he had singled out for particular mention. In the second letter he turned his attention to the future. Within several weeks the troops would have to go into winter quarters, he told Germain, but he was confident that Cornwallis would by then be in possession of the whole of eastern New Jersey, which the British would occupy for the winter. The rebels would undoubtedly destroy as much forage and livestock as they could along the route of their retreat, but the country was fat and there would be plenty left to supply the army in New York. Meantime, he was sending Clinton and Percy to Rhode Island with 6,000 men; if the weather held, they should have little difficulty establishing themselves there. Unfortunately, the onset of winter had forced the northern army under Carleton to backtrack to Canada, but with the coming of spring they would march again toward Albany and with luck would reach it by September of 1777. All of which brought Howe to the main purpose of his letter—a plan for the next campaign, which he fully expected might "finish the war in one year, by an extensive and vigorous exertion of his Majesty's arms."

Quickly, he sketched out an ambitious, threefold program: Clinton, with up to 10,000 troops based in Rhode Island, would move against Boston and into Connecticut; another army of 10,000 would march from New York (leaving another 5,000 behind to defend the city) toward Albany, to effect a junction with an expeditionary force from Canada; and finally, 8,000 men in New Jersey would threaten Philadelphia, against which Howe intended to march in the autumn, provided everything else went smoothly enough so that he could spare the men for it. Meanwhile, he was not forgetting the South: Georgia and South Carolina should be the targets for the winter, he believed, and he estimated that not less than ten ships of the line and another 15,000 soldiers—possibly from Russia and the German states—would be required for the job. All in all, he reckoned, he would need a good many reinforcements to bring the total up to the 35,000 rank and file necessary for what he had in mind, and he urgently requested that Germain also send another batallion of artillery, 300 horses, and some additional Guards officers to him. Having got that off his chest, Howe could turn his mind to other matters.

A considerable part of the city now occupied by the British was a shambles. Shortly after midnight on September 20 a fire had broken out in the neighborhood of Whitehall, spreading rapidly from one shingled roof to another before a strong wind and eventually destroying 500 buildings, including the 180-foot spire of Trinity Church which crashed to the ground in a flaming pyre. Almost the entire area from the Battery to St.

Paul's Church, between Broadway and the Hudson River, and between Broadway and the East River as far as Broad Street, had been gutted, and in the burned-out ruins, shanties made of discarded lumber and sailcloth had risen, to become a slum occupied by prostitutes, runaway slaves, and riffraff. Nor was "Canvass Town" the only depressing aspect of New York these days. A number of dissenting churches had been converted into prisons and hospitals; looters from the army and the waterfront roamed the city; known rebel sympathizers had a big letter "R" chalked on their doors and walked the streets at their peril; and with the onset of winter, nearly every household was beginning to suffer from lack of fuel. British troops had plundered the King's College library of books, scientific apparatus, and pictures, which Judge Thomas Jones had seen "publicly hawked about the town for sale by private soldiers, their trulls, and doxeys." For officers and men alike, it seemed that the only diversions from this dreary scene were gambling, drinking, and whoring, and William Howe was engaged in all three activities. As a matter of fact, despite all that he had to contend with in New York, it appeared that this was going to be a very pleasant war for the general. In the field, everything was going his way, and rumor had reached him that he would be knighted by the king for his triumph on Long Island. The formal investiture had not yet taken place, but it was a happy prospect to contemplate, and Howe was occupied with plans for a series of gala balls and other social events that would break the monotony of the winter's inactivity.

By the time a man reached the rank of lieutenant general in the British army, he was accustomed to an impressive array of perquisites. The system under which the army functioned virtually insured that high ranking officers would be aristocrats and men of considerable wealth—the sons of peers, or relatives and friends of dukes and earls. There was, in fact, no other route to the top, since there were only two ways that commissions and promotions could be had. One was money and the other was influence, and since the aristocracy and the gentry had both, they were the men who got the plums. As a result, social connections frequently got in the way of the military chain of command and there were violent quarrels between officers, based on a spoils system which prevailed in England. Favor counted for a lot more than hard work or ability; a seat in Commons was the instrument for obtaining it, and criticism of a military commander was likely to send him or his patron into the arms of the Opposition. Often enough, the system resulted in a lack of discipline between officers and their men; as Charles Stuart wrote a friend, urging that generals worth their salt be sent to America, those that were here were "a pack of the most ordinary men . . . who give themselves trouble about the merest trifles, whilst things of consequence go unregarded." It was the constant maneuvering of political admirals and generals that prompted Lord North to say that he feared the English generals more than he did the enemy.

The whole command system desperately needed reforming; the king, as captain general, might or might not appoint a commander in chief of the army, and since George III took pride in exercising his military prerogative, there had been none since 1770. The king controlled the price of officers' commissions, and they did not go cheap. To become an ensign—the lowest rank in a regiment of foot—a man paid £400, at a time when it was possible to maintain a family and two servants on £40 a year. If he wanted to be in one of the elite companies, he had to pay £900 for his ensign's commission, and a cornetcy—which was the equivalent of an ensign in the cavalry—would set him back £1,600. There was a reason for all this, of course: the English had never forgotten nor forgiven Oliver Cromwell's military dictatorship, and it was thought that by keeping the purchase system in the hands of civilians the government would be assured of the loyalty and good behavior of officers. Promotion was available as vacancies occurred, either in a man's own regiment or another one, but all officers had to serve in grade for a period of time before they were entitled to advance to the next rank. Even so, this made it certain that advancement went only to the wealthy; a lieutenant colonel, for example, who commanded a regiment in the field, had to pay £3,500 for his rank in the infantry, £5,200 in the cavalry, and £6,700 in the foot guards—this last figure being nearly equivalent to the combined salaries of the first lords of the Admiralty and the Treasury. Without independent means an officer got nowhere, because it was impossible to save money on his army pay. The reverse side of the coin was that wealthy officers advanced fastest; Lord Cornwallis, who was well to do, was a lieutenant colonel at the age of twenty-three and a lieutenant general at thirty-eight. So it went without saying that a lieutenant general like Howe was not only accustomed to the best but lived in a style befitting his rank; he demanded, and received, the finest service, housing, food, and wine, he entertained frequently and well, and, to relieve the tedium of daily life, he maintained an attractive mistress, a "flashing blond" named Elizabeth Loring.

Howe's dark, roving eye had fastened approvingly on Mrs. Joshua Loring soon after his arrival in Boston, early in '75. By all accounts she was an extremely handsome woman, the wife of a grasping Tory who received a lucrative appointment from General Gage not long after Howe met Elizabeth. Loring later got the job of commissary of prisoners—a role that seems to have been admirably suited to his disposition; quick to see the prospect of financial reward in the general's attachment to his wife, he raised no objection to their arrangement so long as he got what he wanted. A man devoid of pride and a sense of honor, he had traveled with the army to Halifax and then to New York, seemingly oblivious to the sneers, innuendo, and gossip swirling around Howe and his paramour. As the acidulous Judge Thomas Jones described the sordid little triangle, "Joshua had a handsome wife. The General . . . was fond of her. Joshua made no objections. He fingered the cash, the General enjoyed Madam." Howe's ménage fascinated a good many people of the time, including Francis Hopkinson, who immortalized it in verse:

> Sir William, he, snug as a flea,
> Lay all this time a-snoring;
> Nor dreamed of harm, as he lay warm
> In bed with Mrs. ———

Suggestions were made at the time, and since, that Howe's dalliance with his mistress held him back from engaging the enemy. Certainly he took his pleasures where and when he found them; he was a heavy drinker, he and Mrs. Loring were habitués of the gaming table, and she was supposedly the best avenue for securing a favor from the general. Charles Lee, who was to see a good deal of Howe, said that he was "naturally good humoured, complaisant, but illiterate and indolent to the last degree, unless as an executive soldier, in which capacity he is all fire and activity, brave and cool as Julius Caesar . . . He shut his eyes, fought his battles, drank his bottle, had his little whore, advised with his counsellors, received his orders from North and Germain (one more absurd than the other)."

Howe was indeed indolent, spent too much time in pursuit of pleasure, and was also a victim of the curious double role the government had demanded of him; but his outlook on life was not markedly different from that of many other officers of the day. And Howe, after all, had not done badly in this campaign. He had nothing but victories to show for his efforts since arriving in New York, and although he could (and would) be faulted for failing to go for the jugular, to eradicate Washington's army when he had the opportunity to do so, he had—by the lights of eighteenth-century warfare—succeeded rather well. Every time he had met the enemy they had been driven from the field or forced to retreat, and while the force confronting him was diminishing with every engagement and with each passing day, his army was still intact, in possession of the principal city in the locale, and with its morale high. That this should have come to pass was, however, only partially attributable to Howe's generalship. He had been fortunate in coming up against an inexperienced, untrained, ill-prepared, badly equipped foe, but he was singularly lucky in having as the tactical instrument which executed his orders an army that was at least the equal, if not the superior, of any in the world.

Long after the event, the vision of the British redcoats that passes through the mind's eye is one of line after line of seasoned veterans, marching in precise parade order, bayonets glinting in the sun, halting on command to deliver a volley at an enemy that was already half-panicked by the awesome display of massed power confronting them. There is enough accuracy in the picture to justify its retention, but the wonder of it all is that the system which created it managed to fashion such a superb fighting machine, given the material it had to work with and the training methods it employed. For if the officers in the army were nearly all from the top stratum of society, the men in the ranks came from the slime at the bottom of the barrel—"the scum of the earth," Wellington was to call them three decades later. With obvious exceptions, most were the very dregs of society—outcasts, thieves, poachers, and ne'er-do-wells who had been recruited while drunk in some grog shop by a non-com who slipped them the "king's shilling" as a bounty for enlisting. Others were recruits from jails and slums, for this was a time when men and boys who would be dismissed nowadays with a fine ran the risk of the hangman for minor offenses. Before the American war, the age limits were eighteen and thirty and the only important physical requirement was that a man must be 5 feet 6½ inches tall. But the demands of the moment had changed all that; now the height requirement was reduced to 5 feet 3 inches and the ages of men in the ranks ranged from sixteen to fifty.

The method of inculcating discipline can only be described as brutality. Drill sergeants literally beat obedience into the men, teaching them to load and fire, form ranks, move into line or column, and march on command like automatons, without thinking, and the punishment for failure to do so was the lash on the bare back—usually twenty-five or thirty strokes laid on by a man who would be similarly punished if he didn't put every ounce of strength into the task. In practice, no army-wide standard of drill prevailed and would not until 1792; each regiment had its own system of maneuver, prescribed by individual commanders. Uniforms also varied according to regiment; the army clothing board prescribed the heavy wool scarlet coat, white breeches, and gaiters reaching above the knee, but different units wore different colored facings on their lapels as a mark of distinction, and wealthier officers liked to trick out their men in more elaborate dress. (Cornwallis, for instance, once spent over £1,000 to supply his regiment with special coats, breeches, drums, fifes, and the like.) If ever a man went into action under difficult circumstances, though, it was the eighteenth-century British foot soldier. The brilliant scarlet coats made ideal targets, knee breeches were so tight they often cut off the circulation in the legs, the wide white belt from which the bayonet hung was worn as tight as possible, a stiff collar and high leather stock restricted movement of the head, and none of the cumbersome hats—some of them heavy bearskins—had a visor or brim to shield the face and eyes. On one side the foot soldier carried an ammunition pouch, on the other his cartridge box, and into the haversack on his back went extra clothing, provisions, a canteen, and various camp tools. When fully dressed and equipped, the British private bore a weight computed at approximately 125 pounds, and with this burden added to his constricting uniform, he was expected to march into battle and fight efficiently.

The weapon on his shoulder was the smoothbore Brown Bess musket, that highly unreliable weapon also carried by many Americans. Aside from the fact that the British firelocks were of uniform construction, they had all the disadvantages of the muskets carried by the rebels, which meant that they were clumsy, slow to load, temperamental, and ineffective at a range of over eighty or a hundred yards. But the volley firing employed by the British with varying success was only a prelude to their favorite tactic, for the Brown Bess was also fitted with a bayonet, as a result of which the redcoat became a spear-carrier like the legionnaire of ancient

Rome. A bayonet charge was guaranteed to have a fearsome effect on an enemy, no matter how experienced he might be; the ranks advanced as one man, gleaming steel bobbing before them, the beautifully disciplined troops coming on steadily even in the face of enemy musket fire, and by the time they reached their objective they had murder in their eyes and lashed out savagely, lunging and slashing with their terrible weapon, cursing and yelling "Hurrah," pressing the assault home with the awful fury of which enraged men are possessed. The British infantry was superb at this sort of thing, the artillery was extremely efficient, and the army's tactical skill may be judged from the fact that in eight years of war the British regulars (not the Hessians or loyalists) lost only a handful of battles to American troops.

It was small wonder that British officers swore by the product of their military system, but few of them ever bothered to ameliorate the conditions under which the poor men suffered. Not only was the training brutal and the horrors of war very real, but the facts of everyday life were abominable. The foot soldier was paid eightpence a day, from which numerous deductions were systematically taken. Funds appropriated for the men's pay by Parliament went first to the London agent of each regiment, from him to the regimental paymaster, and thence to the company captains who paid the troops. And each man took his slice as the melon passed by. Paymasters were not above speculating with these funds, noncoms often appropriated unsuspecting privates' pay on disciplinary grounds, and the army deducted part of the cost of food, uniforms, medicine, transportation, and contributions to the old soldiers' home from the privates' miserable pittance. Company captains found it advantageous to retain as many men on their muster rolls as possible and often swelled the totals with names of dead or non-existent men for whom the regiment (and the captain) continued to receive pay. For many a brave soul, death in battle was merciful compared to the suffering he would have to endure if he were wounded. There were never enough surgeons to go round, and the ones they had were crude, incompetent butchers without adequate supplies or knowledge. Many wounded were left to die on the battlefield, especially if the army had to move quickly, and the unfortunates who made it to the hospital lay there on the ground or on wooden benches, suffering horribly while awaiting their turn with the surgeon, who relied on the saw or some medieval remedy. Hospitals resembled grisly charnel-houses, filled with the hideous stench of festering wounds and the anguished cries of the dying, who were crowded together with men suffering from all forms of disease. (During the Seven Years' War only 1,512 men were killed in action, while the appalling total of 134,000 was lost to disease, mismanaged wounds, and desertion.)

On the march, the army was at the mercy of the ordnance department for its supply of blankets and tents, the quartermaster general for the transport of its baggage, and agents of all shades of honesty who furnished its wagons. Any or all of the army's supplies might turn up missing, for the system was inefficient, unreliable, and riddled with tricksters. Although three hundred wagons had been shipped from England in the spring of 1776, transport was critically short throughout the war. A few four-horse wagons were built in New York, but in general Howe had to rely on vehicles hired by the day or the month—an arrangement that was an endless source of corruption and delay. Commissaries hired their own wagons, and by the end of the war it was estimated that the quartermaster general's department had pocketed some £400,000 from contracts let for this purpose over a five-year period. In a large, unfriendly country, there was always the risk that wagon convoys would be ambushed or attacked, a factor that led Charles Stuart to comment in 1778 that it "absolutely prevented us this whole war from going fifteen miles from a navigable river." What it also meant was that Howe—tied to his supply line and short of land transport—could almost never follow the Americans quickly enough when they retired.

Trailing along behind the army and its impedimenta came baggage of another sort—a disorderly throng of female camp followers, many of them with children by their sides. This motley company of drabs tagged along in the wake of the troops and when they made camp washed the men's clothes, cooked for them, nursed them, and ministered to the needs of the flesh. It was a hard lot, helped not at all by the fact that the women were subject to military discipline. Howe's orderly book records the trial of one soldier named Thomas MacMahon and his wife for trafficking in stolen goods. Both were found guilty, and MacMahon was sentenced to receive 1,000 lashes, while his wife got "100 lashes on her bare back, at the Cart's tail, in Different portions and the most Conspicuous Parts of the Town."

Feeding and maintaining this British expeditionary force was a staggering proposition, by any lights. Every weapon, musket ball, and grain of powder, every boot and uniform button, had to be transported 3,000 miles across the Atlantic in slow, cranky transports. A battalion bound for foreign service was allowed to take sixty women and eighty tons of baggage, but often a general and his staff would appropriate an equivalent amount of space for their own use. For each year the war went on, a third of a ton of foodstuffs—salt beef and pork, butter, flour, and the like—was needed for each soldier, and oats had to be shipped across for the horses. (The government discovered early that it was impracticable to transport livestock, so the army had to depend for its meat supply on raids on rebel farms.)

There were endless problems in the home country: many contractors delivered late, spoiled provisions or faulty containers had to be rejected or repaired, there were delays in assembling individual ships and convoys, the weather blew supply ships hundreds of miles off course, and there was immense waste, corruption, and theft to be reckoned with. The whole thing created a strain of almost overwhelming proportions on the country's shipping facilities, since transports were mostly small vessels of 250 to 400 tons' burden, and three or four troopships were required to move a single battalion. An example of what the government had to contend with was the effort, in the late spring of 1776, to ship 950 horses to America: twenty-one transports were finally assembled and every precaution was taken to keep the animals healthy during the voyage, but by the time the ships arrived only 400 were still alive. The horrors of the trip took it out of the troops, too. Sergeant Roger Lamb never forgot the forty day agony of the crossing from Ireland to the Gulf of St. Lawrence; what little food they got was terrible, the water was slimy, and the soldiers' quarters were cramped, filthy, and almost without ventilation. In older ships the dread ship fever often raged, and continued exposure to salt water produced wholesale outbreaks of boils. As a non-com in one of Howe's brigades described it, "There was continued destruction in the foretop, the pox above-board, the plague betweendecks, hell in the forecastle, the devil at the helm." And the cost in men was scandalous. Returns of regiments sent from the British Isles to the West Indies between the fall of 1776 and early 1780 reveal that of 8,437 troops who embarked, only 7,506 landed —932 men died in passage, an average of 11 per cent lost on each voyage.

Faced with logistical problems of such dimensions, it was little wonder that the ministry and the commanders in the field viewed the conservation of troops as one of their primary objectives. So that Howe, even while proclaiming his objective as "the defeat of the rebel regular army," was realist enough to know that this must be achieved "under circumstances the least hazardous to the royal army; for even a victory, attended by a heavy loss of men on our part, would have given a fatal check to the progress of the war, and might have proved irreparable." This reckoning was behind the fact that all of Howe's movements in 1776 except the attack on Fort Washington had been flanking operations and not head-on assaults. Not for nothing had William Howe led the redcoats up the slopes of Breed's Hill, and the memory of the carnage there was still fresh.

Although Howe may not have suspected it at the time, a good many cards in the deck were stacked against him. There was that unceasing need to preserve his army at all costs. Someone estimated that it took from three to five years to train a man properly in the mysteries of precise order drill, and Howe was not about to fritter away the lives of men who could not be replaced. Nor was this sense of caution unique to Howe; it pervaded the entire officer corps. Frederick Mackenzie, writing in his diary about the battle of Long Island, highly approved of Howe's "cautious circumspect" tactics there. They were "not so brilliant and striking," Mackenzie admitted, but they were "productive of certain and real advantages, at the same time that very little is at stake." He judged that it would be "the height of imprudence in the Commander in chief" to risk his men in any "incautious or precipitate conduct."

Another factor that was working against Howe here in America was the country itself. Captain Sir James Murray commented that it was almost impossible to triumph over a land several thousand miles in extent, covered everywhere by forests, even if there had been no inhabitants; "but when we consider that there are no less than 3,000,000 exasperated to the last degree and inflamed to the highest pitch of enthusiasm," it was folly to think of victory. (That figure of three million aroused partisans would have amused the Congress, but in principle Murray was right). The sheer immensity and wildness, even of the eastern seaboard, was a fact of life even twenty years later, when a visitor remarked that the place was "one vast wood"—travel was so difficult that a detour of a hundred miles by sea and river was preferable to an overland journey of fifty miles. Even from a desk in London, Lord George Germain had a premonition of how the rebels would use the terrain to advantage. "The manner of opposing an enemy that avoids facing you in the open field is totally different from what young officers learn from the common discipline of the army," he had warned. As if reading his mind, George Washington had told Congress in September that his strategy would consist of avoiding a general action, so as never to be drawn into a situation where he would have to risk the cause in an unfavorable battle, implying that he would be content to harass the British at every opportunity, while doing his utmost to keep food and other supplies out of their reach. Howe's letters to Germain and his friends in London were full of references to the difficult terrain and the hardships of moving an army about. Although New York had become the center of British military activities in North America, the army's base remained the Atlantic Ocean and the navigable rivers leading upcountry from it. How fragile that lifeline could be had already been seen in the winter of 1775–76, when, out of forty transports sent from Great Britain, only eight arrived safely in Boston; the rest fell prey to American privateers or were swept south to the West Indies by the prevailing northwest winds and storms. By all that was logical, therefore, the army should have learned to extemporize, to live off the country and fend for itself, but somehow the British never acquired the knack of doing so, perhaps because of Howe's stubborn belief that the war should not be made too painful for the Americans, perhaps because the habit of a regular supply line was too ingrained and the army unable to adjust to a new set of circumstances.

Howe himself was no improviser. Schooled in European warfare— which was an affair of days and weeks, not hours or minutes—he was also a victim of a commonly accepted belief that if the British simply held onto what they occupied in America, the resistance would collapse. This was far from being a theoretical matter, for if the British failed to hang onto what they had won, it meant abandoning the loyalists to the vengeance of the rebels and admitting to everyone that the protection offered by the crown was a perilously frail reed. Howe admitted that "the enemy moves with so much more celerity than we possibly can," but he never fully grasped the notion of mobility, the idea of making his army a self-supporting outfit which traveled light and rapidly. Possibly it was just as well that the Americans never had anything to carry with them. Poverty made travel a good deal faster.

Although he was 3,000 miles from home and in a position to exercise real autonomy, Howe was not one to display the audacity and flexibility the situation might have permitted. Perhaps he could not bring himself to rise to the challenge of campaigning in territory where the discipline and bravery of British troops counted for less than an aptitude for marching and foraging. It was rough, inhospitable country, where the winters were long and harsh, and these factors, rather than provoking Howe to more strenuous exertion, only reinforced his native caution and laziness. Steeped in a formalistic art of war, he seems to have felt that by following the conventional rules and playing it safe he would avoid criticism at home even if he failed. The truth of the matter was that the world was passing him by; for the eighteenth-century concept of war had already received a rude shock in the American wilderness, and something entirely different was now evident in the character of the fighting.

Sergeant Lamb saw it and was bothered by it, but he recognized it for what it was—"a sort of implacable ardour and revenge, which happily are a good deal unknown in the prosecution of war in general." Howe, lacking that "implacable ardour and revenge" and having no instinct for the jugular, was reluctant at any time to take the one extra step that would have made the difference between partial and total victory. That quality simply was not in the man, as he demonstrated once again in the moment of victory at Fort Lee. Another general might have ordered Cornwallis to pursue Washington's beaten army relentlessly, to make the kill then and there before the quarry got away, but Howe did nothing of the kind.

Long years afterward, in another conflict in another part of the world, German Field Marshal Erwin Rommel—who understood better than most military men that sustained, successful pursuit of the enemy is the most difficult action in war, and the most important—remarked that the battle is fought and decided by the quartermasters before the fighting begins. But that conception of warfare was totally alien to a soldier of William Howe's disposition; he was content to sail across the Hudson a few days after the fort had fallen, congratulate Cornwallis and his staff, and discuss with them the task ahead. As his report to Germain made clear, he was planning even then to send the men into winter quarters shortly and the idea of wrapping up the war with one quick, killing blow now seems not to have entered his head. The instinct for hibernation was too strong in Howe, and what he had in mind was the establishment of a chain of posts across New Jersey—a string of strong points that would constitute a threat to Philadelphia at the same time they provided local loyalists with the security of the British presence. And the immediate consequence of Howe's attitude was that Lord Cornwallis, lacking a strong directive to the contrary, took his time about tying up the loose ends around Fort Lee, leisurely moved into Hackensack, and only then began to think about going after Washington.

But the pace of events was about to quicken, as a result of a chance encounter between a Tory and an express rider George Washington had sent to Philadelphia with an important dispatch. It is hard to say how the Tory contrived to get this particular letter away from Washington's messenger, but get it he did and forwarded it to British headquarters, where Howe recognized it at once as a momentous piece of information that called for immediate alteration of his plans.

As a member of Congress ruefully put it after the event, luck had placed in the British general's hands a report from the rebel commander to the Board of War, giving "an exact account when the time of service of all our battalions would expire, and [Washington's] apprehensions that the men would not reinlist without first going home to see their families and friends." Howe was well aware, of course, that American enlistments were running out, but for some reason or other he had been under the mistaken impression that most of the men had already signed up for another hitch and that Washington's strength would remain about the same. What he now knew, after reading the letter, was that the rebel army would soon number no more than 3,000—perhaps less—and that he had a priceless opportunity to pounce on that force before any reinforcements could possibly reach it. Fate had been almost too kind to Howe: all those successes in Long Island, New York, and Westchester; now he had this piece of paper describing so eloquently the pitiable state of the enemy, which lifted the mist of uncertainty that always clouds the vision of an army commander, giving him an insight into Washington's problems and probable course of action as if he had been present at his council of war. What Howe also had going for him, if he chose to take advantage of it, was the happy accident of geography. Since early July some British and Hessian soldiers had remained on Staten Island, that large, rectangular chunk of land that occupies much of New York Bay, and it would be no trick to ferry reinforcements over there from Manhattan now.

North of the island the Hackensack and Passaic rivers flow into Newark Bay, and only a narrow strip of water separates it from the mainland. By crossing Arthur Kill, that little estuary at the northwestern end of the island, the British would be only a short march from Elizabethtown, which lay on the main road leading south from Newark; or, by ferrying troops across at the southern tip of Staten Island, they would be at Perth Amboy. In either case they would be directly astride Washington's line of retreat toward Philadelphia and in a position—since Cornwallis was coming up on his rear—to bottle him up against the mountains to the west before he could escape the trap. General Henry Clinton, Howe's waspish second in command, who was ready to sail for Rhode Island with six thousand men, immediately saw the possibilities offered by the second alternative, and proposed to Howe that the Rhode Island expedition be put off temporarily so that his troops—who were already on board transports in the harbor—could push up the Raritan to head off Washington. Why Howe didn't respond to the suggestion is anyone's guess: it is just possible that he disliked Clinton so intensely that he was determined to rid himself of the man by sending him to Newport; or it may be that his mind was firmly fixed on those plans for the spring campaign, which called for Clinton's army, based on Newport, to attack the New England mainland. Whatever his reasons, he rejected the idea out of hand, and on December 1 the fleet carrying Clinton and his men sailed past the mouth of the Raritan and headed out into the wintry Atlantic. (But not before Clinton, peevish as ever, warned Howe against the possibility of his bases in New Jersey "being broken in upon in the winter, as I knew the Americans were trained to every trick of that country of chicane.")

The ominous prospect of a flanking movement had already occurred to Washington, and on the morning of November 28 he decided he had to abandon Newark; people coming over from Staten Island told him that the British troops there were collecting wagons and preparing to embark for Perth Amboy, so he had no choice but to leave in the utmost possible haste. He was just in time at that. Cornwallis' van marched into one side of town while Washington's rear guard was leaving the other, and the British found all the signs of a sudden evacuation, compounded, Ensign Thomas Glyn remarked with disgust, by the "filth and dirt of the Rebel Troops" in all the houses they occupied.

In the man he had placed in charge of the pursuit, Howe had a general who was in many respects the antithesis of his own personality. Charles, second Earl Cornwallis, was, like Howe and many other officers, an aristocrat who had made a career of the army. He was only thirty-eight years old, a strong, imposing man with a full face, large nose, and heavy-lidded eyes, one of which had a cast from a hockey accident at Eton. But unlike most of his fellow officers, he took his profession seriously enough to have studied and worked diligently at it since his eighteenth birthday. He had traveled about in Europe with a tutor, who was a veteran officer, attended the military academy in Turin, and visited several German courts to observe their armies. For three years he campaigned on the Continent in the Seven Years' War, serving as aide to the Marquis of Granby, who took command of British forces after Germain (then Lord George Sackville) was disgraced at Minden, and when hostilities erupted in the colonies he volunteered for service, much to the surprise of George III and Germain, who called it a "handsome offer." Their astonishment arose from the fact that Cornwallis, between the wars, had sided politically with the Rockingham Whigs and even with "that devil Wilkes" in opposition to the king's policies. But one of Cornwallis' strongest characteristics was a trait of loyalty and obligation, a sense of duty to his monarch that persuaded him to approach Germain and volunteer even though he would not have the top command in America. Despite his record of opposition, both Germain and the king liked him personally and admired him; he was something of a sobersides, a dignified, devoted family man, which counted for a lot with George—and Germain knew that he was a considerable cut above the average military man. He worked hard at being a successful commander, studied tactics, strategy, and the ins and outs of administration, and throughout his long, illustrious career paid more attention to his troops and their needs than most eighteenth-century generals ever dreamed of doing. Intelligent and compassionate, he did not hold with the kind of punishment that was commonplace in the army of his day; the only men he had no patience with were shirkers, for Cornwallis was all duty and seriousness. His men knew he was fair and they loved him for it and would follow him unquestioningly, and he returned the affection with interest (years later, in India, he donated to his troops the entire £42,000 in prize money that was his reward for victory over Tippoo Sahib of Mysore). It was no accident that Cornwallis' own regiment, the 33rd, was described by Sergeant Roger Lamb in 1775 as being "in a high state of appointment, and exceedingly well disciplined." Lamb said he "never witnessed any regiment that excelled it in discipline and military experience."

There was no doubt that Cornwallis was the best general the British had in America during the Revolution. But there was a flaw in his makeup somewhere that kept him from the ultimate success here that he enjoyed later as governor general and commander in chief in India and in Ireland. Maybe he loved his wife too well: she was an elegant, handsome woman who was to die in 1779 of a broken heart, it was said, caused by his protracted absence in America; he missed her all the time he was away and maintained that her death "effectually destroyed all my hopes of happiness in this world." Or perhaps it was something else: he was a brilliant, courageous leader on the battlefield, and in his later campaigns in the South he demonstrated a fierce energy, initiative, and decisiveness that very nearly brought the war there to a close; but he always seemed just to miss bringing the thing off, as if he became bored or distracted during a long period of activity and could not summon up the final dedication necessary to finish the job.†

When Howe gave him his marching orders and laid out the plan of operations in New Jersey, Cornwallis moved off at once. By now his task force of 4,000 had been heavily reinforced; the 2nd and 4th Brigades had come across the Hudson, and on November 28 he was joined by Rall's brigade of Hessians, bringing his total strength to nearly 10,000 men. Off on the flanks and in front of his army, Lieutenant Colonel William Harcourt's 16th Dragoons were ranging all over the countryside, providing

---

† As might be expected, Cornwallis disagreed with the passive strategy of Henry Clinton, who was commander in chief when the former took over the southern theater. Instead of guarding British holdings in Georgia and South Carolina, Cornwallis argued, the southern army should take the offensive, move into North Carolina and Virginia, link up there with the northern army, and end the war. In all this, however, he reckoned without Nathanael Greene, who was his opponent by then and who demonstrated that Cornwallis should have stuck to battlefield tactics and let someone else devise the overall strategy. (Some modern critics of Cornwallis blame his failure, ironically, on too extensive a study of the classic military approach, which kept him from improvising as he should have to counter Greene's hit-and-run campaign.)

Astonishingly, the British public did not blame Cornwallis for the surrender at Yorktown; the unhappy Clinton and the navy took the brunt of the criticism. In 1786 Cornwallis succeeded Warren Hastings as governor general of India, and under his vigorous direction the ancient system of land tenure was changed, elements of the British common law were introduced into the legal system, and the civil service was reformed. A decade later he went to Ireland and then returned to India, where he died in 1805.

Cornwallis with information about the rebel army's movements, and the infantry was coming on fast, despite the muddy roads and the miserable weather. On November 30, when Washington's "wretched remains of a broken army" lay opposite Brunswick on the Raritan, some British detachments were marching in the pouring rain through the town of Mountain Meeting toward the mountains off to the west, while others passed through Elizabethtown in direct pursuit of the rebels, pausing only long enough to swoop up the supplies and twenty tons of musket balls left behind in the retreat. The American general had received "positive information" that Howe intended to move on Philadelphia now that he knew about his critical shortage of men, but he said that if the British decided to risk the attempt, "they will pay dearly for it for I shall continue to retreat before them so as to lull them into security." That, in a letter to Lee (which was intercepted by the enemy, whose patrols were everywhere), was so much brave talk; every man in the army knew that he lacked the muscle to do anything but fall back.

A soldier named John Chilton, describing to a friend the disparity in numbers between the opposing forces, went on to say, "You will wonder what has become of the good army of Americans you were told we had. I really can't tell, they were in some imaginary." The thirtieth, another wretched day, saw the last of the Flying Camp's militiamen, and on the first of December, although the enemy was said to be only two hours' march away, they left camp in droves, running for home and safety. Scouts brought in a report that the enemy had been seen in Bonumtown, just ten miles from Brunswick, collecting horses, wagons, sheep, and cattle—which meant that they planned to keep moving—so Washington ordered his men to fall in at once and cross the Raritan. By 1:30 in the afternoon the British were in sight and soon had artillery on the hill across the river lobbing shells into the town.

There was barely time to destroy part of the bridge before the army got under way (Howe commented that if it had not been damaged, Cornwallis' men could have cut the rebels to pieces right there), but Washington himself remained in Brunswick, too busy to mind the cannon fire, writing another message to Lee to come up, sending a bulletin to Congress informing them that since he had no hope of making a stand in the countryside beyond Brunswick he would retreat to the bank of the Delaware River. And he begged Governor Livingston's assistance in obtaining all the boats that could be found along the Delaware, "particularly the Durham boats used for the transportation of produce," which he knew would "transport a regiment of men." He wanted all of them removed to the opposite shore, hauled out of the water, and placed under guard until he was ready to use them. Twenty-six miles to the southwest lay Trenton, the river, and sanctuary of a sort, and the army tramped off down the road in the waning light of the short December day, passed a crossroads tavern, and made camp near a lonely Dutch church that stood in the fields. Stirling's brigade, which consisted of five Virginia regiments and one from Delaware, was the last to arrive and settle down for the night.

More accurately, the last-named outfit was what remained of the first Delaware Continental Regiment. These boys had been recruited earlier in the year by Colonel John Haslet, a tough, burly Irishman who had practiced medicine in Dover, and when they joined Washington in New York they were the best-drilled and probably the only completely uniformed unit in the army. There were about 550 of them then, handsomely turned out in blue coats, faced and lined with red, sporting white waistcoats, buckskin breeches, white woolen stockings, and round black leather caps with a high peak in front, inscribed with the words "Liberty and Independence. Delaware Regiment." As an extra fillip for the parade grounds, they liked to stick a short red plume jauntily in the left side of their hats, and they cut quite a figure when they marched into the Perth Amboy camp in August 1776, carrying what a Hessian who later fought against them described as the "most beautiful English muskets and bayonets." They were fiercely proud of themselves and when they went into combat they demonstrated they had every reason to be. Before their first fight they were attached to the command of Lord Stirling, and just before the action began on Long Island he gave them a little pep talk there in the front lines. As it happened, Stirling had been present in the gallery in the House of Commons in February 1775 when General James Grant, then a member, rose from his seat and made a widely publicized boast that he could take 5,000 men and march from one end of the American continent to the other. Now Grant's division was facing Stirling and the Delaware regiment across a marsh that lay along Gowanus Creek, and Stirling told his untested troops, "He may have 5,000 men with him now—we are not so many—but I think we are enough to prevent his advancing further on his march over the continent than that mill-pond." Actually, Grant had

7,000 men to Stirling's 950, but Stirling "fought like a wolf" and so did the Delaware and Maryland boys he led, and instead of retreating they dumbfounded the British by attacking six separate times before Grant, reinforced by Cornwallis, finally broke them. Washington, observing the action through a telescope, saw what was going on and groaned, "Good God! What brave fellows I must this day lose!"

By early November a return of the regiment showed only 273 present and fit for duty. They moved over to New Jersey and were out on the front line of the retreat, their ranks decimated every day by sickness, lameness, and fatigue, and by the time they arrived in Brunswick most of those fine uniforms and the cocky red plumes were gone; the men were "broken down and fatigued," Lieutenant Enoch Anderson wrote, and "some [were] without shoes, some had no shirts." Even so, "gloomy as the times were, that very evening twenty-two of our old Regiment, and mostly of our old company, came to me to enlist with me for three years or during the war."

When the British cannon began bombarding Brunswick, Anderson reported, several men were killed and wounded before orders were passed along to retreat. It was nearly sundown and the Delaware regiment was forming up in the rear of the army when Colonel Haslet came back and ordered Anderson to take some men to burn all their fine tents; there were no wagons to carry them. "When we saw them reduced to ashes," Anderson said sadly, "it was night and the army far ahead. We made a double quick-step and came up with the army about eight o'clock. We encamped in the woods, with no victuals, no tents, no blankets. The night was cold and we all suffered much, especially those who had no shoes." Less than 3,000 men left Brunswick, Nathanael Greene noted—"a very pitiful army to trust the liberties of America"—and Lieutenant Anderson observed with pride that while other soldiers were still going off by the hundreds, "Our Regiment, although many of the men's enlistments were up, stuck to." But for all their dogged spirit and determination, there were only 92 of the regiment fit for duty three weeks later, and of the 550 men who had come into Perth Amboy so bravely in August, there remained by the end of December only Colonel Haslet and two other officers, a surgeon, and two privates.

Behind in Brunswick, too weary and hungry to go on, the British dropped in their tracks and made camp. Under those murderously heavy packs they had made a forced march of twenty miles that day through mud that clung to their boots like glue. For seventy-two hours they had had nothing to eat but the flour they picked up from farms along the way, because their wagon trains were still miles to the rear, laboring through the mire, and further pursuit now was out of the question. Cornwallis was criticized later for not attacking the rebels that night, south of the town, but as he said, "I could not have pursued the enemy from Brunswick with any prospect of material advantage, or without greatly distressing the troops under my command . . . But had I seen that I could have struck a material stroke by moving forward, I certainly should have taken it upon me to have done it." What he left unsaid was that his worn and hungry men would have had to ford the icy-cold river at nightfall and attack an unseen foe in unfamiliar surroundings in total darkness. It was too much to ask.

After spending the night under canvas, Washington rode into Princeton between eight and nine o'clock on the morning of December 2, just as his foot soldiers marched into town. He was hoping Lee might be there to meet him, but there was not even a dispatch telling of his movements; for five days, there had been no news from him. As Washington knew, Princeton was no place to linger; it was too exposed, out in the middle of open country, and did not lend itself to defense. And this morning it was also strangely deserted and quiet—a ghost of a place. Originally settled by Friends, the town was best known as the site of the College of New Jersey, founded by Presbyterians in 1746. The school's president, John Witherspoon, was a grave, dignified clergyman—a practical man who had been a leader in the political fight that ousted Governor William Franklin from office. Somehow, in addition to his duties at the college, he found time to be a member of the Continental Congress, where he served on the Board of War and the Committee of Secret Correspondence—which was what they called foreign affairs in those days. On July 2, 1776, when the crucial resolution on independence was being debated, he got to his feet and declared in a heavy Scots burr that the country was "not only ripe for the measure but in danger of rotting for the want of it." His hopes for independence had been realized, but he was beginning to see at what cost: this past September, the college had held its commencement exercises and the once-joyous occasion had been a gloomy, depressing business.

Students were disheartened by the news of one defeat after another, and the lack of a quorum among the college trustees had made it impossible even to confer degrees. As the grim tidings of Washington's headlong flight across New Jersey swept like a brushfire before him, President Witherspoon assembled his undergraduates on November 29 to tell them of the imminent approach of the British, advised them to clear out of town as quickly as possible, and bid them farewell. For the next several days the school was in constant uproar; most of the young men packed their belongings and tried to find transportation out of town, while those who lived at a considerable distance decided there was nothing to do but leave their possessions behind and get out. On the morning of December 2 the shattered American army trailed into sight along the pike, but by then most of the students and faculty had gone, silence had descended on the little college, and the buildings and grounds stood empty. Nassau Hall, which was said to be the largest building in the thirteen states, looked pretty good to the soldiers, and when Washington decided to leave Stirling and 1,200 men in Princeton to guard against a sudden cavalry attack, the men swarmed inside, delighted to have a dry billet for a change.

Ice lay thick on the ponds and streams, and the men made use of it for the only fun they had had in weeks. Some Pennsylvanians had brought in a Tory, an unfortunate fellow who had mistaken them for a party of British regulars, and as Solomon Clift told it, they removed his trousers and, after "giving him absolution by setting him on the ice (to cool off his loyalty), they set him to work bringing in faggots. He seems pleased with his new office, knowing that he got off easy." There were not many moments of levity in store for these soldiers, nor would there be any for the villagers of Princeton in the weeks to come. A few days later, when the redcoats appeared, there began what one resident called the "twenty days tyranny," as British and Hessians went from house to house, looting and dragging off anyone suspected of rebellious tendencies. At least one dwelling was burned to the ground, livestock, grain, furniture, and valuables were taken off, and the regiment quartered in Nassau Hall stabled their horses in the basement and stripped the library of books.

While Washington paused momentarily in Princeton, it was all his men could do to shake off the fear of what was behind them—maybe just over the last rise in the road—the inexorable, deadly approach of those British and Hessian legions. "We are in a terrible situation," Clift wrote, "with the enemy close upon us and whole regiments . . . leaving us. To-morrow, we go to Trenton, where the General is determined to make a stand." But Clift was mistaken; they were leaving at once. Washington was going to take advantage of one of the few good days they had had in weeks and his officers were rounding up all the men who were not going to stay with Stirling and were heading toward Trenton, twelve miles away. The general and his staff reached there in the forenoon, and as soon as headquarters was established and orders issued for moving supplies and equipment across the Delaware, Washington sat down to read a communiqué from Charles Lee, the contents of which were as foreboding as the days of silence that had preceded them.

Nothing George Washington had said so far had moved Charles Lee in the slightest; he was still in Westchester and, as his four-day-old letter revealed, he would not cross the Hudson until December 2, besides which he was persisting in the notion that he would operate independently once he got over to New Jersey. "I could wish you would bind me as little as possible," the free-wheeling Lee said breezily, "not from any opinion, I do assure you, of my own parts, but from a persuasion that detached Generals cannot have too great latitude, unless they are very incompetent indeed." Lee's abrasive demands had finally worn down Heath's resistance. Against his better judgment he had consented to allow two regiments to march with Lee's men into New Jersey, but as soon as Lee exacted this pound of flesh he returned them to Heath, as if to rub his nose in the mud. He seemed to be practicing something of the sort on Washington, too; in another letter, written several days earlier, he minimized the commanding officer's predicament by saying that he had good reason to believe the number of British troops now in New Jersey was "not near so great as you were taught to think."

About the only good news Washington heard in Trenton was that twenty-six dragoons from the Philadelphia city cavalry had clattered into town, bringing word that 1,500 militiamen were on the march behind them. One of the privates in the cavalry troop was Benjamin Randolph, the well-known cabinetmaker, and he stopped in to give Washington news of his wife, Martha. The commander in chief had not seen her since June 5, when he left her at Randolph's home in Philadelphia. At that time she was planning to join him in New York, but Howe's activities had changed all that.

Rather mysteriously, there was no indication that Cornwallis had moved from Brunswick, and Washington took advantage of the respite to write his daily communications to Congress and to Lee, and to see that the sick and wounded and all stores and equipment were ferried across the Delaware to the Pennsylvania side in the boats he had had assembled. On December 4—a day of hard rain that swept across the entire eastern seaboard, halting operations on the river and giving Lee one more excuse not to depart from Haverstraw, to which he had finally crossed on the second —a new recruit showed up at headquarters. He was Matthias Alexis Roche de Fermoy, a Frenchman who claimed to be a colonel of engineers and who had been commissioned a brigadier general in the Continental Army by Congress. But the question was, what to do with the man? As Washington described his dilemma not too subtly to the Board of War, he doubted if the foreigner could "render me that service which, I dare say, from his character, he would was he better acquainted with our language."

Cornwallis's continued inactivity was puzzling, to say the least, and on December 7 Washington decided to retrace his steps and take about 1,200 reinforcements back to Stirling in Princeton. Leaving a guard at the landing in Trenton, he had proceeded about two miles when he met Stirling's van, retreating in some haste from the college town. For several days there had been some confusion in British councils as to what Cornwallis was to do; he understood that he was to wait at Brunswick until further orders. Then Howe came over to New Jersey to check out the situation and, after conferring with Cornwallis, decided to push on at least as far as the Delaware since there was plainly nothing to stop him from doing so. He was still playing this thing by ear, thinking on the one hand that he should go into winter quarters, but on the other, considering the possibility of crossing the Delaware and taking Philadelphia if the weather held and everything continued to go his way.

So the British army was set in motion toward Princeton, and when Stirling got wind of it he decided not to hang around to see what would happen. Washington received a brief summary of what was happening, sent Stirling on toward Trenton, and rode immediately to the rear and took charge. The Delaware regiment had the post of honor there, and Lieutenant Anderson and thirty men were busy "tearing up bridges and cutting down trees, to impede the march of the enemy." Washington collected a group of pioneers and supervised the demolition job himself, telling Anderson to move ahead no faster than he did. After they reached Trenton, the boats shuttled back and forth across the river through the night of December 7 and on into the next day, carrying men to the opposite bank.

Once again, Howe's capacity for delay gave the Americans just enough time to make their getaway; inexplicably, the British lingered in Princeton for seventeen hours, and their advance guards arrived in Trenton at the very moment the last rebels were rowing out into the river and out of reach. By this time, some of Howe's junior officers had begun to wonder if the man who was running things was quite the general he was cracked up to be. "Why not pursue Washington from Brunswick with more spirit?" Stephen Kemble asked himself, for surely at least, "his cannon and baggage must have fallen into our hands." And Charles Stedman noted caustically that Howe seemed almost to have planned when the British would arrive at Trenton; it was "as if he had calculated . . . with great accuracy, the exact time necessary for his enemy to make his escape." Characteristically, Cornwallis wasted no time on recriminations. Now that Howe had given him a green light he gave his men several hours' rest and hustled them up at one o'clock in the morning to march thirteen miles upriver to Coryell's Ferry in hopes of finding some boats there. But the American general's orders had anticipated just such a move and the New Jersey bank had been cleared of all boats for seventy miles.

Enoch Anderson and the Delaware regiment made it to the Pennsylvania side without mishap, but two hours after they landed the British began shelling them from the opposite shore. "This night," he said, "we lay amongst the leaves without tents or blankets, laying down with our feet to the fire. We had nothing to cook with, but our ramrods, which we run through a piece of meat and roasted it over the fire, and to hungry soldiers it tasted sweet."

Geography and the forces of nature accomplished what Washington's army could not and Howe, stalled at last at the wide river's edge, concluded predictably that the campaign of 1776 was over. The search for boats along the entire New Jersey shore of the Delaware produced not one, and as he informed Germain, the weather turned cruelly cold—"too severe to keep the field"—so on December 14 he declared the fighting at an end. "The Campaign having closed with the Pursuit of the Enemies'

Army, near ninety Miles, by Lieut.-Gen. Cornwallis's Corps, much to the Honour of his Lordship and the Officers and Soldiers under his Command," the orders read, "The Approach of Winter putting a Stop to any further Progress, the Troops will immediately march into Quarters and hold themselves in Readiness to assemble on the shortest Notice."

As Howe returned to New York and the waiting arms of Mrs. Loring, one worry kept nagging at him, and he mentioned it somewhat apprehensively to Germain. All those posts strung out through the countryside from Hackensack to Pennington and Trenton were a bit too exposed for his liking. "The chain, I own, is too extensive," he explained, but "I was induced to occupy Burlington to cover the County of Monmouth, in which there are many loyal inhabitants; and trusting to the almost general submission of the County to the southwest of this chain, and to the strength of the corps placed in the advanced posts, I conclude the troops will be in perfect security."

4. The Game Is Pretty Near Up

One reward a victorious general has is the luxury of options. William Howe was able to call a halt to his army's activities, confident that he could afford to live and let live for the duration of winter; but no such choices were available to the American high command. Even when Howe's decision became public knowledge, the rebels sensed that events were rushing toward some sort of climax, as if the hour of destiny was approaching and must be taken at the flood or lost, perhaps forever. The specter that haunted all their waking hours was that the Continental Army would cease to exist on the last day of December 1776, when the men's enlistments expired. Some militiamen would remain, to be sure, but it was hopeless to rely on these short-term men for any serious or sustained business. Washington, in reviewing the harrowing events of the retreat through New Jersey for Congress, blamed much of the catastrophe on the "fatal supineness and insensibility of danger" of the local militia. The country could not and should not depend upon men enlisted for short terms; they were no better than a "destructive, expensive, and disorderly mob" and "the Continent would have saved money" by excusing them from duty. The problem was that "when danger is a little removed from them they will not turn out at all. When it comes home to 'em, the well-affected, instead of flying to arms to defend themselves, are busily employed in removing their families and their effects, whilst the disaffected are concerting measures to make their submission, and spread terrour and dismay all around, to induce others to follow the example."

Two absolutely compelling reasons lay behind the general's determination to make some stroke against the enemy while he still had some means of doing it: most of his remaining veterans would be gone after December 31, and unless he took action before then neither the soldiers, potential soldiers, nor the country at large were likely to see any hope in continuing the struggle. The commander in chief was like a man who has a wolf by the ear—he could neither hold him nor afford to let him go. His army was, as Lieutenant Anderson put it, "crouching in the bushes" on the west bank of the Delaware. Sick, dirty, many were "entirely naked," Washington said, "and most so thinly clad as to be unfit for service." The young painter Charles Willson Peale, who had watched the exhausted men hobble up the bank after crossing the river, described it as "the most hellish scene I ever beheld." While he stood there in shocked disbelief, he was greeted by one soldier who "had lost all his clothes. He was in an old, dirty blanket jacket, his beard long, and his face so full of sores he could not clean it." Not until the man spoke to him did Peale comprehend that it was his brother James. It was the unremitting exposure to such misery that was behind Washington's admission to his brother, John Augustine: "I think the game is pretty near up."

The condition of the army was pitiable enough even if there had been no enemy to contend with, but as things stood, there was no knowing whether the British would cross the iced-over river if the temperature stayed below freezing or construct boats for the purpose if the ice would not hold them. According to Judge Jones, who took a jaundiced view of Howe in general and his conduct of this campaign in particular, there was a lumberyard full of boards directly behind the Britisher's Trenton headquarters, which he "must have seen every time he looked out of his window." Besides, there were barns and warehouses from which timbers for rafts could be taken; but no, the judge said angrily, "the rebellion was to be nursed, the general to continue in command, and his friends, flatterers, mistresses, and sycophants, to be provided for."

Bad news travels fast, and the capital city of Philadelphia was in a state close to panic. David Rittenhouse of the Pennsylvania Council of Safety notified all militia captains in the area that "Vigour and spirit alone can save us," with Washington flying before the enemy. "There is no time for words," he cautioned. "Exert yourselves now like freemen." A growing number of local merchants were refusing to accept Continental currency in payment for goods and the smart money was going into flour, pork, butter, and seed—all the items that would be in short supply when final disaster struck. Those who could get out of the city were leaving, "loading wagons with their furniture &c., taking them out of town . . . Great numbers [of] people moving . . . All shops ordered to be shut . . . Our people in confusion, of all ranks," while the capital was "amazingly depopulated," one man noted. That same unbridled fear was gnawing away at people's loyalties, separating the fainthearted from those who were still determined to stand up to the enemy.

Joseph Galloway, a lawyer and member of the First Continental Congress, had slipped through the lines and gone over to the British at Trenton;‡ so had three members of the wealthy Allen family—one a former member of the Committee on Observation, another a congressman, and a third a lieutenant colonel of the 2nd Pennsylvania Regiment. These four were permitted to continue on to New York, where they were soon spending a good deal of time in the company of Ambrose Serle, Admiral Howe's secretary, taking tea and meals with him and talking by the hour about the situation in Philadelphia and in the country at large. William

‡ Galloway's ostensible reason for joining Howe was that he could serve his country best by helping to put down the present disorder, but there was more to it than that. He was in his mid-forties, a well-educated, prosperous Philadelphian who had married an heiress and was genuinely interested in public affairs, as evidenced by twenty years' service in the Pennsylvania legislature and six as vice-president of the American Philosophical Society. At the time the First Continental Congress met, Galloway seemed certain to become one of the outstanding figures in America, but he was basically a conservative who felt that the difficulties besetting England and the colonies were strictly of a constitutional nature, and he declined to serve in the Second Continental Congress. He moved out of Philadelphia to the country, fearful of what the radicals might do to him, and when he continued to receive threats, fled to New York. When Howe took Philadelphia in 1777 Galloway became civil administrator of the city, but after the rebels recaptured it he fled again—this time to England, where he became a spokesman for the loyalists in exile and devoted much of his time to writing pamphlets criticizing the government's conduct of the war.

Allen, the former military man, informed Serle confidently that three fourths of the people were opposed to independence and that the only reason the rebellion continued was that "the Continent is under the Dominion of a desperate Faction, formed by the worst Characters upon it." Unfortunately, these were the very people who controlled the army. The worst of the lot, Andrew Allen observed, was Samuel Adams, who had for twenty years been spreading his republican ideas among the young men of Boston; he had an infinite capacity for leading and inflaming the mob and his bag of tricks included "vast Insinuation, & infinite Art, by wch he has been able to impose upon most Men." As for John Adams and Benjamin Franklin, Congress had appointed them to meet with Admiral Howe in September only after assuring themselves that Edward Rutledge would be a member of the party, for the truth simply was not in Adams or Franklin and only by having Rutledge present could Congress be sure of learning the facts of what had transpired. But the conversations with Serle went well beyond gossipy chitchat about personalities.

The Allens and Galloway were thoroughly agitated by all that had occurred during the past year and so, they believed, was a majority of thoughtful Americans. John Dickinson, Galloway said, "is almost crazy from the present Troubles" (indeed, the following month Dickinson declined election to Congress on grounds of "a very low state of health," which may or may not have been the real reason). As Serle's visitors saw it—and he saw no reason to doubt them, since he found them eminently sensible fellows who agreed with him in almost every particular—the strength of the rebellion was nearly broken, and although the former colonies would undoubtedly make further efforts to keep resistance alive, these attempts were bound to be feeble and ineffectual. Congress had completely lost the support of the people and just as soon as the British army occupied more of the country, its influence would collapse—a prospect already hinted at in three lower counties of Delaware and Maryland, where the authority of the central government had recently been actively opposed.

Andrew Allen, however, was a moderate man and what lay heavily on his mind was the question of what might now be done to salvage the situation, to avoid the possibility that America would be considered and treated by the British as a conquered country. Did Serle have anything to suggest, or could he find out what the Howes felt about arranging an accommodation? There was a strong hint from Allen that he could find the means of planting important information where it would do the most good, if only the Howes were willing to give him a sign that they would look favorably on negotiations to this end. Serle said it would be presumptuous of him to offer any suggestion beyond the obvious one that the colonies—as he preferred to call them—should, either singly or collectively, make a public renunciation of independence and of the body of men who had declared it or—failing that—seize the ringleaders of the rebellion. Allen replied that the idea of arresting the members of Congress had indeed occurred to "some of the first People" in Philadelphia, but that they discarded it as being too hazardous. (To which Serle responded that the peril might be worth it, since the alternative of prolonging the war was considerably worse.)

A few days later Serle met with Andrew Allen again. He had discussed their earlier conversation with Lord Howe and had a concrete proposal for the Philadelphian: what, he asked, would be the likelihood of persuading the governor of Pennsylvania and his friends to issue a proclamation renouncing the actions of Congress as the acts of a "factious & illegal Body," while urging all men in the state to profess allegiance to His Majesty King George III and to condemn the rebellion and support of the revolutionaries? Even as he described it, Serle realized it sounded suspiciously like the Howes' proclamation of November 30—a one-sided arrangement that he had disliked himself. At the time he had observed that it would only save a few villainous New Yorkers from the halter while alienating the "loyal and suffering Inhabitants." No, he thought, the only effective means of dealing with the rebellion was with the sword, for "to govern America, it must be conquered." And ironically, it would be easier to conquer this country than to govern it. Both he and Allen knew that what he was passing along now wasn't much of an offer, but Allen promised halfheartedly to think it over and get in touch with some of the "leading People" in Philadelphia.

In the meantime, the members of Congress were feeling the hot breath of the approaching enemy, and few of them relished the idea of being present if Howe's army should reach the capital. On numerous occasions Washington voiced his fears for the safety of the city; "I tremble for Philadelphia," he admitted on December 10 after hearing a rumor that the

British were building bridges in Trenton. Now he was offering suggestions for its active defense, and to reassure the residents he sent Generals Thomas Mifflin and Israel Putnam to lend a hand with the preparations. Mifflin was a smooth-talking diplomat who had a way with Congress; Putnam was his exact opposite. Old Put was a legendary hero in the colonies before the war began; he had, it was said, killed a huge she-wolf in her den while a boy, fought in the French and Indian War as one of Rogers' Rangers, been rescued in the nick of time from being burned at the stake by Indians, survived a shipwreck and other near-disasters, and, when the port of Boston was closed in 1774, had driven a large flock of sheep from his Connecticut farm to the town. If anyone could put some spine into the people of Philadelphia, the tough, square-jawed, almost illiterate Putnam looked like the man.* But it was a difficult assignment.

He imposed a ten o'clock curfew and issued an order declaring his intention of executing anyone caught setting fires in the city, but those were halfway measures that could not remedy the underlying sickness. "All things in this city remain in confusion," he confessed to Washington on December 12. Congress had distributed broadsides throughout the outlying districts appealing for troops and then, casting about in a higher direction, recommended that all of the states declare a "day of solemn Fasting and Humiliation" when all citizens should repent and reform and all army officers forbid "profane swearing and all other immoralities" while asking for divine assistance in "the prosecution of this just and necessary war." The Council of Safety was understandably nervous about the presence in the city of enemy prisoners, taken in earlier campaigns, and was preparing to send them down to Maryland, with their blessings. With the tiger nearing the gates, everyone knew or suspected what Washington told John Hancock privately on December 12: "Perhaps Congress have some hope and prospect of reenforcements; I have no intelligence of the sort and wish to be informed on the subject. Our little handfull is daily decreasing by sickness and other causes, and without con-

---

* Although Putnam was an appealing, roughhewn folk hero, it was apparent to Washington by this time that he did not have the stuff to make a field commander. Part of the difficulty may have been that he was over the hill: at fifty-eight, he was an elderly man as age was reckoned in that day. His only real moment of glory in the Revolution came at the battle of Bunker Hill where, although not in command, he was characteristically in the thick of the fight. From then on, however, he seems to have gone downhill in Washington's estimation, and after receiving a stern rebuke for his dilatory conduct in the Highlands in 1777, he suffered a stroke in 1779 which put an end to his military career.

siderable succors and exertions on the part of the people, what can we reasonably look for or expect, but an event that will be severely felt by the common cause and that will wound the heart of every virtuous American, the loss of Philadelphia. The subject is disagreeable, but yet it is true. I will leave it, wishing that our situation may become such as to do away the apprehensions which at this time fill the minds of too many and with too much justice."

So in the final analysis, the only hope that sustained Washington—and a wispy one it was—lay in the possibility that Lee would join him before time ran out. Lee, after crossing the Hudson, indulged himself in a spate of letters covering every conceivable subject but the one George Washington was desperate to hear about. He told the commander in chief to be of good cheer: Lee's army of 5,000 was in good spirits and was considering an attack on isolated British detachments in New Jersey in order to cut their line of communications. He asked the harried Washington to do him a small personal favor: "I entreat you to order some of your suite to take out of the way of danger my favourite mare, which is at Hunt Wilson's, three miles the other side of Princeton." (One of his secretaries wrote in similar vein to Heath, saying Lee had lost three of his best camp horses—a black, a bay, and a sorrel mare—and would Heath please to make inquiries about them among his men.) He got off a letter to Governor Cooke of Rhode Island, advising him on the defense of that state and providing some gratuitous comment on what makes a good commanding officer. ("Theory joined to practice, or a heaven-born genius, can alone constitute a General," Lee observed, pointedly noting that "God Almighty indulges the modern world very rarely with the spectacle.") He boasted to Heath, "I am in hopes here to reconquer (if I may so express myself) the Jerseys. It was really in the hands of the enemy before my arrival."

Washington and most of his officers had become accustomed to this sort of performance from Lee; what was giving them fits was that his march was as rambling and leisurely as his letters. His advance units finally made their appearance in Morristown on December 8, having taken twenty-three days to get there from White Plains, and the last of his troops did not straggle in until the tenth. The unhappy affair had badly undermined the morale of Washington's junior officers and was beginning to affect their confidence in his judgment. As Nathanael Greene frankly told the commander in chief, "I think General Lee must be confined within the lines of some general plan, or else his operations will be independent of yours." Which was what had bothered Washington all along, of course. Despairing of the effort to achieve anything by letter, Washington sent a man in search of Lee. Lieutenant Colonel Richard Humpton finally caught up with him in Morristown and in the course of their conversation made the mistake of mentioning that Washington had been reinforced by several thousand Pennsylvania militiamen. That was all that was needed to send Lee off on another flight of fancy. Had it not been for those reinforcements, he assured Washington, "I should immediately join you; but as I am assured you are very strong, I should imagine we can make a better impression by hanging on [the enemy's] rear, for which purpose a good post at Chatham seems the best calculated."

Now Chatham was about eight miles east, and a little south, of Morristown; a quick glance at the map showed that if Lee went there, he would be in a position to harry the British flank and rear, all right, but he would also be heading away from Washington's camps along the Delaware, away from Philadelphia, and off into a murky no man's land that promised the gravest risk to his army. There was a good possibility that the British would turn on him and deal with him separately before they advanced on Philadelphia. Regardless of what might occur, Washington was determined that anything which prevented Lee from joining him must be avoided at all costs. Swallowing his pride once more, the commander sent another high-level courier to Lee in the person of one of his aides, Colonel Stephen Moylan. "Were it not for the weak and feeble state of the force I have," his message read, "I should highly approve of your hanging on the rear of the enemy," but given the present circumstances, "I cannot but request and entreat you . . . to march and join me with all your whole force, with all possible expedition." Only the utmost exertions would save Philadelphia, and without Lee's support there was no prospect of doing so. But the ambitious Lee was still casting about for some opportunity to pull off a spectacular surprise.

From December 8 to 11 he remained in Morristown, undecided as to whether to join Washington or attack a British outpost at Brunswick or Princeton, examining all the possibilities open to him in hopes of spotting one that would bring glory and personal credit. Having nothing better to do one morning, he twitted Washington on the latter's efforts to collect all the boats on the Delaware: ". . . for Heaven's sake what use can they be of? I hope if you leave Trent Town you will set it on fire." Off on the sidelines of Lee's reckless game of chance, his friend William Duer of the New York Council of Safety was rolling some loaded dice. He had gotten in touch with General Horatio Gates, who was leading the Northern army toward a junction with Washington, and did his best to persuade Gates to disobey orders and join Lee instead. Gates, fortunately, was not interested in the idea.

The uneasy calm that had descended on the wintry plains of New Jersey could not last much longer. Washington, fretting constantly about the immediate difficulties of holding his army together and holding off the enemy, was beginning to sense that the rebellion might suddenly come apart at the seams if all the inner frustrations and fears of the populace came unraveled. In New Jersey the state legislature had disbanded; inhabitants were queuing up in every town occupied by the royal troops, signing loyalty oaths, and accepting pardons; and now farmers, like the merchants of Philadelphia, were refusing to accept Continental paper in exchange for supplies the soldiers tried to purchase. From Pennsylvania came word that certain militia units "exult at the approach of the enemy," which forced Washington to consider how this potential fifth column could be disarmed before it proved dangerous. Putnam warned members of Congress that they should leave the capital, noticeably increasing the legislators' state of jitters. They voted on December 11 to denounce the rumors of their impending departure from Philadelphia and asked Washington to inform his army of their resolve. But the next day discretion got the better of valor, and a resolution provided that General Washington should "be possessed of full power to order and direct all things relative to the department, and to the operations of war," thus conferring on him virtual dictatorial powers in case he wanted to use them. Congress had decided to adjourn and, when next heard from, would be meeting in Baltimore. They had abandoned the capital.

Colonel John Cadwalader was furious when he heard the news. Writing to Robert Morris, who remained implacably in Philadelphia, he asked why in God's name the government had flown. This act of timidity was an open invitation to the enemy to move on the city, it destroyed the nation's credit at home and abroad and left everyone to suppose that only if "the sky may fall, or some lucky circumstance happen, that may give a turn to our affairs. A good face among men in power keeps up the spirits of the people, and one cheerful countenance may do wonders." It was a sentiment echoed by Samuel Morris of the Philadelphia Associators, who observed that the departure of Congress "struck a damp on ye spirits of many."

For his own part, Robert Morris considered the move necessary; he thought Congress ought to stay in Baltimore until the enemy went into winter quarters or retired to Brunswick or New York. Morris, a jowly, unflappable bear of a man, had remained behind when all his fellow delegates fled the capital, to continue the rather mysterious affairs of the Secret Committee of Congress, of which he was chairman. That group, which was often confused with the Committee of Secret Correspondence, with which its maneuverings frequently overlapped, controlled all foreign trade. It imported munitions, medical supplies, blankets, and cotton goods, bought ships and other necessities, dealt with the Franco-Spanish firm of Hortalez & Cie., controlled the movements and activities of American privateers, and was intimately involved in the diplomatic dealings of Silas Deane, Congress' representative in Paris. In the process of conducting his official duties, Morris also kept a beneficent eye on the welfare of his own commercial and banking firm, Willing & Morris, and to no one's surprise, the biggest contracts for importing foreign goods went to Willing & Morris, to relatives and friends of Silas Deane, and to firms connected with other members of the Secret Committee. John Adams was not exaggerating when he stated that Morris had "vast designs in the mercantile way" (Morris possessed a substantial fortune before he became a member of Congress), but whether he exceeded the bounds of propriety while carrying out the essential business of Congress was for the future to decide; what mattered now was that he was virtually the only available civilian in a position of authority to whom George Washington could turn for assistance and guidance, and during the next several weeks the general would rely increasingly on him for both. Meanwhile, Morris took it upon himself to inform the departed congressmen about matters as seen from Philadelphia, one of which was the distressed state of mind of Silas Deane, who was feeling hopelessly out of touch with events, off there in Paris.

Poor Deane, who was doing his level best to secure open French support for the rebellion, had not received Congress' letter informing him about what he called the "Declaration of Independency" until early November. Completely uninformed about that momentous event, he had hemmed and hawed, trying to keep up a bold face with the French court, while the news "had been circulating through Europe for two months." It was essential in the future, Deane said, that more than one copy of a letter be sent him—in fact, "duplicates of every letter should be lodged in every port, in the hands of faithful and attentive persons, to be forwarded by the first conveyance to any part of Europe." Since leaving America, Deane had received only two short letters from Congress, which put him in an impossibly embarrassing position as the American government's agent. All in all, he reported, he found himself in the humiliating situation of being "Without intelligence, without orders, and without remittances, yet boldly plunging into contracts, engagements, and negotiations, hourly hoping that something will arrive from America." Writing on November 28, Deane informed the Secret Committee that a M. du Coudray was en route to America with sufficient stores for 30,000 men, while a certain Baron de Kalb ("who speaks English") would be a useful addition to the army. Both men would doubtless arrive some time in January. What Deane could not know was that there might be no cause left to fight for when they got here.

Early in the morning of Friday, December 13, the snow began to melt and cottony mists hung heavy in lowlands along the Delaware, blanking out the American pickets' view of enemy activities on the Trenton side. There were two important communications in the headquarters mail that day, one of which contained the woeful tidings that Congress had fled from Philadelphia to Baltimore; for a matter of days—perhaps weeks—the new nation was to be without a government, with its capital city abandoned. Then there was a letter from Charles Lee, another of those enigmatic communiqués that raised more questions than it answered, which began with a complaint about the lack of shoes (many of Lee's men were forced to wrap their feet in the fresh hide of beef animals slaughtered the preceding day). Gates's men were on their march, "but where they actually are, is not certain," the message continued. Lee was apparently trying to make up his mind whether to march toward the Delaware and cross it above Trenton or maneuver toward Burlington and make for the ferry below that town. Taken at face value, this meant that he was seriously considering a movement that would take him across the British line of communications and on to a position somewhere on Cornwallis' left flank, where he would have the entire enemy army on his right and rear and a broad river in front of him.

It was an absurd suggestion, and Washington told him so. He was astonished that there should be any doubt in Lee's mind about the route he ought to take; he should march immediately for Pittstown, from where he could go directly to Tinnicum Ferry, below Helltown. Lee was to advise the commander in chief the moment he arrived there and should wait on the Pennsylvania side for further orders. To make certain Lee got the word, Washington sent Lord Stirling off to his Morristown headquarters, where Stirling was also to sound out Lee on the possibility of making a combined attack on the British, using the forces under Lee, Gates, and Heath, along with Washington's own. Apart from the question of how these scattered remnants of the Grand American Army were to find a chink in the British armor which they might exploit, there was just one other problem in connection with this plan born of desperation. Washington was not yet aware of it, but Major General Charles Lee had been captured by a troop of His Majesty's dragoons on the morning of Friday the thirteenth.

5. *A Most Miraculous Event*

The man who captured Lee was type cast for such work. Stocky, red-haired, twenty-two years old, and as aggressively ambitious as Lee himself, Banastre Tarleton had attended Oxford and the Middle Temple before the lure of gambling and London's heady social life got the better of his interest in law and decided him on a more glamorous career. For a young man on the make, the cornet's commission his mother purchased on April 20, 1775, was a long way from the top, but it held the almost certain guarantee of action, since the cornet's conspicuous duty was to carry the pennant in battle. Later that year Tarleton applied for overseas service, which led him first to Charleston with Clinton and Cornwallis and then to New York, where he applied almost immediately for a vacancy in Lieutenant Colonel William Harcourt's 16th Regiment of Light Dragoons.

There is a romantic notion about cavalry that has persisted for a long time, as though the man on horseback were some kind of throwback to those illusory times of knighthood and chivalry. But in plain fact the best cavalrymen were hard, utterly ruthless characters like Tarleton, who enjoyed riding down enemy infantrymen and crushing them under their horses' thundering hooves and hacking them brutally with terrible, swinging sabers. For the next five years this young man's story would be a saga of lightning-quick raids and cavalry charges that left a trail of death and terror across the battlegrounds of America, until he was known to his enemies as "Bloody" Tarleton and the phrase "Tarleton's Quarter" became a bitter term for the kind of mercy one could expect from his British Legion.†

Lieutenant Colonel Harcourt and his troop had arrived in New York on October 3 and since mid-November had been active in the Jerseys, patrolling the roads and half-hidden trails, riding reconnaissance, and serving as Cornwallis' eyes and ears. During the first ten days of December, however, Cornwallis knew less about the whereabouts of Charles Lee than even Washington did and Harcourt was ordered to find him, the general being understandably nervous about having the unpredictable Lee and an unknown quantity of troops somewhere on his flank or rear. In the frosty morning air of December 12 Harcourt trotted out of Pennington, where Cornwallis had his headquarters, followed by an aide, Captain Eustace, two subalterns, Tarleton, and twenty-five privates, to look for Lee. Heading north across the snow-covered terrain, they covered eighteen miles without seeing or hearing anything to indicate where Lee was. Early evening darkness found them in the village of Hillsborough, on Millstone Creek, where they bedded down in a house. About one in the morning the troopers awoke to the smell of smoke and cries of "Fire!"—pounding out of the house, they collected their horses while the building burned to the ground and retired to a nearby hay barn to sleep for what

† Tarleton emerged from the war with a reputation as brilliant in England as it was infamous in America, but his later years were disappointing to those who had hoped for better things from him. As the historian Henry Belcher wrote, comparing him with Lafayette, "Both Tarleton and Lafayette in 1777 were of the age when all is golden and gay. They both shot their bolt young." Tarleton became no more than "a hanger-on of a society in which eccentricity was the chief note of distinction."

was left of the night. At five in the morning they were up and away again, and Harcourt told Tarleton to ride on ahead of the others with six men, which the young trooper said later was "one of the luckiest Circumstances of my life."

Cantering across the countryside through a maze of trails and back roads, the cavalrymen were heading toward Morristown and had proceeded about fourteen miles when they picked up an armed rebel. Two miles further Harcourt learned at last that Lee was about four or five miles away and was told at the same time that his own line of retreat had been cut off by rebels blockading the roads he had just traveled. Captain Nash and four dragoons went back to see if this information was accurate, while Tarleton rode on ahead. Three miles to the north they swooped down on two American soldiers who were afraid to fire at them and who admitted, under threat of death, that Lee was about a mile away. His guard was not large, the rebels informed Tarleton, and "he was about half a Mile in the Rear of his Army. These Men were so confused that they gave us but an imperfect Idea, where Genl. Lee was." With no more than that to go on, the young cornet took two of his men up a hill overlooking the road, where they surprised a mounted American and took him prisoner. Tarleton led the man back to where Harcourt was waiting, threatened him with a saber, and learned that he had just left Lee's headquarters with a dispatch for General Sullivan at Pluckemin. The courier couldn't or wouldn't tell how many men were in Lee's guard, but he admitted that it was not large—probably not over thirty soldiers in all. Then, going back up the hill with them, he pointed out the house where Lee was staying. After a hasty review of their situation, Harcourt told Tarleton to charge the front of the place while he took the rest of the men around to the rear.

For reasons best known to himself (Washington later assumed, probably correctly, that it was "for the sake of a little better lodging"), Lee had decided on December 12 to spend the night about three miles from his army's camp, in a tavern kept by a widow named Mrs. White in the town of Basking Ridge. With him he took a personal guard of about fifteen men, his aide-de-camp Major William Bradford, two French volunteers—Captain Jean Louis de Virnejoux and a lieutenant colonel of cavalry, the Sieur Gaiault de Boisbertrand—and he was joined during the night by Major James Wilkinson, who had brought in some dispatches from Gates. At eight A.M. Lee's army began marching out of Morristown as planned, but Lee stayed at the tavern for about two more hours, intending to catch up with them after breakfasting leisurely and dictating a letter to Gates—a highly remarkable document which revealed the curious direction his mind was taking these days. After commenting sarcastically on the disaster at Fort Washington, he let loose at Washington: ". . . *entre nous*, a certain great man is damnably deficient—He has thrown me into a situation where I have my choice of difficulties—if I stay in this Province I risk myself and army and if I do not stay the Province is lost forever . . . unless something which I do not expect turns up we are lost—our counsels have been weak to the last degree . . . ."

No sooner had he finished this than he heard a commotion outside the tavern. Peering from the upstairs window, he saw British horsemen suddenly appear from the woods at the side of the house and from a garden opposite, riding down two sentries and scattering the men of his guard, who were quartered in an outbuilding. When the dragoons burst out into the open around the tavern, Banastre Tarleton reported, "I went on at full Speed when perceiving 2 Sentrys at a Door and a loaded Waggon; I push'd at them making all the Noise I cou'd. The Sentrys were struck with a Panic, dropp'd their arms and fled. I order'd my Men to fire into the House thro' every Window and Door, and cut up as many of the Guard as they cou'd." The Frenchman Virnejoux was firing at the troopers from the front door while others shot at them from windows of the house, and at this moment the widow White ran outside, threw herself on her knees before Tarleton, and begged for her life. General Lee was inside, she told him to his delight, and as Tarleton later described his reaction, "I carried on my Attack with all possible Spirit and surrounded the House, tho' fir'd upon, in front, flank, and rear." Harcourt and the other dragoons had ridden up a hill not far from the tavern to prevent any surprise attack from units of Lee's army, while Eustace kept in Tarleton's rear to fend off the guard. After about eight minutes the shooting stopped, and Tarleton reined up in the heavy fog of gunsmoke. After firing two shots through the door he shouted that he knew General Lee was inside and that if he surrendered, he and his staff would be safe. If he did not give up immediately, Tarleton would burn the house down and put everyone in it to the sword. At that moment Boisbertrand and several others tried to leave by the rear entrance, but several dragoons spotted them, shot one of the men, and clouted the Frenchman over the head with a saber.

During all the confusion outside and downstairs, Lee paced the upstairs room, looking anxiously out the window to see if there were any sign of reinforcements, and after concluding that there was no hope of saving himself, sent Bradford out to say that he would surrender. Bradford opened the front door and somehow missed being cut down by a hail of gunfire before he had a chance to shout that Lee would give himself up, and in a moment the general appeared, turned himself over to a sentry Tarleton had stationed there, and was led off to see Harcourt, who reassured him he would be treated like a gentleman. Lee requested that Bradford be permitted to return to the house for his hat and cloak, and the major—who seems to have had his wits about him—went inside and coolly changed into a servant's clothing. When he returned with Lee's gear he was mistaken for a civilian and allowed to go back to the tavern, from which he later made his escape. All this time Wilkinson had been hiding in a chimney, and since the British were only concerned about getting out of there with their high-level captive, they did not bother to search the place, so he got away too, with Bradford and Virnejoux.

According to Tarleton, Harcourt put his "noble Prisoner" on a horse and led him off immediately, heading down a different road than the one over which they had traveled before. The high, clear notes of a bugle sounded in the wintry air, the troopers fell in behind Harcourt, and with Tarleton bringing up the rear with the Frenchman Boisbertrand, they clattered off in the direction of Pennington. Out here in the heart of enemy country, every clump of trees and every bend in the road suggested a rebel ambush, and they rode hard, scarcely daring to look back to see if anyone was following. They put thirteen miles behind them without spotting a single American soldier and after they had forded a stream and approached Hillsborough, breathed a collective sigh of relief. "This is a most miraculous Event," Tarleton concluded, "it appears like a Dream." Then, anticipating Howe's announcement of the following day, he declared proudly, "This Coup de Main has put an End to the Campaign."

General John Sullivan, who was about seven miles away from Basking Ridge, in Pluckemin, heard about the capture from Bradford and Wilkinson and sent out a rescue party at once, but by then it was too late. Harcourt had too much of a start on them and convoyed his important prisoner to the home of a physician near the Raritan River, where Lieutenant Colonel Charles Mawhood and an old friend of Lee's from British army days, Major Moyney, were staying. Moyney came out of the house, embraced Lee fondly, and the group went inside for something to eat as though it were a perfectly normal social occasion, after which Harcourt's party saddled up again and rode to Brunswick, where Lee was placed under heavy guard. Outside, jubilant redcoats proceeded to get his horse drunk while they toasted the king and a band played all night in celebration. Lee, wearing an old blue coat trimmed with red, a battered hat, and greasy leather breeches, was an object of pity or contempt to the many British officers who dropped by to see him in prison. Some thought he should be tried as a deserter from the British army and a traitor to the crown (he narrowly escaped this fate because he had resigned from the half-pay roster and was therefore technically no longer on active duty), and one visitor commented that he had never seen a general officer "so dirty and so ungentleman-like." Almost everyone found him extremely dejected—as well he might be—and asking constantly what they thought Howe might do with him.‡

Communications being what they were in the New Jersey no man's land, Washington's first inkling of what had occurred came two days after the event, when he received a letter written by John Sullivan on December 13. "It gives me the most pungent pain," Sullivan began, "to inform your Excellency of the sad stroke America must feel in the loss of General Lee, who was this morning taken by the enemy." Sullivan quickly sketched the facts of the shocking episode, told Washington that he had taken every possible step to retrieve Lee—but without success—and said he would bring Lee's troops over to join the main army as quickly as he could—which was an assurance Washington had never re-

---

‡ There was much consternation in rebel councils following Lee's capture. Congress, hearing that his life was in danger, requested Washington to find out what sort of treatment he was receiving at British hands and arranged to get some money to Lee. When the captive was taken to New York in January, however, his fate was the reverse of what Congress had feared: he stayed in comfortable quarters, and although the place was ringed with guards, he was permitted to have his servant, Giuseppe Minghini, and one of his dogs with him and seems to have had all the wine and good food he wanted —all to the despair of Judge Thomas Jones, who regarded this as one more outrage perpetrated by General Howe. Lee was finally exchanged in April 1778 (it took quite a while for the rebels to capture a British officer of equal rank for the purpose) but was court-martialed for his conduct at the battle of Monmouth two months later and was cashiered from the service in 1780. He died in 1782, heavily in debt and still fulminating against George Washington, whom he called a "puffed up charlatan . . . extremely prodigal of other men's blood and a great oeconomist of his own."

ceived from Sullivan's predecessor. "Unhappy man!" was the commander in chief's observation. "Taken by his own imprudence . . ."

As Washington and everyone else in authority realized, this "melancholy intelligence" might prove to be one blow too many for the country at large, on the heels of all the other bad news. John Hancock, the president of Congress, was especially worried about the effect on army morale; he believed that Lee was "in great measure the idol of the soldiers, and possessed still more the confidence of the soldiery." And a good many men in the ranks agreed with him. After listening to a group chew over the affair around their campfires along the Delaware, Samuel Webb gave his opinion of the "unfortunate Captivity of General Lee" to his friend Joseph Trumbull: "I wish it may not despirit the people: this is what I most fear. His services as an Officer were great, but this in some measure can be made up. The General is much surprised Genl Lee should venture to lodge from Camp in a Country where he must have known we had many Enemies. Indeed we shall have hard work to convince many Officers and Soldiers that he is not a Trayter. I do not speak of this as tho' any at Head Quarters have the most distant tho't of his Integrity, but it's difficult to convince the common people." Yet despite the hue and cry that followed, some Americans concluded that this misfortune might turn out to be a blessing in disguise.

One day late in December Colonel John Cadwalader fell in with a contingent of Delaware militiamen who were marching to join the Continentals and mentioned to Thomas Rodney that Lee's capture had not only lowered morale in the army but made all their future prospects look gloomy. Rodney thought about this for awhile as they tramped along and then told Cadwalader he did not agree. Until now, he thought, Lee's reputation as a general had tended to hold Washington back, as though he were reluctant to exercise his own good judgment without deferring to Lee's opinion. This turn of events might mean that the commander in chief would rely more heavily on his own native abilities, which could turn out to be a healthy thing in the long run. What Rodney was suggesting was particularly appropriate to that particular moment in time, but whether he realized it or not he was touching on a subject of considerable significance for the future.

There is no telling what might have happened had Lee not been forcibly removed from the scene, but certainly he and Washington were fast reaching the point at which someone was going to have to choose between them one way or other. Lee had been chafing for months now about his subordinate role, he had the bit in his teeth and was lining up allies for what looked like a final power struggle with Washington, and on the basis of their respective accomplishments and failures to date, it is just possible that the Virginian might have lost out to Lee in any test of strength. If the Englishman, and not Washington, had received the credit for victories that came later, at a time when many Americans were seriously questioning the commander in chief's military capacity, it is not easy to say what might have happened or what the consequences might have been—during the course of the Revolution or its aftermath. For Lee was a highly opinionated man of very little patience or charity; he was scornful of Washington's habit of constantly deferring to Congress, and he had little use for the principle of military subservience to a civilian government. At the time of his capture, things looked very black indeed for the struggling United States of America, but from the vantage point of hindsight, it is just conceivable that his disappearance from center stage may have been the luckiest possible break for the country.

When word of Lee's capture reached England, Londoners at first thought it too fantastic to be believed and then, when the report was confirmed, spoke of the possibility that this might end the war. George III sent a graceful note of thanks to Harcourt for his exploit (it came as a disappointment, for Harcourt had expected to be made a colonel for pulling off such a coup), and one wit suggested that Lee should be condemned, taken to the gallows, and then pardoned on condition that he agree to marry the republican historian Catharine Macaulay.

In the wake of Lee's unwilling departure, Washington had no time to consider its ramifications except insofar as they affected his immediate plans. How many men in Lee's command—now with Sullivan—were coming up he did not know and would not until they arrived; Lee had stated his total strength variously as anywhere between 3,000 and 5,000, and Washington pessimistically assumed it would be closer to the lower figure. Horatio Gates had written him on December 12 from a place near Sussex Court House, informing him of his route toward the Delaware, but his progress was horribly slow—his army was laboring through deep snow drifts and there was no telling when they might finally arrive. Heath would have to stay in the Highlands with his 600 men, Washington concluded, and Clinton should remain there, too. Making allowances for error, Washington estimated that he might have about 5,000 on hand when all of them reported in, but there would be no more than 1,200 Continentals around after the end of the year.

To provide for the army, the indefatigable commissary general, Joseph Trumbull, was making some progress by darting here and there, gathering up whatever he could lay hands upon, but the beef he was planning to get in New England had not even been slaughtered yet; flour from Virginia was still to be shipped to New England; and Trumbull was continually hampered by a shortage of funds for these purchases. In Philadelphia the citizens were collecting old clothing and blankets for the soldiers, but these essentials were just beginning to trickle into the camps and the men's suffering would be intense before enough were on hand to do any real good, for December 14 had brought a heavy freeze which continued through the following day and no relief was in sight.

Scouts and spies had been sent off in all directions to pick up anything they could learn of the enemy's intentions. Joseph Reed, who had returned to active duty, passed on a succinct report of all he had gleaned from informers, which seemed to add up to the fact that the British would definitely make a landing on the west bank of the Delaware soon. Howe was still with the army, he reported; Cornwallis was at Pennington with a large body of troops—mostly light infantry and grenadiers; the British artillery park contained thirty cannon, and horses were being collected from all over the countryside. Reed believed the attack would come somewhere near Trenton and he expressed concern that there was no possibility of guarding the river adequately to prevent surprise. What was more, "I do not like the situation of things at and above Coryell's Ferry," he said. "The officers are quite new, and seem to have little sense of the necessity of vigilance."

On the fourteenth, Washington moved his headquarters from Thomas Barclay's house opposite Trenton to William Keith's, about ten miles distant, in order to be nearer the main body of his army and to Greene, Stirling, and Knox, who had headquarters in that vicinity. Here he received word from Cadwalader that the enemy had been out in strength on December 15; at least 2,000 Hessians with brass fieldpieces had marched into Bordentown during the afternoon and arrangements were evidently being made for them to go into winter quarters. Five hundred would be stationed at Brunswick (which was to serve as command headquarters), with an equal number at Burlington and Trenton and smaller contingents in less important towns throughout the state. Cadwalader's news about Howe was more recent than Reed's and more reassuring: "Unless the whole is a scheme to amuse and surprise," he reported, the British general had left for New York. Wagon trains had been seen moving in the direction of Perth Amboy, which meant that the enemy was taking all surplus equipment back to Manhattan and leaving only the necessities in the New Jersey posts.

Each passing day brought the storms of winter closer, and the British command was not going to while away the hours in some godforsaken crossroads town; until spring, Howe and his retinue would be in New York. At the front the snows would come, silent and deep, making it more difficult than ever for the chain of garrisons to link hands, while within those lonely bastions hundreds of homesick soldiers could do no more than face the elements and wait and wonder if the rebels would come.

CHAPTER FIVE

1. We Have Not Slept One Night in Peace

William Howe's pronouncement that the 1776 campaign was over was the sign New York had been waiting for; with the gentlemen of the British army freed for more civilized pursuits, the social season could begin in earnest. The general's return to headquarters set off a ten-day round of parties, broken only by preparations for a brilliant series of festivities that would culminate in his reception of the red ribbon of a Knight Commander of the Bath—the honor conferred on him by a euphoric sovereign in a spur-of-the-moment gesture when he learned of the victory on Long Island. Howe's letter of thanks, via Germain, was all modesty—a seemly denial that his "humble endeavours" deserved this "unmerited goodness" —but privately he could take smug satisfaction that he was rounding out a successful year as Sir William Howe. Cornwallis—who was longing to see his wife—was given leave to sail for England on the next ship, and Major General James Grant took command of the troops in New Jersey, with instructions for garrisoning the occupied towns.

In replacing Cornwallis with James Grant, Howe was taking something of a chance, although he had no reason to suppose that the former would be needed before the army took the field again in the spring. But the troops would miss him: as Ensign George Hart said, "the whole Army love him better than all the Generals." Whereas Grant was something else again. A tub of a man, forty-six years old, with the face of a worried pig, Grant was the officer who had maintained so positively in February 1775 that Americans could not fight and that he was prepared to take 5,000 British troops and march from one end of the North American continent to the other with them. His ideas about the locals had been acquired during the French and Indian War, when he had made a thorough botch of things in approaching French-held Fort Duquesne, been ambushed, lost one third of his men, and been captured into the bargain, never realizing that what brought on that disaster was his stubborn unwillingness to listen to anyone who had had experience in wilderness fighting. It was an article of faith with Grant that all provincials were beneath contempt and not worth listening to, and this attitude had only ripened with the passing years into a violent anti-Americanism.

Grant had an eighty-mile-long chain of posts as his responsibility—a southwesterly line stretching all the way from Staten Island to Trenton and beyond: one was at Perth Amboy, one at Brunswick, another—where he established his headquarters—at Princeton, and little pockets of men were strung out like beads on a necklace along six miles of the Delaware, from Trenton down to Bordentown and Burlington. The line, as Howe had admitted, was "rather too extensive," and the distance between posts would have been an invitation to any enemy worth worrying about, but Howe was confident that he had enough strength to counter anything Washington's beaten army could throw at him. With Grant at Princeton were the light infantry, the British 2nd Brigade, and a party of light horse under Brigadier General Alexander Leslie.

This Leslie, with an outslung, belligerent jaw, was a small man who liked to wear his big hat cocked forward so that it almost covered his eyes, giving him a look of permanent aggressiveness. Leslie had seen a good deal more of the rebellion than most other Britishers, his service dating back to the period before the war began, when he had the honor—if that was the word for it—of being involved in an incident that very nearly started the fighting. In February 1775 Gage had sent him from Boston to Salem to seize several brass fieldpieces the Liberty Boys had collected, and what kept the affair from becoming the opening battle of the Revolution was some quick thinking on the part of a Salem clergyman and a willingness on Leslie's part to compromise as long as he could save face by doing so. It seems that the little party of British had gone to Salem by ship and then marched toward the town from a point about five miles distant, which gave the local people plenty of time to prepare for whatever was going to happen. They had assembled in a shipyard—militia under Timothy Pickering all mixed in with armed townsfolk who were determined to make things difficult for the redcoats—and before Leslie arrived they hoisted a drawbridge the British would have to cross in order to get into the town. When Leslie saw what was going on he demanded that the bridge be lowered into place so that he could march his men into Salem, and there was a brief scuffle during which a few of the townspeople were pricked with bayonets before a minister made his way out of the crowd and spoke to the colonel. He told the British officer that if he forced his way across the stream he was certain to be overwhelmed by all those angry people on the other side. That might be, said Leslie, but he had his orders and they included crossing that stream. Well, the minister suggested, he thought he could persuade the people to let Leslie carry out his orders on one condition: that Leslie would agree not to advance more than thirty rods beyond the bridge and then, if he found no cannon, return to Boston. Leslie thought about this, considered the odds against him, and said he would accept the terms; so he led his men across the bridge, which had been lowered, halted them thirty rods from the stream, looked around and saw no guns, turned about, and headed down the road toward their ship, his orders fulfilled and British face somewhat askew but more or less intact. Afterward, Leslie had fought on Long Island and at Harlem Heights and led several regiments at White Plains in an ill-considered attack that was thrown back with heavy losses, so he was beginning to realize that things might not proceed as smoothly as General Grant liked to say they would.

Before making his final disposition of troops, Howe had given thought to the somewhat delicate relationships that existed between British and German troops and, in order to prevent any jealousy from breaking out between them, decided to take the easy way out by letting the Germans, who had originally been on the left of his army marching into New Jersey, retain that position and occupy the posts on the left of his chain. Accordingly, they would hold the most exposed towns along the Delaware from Burlington to Trenton, immediately opposite the rebel army. These soldiers were placed under the over-all command of Colonel Carl Emil Kurt von Donop, who seems to have been one of the few German officers who regarded the American troops with anything like respect. But Donop began to have difficulties almost from the moment he established headquarters in Bordentown and took charge of the area. Howe expected him to protect the large number of loyalists in that town and in Burlington, but the colonel spoke no English, had a hard time knowing which civilians he was supposed to protect, and was not likely to be a good judge of the importance of information brought in by informers. Donop had a nasty march from Trenton to Bordentown, since roving bands of rebels had destroyed the bridges along the route and harassed his columns with rifle fire from a range at which his own men's muskets were useless, and shortly after he left the town he became aware that further problems were in the offing.

Bordentown is located at a point where the Delaware, flowing down from the northwest, makes nearly a right angle turn and runs off to the southwest toward Philadelphia. Below it the main road from Trenton made a large arc, following the general direction of the river to Burlington, while another road ran due south, passing through the towns of Rising Sun, Mansfield Square, and Black Horse, going on eventually to Slab Town and Mount Holly. Since Burlington was approximately equidistant between Trenton and Philadelphia and was only eighteen miles from the rebel capital, there was a good possibility that it would be an extremely vulnerable position, as Donop soon discovered. When he arrived on the outskirts of the town, where he intended to billet about 1,500 men, he met a delegation of citizens led by the mayor, John Lawrence (whose son James was to become a naval hero of the War of 1812), who pleaded with him to pass their town by. If he occupied it, they said, some American vessels lying offshore in the Delaware River were going to open fire on the place.

This little flotilla of galleys was commanded by Commodore Thomas Seymour, who had been stationed there by Washington on December 10, and Seymour had given the Burlington people fair warning of what would happen if the Hessians showed their faces in the village. After listening to their appeal, Donop accompanied the burghers to Mayor Lawrence's house, where they had lunch and tried to see if a meeting with Seymour could be arranged. Unfortunately, some American sailors out on the river saw Donop's personal guards strolling about the streets, came to the logical conclusion that the enemy had moved in, and before anyone could do anything about it began lobbing cannon balls into the town. Lawrence and others ran down to the river's edge and waved their hats and shouted at the seamen to stop firing, but to no avail; all afternoon the bombardment continued and a number of houses were hit before Lawrence was finally rowed out to confer with Seymour. The commodore informed the mayor firmly that he was under orders to show no mercy if the Hessians were quartered in Burlington, and when Lawrence reported back to Donop the colonel agreed to withdraw, since he had no guns large enough to match those on the ships. The result was that Donop decided to station Lieutenant Colonel Thomas Sterling's regiment—the 42nd Highlanders who had fought so well in the attack on Fort Washington—out at Black Horse, along with Block's grenadier battalion, where they would be out of range of the American fleet, while he proceeded back to Bordentown with the Linsing and Minnigerode grenadier battalions and several detachments of artillery, sending several companies of jägers to look for quarters in smaller, outlying communities. There appeared to be no other choice, although Donop didn't care for the arrangement; it dispersed his forces and put quite a few of them in places where they would be a lot closer to the Americans than they were to Grant at Princeton.

Donop's woes were far from over. Back in Bordentown he found housing facilities so inadequate that he was forced to parcel out his men a dozen or so to a farmhouse, scattering them all over the place. (A good many of the inhabitants having fled, taking blankets and bedding with them, the soldiers also had to sleep in straw on the floor.) Since he spoke or wrote no English, he had a terrible time communicating with Grant, and he was constantly badgered with reports from Rall in Trenton and from loyalists in Bordentown indicating that the rebels were planning an attack and that there was a noticeable intensification of guerrilla activity all along the riverside. On December 16 an alarm caused him to send out patrols to catch a party supposedly consisting of 300 mounted rebels (the number was magnified to 4,000 as the hours passed) and on December 22 he was informed that American troops were in Mount Holly. Donop rode down to Black Horse, where several inconclusive little skirmishes were fought that day and the next, but as far as he could tell the rebels were not out in real strength.

Donop's sector included the town of Trenton, and there Colonel Johann Gottlieb Rall was in command of three regiments of infantry—his own, and the Knyphausen and Alt von Lossberg units—plus some jägers, a detachment of artillery, and twenty dragoons from Harcourt's 16th Regiment, the whole force totalling about 1,400 men. Howe had some misgivings about assigning this post of honor to Rall, but he acquiesced on the grounds that the colonel had earned it by his courageous behavior at White Plains and Fort Washington. The obvious trouble with Rall, as Stephen Kemble had noted, was that he was noisy, unacquainted with the language, and a drunk, but what Howe did not know was that the German officer was nothing more than a battlefield slugger, and no man to put in charge of an important post. He had a professional soldier's disdain for the American amateurs he had already beaten on several occasions and his personality was such that he could serve no useful purpose in dealing with the loyalists of Trenton.

To compound their commander's inadequacies, the German troops were severely handicapped by the fact that they had come to America with a fearful reputation which their subsequent behavior had done nothing to diminish. Early in November, while the army was still in Westchester, Stephen Kemble noted in his journal that the countryside was being "unmercifully Pillaged by our Troops, Hessians in particular, no wonder if the Country People refuse to join us." The Hessians, he said, were "Outrageously Licentious, and Cruel to such a degree as to threaten with death all such as dare obstruct them in their depredations." Kemble observed distastefully that there were examples of insolence to British officers and he was deeply ashamed of that ugly incident at Fort Washington, where the Germans had stripped the captive Americans of their clothing before the British put a stop to it. According to General James Robertson, who was one of the witnesses later questioned in the House of Commons about the practice of looting, the Hessian soldiers had reputedly been told before they left Germany that they were going to a country that was rich in plunder, and it was Robertson's opinion—since few of those soldiers spoke English or could distinguish between friend and foe among the civilians they encountered—that they regarded all Americans as fair game and took from them what they wanted, following the practice they had known in European wars. Robertson assured the House that Howe had done all he could to prevent the plundering, which, quite naturally, "would lose you friends and gain you enemies," but repeated orders against it had had little effect. Robertson could further certify that he had seen, upon his arrival in the country, many well-stocked farms, but when he visited them later "found nothing alive." As a committee appointed by the Continental Congress to investigate British and Hessian atrocities reported, "The whole track of the British army is marked with desolation and a wanton destruction of property . . . and the general face of waste and devastation spread over a rich and once well-cultivated and well-inhabited country." Churches had been ransacked as outrageously as homes, people had been murdered, and there were "many instances of the most indecent treatment and actual ravishment of married and single women." On December 11 a group of American soldiers on the Pennsylvania side of the Delaware saw a number of women on the opposite shore calling for help, and when they went over in boats to assist them discovered that all the women had been abused by the enemy and that one, a girl about fifteen years old, had been raped that morning by a British officer.

Hopewell and Maidenhead were two of many New Jersey villages exposed to the wrath of the invaders; houses had been stripped of furniture, cattle and sheep driven off, families bullied about and left destitute; and when the Germans pulled out, their horses and wagons were loaded down with belongings from every household. Dr. Witherspoon and his wife fled Princeton in time to escape the British army—he on a sorrel mare, riding alongside an "old family chair" that carried Mrs. Witherspoon—but their house was left a shambles, its valuable furnishings taken off or ruined, his library of rare books ransacked, while the contents of Nassau Hall—books, scientific apparatus, and a "celebrated orrery," a planetarium reputed to be the best in the world—had disappeared. The natural effect of all this, as the British high command was acutely aware, was to magnify the existing hatred of their army beyond anything that had existed before, providing one more piece of evidence that the vacillating policy of carrot and stick was not working as the king's ministers had supposed it would.

Sir Henry Clinton, who had just seized the town of Newport, Rhode Island, learned what was going on in New Jersey and was incensed. "Unless we would refrain from plundering," he commented, "we had no business to take up winter quarters in a district we wished to preserve loyal. The Hessians introduced it." Meanwhile, New Jersey's collaborators, who were horrified by all they saw and heard, began to realize that they were not likely to fare any better than their neighbors who supported the rebel cause, since the protection the oaths of allegiance were supposed to afford them was non-existent—the papers were disregarded or ignored by redcoats and Germans alike.

While there was a good deal of understandable outrage expressed by all

those affected, it is hard to see how the British could have expected much
different from the mercenaries they had hired, considering their background. In that patchwork quilt of petty princedoms which constituted
the map of eighteenth-century Germany, there were nearly 300 separate
sovereignties along with 1,400 estates of imperial knights who held some
measure of authority over their respective subjects, and no prince was
worth his salt unless he had his own little court and army. Those who held
the whip hand were usually despots, treating the peasantry like the serfs
they were and regarding them as little more than cattle to be traded or
sold for money with which to supplement the precarious finances of the
court.

Inevitably, there were caricatures of monarchs, nobles who lorded it
over a world that seems now like the setting for comic opera had it not
been so lamentable: Prince Frederick Augustus of Anhalt-Zerbst, for example, spent the last thirty years of his life in Basle and Luxembourg and
forbade his servants—by printed order—to trouble him with the affairs of
his principality, on pain of dismissal. This was the sort of stewardship accorded a land and people already beset by famine, plague, floods, and in-
termittent warfare. Because the land of Hesse-Cassel was so poor, the
landgraves had turned to the vastly more fruitful business of dealing in
men, filling the ranks of their rental armies with poverty-stricken peasants
who had no choice but to serve. The country was divided into districts,
each of which had its quota of recruits, and no one in the lower classes
was immune from the recruiting officer nor questioned the means by
which some poor lad was led off to military servitude. When the Virginian Arthur Lee visited the court of Frederick the Great, he saw at
Potsdam the model which all these minor princes of Germany were so
eager to emulate. Frederick's regiments were in the field every day, Lee
observed, and every soldier was required to leave the ranks alone and pass
in review before several different officers, "who beat his limbs into the position they thought proper, so that the man appears to be merely a machine in the hand of a workman." Even British regulars, who were hardened to floggings administered as the result of a court-martial sentence,
cringed at the sight of the casual beatings given the rank and file by Hessian non-coms, who carried canes for that purpose. Understandably, desertion was common, but terrible punishments awaited the German civilian
who dared harbor or assist a runaway: conviction could bring loss of civil
rights, imprisonment at hard labor, and merciless floggings for this crime;

and when a soldier escaped, the town in which he had disappeared was required to furnish a substitute (one refinement of the system was that sons of the leading inhabitants were dragged off first).

The wonder of it all was that the poor devils, taken from their homes by a press gang, brutalized by officers and non-coms, and sent off to fight in a strange land for a king and cause they neither knew of nor cared about, were not a good deal worse than everyone made them out to be. The reasons for this particular war did not concern them much; about all most of them knew was that the Americans had rebelled against their king, and being dutiful folk who had been taught to respect authority of every kind, the Germans understood that this sort of transgression had to be punished. That was enough reason for them. They were, by and large, thoroughly disciplined soldiers—as Howe and other British commanders attested—and the looting of which so many Americans complained was part of a system they had been schooled to accept, in which booty taken from the enemy was part of the victor's due. Assured that America was a land of milk and honey, they saw nothing after their arrival here to alter that promise. One lieutenant said flatly that the countryside around New York was the most beautiful he had ever seen, and Captain Carl Leopold Baurmeister, the first adjutant to the Hessian commanders, noted pleasurably that Long Island resembled the Westphalian farm districts: "The houses are beautiful and are furnished in better taste than any we are accustomed to in Germany . . . everything is so clean and neat that no description can do it justice. The women are generally beautiful and delicately brought up. They dress becomingly according to the latest European fashions, wearing Indian calicoes, white cotton goods, and silk crepes. There is not a single housewife who does not have an elegant coach and pair. They drive and ride with only a negro on horseback for an escort."

Anything that appeared so alluring to a sophisticated, wealthy officer must have looked positively irresistible to the thousands of former serfs in the ranks, and they methodically proceeded to take whatever they could lay their hands on. And it followed quite naturally that British regulars, seeing the Hessians looting, saw no reason not to go and do likewise, which bothered the more doctrinaire military men like Clinton, who regarded such behavior as highly improper among Englishmen. The consequence, an American perceived, was that "the Hessian and British troops disagree and are kept entirely separate. The latter do not like the former's being allowed to plunder while they are prohibited from doing it. Those rascals plunder all indiscriminately; if they see anything they like, they say, 'Rebel, good for Hesse-mans,' and seize it for their own use. They have no idea of the distinctions of Whig and Tory."

In making off with everything from jewels to furniture to forage, the Germans were doing what came naturally to them as soldiers, and being well-drilled, skillful fighting men as well, they regarded war as the business of killing, without many of the niceties. What they had seen on Long Island made them contemptuous of the undisciplined amateurs Washington put into the field. Colonel von Heeringen, who fought there, told of rebel riflemen "spitted to the trees with bayonets," and said that "These frightful people deserve pity rather than fear. It always takes them a quarter of an hour to load, and meantime they feel our balls and bayonets." Not only were the enlisted men cowardly, Heeringen observed, but colonels and other field-grade officers lay down their arms with whole troops of men, and on one occasion he saw a group of sixty rebels, bearing a red damask flag with the motto "Liberty" stitched onto it, surrender to Rall. "They had all shouldered their guns upside down, and had their hats under their arms. They fell on their knees and begged piteously for their lives."

Given the Hessians' reputation, it was understandable why Donop and other German commanders in the forward area were experiencing difficulties quite beyond anything they might have anticipated. In what was increasingly a guerrilla war, the residue of fear and hatred for these mustachioed, ferocious-looking foreigners in their bizarre uniforms was bound to erupt in various ways. So when Rall's German regiments marched into Trenton to take up quarters there—colorful banners flapping in the wind and big brass kettledrums rolling out a deep, steady cadence like the knell of doomsday—there had been no rejoicing by those who had remained in town, whether they were British sympathizers or not. Rall's situation was made no easier by the rising hostility of the populace, but at least his troops were fairly comfortably fixed by comparison with Donop's and he was able to billet all of them within the village limits.

Trenton was a prosperous little town at the head of navigation on the Delaware and it had about a hundred houses—many deserted by their owners—and a two-story stone barracks that had been erected in 1758 for the use of itinerant militia companies during the French and Indian War. Originally designed to hold about 300 men, the building could accommodate half again that many in a pinch, and some of Rall's troops shared it with a number of Tory refugees who had come in from the country seeking British protection. All things considered, the village was a good place to be: it commanded the upper reaches of the Delaware and it lay astride four principal highways, which formed a shape rather like a three-pronged pitchfork, with the handle at the bottom. From the northwest came River Road, meandering through low ground behind the numerous ferry landings along the Delaware to carry traffic to the town's busy marketplace and mills. Out of the north a thoroughfare from Pennington led into the junction of King and Queen Streets, the two main roads in the village. The Princeton Road headed northwest from Trenton via Maidenhead, Princeton, and across the Raritan River, while the Bordentown Road—which formed the handle of the pitchfork—was a continuation of Queen Street, which crossed Assunpink Creek at the southern edge of town, passed the Blazing Star Ferry road, and swung off in an easy, curving arc toward Bordentown. Trenton, in short, was an important road junction in that tenuous line of posts Howe had established across the flat plains of New Jersey, but there was a growing sense of uneasiness within the garrison that Johann Rall might not be the man to defend it.

He had the bully's contempt for the man he has already licked in a fight and when someone suggested that he fortify the town against possible attack he exploded: there would be no earthworks while he was in charge, and if the Americans came, the men would go at them with the bayonet. Junior officers complained that he seldom consulted them, that he almost never visited the picket lines to see what was going on, that he was cavalier about requests for warm clothing from the men. And they were sick to death of his endless preoccupation with useless drill and inspections; every day the guard and the cannon, led by the band, marched around the churchyard "like a Catholic procession," Lieutenant Andreas Wiederhold wrote, "wanting only the cross and the banner and chanting choristers to lead." Evidently Rall liked music inordinately, for he followed the parade every day just to listen to the band play. "The cannon," Wiederhold went on, "instead of being out at the head of the streets where they could be of use, were in front of his quarters and two of them had to be paraded to the lower part of the town every morning and back again so as to make all the display possible." The worst of it was that Rall was a carouser; he stayed up till all hours of the night, slept until nine in the morning, and when the guard arrived at ten to parade in front of his quarters they often had to wait half an hour in the cold while he finished his bath.

As Christmas approached, Tories drifted into the town with reports that the enemy was planning something. Several American deserters said that cooked rations were being prepared for the rebel army across the river, indicating that a movement of some sort was in the wind, but Rall dismissed this as idle, old woman's talk. Yet there was another side to the colonel which, with that thick layer of bluster and braggadocio, he concealed from his officers and men. As his letters to Grant and Donop reveal, he was becoming almost pathologically nervous about those continuing flurries of. activity along the perimeter of his sector and he was reacting to them about the way a man would who was standing on a little piece of dry land surrounded by water, seeing the waves come a little closer each day, licking at the ground, eating away a piece here and a piece there until soon there would be no safe place left. On December 18 a party of rebels made a landing upriver from Trenton, killing one of the light dragoons; two days later on the road to Maidenhead three men from the Alt von Lossberg Regiment were captured, a patrol four miles from Trenton was fired on by a party of 150 men, and Rall nervously told Donop that "my right wing is too much exposed," while requesting that Grant post some troops at Maidenhead to keep his line of communications open. Grant informed Donop waspishly that he had had three letters in one day from Rall and expressed annoyance over the colonel's display of timidity in sending a hundred men and a cannon to convoy a dispatch from Trenton to Princeton. As the British general remarked sarcastically to Rall, the latter could take heart from the fact that the entire rebel army in Pennsylvania—which now included Lee's and Gates's corps—"does not exceed eight thousand men who have neither shoes nor stockings, are in fact almost naked, dying of cold, without blankets and very ill supplied with Provisions. On this Side the Delaware they have not three hundred men. These stroll about in small parties, under the command of subaltern officers none of them above the rank of Captain, and their principal object is to pick up some of our Light Dragoons."

All of which was cold comfort for Rall, sitting there in the exposed outpost of Trenton nervously eying the ominous flickers of action that were bursting out all around him, and on December 21 he advised Donop that he was "liable to be attacked at any moment." Curiously, however, he had not constructed redoubts or other fortifications—an omission he blamed on the unremitting pressure of the enemy, which was "before me, behind me and at my right flank." Other Hessian officers were beginning to share his fears. One of them recorded in his diary the incidents that involved action with the enemy and by Christmas it read, in the aggregate, like an account of constant guerrilla warfare—rebels crossing the river here, then there, an English trooper badly wounded one day, another killed the next, two Highlanders and a Hessian grenadier wounded the day after that. "We have not slept one night in peace since we came to this place," the entry for Christmas Eve read. "The troops have lain on their arms every night, but they can endure it no longer." Yet the author of the journal wondered if these fears about the rebels were not exaggerated; he couldn't believe that an army in their condition could put up any dangerous resistance. "That men who will not fight without some defense for them, who have neither coat, shoe nor stocking, nor scarce anything else to cover their bodies, and who for a long time past have not received one farthing of pay, should dare to attack regular troops in the open country, which they could not withstand when they were posted amongst rocks and in the strongest intrenchments, is not to be supposed."

Christmas Eve was cold and in the houses men drew closer to the fire, while the sentries outside stamped their feet and hugged themselves against the piercing wind. Late that evening General James Grant received a visitor, a Tory who had brought him news before and whose intelligence he had come to rely on, and at 11:30, after talking with the man, he sent off a dispatch to Rall. Washington, he had been told, had held a council of war on December 22 at which the British weakness at Trenton and Princeton was described and plans for possible offensive action discussed. Although the information was almost certainly accurate, Grant said, he very much doubted if an attack would be attempted; nevertheless, it would be well for Rall to be on his guard, just in case. When Rall received the general's letter he had already been out for much of the day on horseback with some light dragoons and two patrols of a hundred men each, and they had separated and taken two different roads toward Pennington to see if there was any enemy activity in that direction. At one ferry landing they chased about thirty rebels back to their boats, wounded several of them, and then retired to Trenton when the American artillery opened fire from the opposite bank. When Grant's letter came in, Major Friedrich von Dechow of the Knyphausen Regiment urged Rall to send away the Hessians' supplies and spare equipment, which would be highly vulnerable in the event of an attack, but Rall, for reasons of his own, was no longer nervous about the situation; like Grant, he did not think the rebels would try anything.

There was snow on the ground in Trenton on Christmas morning, but as a cheerless sun came up the temperature rose to a point just above freezing. By noon the Delaware River was full of floating cakes of ice, which had broken up in the little tributaries and along the river's edge during the relatively warm days earlier, and they were floating past the town, bound for the sea. From Grant, Rall got word that Lord Stirling and some rebels had been seen in the area, but again the colonel was not overly alarmed. He rode out along the outskirts of town and talked with the sentries there and in the late afternoon returned to headquarters on King Street, where he sat down to a game of checkers with his host, Stacy Potts, who owned a tannery and an ironworks in Trenton. They were still playing about seven o'clock when the sound of firing was heard—first a volley, then a few scattered shots, then silence—and Rall got up from the table at once to find out what was happening.

His own outfit was the duty regiment, which meant that the men were standing by ready for action (the orders were that men in the regiment of the day could unbutton their leggings and remove cartridge belts, but otherwise they had to be fully dressed), and Rall marched them to the intersection of the Pennington and Princeton roads at the head of town and learned that some two or three score rebels had attacked the guards stationed on the Pennington Road, wounding half a dozen of the Lossberg men, and then had vanished into the darkness toward Johnson's Ferry, as McKonkey's Ferry was called on the New Jersey side. While other Hessian regiments fell in outside their quarters, Rall sent a patrol up the Pennington Road after the rebels, but they brought back word that they had gone two miles without seeing a sign of the enemy. Rall was in the process of ordering all the men back to their billets when Dechow came up and urged him to send patrols out on all the roads, as far as the ferry landings beyond the town, but Rall said there was no need of that—it could be done the next morning, and anyway, what had appeared to be an attack was probably no more than a gang of farmers trying to stir up some trouble. The major wasn't happy with this decision, so he took care, before retiring for the night, to see that a sentinel was posted outside each house occupied by the men in his regiment and left orders that the troops should stay inside, ready for anything that might happen. Dechow had the duty the next morning and he planned to have his patrols keep an extra sharp lookout. Rall's adjutant, Lieutenant Jacob Piel, saw the colonel about ten o'clock and was told that there were no special orders for the night. The Hessians returned to their quarters to sing and drink and look at the evergreen trees they had cut and brought indoors to remind them of Christmas at home, while Rall went off to the home of Abraham Hunt, where a party was going on.

Hunt was somewhat of an oddity in the town where he served as postmaster and had acquired considerable wealth as a merchant. Somehow or other he had managed to straddle the political fence so adroitly that neither the rebels nor the British ever quite decided which side he was on, and the result was that he fraternized rather freely with men of both persuasions. There is no indication that he requested protection from the British during the war, yet they left his house and goods alone as long as they were in the vicinity, and afterward, when the Americans took over Trenton, his property was not confiscated as it would have been had he been known as a loyalist, and he held his office as postmaster for years under the national government. What was even more perplexing was that Hunt held a commission during the war as a lieutenant colonel in a rebel militia regiment commanded by Isaac Smith, and none of the records show that he was anything but a satisfactory officer on those occasions when his outfit was on active duty. On the surface, at least, Hunt was one of those friendly, gregarious souls whose house was open to friends, no matter what their politics—a place where good company and hospitality were always available. There is no reason to believe that Hunt was doing anything more than acting the genial host on Christmas night in 1776, but on the other hand, given his close contact with the New Jersey militia, his insight into the situation around Trenton, and his probable knowledge that something important was shaping up in the American camps across the Delaware, there is some cause for suspecting that Abraham Hunt had an ulterior motive in seeing that Johann Rall whiled away the long night hours playing cards and drinking.

Late that night there was a knock on the door of Hunt's house and a Negro servant answered it to find a Tory farmer standing outside in the cold; the man said he had come across the river from Bucks County with a message for Colonel Rall. Whether on Hunt's instructions or not, the servant told the man that Rall was busy with friends and could not be disturbed, so the farmer scribbled a few lines on a scrap of paper, gave it to the servant, and walked off into the night, doubtless feeling that he had done his bit as a loyal subject. The Negro made his way into the room where the card game was going on, slipped the note to the Hessian colonel, and went away. But Rall, without glancing at it, stuck the paper into one of his vest pockets, picked up his cards, and went on with the game.

2. The Snow Was Tinged with Blood

Johann Rall's relative peace of mind in the face of Grant's warning has been attributed to a curious incident that is almost impossible to document except through the testimony of several people who claimed to know something about the circumstances and revealed them many years after the event. According to these accounts, a Scotch-Irish cattle dealer who plied his trade in and around Trenton and was a familiar figure there came to Rall's headquarters a day or so earlier with a story of how he had been captured by the rebels and had seen with his own eyes the pitiable state of their camps before making his escape. No one who had witnessed these deplorable conditions, he said convincingly, could imagine that there was the slightest danger of an attack, and since the cattleman's tale was partially corroborated by Hessian pickets who had picked the fellow up, half frozen from a drenching he got in the Delaware River after eluding the Americans, it was good enough for Rall. What Rall did not know, however, was that he had been told only part of what was a very strange story.

Out on the deserted, uncertain fringe of war, just beyond the armies' lines in countryside too perilous for all but the foolhardy or fearless to visit, life of a sort went on, but since anyone found there was presumed to be on questionable business, not many risked being seen during daylight hours. It was mostly at night that individuals hurried along the obscure byways on their mysterious errands, but in the afternoon of December 22 two American horsemen posted as lookouts on the New Jersey side of the Delaware, across from the rebel camps, heard a sharp cracking sound and were surprised to see what looked like a farmer with a coil of rope in one hand and a long whip in the other, walking across the fields beyond them.

Crossing the frozen, crusty snow, he moved toward a fence where a cow stood, and as he approached the animal she ran and he went after her, shouting and cracking his whip. The cavalrymen leaped on their horses and ran him down, whereupon the fellow slashed at them with his whip and turned to flee when one of the horsemen jumped on his back and threw him to the ground. Before the other rider could dismount the farmer shook loose, ran, slipped on the ice, and fell again. This time the cavalrymen held onto him, trussed him up with his own rope, took him across the river with a pistol at his head, and led him to Washington's headquarters. Then a very odd thing happened. The general thanked the two troopers for their work, asked all of his staff members to leave the room, and after telling the sentries outside that they were to shoot the fellow if he tried to escape, said that the farmer was to be left alone with him.

To the bewilderment of everyone, Washington closed the door and remained closeted with the captive for half an hour before emerging and turning him over to the guards, with orders to lock him up. And that, apparently, was that. Except that after dark some hay that was piled near the guardhouse somehow caught fire and the sentry dashed over to help put it out. When he returned to his post he discovered to his dismay that the door of the guardhouse had been mysteriously unlocked and the prisoner was gone; he set up a yell, roused some other sentries, and someone caught sight of a figure running off through the woods and fired at him, but the fugitive made it safely to the river, crossed as far as he could on the ice, and then waded the rest of the way to the New Jersey shore, where he was picked up by Rall's pickets on the River Road. The next morning when Washington was told that the prisoner had gotten away during the night he was said to be furious about it, but he seemed strangely preoccupied when Dr. Benjamin Rush paid a call on him a little later. While Rush talked, the general kept writing words on scraps of paper, one of which fell to the floor; Rush bent over to pick it up, glanced at it, and saw that it bore the words *Victory or Death.*

Although no one else in the army knew it, Washington had first met the purported cattle dealer in Philadelphia, just after he was named commander in chief of the army. The man's name was John Honeyman and he had taken up the weaving trade after serving involuntarily in the British army during the French and Indian War, where he had been assigned for a time as bodyguard to General James Wolfe. Honeyman didn't like the British and he wanted to do something about it now that there was fighting going on, and what he had in mind, he told Washington, was to serve as a spy. So the two men worked out a plan whereby Honeyman would pose as a cattle dealer and butcher, at which he had had some experience, while collecting information that might be useful to the American army. Whenever he learned something of special importance he was to arrange to be captured, doing it in such a way that his real business would not be discovered, after which his escape would be arranged. Apart from Washington, the only person privy to this secret was Honeyman's wife, an Irish girl with whom he lived in Griggstown, near Princeton, with their four children.

Throughout the war years, Washington maintained a remarkably effective secret service, and one reason for its success was his insistence that "the persons employed must bear the suspicion of being thought inimical." If they were captured by Americans, in other words, it would not be possible for them to declare their innocence, since that would destroy the whole fabric of their double life. So Honeyman himself while posing as a loyalist would have no protection—but for the sake of his family's well-being Washington gave him a letter stating that "the wife and children of John Honeyman, the notorious Tory, now within the British lines, and probably acting the part of a spy," were to be spared from harm. (Throughout the war, John Honeyman plied his precarious trade, despised by his Whig neighbors, indicted several times for high treason and for aiding the enemy, and on at least one occasion his wife had to resort to using the paper signed by George Washington to save their home from a mob of irate citizens who threatened to burn it unless her husband came out. Honeyman was a taciturn man who kept his own counsel, and so far as is known he received no reward for his efforts until 1783, after the war had ended; his daughter Jane remembered as long as she lived the day a party of mounted officers came up the road and stopped in front of their house while General George Washington walked up to the porch, extended his hand to John Honeyman, and thanked him warmly for his services to his country.)

What Honeyman undoubtedly gave Washington, during their whispered conversation behind the closed door of the Keith house, near the Delaware, was a detailed description of the situation in Trenton, including Rall's troop dispositions, and the vital information that no boats were being built nor fortifications erected. Almost equally important, after he was permitted to escape he planted with Colonel Rall the word that Washington wished him to have—that the American army was in no condition whatever to launch an attack. So, in the sense that the rebels were planning an attack and the British, through their own informers, knew it, it might be said to be a standoff. But not quite. For the British— or Rall, at least—were inclined to pooh-pooh the possibility and furthermore, they did not know where or when it would occur. Which meant that Washington, for the first time in months, had an opportunity to seize the initiative if only he could find the means to do so with the remnants of his little army.

For a week or more the general had been turning the idea over in his mind and had thrown out a few hints here and there that something was brewing. To Governor Trumbull of Connecticut he wrote that the British were settling down in their scattered posts, lulled into a sense of security by the approach of winter and the impending collapse of the rebel army, which virtually invited the possibility of making some stroke, a "lucky Blow" which would be "fatal to them, and would most certainly raise the Spirits of the People, which are quite sunk by our late misfortunes." He would bide his time until Lee's and Gates's men came in, he said, and then see what might be done; but that was as far as he would commit himself. Meantime, he had taken precautions to see that the likeliest crossing places on the Delaware were watched day and night, for he was still fearful that Howe might move against Philadelphia if the river froze solid (he had just received an intercepted letter indicating that this was indeed Howe's intent). Until and unless the ice formed, however, the Americans possessed the only boats on the river, and as long as the weather held they could cross while the British could not.

While waiting for reinforcements, Washington had arranged his army in three divisions along the west bank of the Delaware. From Coryell's Ferry at the north to Trenton Ferry to Dunk's Ferry at the south, the river follows a course that looks on a map like the pointed end of an arrow aimed at Bordentown. At the northwestern or upper end of the arrowhead, camped along the riverbank between Coryell's and McKonkey's ferry landings, was the main force, consisting of most of the veterans of the New Jersey retreat—the brigades of Generals Stirling, Stephen, and Mercer, along with a battalion of Germans recruited during the past few weeks in Pennsylvania and Maryland under the command of Colonel Nicholas Hausegger. Gates had come in with about 600 rank and file, but those "5000 good troops in spirits" that Lee had said he had turned out to be no more than 2,000, and most of the brigadiers now under Sullivan were either sick or absent. On December 22 this body of men was augmented by the arrival of units led by Colonel John Glover, Colonel Paul Sargent, and Brigadier General Arthur St. Clair. Below them, at Trenton Ferry, Brigadier General James Ewing commanded a contingent of Pennsylvania and New Jersey militiamen that was sprawled out between Yardley's Ferry and the area opposite Bordentown. And at the southwestern extremity of the arrowhead was Colonel John Cadwalader, senior officer of the Pennsylvania Associators, whose 1,800-man command included a number of fresh, newly equipped militiamen from Philadelphia and some very weary New Englanders under Colonel Daniel Hitchcock.

Although the regular army's return of December 22 showed more than 11,000 officers and men, what the paper did not fully indicate was their condition of readiness. Nearly half were sick, wounded, or elsewhere on duty, leaving only about 6,000 effectives on hand, to which could be added about 1,400 of the Pennsylvania and New Jersey militia. It was an odd assortment, this lot of men from various parts of the land who had been thrown together in a venture that would determine the new nation's survival. About the only ones who could be said to be in a state of real fitness were the Philadelphians, recently recruited and well turned ·out and happily operating fairly close to home, but it remained to be seen how these green troops would stand up in their first battle. Hitchcock's brigade at Bristol had almost no camp equipment, blankets, or stores of any kind, and neither did the militiamen around Trenton Ferry, who had been sent off in expectations that they would serve only for a few weeks before returning to their homes. As for the Continentals, there was little to be said beyond the fact that they had survived the long retreat across New Jersey somehow or other and were almost totally without clothing or equipment of any sort; just now their supply officers were combing the countryside in search of old clothing and blankets to keep them warm.

There was also—in addition to this force, but by no means part of it—a small command of about 600 militiamen and volunteers that had been stitched together somewhat impromptu under Colonel Samuel Griffin. Israel Putnam, in Philadelphia, had come up with the idea of sending this outfit across the river into southern New Jersey, below the furthest Hessian outpost, to see if it couldn't divert the enemy's attention from what was likely to be the main effort around Trenton. Although Griffin was taken sick almost as soon as he got into the field, leaving the miniature army leaderless and almost totally ineffectual, the presence of this minor expeditionary force down in Moorestown did succeed in drawing Donop's attention for several important days; he took about 2,000 Hessians to Mount Holly and threw Griffin's militiamen into a panic, but instead of returning at once to Bordentown, Donop remained there in the boondocks beyond Burlington for two more days, eighteen miles from Rall in Trenton.

Joseph Reed had gone down to Burlington at Washington's request to see if he could enter into negotiations with Donop to save the town of Burlington—this being an ironic twist, since the only reason the place would be destroyed was by Washington's orders to Commodore Seymour, whose flotilla of gondolas was still sitting out in the river ready to open fire if the Hessians entered the place. A meeting between Reed and Donop was arranged, however, Donop agreeing to sit down and talk with Washington's aide at noon on the twenty-fifth of December at John Antrim's house midway between Mount Holly and Burlington. But Reed was not there when Donop's letter of acceptance arrived in Bristol; he had gone to Philadelphia to see what Israel Putnam could contribute in the way of support for Washington (Putnam, unhappily, had no troops to send), and then Reed had ridden hard for Washington's headquarters, arriving there on Christmas afternoon. Before that, however, Reed had written a long letter to the commander in chief from Bristol, describing the situation as he saw it and making some strong recommendations as to the course of action that might be taken. He already knew that Washington had something up his sleeve, but his seeming reluctance to make a move disturbed Reed. Something, he pleaded, "must be attempted to revive our expiring credit, give our cause some degree of reputation, and prevent a total depreciation of the Continental money." Putting it bluntly, he went on to suggest that "even a failure cannot be more fatal, than to remain in our present situation," with the Continental army about to vanish and the newly recruited militiamen sure to lose heart. Wouldn't it be possible, he asked, to "make a diversion, or something more, at or about Trenton?" As things stood now, Reed added, the cause was desperate and hopeless: "Our affairs are hastening fast to ruin if we do not retrieve them by some happy event. Delay with us is now equal to a total defeat." Having said all this, he remembered his place and asked the general's pardon, laying his outburst of emotion to "the love of my country, a wife and four children in the enemy's hands, the respect and attachment I have to you, the ruin and poverty that must attend me, and thousands of others [who] will plead my excuse for so much freedom."

What Reed did not know until he arrived at headquarters was that Washington had made his plans and would act on them that afternoon. Once Honeyman had briefed him on the situation in Trenton, he was ready to move, and precious little time was left; as he had informed John Hancock on December 20, "ten days more will put an end to the existence of our army."

Orders had gone to Commodore Seymour down on the river to bring his odd assortment of vessels upstream as far as Bordentown, and under cover of a fierce snowstorm on December 23 they got under way and tied up along the stretch of water between Bordentown and Burlington. On Christmas Eve Washington and a group of officers rode over to Greene's headquarters to have supper, and after the meal Greene asked the Samuel Merrick family, in whose house he was staying, to leave. Seated around the table, the commanders had their final council of war to work out the details of a plan they had been discussing for the past several days: Sullivan, Mercer, Stirling, Knox, and several other officers were there, and the group included one civilian—a minister named Alexander MacWhorter, of the Presbyterian Church of Newark, who had remained with the army on its retreat through New Jersey. In its essentials, the scheme was this: the attack would be made on Rall's garrison at Trenton after the army had crossed the Delaware at three separate points. Cadwalader would attend to the Hessian outposts at Mount Holly, Black Horse, and Bordentown; Ewing, crossing at Trenton Ferry, would hold a position on the lower side of Assunpink Creek to close off Rall's escape route and prevent Donop from reinforcing him; and Washington, with the Continentals—about 2,400 men—would cross at McKonkey's Ferry, march against Trenton, and then push on toward Princeton and Brunswick. All the men at the table knew the importance of the Christmas festival to the Germans, so the attack was planned for Christmas night, when the effects of the traditional feasting, drinking, and revelry might put the enemy off guard.

Early on Christmas morning detailed orders were issued. Each brigade, accompanied by two guides, had a specific mission: Stephen's party would form the advance and would attack the enemy's pickets and guards in the town, set fire to any buildings where there was resistance, and carry off or spike the Hessian cannon; Nathanael Greene would command what was called the second division, or left wing, with Mercer and Stirling accompanying him on the march to Trenton by way of Scotch Road, which joined the Pennington Road just above the town; and the first division, or right wing of the army, under John Sullivan, would include St. Clair's, Glover's, and Sargent's brigades and would travel by the River Road. Knox, in charge of the artillery, would see that four pieces were at the head of each column, three guns in the center, and two with each reserve outfit. During the afternoon the troops were to be paraded a mile back of McKonkey's Ferry and as soon as night began to fall they would march to the ferry and begin embarking in the boats under the direction of Knox.

There followed a number of explicit directions concerning the order of embarkation, an assignment to the French General Fermoy to secure the roads between Trenton and Princeton, orders for a troop of forty cavalrymen under Captains William Washington and John Flahaven to fan out in front of the infantry and seize the road junctions outside Trenton, and arrangements for a detail to form a chain around the landing place to keep out unauthorized persons. Each man in the army was to carry a blanket, cooked rations for three days, and forty rounds of ammunition, and they were given a final word of caution: "A profound silence to be enjoined, and no man to quit his ranks on the pain of death."

It was all very carefully thought out except for one crucial element—the weather. During the night of December 19 and into the morning hours of the next day, heavy snow had fallen continuously, piling up slowly on the flatlands and drifting into ravines and gulleys along the river, lying heavily on the branches of trees. Then there had been a partial thaw, followed by two days of extreme cold when the Delaware began to freeze. Off in the distance snow clouds were beginning to pile up ominously, and the wind had shifted around to the northeast—the promise of a storm. How solidly the river might freeze was anyone's guess, but if the ice was too thick it would make it impossible for the boats to move, while if it was too thin it could not support the weight of men and horses and cannon. So for all of Washington's careful calculations, he was going to be at the mercy of nature. Nor was that the end of it. His plan meant that three widely separated bodies of men, most of them poorly trained and lacking the experience and discipline required for a maneuver of this sort, would cross a wide river choked with ice, in the dead of winter and in darkness, and move in such careful co-ordination that each element would reach its destination at the right moment—not too soon, not too late—in order to achieve a surprise attack on an army of seasoned professionals. It was tempting fate and Washington knew it, and his willingness to proceed with the complicated plan indicated how desperate his situation was. If the amphibious movement succeeded there would be bloody work at the end of the march, and he sent an express rider to Bethlehem, Pennsylvania, to request Dr. Shippen and his assistants at the hospital there to join him as soon as possible. To make the task of co-ordination as near perfect as might be, he ordered all the officers to set their watches by his own, wished them luck, and said good-night.

For the past ten days three New Jersey militia officers had been scouring the upper Delaware and Lehigh rivers for more boats and hiding what they collected behind the thickly wooded banks where the others had already been concealed. Captain Daniel Bray and another man located twenty-five assorted craft during this period, and all of the boats were now assembled upstream from McKonkey's Ferry, waiting for the operation to start. Although the thought may not have crossed Washington's mind, he could thank the discovery of iron ore in Bucks County for one of the most important assets at his disposal. Near Riegelsville the Durham Iron Works had been established in 1727, and about 1750 the rivermen had begun building a special type of boat named for the little company. These were employed to haul loads of ore and pig iron down across the rapids of the Delaware River to Philadelphia. The big, black Durham boats ranged in length from forty to sixty feet and were shaped much like a canoe, with two blunt, slightly pointed ends. Loaded with ore, grain, whiskey, and produce from upcountry, they coasted downstream on the current, manned by half a dozen men, then disgorged their cargo in Philadelphia and loaded up again with manufactured goods, and were poled back up the river. The steering sweep, manned by the captain, could be fixed to either end of the boats, and two men with setting poles walked up and down each side, pushing the boat forward its full length, then going forward to repeat the operation. For Washington's purposes the beauty of these open boats was that they had an eight-foot beam and a very shallow draft; empty, they drew only five inches, and when loaded with fifteen tons, only thirty inches, which meant that they could haul a large number of men and heavy equipment across the shallow river.

There was neither time nor opportunity that Christmas Day for celebration on the west bank of the Delaware, but over in Trenton the Hessians were observing the festival, and off in the Highlands, in the area around Ramapo and Closter, the Americans under George Clinton forgot the war for a few hours; night scouting parties were cancelled and, as one soldier recorded in his journal, "The evening ensued with delightful sports, full flowing bowls and jolly souls, spirits elevated with liquor and hearts enflamed by the beauty of woman." All that Washington's men had to elevate their spirits were the words of Tom Paine's *Crisis*, which had been published a few days earlier in Philadelphia and which Washington ordered read to them while they stood quietly in the cold, waiting to move down to McKonkey's landing. About two o'clock in the afternoon the first units got underway and an hour later the entire army was marching toward the river. Watching them pass by, the commander observed again how many were barefoot and clad only in rags, and Major James Wilkinson, who had been with Lee when he was captured, remembered ever after that their route to the river, covered with snow, was "tinged here and there with blood from the feet of the men who wore broken shoes."

At the water's edge, William McKonkey's graceful, three-story stone house sat beside the ferry landing, and here the troops lined up patiently, quietly awaiting their turn to board the boats. Looking across the stream they could barely make out the shadowy, tree-lined bank on the other side; there the land rose more sharply from the river than on the side where they stood, and the River Road ran along about seventy-five or a hundred feet above water level. In front of them ice covered the gradual slope of the riverbank where the boats were drawn up in ranks, and off to the left, about 150 yards from McKonkey's house, a long, narrow finger of land ran parallel to the shore, sheltering the embarkation point in its lee from the wind and current sweeping down the river. The Delaware had been virtually free of ice floes on Monday and Tuesday, but on Wednesday the twenty-fifth, just before noon, the water began to fill with huge cakes of floating ice that had broken up farther north and were drifting ominously downstream on the swift current, interrupted only here and there by patches of black, open water. Washington rode down to the shoreline and while he waited there, watching the boats, James Wilkinson came up with a message.

"What a time this is to hand me letters!" the general remarked, to which Wilkinson replied that General Gates had instructed him to deliver a message.

"General Gates?" Washington asked, "Where is he?"

"I left him this morning in Philadelphia," the major said.

"What was he doing there?"

"I understood that he was on his way to Congress."

"On his way to Congress!" Washington exclaimed, wondering what in the world the man could possibly be doing that was more important than this night's work. With Lee gone and Gates and Putnam in Philadelphia, it meant that his senior officers were Hugh Mercer and Stirling, both in their early fifties, while nearly every other officer was young, relatively inexperienced and largely untried. Nathanael Greene once remarked that officers are the soul of an army, but at this precarious moment, after more than a year and a half of war, Washington still had not much way of knowing how many of these young fellows had the stuff to provide that soul. Some, like Greene, Stirling, and Knox, he had been able to observe personally, but most of the junior officers remained an unknown quantity and there was a very real question whether he could count on them or not. Henry Knox, who gave considerable thought to the problems of command, appreciated the dilemma; he realized that Washington, for all his abilities, could neither do everything nor be everywhere at once, but he also knew that the "most radical difficulty" in the army continued to be the lack of good officers. The trouble with most of them was that they were "a parcel of ignorant stupid men, who might make tolerable soldiers but who are very bad officers," and until Congress established some sort of academy for teaching them the art of war, the army would continue to be "a receptacle for ragamuffins." And Knox, for one, was not eager to risk his life and reputation on "so cobweb a foundation." *

All things considered, however, and despite the concern Washington and Knox felt, the crowd of men standing there on the bank of the Delaware River included an extraordinary array of talent. Several of them— like the twenty-six-year-old Knox himself, the young artillery Captain Alexander Hamilton, and a quiet, eighteen-year-old lieutenant from Virginia named James Monroe—would serve the country in other ways once the war was over. Others had that special aptitude for leading men in battle—men like Greene, who would turn out to be the best field commander the Americans had, after Washington; the cavalryman William Washington; Edward Hand, who led the Pennsylvania riflemen; Delaware's John Haslet; ornery John Stark of New Hampshire; a stubborn Pennsylvania artillery officer named Joseph Moulder; and Colonel John Glover—all of whom were, when the chips were down, capable of delivering the best any general could demand.

Glover just now was being asked to rise to the occasion as he had several times before and perform some kind of minor miracle. He was a fine-looking man with a high forehead, outthrust jaw, and the clear, deep-set blue eyes of one who had spent years at sea. A Marbleheader, Glover had been a successful merchant and shipowner before the war, and in June, 1775 he had recruited ten companies of men—mostly fishermen and sail-

---

* Not all of Knox's peers regarded him as an expert artilleryman, but there was no doubting his administrative ability or the esteem in which he was held by most other officers and his own soldiers. And certainly the American artillery, despite limitations of resources and experienced men, improved steadily with each battle until the triumph at Yorktown. After the fighting was over, Knox's wartime estimate of his fellow officers tended to soften in a haze of nostalgic camaraderie, and he was instrumental in founding the Society of the Cincinnati (to which numerous republicans took exception, since it was an exclusive military order and a hereditary one, at that). To him also goes much of the credit for the idea of establishing a national military academy, and he served in Washington's cabinet as the first United States secretary of war. There was a streak of pomposity in Knox, his wife Lucy enjoyed playing the "lively and meddlesome . . . leader of society," and this post satisfied their longing for social position and their aptitude for high living (Knox's salary was £980 in 1790, his expenses over £1,300). In 1794 he retired to their "palace in the woods," as a contemporary called the estate Lucy had inherited in Maine, where he lived in something resembling baronial splendor, speculated in land, and died in 1806 at the age of fifty-six after swallowing a chicken bone.

ors from his home town—and been named colonel of the Continental Army's 23rd Regiment. Back in August of 1776, when Washington's army was hemmed in on Brooklyn Heights after the disaster on Long Island, there was only the shadowiest glimmer of hope of saving the troops and Washington leaped at it: ordering every available boat to be brought to the Manhattan side of the East River, he summoned John Glover and his Marblehead regiment and Israel Hutchinson's Salem command to man the boats and ferry his men to safety under cover of nightfall and the rain and fog that obscured their activities from the British.

Through the hours of darkness the Massachusetts seamen rowed and sailed silently back and forth across the treacherous tidal river within earshot of the enemy, and by daybreak had rescued 9,500 men, with all their horses, baggage, cannon, equipment, and provisions; the only soldiers to fall into Howe's hands were three stragglers who had remained behind to plunder. Six weeks later, when a picked force of Hessians and British regulars came ashore at Pell's Point to strike inland and cut off the American army from the mainland at Westchester, it was Glover again who saved the day. Washington had sent him with four Massachusetts regiments to hold off the enemy while he hastily evacuated his Harlem lines, and Glover did his job superbly. When he first saw the size of the force he was supposed to stop (he counted more than 200 sail out in the waters of the Sound), he admitted that he "would have given a thousand worlds to have had General Lee, or some other experienced officer present, to direct, or at least to approve of what I had done." But there was something of the terrier about the tough, stocky Marblehead colonel, in addition to which he possessed courage and a lot of common sense. "I did the best I could," he reported later, "and disposed of my little party to the best of my judgment." By which he meant that against 4,000 troops—nearly five times his own number—he held out all day, firing and falling back, forcing the British to retreat several times and gaining a three-day respite for Washington, who was altering his entire front from south to east and occupying a position that stretched across eighteen miles from the King's Bridge to White Plains. By the time Howe's troops advanced gingerly to New Rochelle, the rebels were no longer in the same danger of being trapped; while Glover's brigade screened their march, Washington's long, straggling column had fallen back to White Plains.

Now Washington was turning once more to Glover and his seamen to man the boats that would get his army across the river to New Jersey. Jagged chunks of ice were banging into the sides of the Durham boats as they were poled out into midstream, making it almost impossible to keep them on a steady course; the wind was rising, the swollen current running strong, and it seemed to take forever to load the eighteen cannon into the big boats. The wintry moon was dim, as if behind a scrim, and as the hours wore on it was entirely obscured by the cloud formations of a big storm that was coming up, one which broke in full force about eleven o'clock.

"It was as severe a night as I ever saw," Thomas Rodney remembered. "The frost was sharp, the current difficult to stem, the ice increasing, the wind high, and at eleven it began to snow. It was only with the greatest care and labor that the horses and the artillery could be ferried over the river." Knox, who had a powerful deep voice, was roaring orders into the gale, trying to speed up the loading of men and cannon, but "the floating ice in the river made the labor almost incredible," he said. Stephen's brigade had reached the opposite shore about seven o'clock, to find that a number of men from Hopewell—one of the towns the British had treated so roughly—were there to help unload the boats and serve the army as scouts on the way to Trenton. A little later Washington went over to wait for the rest of the men and the guns to arrive; he got off his horse and sat down on a box that had contained a beehive in warmer weather and remained there, wrapped in a cloak, silent and patient despite the realization that the army was badly behind schedule: he had expected to begin marching by midnight and reach Trenton before daybreak, but it was almost 4 A.M. when the troops finally formed up. If anything, the weather had turned worse; it had been sleeting hard for several hours—a terrible wind out of the northeast blowing it into the men's faces so it cut like tiny knives—and a violent hailstorm began just before they stepped off on the road that led to Bear Tavern, east of the river. There they turned right, and although there was no letup in the storm, it was now at their backs and, Henry Knox noted, would be in the faces of the enemy.

Officers kept moving up and down the ranks, speaking softly to the men, telling them again to be as quiet as possible, reminding them that the password Washington had chosen for the night was "Victory or Death." One of Knox's battery commanders, Alexander Hamilton, was a small, delicate youth not quite twenty years old, and he rode along beside the guns, lending his horse now and then to help pull a cannon over a rough spot while he walked alongside, patting the gun's barrel from time to time as if it were a personal acquaintance. Just a few of the men carried lanterns; artillerymen had fixed torches to the gun carriages and the flames flickered and danced in front of the marching men, making small circles of light that bobbed along through the falling snow, illuminating the black trunks and branches of ancient oaks and hickories that lined the roadside. There were nearly nine miles to go and Washington rode up and down the lines, calling, "Press on, press on, boys!" (It was fatal to stop; two soldiers who dropped off to sleep during a halt could not be wakened.) Past a few silent farmhouses they tramped, feet crunching and slithering on the ice, cannon squeaking along, and it took the better part of two hours to reach Birmingham, where Greene's division turned left toward the Scotch Road and Sullivan's men continued straight ahead on the River Road. After giving orders that no one was to show a light from this point on, Washington got a message from Sullivan: one of his guides, who had been walking ahead of the troops, noticed that his priming powder was wet, and when Sullivan checked with other men in the line of march he discovered they all had the same complaint. As Washington rode ahead with Greene, Samuel Webb was sent back with word for Sullivan: "Use the bayonet. I am resolved to take Trenton."

The first signs of daylight were visible when Washington trotted back along the column to speak again to the men. "Soldiers, keep by your officers. For God's sake, keep by your officers!" One Connecticut man remembered seeing the general's horse lose his footing on the ice and admired the way the commander in chief seized the animal's mane as if to pull him upright again. Then there was a shout somewhere up ahead, and Washington put his spurs to the horse; off to one side of a narrow lane a group of men were walking toward them across a field, and to the general's astonishment they proved to be a party of Virginians. What were they doing here? he demanded of a captain, who identified himself as Richard Anderson. The young man explained that General Stephen had sent them out to reconnoiter on Christmas day and they were only now returning from one of the Hessian outposts where they had shot a sentinel. For a moment the anguished Washington lost control of his temper and told the captain that he had very likely ruined his plans for a surprise; then he simmered down and told Anderson that as he and his men must be tired after their night's work they should come along with him rather than go to the rear of the column.

By now the guides estimated that they were within a mile of Trenton. It was half an hour after daylight, and the nearest enemy outpost should be about 800 yards off. Pushing on through the storm at a "long trot," the Americans emerged from the wooded Pennington Road at just eight o'clock and saw, in the cleared fields beyond them, Richard Howell's cooper shop, which the Germans were using as an advanced post. At the moment they caught sight of it, the men in the front ranks saw the door open and a Hessian officer come out.

3. I Wanted the Victory Complete

Lieutenant Andreas Wiederhold was a bright, intense young man of twenty-four, sure of himself and inclined to carp privately at his superiors' shortcomings, and in the manner of other bright, intense young military officers he often felt that things would go a lot better if only he could handle them in his own way. The lieutenant had just put in a rather anxious night, and before the day was out he would be handed the opportunity to see what he could do under circumstances infinitely more trying.

The evening before, directly after the alarm was raised in Trenton, Wiederhold had taken ten men from the Knyphausen regiment out to Howell's cooper shop about a half mile from town and found himself the senior officer present at this little advanced post. His reinforcements brought to twenty-one the number of soldiers crowded into the place, and during the night, despite the weather, he sent out frequent patrols, telling them to be on the alert for any signs of an attack. About an hour before dawn his first morning patrol came in, shook the snow off their overcoats, and reported that everything was quiet in their sector and that the company of jägers over on the River Road had just called in their night pickets. The lieutenant, who was inclined to doubt the vigilance of his men, decided to step outside and have a look around himself, and as he opened the door and peered out into the storm, wondering whether the patrol from the Princeton Road would be coming along soon, he made out what he took to be about sixty men coming out of the woods to the north of him, trotting along the Pennington Road. Assuming that they were one of the roaming parties of rebels that had been so active lately, he hailed his men, who came running out of the house pulling on their overcoats.

There was a volley from the Americans, then a second and a third, but Wiederhold could see that the range was too great and his men held their fire until the third round had been fired, when the rebels were close enough to hit. But as his first volley went off in the roaring storm, Wiederhold realized that this was something a lot bigger than a party of raiders; off to his left what appeared to be several battalions of rebels ran by and he and his men abandoned their post and ran off across the fields, heading for the picket post in their rear where one of the Lossberg regiments was quartered. Here Captain von Altenbockum had drawn up his men when he heard the shooting out near the cooper's house, and Wiederhold, retiring under heavy fire, led his men over and formed them up on the right flank of the Lossberg men. It was evident that this was no place to stand and fight either—the Americans kept coming in ever-increasing numbers, and the Hessians were forced to fall back, moving toward the town in good order, keeping up a continuous fire as they retreated from house to house.

The first shot had been fired at Wiederhold at eight o'clock, and George Washington noted with satisfaction that it was just three minutes later when he heard firing off toward the River Road, which meant that his two divisions had timed their attacks perfectly. He had ordered Sullivan to halt for a few minutes along his route in order to give Greene, who had the longer march, time to catch up, and Sullivan first encountered the Hessians at the Hermitage, Philemon Dickinson's home, about three quarters of a mile outside of town. Sullivan's advance, led by Captain John Flahavan, came upon the Hessian outpost here and quickly drove in the pickets, who were pursued closely by some of John Glover's men.

Lieutenant Friederich Wilhelm von Grothausen was in command at the Hermitage, and as soon as he heard the gunfire he and a dozen jägers ran toward the sentry post, leaving Corporal Franz Bauer to take a position in the road behind him. Bauer's men stationed themselves behind trees and fences, trying desperately to make out the enemy movement through the raging sleet storm and they suddenly found themselves under cannon fire from the opposite shore of the Delaware River; the artillery there—under the command of Phil Dickinson—had opened up on Dickinson's own house. When hundreds of running figures materialized out of the snowstorm Bauer decided to make a dash for the town, realizing that he was badly outnumbered. He and his men had no time to go back to the Hermitage for their knapsacks—they simply took their muskets and sprinted from where they were—and as they pounded down the road they were joined by Grothausen and his group, who had gone no more than halfway toward the sentinels' post before seeing the rebels booming along to their left down the River Road. It was every man for himself until they reached the old barracks in Trenton, where they picked up a handful of reinforcements and turned to open fire on the Americans, but the attackers were coming in fast here, too, with bayonets fixed, so the Hessians turned tail again and ran for the bridge that crossed Assunpink Creek. Along the way they could see that the rebels were already in the streets of the town, pouring in from yet another direction, and they did not look back again until they had crossed the bridge.

While Sullivan's men were driving these Hessians through the lower part of town, nearest the Delaware River, Washington and Greene watched their troops push back Wiederhold and Altenbockum at the junction of the Pennington and Princeton Roads, those two highways intersected by King and Queen streets at the head of the village, and Washington rode up onto high ground where he could see the whole of Trenton. From here he observed German troops dashing out of houses, pulling on their uniform coats and caps and forming in groups in the narrow streets, while off to his left, to the east, another larger party of the enemy was just visible. It was impossible to tell what they were attempting to do, but he gave orders for the infantry under Stirling and Stephen to form a battle line and move to the left to prevent the Hessians from retreating to the Princeton Road and paused long enough to see Knox's artillery brought into position at the head of King and Queen streets.

A bird's eye view of Trenton showed a street plan something like an elongated race track, with King and Queen streets forming the two long

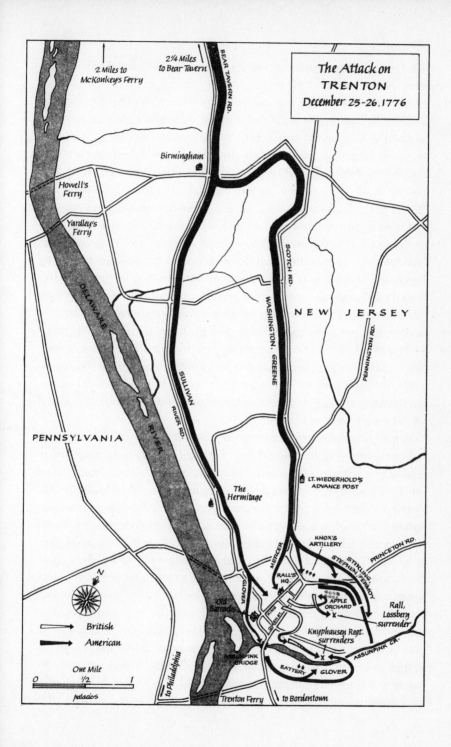

2 Miles to
McKonkey's Ferry

2¼ Miles
to Bear Tavern

BEAR TAVERN RD.

**The Attack on
TRENTON**
December 25-26, 1776

Birmingham

Howell's
Ferry

Yardley's
Ferry

DELAWARE

RIVER

SCOTCH RD.

WASHINGTON, GREENE

NEW JERSEY

SULLIVAN

RIVER RD.

PENNINGTON RD.

PENNSYLVANIA

The Hermitage

LT. WIEDERHOLD'S
ADVANCE POST

KNOX'S
ARTILLERY

MERCER

RALL'S
HQ.

STIRLING
STEPHEN, FERMOY

PRINCETON RD.

GLOVER

KING

QUEEN

APPLE
ORCHARD

Rall,
Lossberg
surrender

Old
Barracks

Knyphausen Regt.
surrenders

ASSUNPINK
BRIDGE

BATTERY   GLOVER

ASSUNPINK CR.

N

to Philadelphia

British

American

One Mile

0   ½   1

palacios

Trenton Ferry   to Bordentown

sides and coming together at the top, just below Washington's vantage point. At the bottom of the oval the streets joined again, and a tail like that on the letter "Q" ran off toward the bridge over the Assunpink. Forming a double belt across the middle of the oval were two little thoroughfares connecting King and Queen streets. So the situation, as near as Washington could determine from the high ground above the town was this: Stirling and Stephen were holding the main intersection there and lining their men up in battle formation in a line that slid off to the east, more or less parallel to the Delaware; several batteries were now in position at this intersection and were beginning to fire down the two long sides of the oval, sweeping these main lanes; off to his right, Mercer's brigade had come cross-lots and were boiling into the west side of Trenton back of King Street; and at the foot of that avenue Sullivan's boys were driving Grothausen's jägers toward the foot of Queen Street and onto the bridge over the Assunpink. The Americans, in other words, were attacking along the western side and at the top and bottom of the town, so that the only possible line of defense that would remain to the Hessians in a matter of minutes would be in the open fields east of Trenton, bounded by the Assunpink. Although nothing had been heard so far from Ewing, it was his responsibility to take up a position on the other side of the creek and seal off the escape route at the bridge.

What made the surprise so complete was that Major von Dechow, who had been worrying like an old hen the night before, badgering Rall to send patrols out in all directions, had apparently had second thoughts and decided on his own hook to cancel the regular dawn patrol because of the severity of the weather. At five o'clock that morning Rall's adjutant, Lieutenant Jacob Piel, was up and about; he walked next door to the colonel's quarters about six, found him sleeping, and went about some other business. Nearly two hours later Piel heard the sound of musket shots above the howling of the wind and ran across the street to inquire of the duty watch what the trouble was. Because of Dechow's kindheartedness they were still indoors and knew nothing about it, so he ordered them out on the double in the direction of Wiederhold's picket post while he went over to bang on Rall's door. Piel yelled three times before the colonel appeared at an upstairs window in his nightclothes, leaned out, and demanded, "What's the matter?" and Piel told him he had heard gunfire somewhere toward the Pennington Road. "I will be out in a minute," Rall replied, and while Piel waited he watched some artillerymen dashing from a stable with their horses and pulling them toward the guns which were parked about fifty yards away.

Lieutenant Colonel Scheffer, who had been sick in bed for nearly a week, was rounding up the men in one company, and Piel saw several of those soldiers coming from a nearby church carrying the regimental colors. Just as Rall barged out of his front door and prepared to mount his horse there was a deafening cannon blast from the head of King Street and Rall ordered his own artillerymen under Lieutenant Engelhardt to open fire. They manhandled one gun into position, got off a shot, and then hitched some horses to the cannon to pull it closer to the enemy, even though they still had no protection from infantrymen. Rall's regiment, which was still the duty outfit and therefore in a ready state, was billeted down the street from the colonel's headquarters, and he rode off to meet the troops who had already formed and were marching up the street. But these fellows were in a bad way almost before they started and they were going nowhere; the rebel artillerymen knew that their moment had come and they were making the most of it. Loading with grapeshot, they fired almost in unison and were raking the entire length of King Street up which the Rall regiment was starting to march. Henry Knox had not had many opportunities like this before, and as he told the story, after driving the enemy pickets in, Greene's troops had entered the town "pell-mell," creating a scene of confusion in which "the hurry, fright, and confusion of the enemy was [not] unlike that which will be when the last trump shall sound. They endeavoured to form in streets, the heads of which we had previously the possession of with cannon and howitzers; these, in the twinkling of an eye, cleared the streets. The backs of the houses were resorted to for shelter. These proved ineffectual: the musketry soon dislodged them."

The German infantrymen had no chance whatever against the shattering fire from the American cannon, and to make matters worse they were now being attacked on their left flank by Mercer's skirmishers, who were running in from the west, firing from the cover of houses into Rall's corps. Scheffer, the lieutenant colonel of Rall's regiment, had a horse shot from under him and, because he had been so ill he could hardly walk, sent for another, leaving Major Johann Matthaus in charge temporarily. Men in the ranks were falling, some were running off through the alleys toward Queen Street to escape the withering crossfire, and Matthaus shouted to Engelhardt to move his cannon forward and put those American guns out of action. "My God!" Rall yelled, "the picket is already coming in! Push your cannon ahead!" The artillerymen had some horses hitched up now and got them plunging forward up the icy street, but there was little hope of accomplishing much—these men were facing the same deadly combination of cannon and musket fire that had broken Rall's infantrymen—but Engelhardt gave it all he had and managed somehow to fire off thirteen rounds before he called it quits. By then over half his men were down, most of the horses had been killed, and there was simply no way to move or handle his battery; the few gunners who were left dropped their rammers and sponges and made a dash for the alley where most of the Hessian foot soldiers had taken cover.

Up at the head of the street where Knox's battery was hammering away, a regiment of Stirling's under the command of Colonel George Weedon was standing by, waiting for orders. Weedon was a tavernkeeper from Fredericksburg, Virginia (where he acquired the name "Joe Gourd" because of his habit of serving rum punch from a gourd), and Henry Knox went over to him and asked if he thought some of his men could get down the street and capture the Hessian cannon. Joe Gourd turned and gave an order to Captain William Washington, who with young James Monroe and a Massachusetts sergeant named Joseph White and several other men, lit out along the west side of the street, keeping close to the houses and running for all they were worth in the direction of the guns. "I hallowed as loud as I could scream to the men to run for their lives right up to the pieces," White said, and he was the first soldier to reach them. There was only one Hessian left there when he raced up, and the man ran when White drew his sword back over his head to take a swipe at him. The rebels swarmed around the cannon and began turning it toward the Hessians who were crowded into the alley; William Washington by this time was wounded in both hands, and Monroe's shoulder was bleeding profusely from a ball which had cut an artery.

Engelhardt found Rall over in the alley, mounted, with a sword in his hand, and told him that there was still time to save the cannon, but the colonel seemed bewildered by what was going on; down at the foot of the town the firing was intense, rebel cannon were thundering off to his right, and directly across the street Mercer's men were shooting at anything that moved. "Lord, Lord, what is it, what is it?" Rall kept repeating. Finally he seemed to get a grip on himself and ordered his men forward, but most of those troops had seen all they wanted of this action and some of them turned and ran in the direction of the bridge while others simply hung back, so Rall decided to lead the remainder to the east side of town where there was an apple orchard that would afford some cover and from which point he might make a dash for the Princeton Road and safety. About this time he encountered Lieutenant Wiederhold, making his way through the melee with the remnants of his little command to find his own regiment, the Lossbergs, and Wiederhold told the colonel somewhat unnecessarily not to underrate the enemy, who "are very strong." What Rall's reaction to this piece of advice was is not recorded; by then he had been joined by men from the Lossberg and Knyphausen regiments, the latter coming up Queen Street from their post near Assunpink Creek, and with this body of men he headed out into the open field.

Behind him the narrow village streets were an inferno of confusion and racket, with small clumps of Hessians here and there, firing from houses at the attacking rebels, with Americans coming in from three sides at once, shooting from the cover of buildings, smoke and snow and shouts and explosions all mixed together in the wild swirling of the storm.

At the south end of town Sullivan's brigades were closing in on the Knyphausen Regiment, with John Stark out in front leading them on. Stark was a tough, cantankerous fellow from New Hampshire, a tall man with a big nose and high cheekbones that made him look like an Indian, and if ever there was a determined officer who knew precisely what he intended to do in a tight situation, it was John Stark. He had been in the thick of the fight for Bunker Hill, and not all the cannon and musket fire the British had thrown at him had disturbed him in the slightest degree; marching out to the front lines with broadsides from the British fleet falling on all sides of him, Stark had been approached by another officer who suggested nervously that they should quicken their pace, and the New Hampshireman had fixed him with a withering glance and said, "Dearborn, one fresh man in action is worth ten fatigued ones," and walked on, unconcerned. Now Stark was in the thick of a stand-up fight again and he seemed to be everywhere at once, driving his men to take advantage of the surprise they had achieved. Seeing a chance to hit the Knyphausen Regiment from the flank, he sent a beefy captain named Ebenezer Frye broadside at the marching enemy with sixteen men and to nearly everyone's astonishment Frye returned with sixty prisoners who didn't know what had happened, it had all been so sudden.

Washington, seeing more and more Hessians move into the field and into the apple orchard, feared that they might break through to the Princeton Road, and sent Stephen's and Fermoy's brigades farther over in that direction to prevent their escape. These units planted their left flank on the Assunpink Creek while forming a strong double line north of the orchard. The moment that Rall perceived he was cut off on that side he again seemed incapable of deciding what to do, until an officer came up and told him that their only hope was to try and retake the town; otherwise they would have to make a run for the bridge, which could turn into a hideous bottleneck. So Rall and Scheffer ordered their men to wheel about and prepare for a bayonet charge. Lieutenant Piel heard one of the Knyphausen officers inquire of the colonel if his regiment should "march about left," to which Rall replied affirmatively, but when the Knyphausen troops stepped off it was immediately clear that the officer had fatally misunderstood his commander's intentions, for instead of heading toward the streets of the town they went in the direction of the Assunpink bridge and were almost immediately cut off from Rall when St. Clair's brigade came swarming into them from the River Road. Meantime, Rall's troops were meeting a shattering fire out of the houses along the eastern edge of the village; as dead and wounded men fell to the ground the officers ordered the survivors to close ranks and keep moving, and all the while the brigade's band was playing, fifes tootling, bugles blowing, drums booming to give them heart.

These badly rattled Hessians needed more than band music to help them; Mercer's men were ahead of them, firing from houses, from cellarways, and from behind fences, and Stirling's troops were charging down on their right flank while cannonballs pounded into the ranks. The visibility was terrible; a heavy rain mixed with the snow caused the men's guns to misfire frequently and made it virtually impossible to distinguish friend from foe. Rall was hit, and although he told Major von Hanstein that it was only a slight wound, he quickly began to grow weak from loss of blood. He was still on horseback, shouting orders at his men, but he was now nearly surrounded and the little crowd of Hessians around him was being pushed into a smaller, more compact mass. Officers and men were down all over the place, the two German regiments were hopelessly mixed up, out of touch with their own officers, and it finally dawned on them that there was almost no hope of breaking through the determined Americans.

Rall's adjutant Piel suggested that they try to make it to the bridge, which Major von Dechow was holding open as a last resort, and Rall sent him to see if they could get through. Piel ran toward the creek and saw a lot of men at the bridge and assumed that they were the Knyphausens, although it was impossible to tell in the storm. Not until he was within thirty paces of them did he realize that they were rebels, so he hotfooted it back to inform Rall that the escape hatch had been closed off. Rall was now being fired on by two cannon of Joseph Moulder's battery, which had been brought into Queen Street to open up at almost point blank range, and the Americans were closing in from all sides. There was only one direction left to go, and Rall ordered a retreat again to the apple orchard, but just as he gave the command he fell from his horse with two terrible wounds in his side. Two soldiers helped him to his feet and half-carried him toward a Methodist church on Queen Street while the battle raged on. Somehow or other, the three remaining Hessian field officers managed to get the remains of their troops out to the orchard again, held a brief council of war, and decided to make a break for it across the upper fords of the Assunpink. Through the swirling haze of rain and snow they could just make out a long line of Americans under Stephen and Fermoy out there in a big half circle with cannon trained on them, and before they had an opportunity to move they were suddenly hit by a galling fire that burst into them "like a swarm of bees." Fermoy's men were closing on them, firing at Scheffer's command from a distance of fifty paces, and as they drove in for the kill the Hessians heard the rebels shouting in German and English to throw down their arms and surrender. Scheffer called to an American officer and asked for quarter, and within moments George Baylor, one of Washington's aides, rode up, spoke to Scheffer and Hanstein, and trotted back to the American general to tell him that they had surrendered.

The Rall and Lossberg standards were lowered, several Hessian officers put their hats on the tip of their swords and held them high in the air to indicate they were submitting, while the infantrymen grounded arms and Stirling himself rode up to take the officers' swords. While this little pantomime was taking place, the Knyphausen Regiment was still trying to reach the Assunpink bridge, but they were having a rough time of it.

They were aware that the Rall and Lossberg man were already on the verge of surrendering, and ahead of them enemy troops controlled the bridge, but they were determined to break through and reach the road to Bordentown. The trouble was that although the men were willing their cannon had perversely gotten mired down in swampy land that lay along the creek. Some of their stragglers had been swept up by St. Clair's and Sargent's men, several officers were badly wounded, and extricating the cannon from the mud took so much time that the Americans had a chance to get a battery into position on the opposite side of the creek and began to lob shells into their ranks. The Hessians were still putting up a fight, although Major von Dechow, the commanding officer, was seriously wounded in the hip and, unable to sit his horse, was leaning against a fence, from which point he could see the two other Hessian regiments laying down their arms. Knowing he couldn't last much longer, he had turned over the command to Captain von Biesenrodt, and when he saw the other regiments give up he ordered Biesenrodt to do likewise. But the captain and several other officers had no intention of that, and while the mortally wounded Dechow hobbled off toward the town, assisted by a corporal who carried a white handkerchief tied to a spontoon, some of them plunged into the icy water of the creek and swam or waded in water up to their chins to the other side. A larger group, fearing that the water was too deep, headed upstream to look for a shallower crossing, but at the first ford they were met by Colonel John Glover's men, who had come around the creek on the opposite bank and crossed over to cut them off. The Knyphausen Regiment was completely surrounded.

A few of them disappeared into the brush lining the stream and attempted to cross; some made it, but some did not. By then St. Clair's brigade and two of Moulder's cannon were within forty paces of the survivors and James Wilkinson walked out in front of the lines and tried to attract Biesenrodt's attention. The captain told him not to come any farther or he would shoot, and then sent Lieutenant Andreas Wiederhold, whose long, trying day was finally ending, to talk to Wilkinson. Wiederhold returned to tell Biesenrodt that St. Clair had given him orders to surrender. But the captain refused. Once again Wiederhold went back to speak to St. Clair, who explained that further resistance was futile—the

Germans were surrounded and all roads, bridges, and fords across the stream were in American hands. If that didn't convince him, St. Clair said bluntly, "Tell your commanding officer that if you do not surrender immediately I will blow you to pieces." That did it; the German captain agreed to talk with St. Clair, with Wiederhold acting as interpreter, and said he would surrender provided his officers could keep their swords and baggage. As soon as the two commanders shook hands, James Wilkinson —who had carried that extraordinary message from Charles Lee to Gates and the strange letter from Gates to Washington on the night before— rode off in search of General Washington with another important report. It was the best possible news he could have delivered.

Washington had heard the battle sputtering to a stop and was just then riding down King Street to inspect the town. On the way he passed by several Germans who were assisting the grievously wounded Rall into a church, and at that moment Wilkinson drew up to report that the last Hessian regiment had laid down their arms. Washington reached for his hand, smiled, and said, "Major Wilkinson, this is a glorious day for our country."

Nothing in any account of the battle indicates that the rebels went wild with joy, as they might have done, knowing they had won the first real victory of the Revolution—their only solid battlefield triumph in more than a year and a half of war. Perhaps it was too much for them to comprehend just then, and certainly no one who had come through this twenty-four-hour trial by fire and ice had strength to do more than make his way back to camp on the other side of the Delaware. At a conference with his officers Washington put the question of whether or not to follow up the victory as he had originally planned, by going on to Princeton and possibly even Brunswick. Greene and Knox were all for it—the element of surprise was still in their favor, they argued, the army was still intact (astonishingly, after all the fighting, only two officers—William Washington and James Monroe—and two privates were wounded) and should capitalize on the momentum of victory. But these two were in a minority. The others pointed out that all the men were hungry, cold, and exhausted, and even though the officers had staved in forty hogsheads of rum a good many soldiers were drunk, having found other stores of liquor in the town. Besides, there was no sign that either Ewing or Cadwalader had crossed the river as planned, which meant that there might be a superior Hessian force under Donop out there to the southeast that would have to be reckoned with, and another strong, fresh body of men at Princeton. The soldiers had done all that humans could be asked, and they still had to retrace their steps, cross the river, and bring off all the prisoners, cannon, and other booty. There was another consideration, perhaps the most important of all: for the sake of the country at large, the psychological impact of this triumph must not be jeopardized. They dared not lose what they had just gained. So it was decided that the army would return at once to the camps in Pennsylvania and the troops assembled once again in marching order. As a young captain recalled, "We did not get to our tents till next morning—two nights and a day in as violent a storm as ever I felt." But there were three men, at least, who never made it to their tents. They froze to death in the boats on the return trip across the Delaware.

After the fighting ended, Sergeant Joseph White had picked his way over the field of battle and his "blood chill'd to see such horror and distress, blood mingling together—the dying groans, and garments rolled in blood. The sight was too much to bear," he said. "I left it soon." Heading back toward Queen Street he came across a dead German officer, took an "elegant sword" from his belt and put it on. (The sword stayed with him the rest of the time he remained in the army, but on his way home he met up with a young officer who took a fancy to it and offered him eight dollars for the prize. The temptation was too much, and White let him have it.) Over on King Street, where he had helped capture the Hessian cannon, White went back to the spot where his battery had been stationed and looked dolefully at his favorite gun—"the best in the regiment." While he stood there, staring at the axle tree which had been shattered by enemy gunfire, trying to figure out how he could fix it sufficiently to get it back across the river, Henry Knox rode up and told him he had better forget the gun, since the army was going to pull out immediately. But White loved that cannon and he was determined to bring it off; he rounded up four men—one of them a seaman—and between them they managed to patch up the axle so that the gun could be moved. They were starting off when Knox came up again to say there was no time to waste and they should leave the gun behind. "I told him I rather ran the resque of being taken, than to leave now, we had got so far," said White, and the party moved on laboriously with the ailing weapon.

Long, straggling lines of infantry slogged by, too weary even to glance their way, and finally the rear guard came abreast, passed, and disappeared into the mist ahead, leaving the five men to struggle on through the gloom. Joseph White was a matter-of-fact sort of fellow who took things pretty much as they came, but he was beginning to realize what this war was going to be. It wasn't quite the same as advertised on that bright morning in May 1775 when he had signed up for an eight-month hitch, when all the talk was of liberty and the glory to be won and you marched to the skirl of fife and drum and the promise of pretty. girls' smiles. No, what it amounted to in the long run was unutterable weariness and discomfort and the bone-breaking effort of hauling and shoving a cranky, unco-operative cannon down a lonely road in a blizzard.

What daylight remained was fading, rain and snow made the road all but impassable, and McKonkey's Ferry and a warm bed and home all began to seem equally unattainable. From far to the rear came a noise, indistinct at first, then unmistakably the sound of mounted men—hoofbeats thudding and clattering on the frozen ground, the jingle of bridles, the squeak of leather—and White and his buddies peered through the murk, certain that this must be the enemy's cavalry coming up to harry the rear guard. Then the riders materialized, ghostly figures swathed in dark cloaks and wearing mysterious white hoods on their heads. As they came closer White finally decided this must be a party of old Quakers, for he now saw that they had handkerchiefs tied babushka-style around their hats.

Not until they were almost on top of him was he able to see who they were. "They happened to be all the Generals," he discovered, who were on their way to the ferry landing, and they had worn those handkerchiefs to keep their hats as dry as possible.

Once again Colonel Knox came over and spoke to White, asking about the cannon they were manhandling along the road. It was the same one Knox had ordered left behind, White admitted, but he just couldn't bear to part with it. "I wanted the victory complete," he said.

"You are a good fellow. I will remember you," Knox told him before he rode off to join the others, and in a moment the generals were swallowed up in the darkness, only those triangular bits of white bobbing up and down, growing smaller and smaller until they finally disappeared from sight. It was a long while before White and the others reached

McKonkey's Ferry where they waited for a boat to take them to the other side, and he was cruelly aware that it had been a nearly endless day. "I being weary," he said, "laid down upon the snow and took a nap; the heat of my body melted the snow, and I sunk down to the ground."

4. The Army Was in the Most Desperate Situation

General James Ewing had not crossed the Delaware River on Christmas night. As Washington told the president of Congress, "the quantity of ice was so great, that though he did every thing in his power to effect it, he could not get over." Whether the crossing was indeed so much more hazardous below Trenton or whether Ewing's determination was less than that of the commander in chief is hard to say, but the fact that he did not carry out his assignment meant that the Hessians' escape route below Assunpink Creek had not been sealed off and 400 enemy soldiers got away. Fifty men and three officers of the Knyphausen Regiment forded the waters of the stream just before the final surrender and, after losing their way and suffering "incredible fatigue," stumbled into Princeton about eight o'clock, bringing news of the disaster to General Leslie. One of the officers, Lieutenant Jacob Baum, was sent on to Brunswick to inform Grant, who gave the poor fellow no rest and directed him to travel on to New York to report in full to General Howe. All things considered, however, Ewing's failure to cross over may have been a blessing. Had his men disembarked on the New Jersey shore on Christmas night, he would have had to keep them out of sight and earshot of the Hessians at least until eight o'clock the next morning, when Washington's attack began. Down in Ewing's sector there were pickets all along the river who might have detected his landing, and the element of surprise, which had worked so providentially in Washington's favor, could easily have been canceled out, with consequences no one could calculate. (Actually, there is no telling whether Ewing's men would have been spotted; one Hessian who was stationed in that area said later that the storm was so severe he had not even heard the sounds of the battle and did not know whether to believe the accounts given him by some civilian refugees from Trenton "who arrived on their horses in a hellish chase"—news that was not confirmed until an hour later, when a few Hessians who had escaped the debacle turned up.)

With Colonel John Cadwalader, the story was slightly different. He had intended to negotiate the river above Bristol, but when he saw that the concentration of ice there made it impossible he had gone to Dunk's Ferry, reassembled all his boats, and ferried his infantrymen across after dark. Then there had been a first-rate snag: loading the two fieldpieces proved to be àn impossible task, and all his officers agreed that it would be foolhardy to attack Donop without them. So Cadwalader brought his 1,800 men back across the river, completing the job about four in the morning, and all the while supposing, as he wrote Washington, that "the badness of the night must have prevented you from passing as you intended."

If the rebel commander in chief was disappointed by the failure of these two officers to get over the river, he did not show it; he had, after all, won a victory without them, and he seems to have believed that they had done their best. Besides, he saw something in Cadwalader's letter that started him thinking that this man possessed a quality he had not suspected—he had an aggressiveness Washington had not discerned in most other militia officers. Here was Cadwalader, despite the cruel weather and the conditions on the river, proposing to cross over to New Jersey again, join forces with 400 New Jersey militiamen and some troops Putnam had supposedly sent into the state, in order to create a diversion that would draw the enemy away from any movement Washington might be contemplating. When he suggested this, Cadwalader had no idea that Washington had even attacked Trenton, and the next day—still in the dark about the main army's success—he wrote again, informing the general that he planned to cross the Delaware on the twenty-seventh, seize a force of 200 enemy troops in the town of White Hill, and surround the post at Bordentown. His Pennsylvanians were spoiling for a fight, Hitchcock's New England troops had at last been issued some clothing and shoes, and Cadwalader was ready to go. "If possible," he added to Washington, "I should be glad to hear from you before we set off."

It was just the sort of imaginative, independent action that appealed to the commanding general, and while he was pondering how to put Cadwalader's boldness to good use, the army was totting up the fruits of victory at Trenton and the shock waves from that event were spreading out in ever-widening circles, to Philadelphia and New York, to London, and eventually to the tiny German principalities deep within the continent of Europe. At army headquarters in Bucks County the rebels found they had taken prisoner 30 officers, over 90 non-coms, 29 men who could not be readily categorized (musicians, drummers, surgeons' mates, and the like) 25 servants, and 740 rank and file—a total of 918. Astonishingly, despite the ferocity of the two-hour battle, only 25 or 30 Germans had been killed (an American officer estimated that 80 were wounded), and even though a sizeable number had been permitted to escape, the quantity of captives taken avenged in part the humiliating loss at Fort Washington.

Rall, the hero of that affair, had been left to die at his headquarters in Trenton, and when his uniform was removed someone discovered in his vest pocket the warning note which had been scrawled on a piece of paper by the Tory farmer, standing outside the door of Abraham Hunt's house on Christmas Eve. Rall looked at it for a moment, realized its significance, and then said simply, "If I had read this at Mr. Hunt's I would not be here." He was no sooner laid to rest in an unmarked grave than it became clear that no one had anything good to say for Colonel Johann Rall. General Grant, who was one of the first to hear the news, sent a letter to Donop in Bordentown, clucking over this "most unfortunate business" and, true to form, expressing wonder at the event: "I did not think that all the Rebels in America would have taken that Brigade Prisoners." If Donop had been there, Grant stated with assurance, he would have contrived to get his men across the bridge and onto the road to Bordentown. Donop, all of a sudden feeling very much alone in the New Jersey hinterland, sent an anxious letter to General Knyphausen informing him of the shocking defeat and adding a postscript that was unlikely to enhance Rall's memory. He could not judge whether the affair was an accident or a mistake, he said, but all the men who escaped agreed that if Rall had only retreated over the bridge and then destroyed it, he could have saved his command instead of fighting against such heavy odds. Knowing what usually followed in circumstances of this kind, Donop closed with the wish that Rall's death might obviate the need for "a painful investigation, for he would have had to answer for this grave responsibility." Then Donop, to his considerable relief, received orders to proceed to Princeton —a move he made at once, since his ammunition had run low and panic-stricken refugees from Trenton reported the presence of "many thousands" of rebels there. Abandoning most of his stores and leaving his sick and wounded behind, he beat a hasty retreat for the college town and safety.

General Howe was stunned by the news, but when he informed Lord George Germain of the loss he minimized its importance and misrepresented the facts by stating that Rall had regrettably quit his post and advanced to the attack instead of defending the town. "If he had obeyed the orders I sent to him for the erecting of redoubts," Howe said piously, "I am confident his post would not have been taken." But there was really no way to put a good face on the matter and the news spread like wildfire, mortifying British and Tories alike. The loyalist governor of New York, William Tryon, told Germain that it gave him more chagrin than any other circumstance of the war—"the moment was critical," he realized, "and I believe the Rebel Chiefs were conscious that if some stroke was not struck that would give life to their sinking cause, they should not raise another army." Cornwallis, having seen the courage of the German troops in the assault on Fort Washington, could only suppose that the defeat "was owing entirely to the imprudence and negligence of the commanding officer," while Clinton, off in Newport, Rhode Island, considered that Howe and Grant, both of whom he cordially detested, should share the blame—Howe for having strung those isolated outposts across the state of New Jersey, Grant for not having "visited his posts, given his orders, and seen they had been obeyed."

Howe's summary of the battle did not deceive Germain. The secretary for the American colonies would have reason to reflect at length on this particular disaster, but his immediate reaction was a starchy letter to General Leopold Philip von Heister, the commander of the Hessian troops, expressing the regret he and George III felt "that the officer who commanded this force and to whom this misfortune is to be attributed has lost his life by his rashness." There was a lesson here, Germain pointed out to Heister, and he sincerely hoped that "the dangerous practice of underestimating the enemy may make a lasting impression on the rest of the army." The memory of Trenton would remain with Germain for a long,

long time, and more than two years later, during a debate in the House of Commons on the American war, he expressed the opinion that Howe should have followed up "the tide of success, which run so strongly in his favor" by crossing the Delaware in December when he had Washington on the run and seizing Philadelphia. Had he done so, Germain believed, the war might have ended then and there—"But," he added regretfully, "all our hopes were blasted by that unhappy affair at Trenton."

What was uppermost in the minds of the top Hessian commanders was the repercussions this would have at home. General von Heister, the man who was ultimately responsible for the performance of the regiments in America, wrote an anguished letter to the ruler of Hesse, addressing him optimistically as "Merciful Father of the Country" and—reminding him of the inconstancy of war—suggesting that since the defeat was attributable to Rall's hotheadedness and stubbornness, the colonel's death should do away "with many investigations and many complications." Then he let the other shoe drop: he had to report, he said, the loss of fifteen regimental flags and six cannon in addition to the men killed and taken prisoner. And this, as Heister knew it would, threw His Serene Highness into a rage.

The Landgrave was not about to be put off with letters of apology; he wanted the full details of what had happened, he wanted punishment meted out to those responsible for the humiliation, and, predictably, his eye fixed immediately on General von Heister. To Knyphausen he commented ominously that since the climate of America did not seem to agree with Heister's health he should return home at once and transfer his command to Knyphausen. Rall's death had unfortunately "taken him away from my wrath," but it was obvious to the prince that an utter disregard for discipline was to blame for the disaster; otherwise none of his men would have surrendered but would have fought their way through the American lines and made their escape. Alluding again and again to the shame and disgrace he felt, he promised that a full investigation would be held to determine where the guilt lay, so that an example could be made of those officers; meanwhile, "these regiments will never receive any flags again, unless they capture from the enemy as many as they have lost in such a disgraceful manner." His Serene Highness meant every word of the threat—he was not the merciful man Heister hoped he would be— and for over five years the gathering of depositions and facts occupied his officers, and the ensuing courts-martial dragged on, finally producing, in April 1782, a Report of the Hessian War Commission in which all the details of that unhappy day were set forth. The commission's recommendation was that all officers but Colonel Rall and Major von Dechow should be pardoned. Only those two—who had been mortally wounded in the battle—had acted culpably and "laid the foundation for the ill fate of the brigade," the court found, and it was therefore urged that His Highness show clemency and give the regiments permission to carry new colors.

In the days and weeks following the battle, the captured Hessian officers were accorded the polite treatment customarily given ranking prisoners of war; although they complained that they had to spend the first night "very miserably without anything to eat or drink," a number of them were taken next day to visit Washington, with whom they dined, and were sent off to Philadelphia in canvas-covered wagons driven by Pennsylvania farmers, put up at an inn, and given "a grand supper, with plenty of wine and punch at the expense of Congress." On New Year's Day there was a pleasant visit with Israel Putnam, and on January 6 they were taken to Baltimore and turned over to Congress's Board of War. Finally they went off to Virginia, where they remained comfortably until they were exchanged in the spring of 1778.

No one, as usual, gave much thought to the enlisted men who were captured, but considering the circumstances, even they fared better than might have been expected. The first order of business was to capitalize on the effect their defeat would have on Americans everywhere, so they were marched to Philadelphia and paraded through the streets of the city, followed by their banners and arms. As one old gentleman wrote, "They made a long line—all fine, hearty looking men and well clad, with large knapsacks, spatterdashes on legs, their looks were *satisfied*." Alongside marched their guards, presenting an almost ludicrous contrast—the Americans were "mostly in summer dress, and some without shoes, but stepping light and cheerful." As one of the Hessians described the procession, everyone in the city, young and old, turned out to see what manner of men these foreigners were, and on all sides the crowds peered closely at them, pressing in despite the guards as if to reassure themselves that they were not giants or ogres after all. A few kind souls brought bits of bread and other food to give them, but as the Hessian reported, "the old women" would not permit it—they "screamed fearfully and wanted to choke us because we had come to America to deprive them of their liberty."

Until 1777 these German prisoners were detained in Virginia, and that year a party of them were sent back to New Jersey to work in a Morris County forge owned by John Jacob Faesch, who was manufacturing cannon for the Continental Army. Some escaped, of course, and settled down in the rich farm country of Pennsylvania and Virginia, and all who did so were listed as "missing" and charged to the mounting debit account of Great Britain. (During the course of the war nearly 30,000 German troops came to America, and more than 12,000 of them—or over 40 per cent—never returned to their homeland.) It was not a bad ending for them, after all—particularly for members of Rall's beloved band, to whom the citizens of Philadelphia also took a great shine. The people in the capital were partial to military music, and the bandsmen were detained there after all the other Hessians had marched off to prison camps, serenading the townspeople on soft summer evenings and playing some rousing tunes on July 4, 1777, the first celebration of the Declaration of Independence.

For the man whose reputation had been on the wane ever since the defeat at Long Island, whose position had been seriously threatened by the rising popularity of Charles Lee, the victory at Trenton marked a turning point. Suddenly the country and the army altered their opinion of him, sensing that only some sort of military genius could have fashioned this triumph out of the miserable resources he possessed and against such long odds. But Washington, after entertaining the Hessian officers, had little time to think about them or the battle that had put them in his hands, for he was still contemplating that awesome deadline of December 31 and turning over in his mind once again the possibility of striking the enemy before the enlistments ran out.

The day after the battle he published a victory message to the troops, thanking them for their gallant and spirited conduct and promising, by way of reward, to divide among them the value of all spoils taken. One immediate consequence of victory was that the short-range prospects of reinforcement now appeared brighter: a regiment of light horse was on its way from Virginia, Benedict Arnold expected to send Washington some militiamen from New England, and the president of the Pennsylvania Council of Safety reported that new levies were being dispatched from

Philadelphia "in hopes this very important blow may be followed up." Yet until these troops arrived the situation would remain exactly the same as it was before Trenton: the army was on short rations, the men desperately needed shelter and clothing, and until they were fed and rested Washington saw no hope of doing anything until December 29. Which left just two days for any action he might be contemplating. On the first day of the new year he would be able to muster only the men in Cadwalader's Pennsylvania militia companies and the remains of a few Virginia regiments. That was all. With this handful of troops he would have to confront an aroused British and German army that had been diminished only by the number of troops captured at Trenton.

What to do then, to take advantage of what Cadwalader was proposing? At a council of war on December 27 two rather tentative decisions were made: on the one hand, if enough men could be persuaded to stay beyond their time, Washington would lead them across the river again and look for an opportunity to hit the enemy; on the other, if he was left with only those few Virginians in the Continental Army, he would march to Dunk's Ferry and combine forces with all the Pennsylvania militia that could be assembled and see what they could concoct. In either event, he was determined to get over to the other side of the river again, in the hope of "driving the Enemy entirely from, or at least to, the extremity of the province of Jersey." Meanwhile, there was the Delaware to be considered: "Please give me," Washington wrote Cadwalader, "frequent information on the state of the river and whether it is to be passed in boats of whether the ice will admit of a passage."

By that time, Cadwalader had already departed. Taking about 1,500 men he crossed the Delaware on the morning of the twenty-seventh, expecting to find Washington and the main army in New Jersey, and as soon as he learned that they had returned to Pennsylvania with the Hessian prisoners, he decided to stay where he was. Joseph Reed was with him, and the two had determined that Cadwalader should occupy Burlington, since the enemy had abandoned the important road junctions at Black Horse and Mount Holly. "They went off with great precipitation," Cadwalader reported to Washington. "I am told many of them are gone to South Amboy. If we can drive them from West Jersey, the success will raise an army by next spring and establish the credit of the continental money to support it." Still, there was nothing Washington could do but mark time; by December 29 the commissary wagons had not yet arrived with bread and meat and the ice on the Delaware was too thin to support a crossing on foot and too thick to permit boats to move. Nevertheless, orders were issued for a move into New Jersey on the thirtieth, requests were sent to Heath and the commanders of other units in the north to create any diversions they could to occupy the enemy, and on the morning of December 30 the second crossing of the Delaware began. Washington was going whether the troops abandoned him or not, and those with him noticed that there were "one half the number less than we had when we had retreated over the river Delaware," as Sergeant White said.

Snow lay six inches deep on the ground and the cold was more severe than men could remember. If anything, the crossing was more difficult than on Christmas night, even though it took place in daylight; all day and through the hours of darkness the boats beat their way against the current and the chunks of floating ice before the last man was finally put ashore in New Jersey. There was no sign of the enemy on the road to Trenton, and Washington could discover little about them beyond the almost certain probability that Howe was concentrating his forces somewhere and would be fortifying Princeton against attack. The Philadelphia Light Horse was dispatched in that direction to reconnoiter while the army pushed on to Trenton, where the general posted his men in a line on the south side of Assunpink Creek where they would be secure from surprise attack. There, on December 30, George Washington played the last card that remained in the deck.

All but a handful of men had one day of service remaining before they headed for home, and it was difficult for them to imagine what the general had in mind to do with them in the twenty-four hours that were left. For days rumors had been coming in to the effect that reinforcements were on the way from Pennsylvania and New Jersey, and the soldiers who had suffered through these past twelve months figured it was time for someone else to take their places and do their part for the cause. From the commander in chief's point of view, however, it was essential that these men who were thinking only about going home should remain with the army. "A body of firm troops, inured to danger," he had written to Congress, "were absolutely necessary to lead on the more raw and undisciplined," and the moment at hand was his final opportunity to persuade them to stick with him.

Now Washington was no orator. He did not have the facility of a Patrick Henry or a Tom Paine to articulate the words that inspired men; even as a member of Congress he had been reluctant to get to his feet and speak unless driven to it. Nor was he the type of man to harangue his troops before a battle and fire them up as so many other officers in the eighteenth century liked to do. He led his men by example and by deed, and when it came to issuing orders or addressing the troops he liked to handle it through the chain of command. Years afterward, when veterans of the war were asked what he was like, they would remember first his distance and reserve and the·fact that he almost never laughed or changed expression; then they would come out with the remark, "But we loved him. We'd sell our lives for him." So what Washington had going for him on this momentous day on the bank of a frozen New Jersey stream came down to a quality no one could quite put his finger on—it was not a magnetic personality, not an ability to affect men with rhetoric, only some rather vague characteristics that might be described inadequately as the ability to inspire respect and admiration and love. And whether this would be enough was the question that would be answered right now.

The air was bitter cold and after the drums beat for one of the New England regiments to form up, the men's breath made staccato clouds of mist up and down the lines as they dressed ranks. They knew something was up: off to one side was General Washington, seated on his horse, alone, waiting to speak to them. The ranks were much thinner now than they had been a year ago when these fellows signed up; a lot of comrades had fallen to enemy bullets or disease or had gone over the hill, weary of the struggle and willing to fight no longer, and the men who were left looked tired and old, with a hollow expression about the face and eyes that spoke mutely of the exhaustion and malnutrition and grinding hardship they had endured. They had seen all they wanted of war during the past twelve months and were ready to let others take on the burden of fighting. They still had no uniforms worth mentioning, just dirty, dun-colored rags that hung limp on their backs; many were barelegged, others had bits of old blankets wrapped around their feet in place of shoes, and as they stood there in the new-fallen snow, shivering, it may have occurred to some of them that all the brave talk and the high-flown phrases about liberty had come, after all was said and done, to this—to a pathetic little band of hungry, desperate men trembling in the cold, far from home.

When they were all at attention the general rode forward, reined up in front of the line, and began to speak. Briefly, he praised them for the success at Trenton and told what it had meant for the country and why they, the veterans of the army, were still needed. They were the soldiers Tom Paine had written about—the ones who had carried the Revolution on their shoulders while others stayed at home—and if they would just remain with him for a few more weeks, he said, they could do more for their country than they ever might again. As a special inducement, he was prepared to offer them a bounty of ten dollars in addition to their pay for sticking with the army for six more weeks. One sergeant who heard him recalled years later that it was "in the most affectionate manner [he] entreated us to stay." When he was through speaking, he rode off to the side of the line to wait while the regimental officers took charge, calling on every man who would accept the bounty to step forward. There was another roll of the drums and then an awful stillness hung in the winter air while Washington and the other officers looked down the line of faces to see what the response would be.

Not one man moved.

Washington, aware that their silent refusal meant the end of everything, could not believe his eyes and something seemed to take hold of him. He wheeled his horse around and rode once again before the line of quiet, embarrassed men and spoke words that seemed to pour from his heart. As the sergeant remembered it, he said, "You have done all I asked you to do, and more than could be reasonably expected; but your country is at stake, your wives, your houses, and all that you hold dear. You have worn yourselves out with fatigues and hardships, but we know not how to spare you. If you will consent to stay only one month longer, you will render that service to the cause of liberty, and to your country, which you probably never can do under any other circumstance." What we are facing today, he concluded, is "the crisis which is to decide our destiny." And then he had finished—told them all he could think to tell them—and. there was nothing left to do but ride off to one side again and wait for the response. A few of the men shifted from one foot to the other, looked at one another uncomfortably, and then a lone veteran stepped forward, saying that he could not go home when the army needed him; then others took the step, and others, until only those who were too feeble or naked to face anything more remained in the original line.

Elsewhere in New Jersey the same scene was being repeated. Henry Knox appealed to another body of troops; Thomas Mifflin, "on a noble looking horse, in a coat made of a rose-colored blanket, with a large fur cap on his head," spoke eloquently to the "animated scarecrows" from Massachusetts and Rhode Island since their colonel, Daniel Hitchcock, was in the last stages of consumption that would take his life in two weeks' time and could scarcely mount a horse. When they had had their say, about 1,200 Continentals agreed to stay on. (To everyone's disappointment, a majority of Glover's Marbleheaders, tempted by the lure of privateering, decided to leave camp with their colonel.) One officer was so elated by the response that he called for three cheers and ordered a gill of rum issued to every man who had signed up for extended service. "Never were men in higher spirits than our whole Army is," another commented, and Nathanael Greene told his wife, "God only knows what will be the issue of this campaign, but everything wears a much better prospect than they have for some weeks past."

What few men knew at the time was that Washington, in promising the bounty to his soldiers, had violated one of the cardinal principles of his office: he had pledged the public credit with no authorization whatever. But as he wrote John Hancock by way of explanation, "What could be done?" He was willing to back up the pledge with his own private resources, if need be, hoping that he would be supported by other responsible citizens, but under the circumstances no other choice had been open to him. As a matter of fact, some of the troops were grumbling that if there was to be a bounty it should be handed out now, and to meet this demand Washington had dispatched a messenger to Robert Morris in Philadelphia, begging him to send £150 immediately. Morris was having his own difficulties in the capital, having sent considerable amounts of hard money to Congress, and, as he told Washington, collecting more was no easy matter. He was pressing the Commissary, Carpenter Wharton, to come up with $40,000 for Washington's needs and said that he would do his best to "add springs to his movements," but for the moment all he could send was contained in "two canvas bundles" which were being sent to the commander in chief at Trenton. (There was a small bit of personal good news for Washington, too. "Hearing that you are in want of a quarter-cask of wine, I have a good one, which Mr. Commissary Wharton will send up," Morris said.) Before noon on January 1,

1777, the bulky canvas bags arrived in Trenton, and it was interesting to see what Morris had managed to scrape up. They contained "410 Spanish milled dollars . . . 2 English crowns, 72 French crowns, 1072 English shillings," which was all the hard money America's leading financier was able to locate in the nation's capital.† Happily for Washington's peace of mind in this matter, an express from Philadelphia had arrived on the last evening of 1776, bringing him a series of resolves adopted by Congress on December 27 in Baltimore.

It seemed that the members, "having maturely considered the present crisis," had reached the same conclusion as Washington, and they authorized him to resort to anything—including bounties—to prevail on the troops to stay with the army as long as they were needed. Nor was that all of it, by a long shot. They had also conferred upon the general the powers of a military dictator, giving him authority to raise sixteen additional battalions of infantry, 3,000 light horse, three regiments of artillery, and a corps of engineers and authorizing him to decide on the proper rate of pay for the men and officers, to appoint officers, and to appeal to the states for militia as the exigencies required. "Wherever he may be," the long catalogue of powers continued, he could take "whatever he may want for the use of the army," and if the inhabitants of those parts would not sell him what he wanted he could arrest them. What had finally brought this about, of course, was the realization by members of Congress that, as Washington had put it, "the game is pretty near up," and that unless something were done quickly the war and the dream of independence were over.

Not only that; it was foolhardy to think that the commander in chief of

† It did not take a war to bring on this shortage of currency; the situation had existed for a long time in the colonies. Before the Revolution, coins from Spain, France, Portugal, and Holland, as well as English money, were accepted as legal tender since the need was so acute; and the scarcity led several colonies to mint their own coins and print paper money, despite English resistance to the idea. In June 1775 the Continental Congress decided to finance the war by issuing paper money and declared that these bills of credit would be backed by the Spanish milled dollar, which was minted in the New World and was the most common coin in the colonies. (The *peso duro*, or hard dollar—sometimes known as a piece of eight—bore approximately the same relation to the English pound as the later American dollar did for many years. That is, $5 was equal to £1.) There were, however, nowhere near enough of these or any other kinds of coins in hand for Congress to make good on its promise, and inflation was the inevitable consequence. By January of 1777 the value of Continental currency was a third less than that of specie; two years later it was 90 per cent lower than its face value; by 1781 it collapsed utterly. That was when the phrase "not worth a Continental" came into existence.

the army on which all these hopes rested should have to appeal to Congress—which was now several days' ride away from him—before he could make a move on which the future of the cause might depend. It cannot have been easy for the civilian representatives of the various states to reach this conclusion, determined as they were that the army must remain under their jurisdiction, but a combination of dire necessity and the character of the commander in chief made it tolerable to them. By now they knew their man. As a passage in the letter of transmittal read, "Happy is it for this country that the General of their forces can safely be entrusted with the most unlimited power, and neither personal security, liberty or property be in the least degree endangered thereby." Even so, Congress had not gone overboard entirely; the civil arm of the government had every intention of retaining the reins, and it was stipulated that the powers vested in the general were for a period of six months, "unless sooner determined by Congress."

It was a remarkable honor, nonetheless, a gift of such confidence as no other American had ever received, and authority and responsibility the likes of which only a Charles Lee might have imagined. Yet Washington's response was so characteristic that the members of Congress might have written it for him: "Instead of thinking myself freed from all *civil* obligations by this mark of confidence," he said, "I shall constantly bear in mind that as the sword was the last resort for the preservation of our liberties, so it ought to be the first to be laid aside when those liberties are firmly established." He would begin, he added, by making the most necessary reforms in the army, although he doubted if he could make much progress "as if I had a little leisure time upon my hand." The future would have to wait upon the present, for as the last hours of 1776 ticked away some uncertainties were coming into focus and Washington's rather vague notion of what he would do was taking shape.

Since nothing in his letters or orders reveals any clear-cut plan of action, it is almost impossible to say what the general had in mind to do, beyond the half-formed idea of bringing the enemy to battle in some way and at some place that would be advantageous to his own army. At times like this he was inclined to be an opportunist, watching for the situation to develop to a point where he could see his way clear for a quick, bold thrust that would catch the British off balance. In any event, only two general schemes were open to him: one was to take the field and move rapidly on an isolated enemy outpost in hopes of surprising the foe as he had at Trenton; the other was to remain where he was and force the British to come to him and fight on ground of his own choosing. Always, in the back of his mind, there was the knowledge that this would likely be his last chance to accomplish anything until a new army was raised in the spring.

On the thirty-first of December he still did not know how many of the old Continentals he would have after those who had refused the bounty left camp and went home; what he did know was that those who stayed with him—the backbone of the army, on whom he could rely in any action—were almost at the end of their rope, exhausted by lack of sleep and the hardships they had undergone during the past month, more fit for the hospital than for active duty, and that they would follow him more through some inner resource than by any discernible stores of vitality and strength. He did have some fresh troops available: Cadwalader was at Crosswicks with about 1,800 militia, and Mifflin had somehow coaxed another 1,600 to follow him from Philadelphia to Bordentown. These men were raring to do something, and they were well clothed and reasonably well fed, but it was hard to say what they would be like in battle, for they had had no training whatever—they were simply farmers and mechanics newly come from fields and shops who knew absolutely nothing about soldiering. The more Washington considered his available resources, the surer he was that he would have to stand and fight at Trenton, and on December 31 he ordered Cadwalader to join him there immediately.

Experience on the frontier and in this war had taught the general about the men he led. As he had observed before the battle on Long Island, "Place them behind a parapet, a breast work, stone wall, or any thing that will afford them shelter, and from their knowledge of a firelock, they will give a good account of their enemy; but I am as well convinced, as if I had seen it, that they will not march boldly up to a work nor stand exposed in a plain." What he saw on Long Island and elsewhere made him even more positive about their shortcomings: it would be foolhardy, he said, "to draw out our young troops into open ground against their superiors both in number and discipline," so he had "never spared the spade and pick-axe." Now the question was whether the enemy would permit him to choose his weapons or the time and place for the duel. All the advantage of surprise had been dissipated during those days of waiting on the other side of the Delaware, and word soon reached headquarters that the British were about to move.

Joseph Reed had ridden toward Princeton with twelve of the Philadelphia Light Horse, and they had had a most interesting excursion. Heading along Quaker Road, they stopped about three miles outside town to ask some farmers about the situation in Princeton, but the local people said they stayed away from there as much as possible and didn't know what was going on, so Reed and the troopers rode on until they reached a farm owned by a fellow named Wilson, almost within sight of the college. Just as they arrived they spotted a British soldier walking between the house and the barn, so they spurred their horses, surrounded the place, and quickly captured twelve dismounted men of the British 16th Dragoons, who were in Mrs. Wilson's kitchen "Conquering a Parcel of Mince Pyes." Reed's men disarmed the redcoats, put one man on each horse behind a cavalryman, and galloped back to headquarters in Trenton, where the prisoners were interrogated separately and gave up the information that there were about 6,000 British and Hessian troops in Princeton who were preparing to march on Trenton. A spy had conveyed much the same tidings to Cadwalader, supplying him with a detailed description of the placement of artillery and the location of defenses in the college town, and Cadwalader incorporated all this into a rough map which he forwarded to the commander in chief. Although the situation was not entirely clear, it appeared that the British in Brunswick and Princeton would soon be reinforced by at least 1,000 additional men whom Howe had sent over to New Jersey on the heels of the Trenton disaster; they had landed at Perth Amboy several days earlier and were now on the march.

On the first day of the new year—a mild, rainy day—the opposing camps were alive with activity. In the lines around Trenton, soldiers who had turned down the bounty were packing their gear and forming up into miniature companies to make their way home, leaving behind just about half the veterans who had made the second crossing of the Delaware. Some regiments, reduced further by sickness, mustered no more than 100 men after the others had departed; Haslet's Delaware Battalion had ceased to exist; and Washington would have no more than 1,200 seasoned troops with which to bolster the 3,400 militia. On that same day Major General James Grant led an army out of Brunswick to join Leslie and Donop in

Princeton, leaving behind only 600 men to guard his stores and a military chest estimated at £70,000.

In his wake rode the ablest general the British had—Lord Cornwallis, who had barely reached New York, intending to board the next ship to England, when news of Trenton arrived. Howe had told him to drop his plans to go home and had sent him off to New Jersey again, "to bag the fox." Cornwallis made a killing march of fifty miles from Perth Amboy to Princeton, arriving there late in the evening of New Year's Day at the head of some of the best troops in the British army, and immediately took command of the combined force of about 8,000 men and a train of artillery, issuing orders that the army would march before daylight the next morning.

There was a good deal of understandable uneasiness among the rebels about the position Washington had chosen to defend. The army was throwing up earthworks along a ridge that paralleled the south bank of Assunpink Creek, and while the site itself was strong enough, with the waist-deep stream providing a natural barrier against attack, it looked as if there would be no way out of the place if the enemy got over the brook and stormed the ridge. The lines extended for about three miles, so that the left was planted on the Delaware and the right, as it were, in the air. Joseph Reed, who knew the area well, pointed out that there were several fords upstream on the Assunpink that might be used by the British, who would then be in a position to drive in Washington's right. The army's back would be to the Delaware, and since all the boats had been left miles upriver at the crossing, the only line of retreat lay along the New Jersey bank of the river, which would mean another battle, somewhere out in the open, or a difficult retreat across the lower Delaware to Pennsylvania. When Washington posted his army here on December 30, he was still playing things by ear; he told his officers that he expected to pull out soon and that they should "hold themselves in complete readiness to advance at a moment's warning." At that moment he seems to have regarded the position as no more than a temporary bivouac, a staging area for some offensive move, but then he changed his mind and elected to stand and fight. So the men in the ranks were discovering that they were in a very prickly spot, once they learned that the British were heading toward them.

As a soldier named Stephen Olney wrote, "It appeared to me then that our army was in the most desperate situation I had ever known it; we had no boats to carry us across the Delaware, and if we had, so powerful an enemy would certainly destroy the better half before we could embark." Olney assumed it would be impossible to break through the enemy's line of march between Trenton and Princeton and he guessed there was scant hope for the army in south Jersey, where there was little support or sympathy for the rebel cause; yet, to his astonishment, the officers he talked to seemed in remarkably good spirits. He couldn't quite fathom the reason for this, and he went to his lieutenant, a man named Bridges, and asked obliquely what he thought now about "our independence." Bridges knew what was troubling him, and after turning it over in his mind for a moment he said, quite cheerfully, "I don't know, the Lord will help us."

CHAPTER SIX

1. We'll Bag Him in the Morning

Charles Cornwallis operated on the theory that an army's function is to get at the enemy in the speediest possible way and destroy him, and the night he arrived in Princeton things began to hum. From Morven, the lovely, big house that belonged to Richard Stockton, where he set up headquarters, a stream of orders flowed out at once. The baggage train was to roll immediately to Brunswick, where it would be more secure, and the general pushed his outposts as far as Eight Mile Run, well beyond the town, to be on the lookout for rebel activity. Colonel Charles Mawhood was instructed to hold three infantry regiments that made up the 4th Brigade—the 17th, 40th, and 55th—plus fifty dismounted troopers and a number of cannon in Princeton as a rear guard, and then to join the main army on the following day with two of these infantry regiments. All other outfits were to be ready to march before daylight, after biscuits and brandy were issued to them.

There had been a marked change in the weather on New Year's Day— it had turned unseasonably warm, with rain that continued through the night—and Cornwallis discovered as he marched out of Princeton before dawn on January 2 that it was going to take a good deal longer to cover the eleven miles to Trenton than he had anticipated. There were twenty-eight cannon in the train of artillery, ranging in size up to twelve-pounders, and the big wheels squished into the soft red clay, choking the spokes and axles with mud, turning the road surface into a quagmire through which the horses heaved and tugged. The soldiers marched in three columns, sinking halfway to their knees in sloppy clay with every step, and

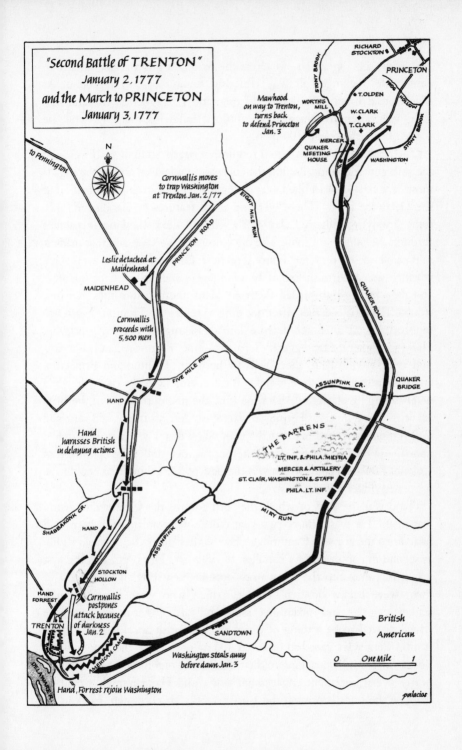

"Second Battle of TRENTON"
January 2, 1777
and the March to PRINCETON
January 3, 1777

N

to Pennington

Cornwallis moves
to trap Washington
at Trenton Jan. 2/77

Mawhood
on way to Trenton,
turns back
to defend Princeton
Jan. 3

RICHARD
STOCKTON

PRINCETON

T. OLDEN

W. CLARK

T. CLARK

WORTH'S
MILL

STONY BROOK

FROG HOLLOW

STONY BROOK

QUAKER
MEETING
HOUSE

MERCER

WASHINGTON

PRINCETON ROAD

EIGHT MILE RUN

Leslie detached at
Maidenhead

MAIDENHEAD

Cornwallis
proceeds with
5,500 men

QUAKER ROAD

FIVE MILE RUN

ASSUNPINK CR.

QUAKER
BRIDGE

HAND

Hand
harasses British
in delaying actions

THE BARRENS

LT. INF. & PHILA. MILITIA
MERCER & ARTILLERY
ST. CLAIR, WASHINGTON & STAFF
PHILA. LT. INF.

SHABBAKONK CR.

HAND

ASSUNPINK CR.

MIRY RUN

STOCKTON
HOLLOW

HAND
FORREST

Cornwallis
postpones
attack because
of darkness
Jan. 2

TRENTON

AMERICAN CAMP

SANDTOWN

British

American

DELAWARE R.

Washington steals away
before dawn Jan. 3

0   One Mile   1

Hand, Forrest rejoin Washington

palacios

they were soon sprawled out across the road and into the open fields on either side, picking their way tediously along the sodden ground. At Maidenhead Cornwallis detached Leslie and 1,500 men of the 2nd Brigade with orders to remain there until the following morning, while he pushed on with about 5,500 men.

The road from Princeton to Trenton ran nearly straight southwest and the soft, gentle country around the college town leveled out, becoming almost dead flat—a plain tilted ever so slightly downward in the direction of the Delaware River. There were no sharp features in this terrain, only some low-lying hills, red clay of the cleared fields showing in patches through the punky old snow, and big clumps of wooded land that made it impossible to see very far in any direction. Out in front of Cornwallis's advance was a skirmish line of Hessian jägers and British light infantry, and they had not proceeded far from Maidenhead before they ran into trouble. Two days earlier, after deciding to remain at Trenton, Washington had posted an outer defense line consisting of Fermoy's brigade, Hand's regiment, Hausegger's Germans, some Virginians, and two cannon at Five Mile Run, about halfway between Trenton and Princeton, and their instructions were to hold off the enemy as long as possible while determining his strength. About the time the first outrunners of the British army came in sight, Fermoy mysteriously left his troops and returned to Trenton (it turned out that the man was a drunk and not to be relied upon), and his unexpected departure put his men under the command of Colonel Edward Hand, which was the best possible thing that could have happened under the circumstances.

Hand was the stuff of which the hard core of the Continental Army was made. He was a thirty-two year old Pennsylvanian, Irish-born, and had joined the army in Cambridge, shortly after the battle at Bunker Hill, as second in command of a battalion of riflemen. This outfit was the first group to come into the army from outside New England and most of them were backwoodsmen—tall, lean men who wore hunting shirts, leather leggings, and Indian moccasins, and carried that deadly long rifle which proved to be a thing of terror to the British and Hessians. Hand and his Pennsylvanians had marched 400 miles to reach the camp outside Boston in 1775, bivouacking in their blankets at night; they had fought in nearly every important engagement since, and Hand himself would be there at the end—storming the British works at Yorktown. He was an amiable, soft-spoken fellow who had the unlimited confidence of his men and his superior officers, and when he caught sight of the British and Hessian skirmishers moving toward him outside Maidenhead he began to handle his troops in the way he was superbly equipped to do.

Cornwallis' men first learned of his presence when a mounted jäger fell dead from his horse at the same moment they heard the dreaded crack of the American rifles, which neither the Brown Bess nor the short German rifle could match at long range. Taking advantage of every kind of cover —woods, ravines, bends in the road—the riflemen popped away at the approaching enemy, forcing the main body to halt again and again while troops of the advance guard were deployed to drive off the unseen Americans. Each time the British formed a battle line the rebels would melt into the deep woods, falling back to another position and firing from cover as they were accustomed to do on the frontier. When Hand was forced to abandon the position along Five Mile Run, he withdrew to a heavily wooded area on the south bank of Shabbakonk Creek, pulled down the wooden bridge there, and deployed his riflemen again; from the trees his volleys were so effective (they were delivered almost at point-blank range as the redcoats came across the stream) that the British thought they were up against the whole American army. Once more they formed up for the attack, brought up their artillery, and "scoured the woods for half an hour." But Hand had already pulled back again, and when Cornwallis' men clambered up the bank and advanced toward the treeline, no one was in sight. Hand began his delaying tactics at ten in the morning and it was three in the afternoon by the time the British skirmish line reached a ravine known as Stockton Hollow, about half a mile from Trenton, where the rebels were forming another line of defense. Washington was determined to hold off the enemy until darkness made it impossible to attack the position on the other side of Assunpink Creek, and Hand's men, supported by two fieldpieces under Captain Thomas Forrest, held out as long as they could.

The British artillery was in place now, though, and it was evident that the whole enemy army was preparing to attack, so Hand gave ground slowly and stubbornly, withdrawing into the town of Trenton about four o'clock, his men retreating down King and Queen streets where they had fought the previous week, keeping up a steady fire at the British from behind houses while they backtracked toward the lines on the south side of the creek. Washington, Greene, and Knox had gone out to encourage the men as they fell back, and American artillery had opened on the British by this time. But at the last there was no holding off the attackers, and it was a near thing as the Virginians made their way across the bridge in the fading twilight, muskets and rifles flashing fire in the gloom, cannon booming from the hill above the creek while the New Englanders opened ranks to let the riflemen through. As Hand's men moved across the narrow bridge they were treated to the sight of the commander in chief at the far end of the span, seated calmly on a big white horse, completely composed, waiting for the last man to cross safely. Cannon were firing from both sides of the stream and muskets continued to pop for another fifteen minutes or so; the British had no idea of the size of the force on the opposite bank of the creek, and one of their columns was driven back at the lower fords and another attack was beaten off even though British and Hessian officers were hitting their men with the flat of their swords to drive them on.

Sergeant Joseph White was up on the hill with the artillery and saw the enemy advancing in solid columns, looking for all the world like an army on parade. "We let them come on some ways," he said, "then by a signal given, we all fired together. The enemy retreated off the bridge and formed again, and we were ready for them." Again the cannon raked the columns, and a third time—now with canister—"and such destruction it made, you cannot conceive. The bridge looked red as blood, with their killed and wounded, and their red coats."

Some 1,500 men in the British advance had taken the brunt of all this fighting, since the main body had been delayed so long by the wretched condition of the roads, and their losses were heavy—estimates range from 150 to 500. One of the mortally wounded was Lieutenant Friedrich Wilhelm von Grothausen, who had commanded the picket post on the River Road outside Trenton on the morning after Christmas. In the skirmish along Shabbakonk Creek a group of Hand's riflemen had come out of the brush and signaled to the Germans, as if they intended to surrender, but when Grothausen and several others ran toward the Americans the lieutenant was shot in the chest before the riflemen disappeared again into the woods. So effectively had Hand done his work that it was dark when Cornwallis rode into the village with the main body. Most of the musket fire had ceased, but cannons were still booming away occasionally and the

British general faced the decision of whether or not to attack, even though night had fallen.

When Cornwallis called a council of war to sound out his officers, Sir William Erskine, the quartermaster general, argued that they should strike right away while they had some momentum going for them. "If Washington is the general I take him to be," he said, "his army will not be found there in the morning." But Grant didn't agree. There was no line of retreat open to the rebels, who had no boats to cross the river, and the British were worn out after their trying ten-hour march. The thing to do, he thought, was to get some rest and storm the rebel lines the next morning; they had Washington where they wanted him—in a trap—and the men might as well be fresh when they set about their business. Cornwallis, pondering these opposing points of view, was fully mindful of the physical obstacles that increased the risks of a night attack. He didn't much like the idea of delaying until morning—postponing an action always rubbed him the wrong way—but neither did he relish the thought of sending troops into battle blindfolded, and that was just what it would be like if he tried to turn Washington's flank out there in the blackness along the Assunpink, where his men would have to travel over completely unfamiliar ground, locate the right wing of the rebel army, cross the stream, and attack an entrenched position. The only alternative was to make a frontal assault across the swollen creek in the face of artillery and against a foe that had had plenty of time to dig in, and he concluded finally that Grant was right. "We've got the old fox safe now," he said. "We'll go over and bag him in the morning." (Erskine was convinced then and ever after that Cornwallis made a grievous mistake in not following his advice: "What followed wrecked the British plans for the winter of 1776–77," he wrote glumly.)

So the British retired to the hill north of town from which Washington had surveyed the battle of Trenton, set up their tents, and built huge bonfires to keep out the growing chill of night. During the evening the soldiers wandered about the streets idly, looking at the shops and houses and inspecting the damage from the previous week's engagement, all the while Knox's cannon continued to lob shells into the town to keep them on the jump. Across Assunpink Creek the Americans had set fire to huge piles of cedar rails all along their lines, and British sentinels, only 150 yards off, could hear the chunking sound of picks and shovels that meant the rebels were digging, strengthening their earthworks against the morning assault. Over on the ridge, parties of unseen men could be heard moving about constantly, patrolling the front, but by the time the gunfire finally sputtered out an uneasy stillness descended on the town, a wind from the north blew up, and by midnight the air was numbing cold. The ground was beginning to freeze. Cornwallis had sent a dispatch to Leslie in Maidenhead and Mawhood in Princeton ordering them to join him as early as possible the next morning, but for some reason or other he neglected to send out cavalry to probe for Washington's right wing and to patrol the roads and fords in that direction. Donop apparently advised him to post some men where the American right was thought to be, in order to warn of an impending attack on the British from that direction, but Cornwallis was as confident as Grant that they had the rebels in a cul-de-sac from which there was no breaking out.

January 3 dawned "bright, serene, and extremely cold, with a hoar frost which bespangled every object," Thomas Rodney wrote. But at break of day neither Rodney nor any other American was in the trenches along the Assunpink. When Cornwallis and his staff emerged from their quarters to greet the day and survey the rebel lines, they looked through the wisps of morning fog lifting from the creek and saw not a single cannon or soldier on the ridge beyond. Except for mounds of freshly dug earth and the smouldering coals of countless campfires, there was no sign that an army had occupied the place. The fox that Cornwallis intended to bag had stolen away in the night, and not until eight o'clock, when the distant rumble of artillery was heard off to the north, did the British general have the vaguest idea where he had gone.

2. *It Seemed to Strike an Awe upon Us*

While Henry Knox's guns were slamming round shot into the streets of Trenton, Washington summoned a council of war to meet at St. Clair's headquarters since his own lodgings were well within range of British cannon. By now he had almost certainly decided on a course of action, but he had long ago formed the habit of talking things over with his officers to get their views, and he put the question to them: should they stand and fight in the morning or should they retreat down the New Jersey bank of the Delaware and take their chances on crossing over to Pennsylvania somewhere? Or—as a third possibility—was there an alternative to battle or retreat? As things stood now, not more than several hundred yards separated them from a much superior force, led by a remarkably energetic general who intended to surround and destroy them between the Assunpink and the Delaware, and it was plain to every man at the meeting that they were in a highly vulnerable position. They all knew the strength of the American lines was deceptive, for although the bridge over the creek could doubtless be held, it was, after all, a very small body of water, and it would be almost impossible to hold the fords above the bridge against a determined attack. The most worrisome aspect of the situation was that the army was composed predominately of militia, who could not be counted on to hold the trenches along the Assunpink against a concentrated artillery barrage and the inevitable bayonet charge and were unlikely to stand up to the regulars in open country. Either way, the army was almost sure to be trapped between the enemy and the river.

Washington had had some conversations with Joseph Reed, Philemon Dickinson, and Arthur St. Clair, who knew this area well, and he was aware that there was a combination of roads leading off from the army's right wing by which it was possible to get to Princeton. From the map

Cadwalader had drawn for him he had also discovered that this route would take him to a little used road that ran along "the back part," or eastern side, of the college town, which was the vulnerable edge of the enemy position there. St. Clair later took credit for proposing that the army make a flank march to Princeton, but it is hardly credible that the idea had not already occurred to Washington as a means of extricating his men from the trap they were in. Further support for the fact that he had such a plan in mind was that some troopers of the Philadelphia Light Horse were posted on that road, on the outskirts of Princeton, from the evening of January 1 on, with explicit orders to warn of any movement of British forces on or near the route. From the time he crossed the Delaware into New Jersey for the second time, Washington's intention had been to strike the enemy somewhere, somehow, and although he could not take on the whole British army with the force at his disposal, a surprise blow at Princeton—where, as he said, "they could not have much force left, and might have Stores"—was very much in keeping with the hit-and-run tactics he had employed at Trenton the previous week. And finally, the commander in chief realized that an attack on Princeton would "avoid the appearance of a Retreat"—a factor that held considerable weight with him.

The key to the plan that was adopted was Cadwalader's map, which showed precisely where the enemy was weakest in Princeton and how that weak point could be reached and exploited. Yet the movement invited catastrophe, for there would be all hell to pay if the British sentinels got wind that the army was pulling out of its lines; it would not take long to get cannon into position and the enemy infantry could storm across the fords and come driving into the middle of the long marching column, cutting the army in two. As daring and risky as the plan was, however, there was really very little choice in the matter when they came down to it, and so it was decided: they would make a night march to Princeton and pray that they could bring it off undetected. Several civilians who lived on or near the route they would take were called in to the meeting and asked what they thought of its practicability, and when they said it was feasible and volunteered to guide the army, the thing was set in motion.

The first problem was to dispose of all excess baggage and stores, since a train of 150 wagons would delay the march intolerably, and Washington decided that they should be moved to Burlington, where some troops dispatched by Israel Putnam could take charge of them and get them to the Pennsylvania side of the river. But artillery was another matter: the army could not fight without those guns. While the officers were discussing what might be done, someone brought word that it had suddenly turned cold and the ground was beginning to freeze, and only this "providential change of weather," as Washington described it later, made it possible to move the artillery over ground on which the guns would have sunk up to the carriages a few hours earlier. By midnight all arrangements were complete. The baggage and three of the heaviest guns rumbled off toward Burlington; the wheels of the cannon that would travel with the army were wrapped in heavy cloth to deaden the racket they would make on the freezing ground; and about 500 men (plus two iron cannon, "to amuse the enemy") were left behind to make a show of patrolling, keep the fires burning bright, and work with picks and shovels to make the enemy think the army was still digging in. Before dawn this working party would pull out of the lines and follow the tracks of the main army.

Those who would march were warned to preserve the utmost silence ("Joe Gourd" Weedon said they managed it so well that the rear guards and sentinels did not even know they had left, and Stephen Olney recalled that orders were delivered so quietly "that some of the Colonels were at a stand which way to move their regiments"). Inevitably, a few souls never got the word at all; since no one below the rank of brigadier was privy to the plan, officers who were quartered in outlying farmhouses awoke the next morning to find the army gone, and they only caught up with their regiments with the utmost difficulty.

It was almost pitch black, only a few stars showing dim in the sky when the march got under way. Some of the light infantry and a company of Philadelphia militia led the van, followed by the artillery and Hugh Mercer's brigade. Colonel John Haslet, who had orders in his pocket detaching him from duty in order to recruit another Delaware regiment, had decided to stick with the army for one more battle, and despite the pain in his legs (he had fallen into the river during the Delaware crossing on Christmas night and his limbs were badly swollen) he walked along beside Mercer's horse, talking quietly to the general. Then came St. Clair's brigade, Washington and his staff, and the rest of the army, with three more companies of Philadelphia light infantry militia bringing up the rear.

By two A.M. the entire rebel army was in motion, stealing off to its right behind the line of trenches, heading eastward in a long column that crossed a little tributary of the Assunpink, passing four or five log huts that made up a hamlet called Sand Town, then fording Miry Run and entering a desolate, gloomy stretch called the Barrens. Somewhere along the way a rumor spread that they were surrounded, and a group of Mifflin's nervous militiamen ran off into the night, never stopping until they reached Philadelphia, but it was a false alarm and the rest of the army kept going. Because of darkness and the condition of the roads there was no rhythm or regularity to the march; portions of the route ran through dense woods where trees had been cut to make a lane, and invisible stumps would bring a cannon to a jarring stop so that men walking behind it, unable to see that the column had halted, would pile into the gun and the soldiers walking ahead of them without warning. Horses slid and fell on the slippery ground, the men broke through ice that lay on little ponds and were soaked to the skin, they scuffed their feet continuously on clods of frozen dirt, and once again there was the all too familiar track marked with blood from their feet. As one soldier described the march, "We moved slow on account of the artillery, frequently coming to a halt, or stand still, and when ordered forward again, one, two or three men in each platoon would stand, with their arms supported, fast asleep; a platoon next in the rear advancing on them, they, in walking or attempting to move, would strike a stub and fall."

Sergeant White, with the artillery, was walking beside Captain Benjamin Frothingham and went to sleep and fell down several times along the way. "You are the first person I ever see sleep while marching," Frothingham told him and then, thinking it might revive the sergeant, brought up another subject. Did White know that in the morning he was going to be in charge of that cannon he had rescued at Trenton? There was bound to be hard fighting where they were headed and Knox, who had just been appointed a brigadier general, had remembered White's obstinate courage at Trenton and was placing him in command of that gun. White was fussed by this news. "I do not think I am capable," he said, "the responsibility is too great for me. I cannot think why he should pitch upon me." But as they trudged along and he turned it over in his mind, he had second thoughts: "I began to feel my pride arising, and I said no more."

The hour before dawn was colder than the night had been and the darkness seemed endless to those who were struggling to keep up. Cadwalader's and Mifflin's troops had had no sleep for two nights, having made a forced march the night before "through the worst roads that were ever seen" in order to reach Trenton, while Hand's men and the others who had delayed Cornwallis' army had fought and maneuvered for eight solid hours the previous day and had had no rest since. Crossing the Quaker Bridge over the Assunpink, so cold and exhausted they could barely take another step, they managed to move along slowly—north- westerly now—and as the first glow of dawn lit the sky they approached a stream known as Stony Brook. The road crossed the waterway, paralleled it for a way, and then made a long, sweeping arc to the right. Just here was a fork which was the key to Washington's plan: the well-traveled route they had been following continued along the tree-lined bank of Stony Brook for about a mile, where it intersected the Post Road between Trenton and Princeton; but off to the right an unused track, indicated on Cadwalader's map, led across Thomas Clark's farmland in a direction more or less paralleling the Post Road. Almost concealed from view from the Post Road by a hill that lay between them, it rounded the corner of a wooded copse, headed in a northeasterly direction past the Thomas Clark house, and ran through cleared land all along the back of the town. From this lane the village could be entered at any point; there were few fences or other obstructions in the way, and the road completely bypassed the defenses which the British had erected on the main highway.

As at Trenton, Washington was running behind schedule. He had planned to attack the British outposts before daylight and capture the gar- rison not long afterward, but when the day broke bright and clear he was still two miles from his objective. Every tree and fence rail was glistening with morning frost, the air was still, there was not a cloud in the sky, and all hopes of achieving a surprise had flown on the wings of that beautiful morning. Having spent some time in Princeton several weeks earlier, Washington knew the lay of the land and had already ordered Hugh Mercer to destroy the bridge where the Post Road crossed Stony Brook. There, in a steep ravine formed by the river, was a stone building known as Worth's Mill and the bridge, and to get there Mercer would have to leave the main army and follow the road that paralleled Stony Brook to the intersection. He had about 350 men with him—veterans from Mary- land and Virginia and a sprinkling of Delaware men—and their objective in tearing down the span was a double one: first, to close off that escape route for the Princeton garrison and, second, to delay Cornwallis' return from Trenton, for the British would be on the march as soon as they discovered that the American army had flown the coop.

Shortly before eight o'clock the main army wheeled to the right and set out along the back road. First went Sullivan's division, consisting of St. Clair's and Isaac Sherman's brigades (the latter was what remained of John Glover's old outfit). Quite a way behind was Cadwalader, who would follow them, with Hitchcock's brigade bringing up the rear. Mercer's men filed off through the trees along the river and as soon as they passed the Quaker Meeting House were lost from sight, since the copse of trees obscured the two separate columns from each other. Not long after they had disappeared, Major James Wilkinson, who was with St.Clair, happened to glance off to the west toward a rise that lay about a mile away, above the route Mercer was taking, and caught a glimpse of sunlight gleaming on steel. He looked again and, realizing that what he had seen could not be the movement of Mercer's men, saw the bayonets of a column of British troops who were climbing the Post Road beyond Worth's Mill, heading toward Trenton. While he watched, two horsemen leaped a fence on the hillside, stared at St. Clair's marching men, and turned about and galloped back toward the enemy ranks. Within a matter of minutes, Wilkinson could see the regulars face about and head down the hill on the run toward the bridge.

Lieutenant Colonel Charles Mawhood had followed his orders from Cornwallis to the letter. Leaving the 40th Regiment behind to guard the town, he marched out of Princeton at five o'clock that morning with the 17th and 55th regiments and their wagons, en route to join Cornwallis. His men had just climbed the hill on the south side of Stony Brook when several troopers, who were leading the column, caught sight of moving figures off to the east, rode out on the hill to have a better look, and returned at once to inform Mawhood that rebel troops were moving along the back road toward Princeton. As Henry Knox said later, "I believe they were as much astonished as if an army had dropped perpendicularly upon them." But as yet Mawhood had no idea that it was in fact an army; it was almost impossible to determine the size of the American force because the wooded hills permitted only an occasional glimpse of movement, but the colonel immediately thought of the 40th Regiment back there in town, sent off a rider to alert them that an enemy party was approaching, and ordered his men to turn about and head for the hill across the stream on the double.

Mawhood's anxiety was something more than a sudden emotion. The map Cadwalader had given Washington, based on information brought in by an American spy, suggested that a state of nerves had prevailed in Princeton immediately after the battle at Trenton. Leslie and Grant had posted a hundred men at Worth's Mill, near the bridge over Stony Brook; there were two cannon between there and the village, in the road near the Thomas Olden house; and these were supported by a battery of eight six-pounders and·a line of breastworks in front of Richard Stockton's home, where the village proper began. Two more guns were sited in front of Nassau Hall, facing northwest, there was another four-gun battery farther on, and here and there around the town the troops were constructing earthworks. Then the arrival of the army under Grant and Cornwallis had given the garrison a temporary sense of security, and by the time Mawhood struck out for Trenton on the morning of the third, he was beginning to view it as something of a lark; as the troops stepped off in the crisp dawn air, he pranced along on a brown pony with several pet spaniels yapping at his side.

By an ironic coincidence, that feeling of ease and safety that had prevailed since the arrival of Cornwallis had the same soporific effect on the British that the weather had produced on the Hessians at Trenton. The previous night Mawhood had called off the patrol that normally scouted the roads in the vicinity of Allentown—the direction from which Washington marched—making it possible for the Americans to approach completely unobserved and giving the garrison no time at all to prepare for an attack. So when the troopers brought word to Mawhood that they had seen some rebels off to the east, the colonel's first reaction was that this must be a raiding party or possibly a group of men that had fled in the path of Cornwallis' march to Trenton. But what Mawhood did not know was that another American force—Mercer's—was a good deal closer to him than the one he had sighted.

Mercer's skirmishers saw the redcoats pouring across the bridge and charging up the hill that led to Princeton, got word back to Mercer, and he immediately led his column to the right, hoping to head off the British and hit them before they confronted the main army. Between the river road and the crest of the hill on Mercer's right was a steep bank about sixty feet high, covered with nearly a foot of hard-crusted snow, and while he waited for the two fieldpieces to be hauled up, the general sent a couple of scouts to the summit to check on Washington's whereabouts. What these men saw, in addition to Sullivan's division, about 500 yards away and well in advance of the rest of the army, was a British cavalryman, standing near an apple orchard and looking straight at them.

The trooper immediately wheeled around and charged off in the direction of the Thomas Olden house, which was located on the Post Road at a point where it turned slightly left to enter the village of Princeton, and there he caught up with Mawhood and informed him that more rebels were coming up in his rear. By now Mercer had reached the top of the hill and saw that he could not catch up with the British column, so he decided to join Sullivan and led his troops toward the east, across William Clark's fields and orchard. From a window of the Olden house an aged man stared at the redcoats running along the road and then walked out into the dooryard, joining several women and a neighbor, to watch the British turn into the field, drop their packs in a corner of the garden, and head off in a quick march toward Clark's wheat field, about 400 yards away.

Mawhood had been compelled to make a quick decision. Once he knew that Mercer was in his rear, he either had to turn on him or continue on in hopes of intercepting Sullivan before he reached the town. From what he could tell, Sullivan's force looked to be considerably larger than Mercer's, which meant that the 40th Regiment was going to have hot work of it if he didn't relieve them. On the other hand, by ignoring Mercer he would lose the opportunity of eliminating one detachment of the rebels. So he decided, in effect, to do both: detaching part of the 55th Regiment, he ordered them to join the 40th in the village, while he took the rest of the 55th, the 17th, fifty cavalrymen, and two fieldpieces to attack Mercer. Speed was vital if Mawhood was to prevent Mercer from rejoining Sullivan, so he ordered the troopers to ride out and delay the enemy while he brought up the other detachments. As Captain Truwin of the British light horse cantered into the fields, he saw Mercer's men entering the Clark orchard; the trees were bare, and a picket fence surrounding them was no obstacle to the men, so Mercer was marching right through them rather than detouring to right or left. This grove of fruit trees was roughly square, and the William Clark house sat in the south-east corner, at the opposite end of the orchard from the barn and several other outbuildings.

Sergeant White's favorite gun was rumbling across the wheat stubble in support of Mercer. During the halt back on the creek road, before they left the main army, White's friend Captain Frothingham had sent over a non-com with two buckets—one filled with gunpower, the other with rum—and ordered every man to drink half a gill of the liquor. A few minutes later the captain joined White and asked if he had had a drink. No, the sergeant replied, but he would take a little now if the captain insisted on it. So they both took a swallow from the bucket and were heading along the road when the scouts first caught sight of Mawhood's redcoats. They had a dreadful time hauling the gun up the steep hill—White and his men unhitched the limbers and pulled the cannon up the slope with dragropes—and they had just crossed the open ground and were moving into the apple orchard when the British light troops opened fire. White turned and got his first view of the enemy: "The sun shone upon them, and their arms glistened very bright," he noticed. "It seemed to strike an awe upon us." Fortunately, the first shots were high—they "passed over our heads cutting the limbs of the trees," another sergeant observed.

This fire took Mercer by surprise; from where he stood the light troops were screened by the trees and by a bank that fell away from the upper side of the orchard, but the fact that the volley went wild gave him a chance to wheel his men around to the left into battle line, from which they began to advance, shooting as they went. (An American officer, watching from a distance, noticed how the smoke from the muskets and rifles rose in the clear, still air "in one beautiful cloud.") Captain Truwin hadn't enough muscle to stand up to the Americans, so he fell back as Mercer's men trotted up to the picket fence at the upper end of the orchard, but by then Mawhood and the British infantry were in position beyond them, with two fieldpieces ready on the right of the line. No more than forty yards separated the two forces here and the two American cannon—one in Sergeant White's care, the other commanded by Captain Daniel Neil of the New Jersey Artillery—were directly opposite the British battery.

The American gunners were the first to fire (White recalled that they loaded with canister, which "made a terrible squeaking noise" as it flew

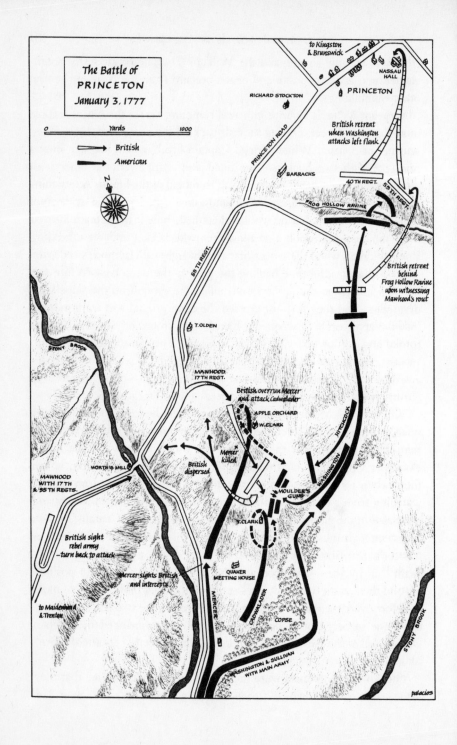

The Battle of
PRINCETON
January 3, 1777

0   Yards   1000

→ British
→ American

N

to Kingston
& Brunswick

NASSAU
HALL

PRINCETON

RICHARD STOCKTON

British retreat
when Washington
attacks left flank

BARRACKS

40TH REGT.

55TH REGT.

FROG HOLLOW RAVINE

British retreat
behind
Frog Hollow Ravine
upon witnessing
Mawhood's rout

55TH REGT.

T. OLDEN

STONY BROOK

MAWHOOD
17TH REGT.

British overrun Mercer
and attack Cadwalader

APPLE ORCHARD

W. CLARK

HITCHCOCK

Mercer
killed

British dispersed

WORTH'S MILL

MAWHOOD
WITH 17TH
& 55TH REGTS.

MOULDER'S
GUNS

WASHINGTON

T. CLARK

British sight
rebel army
–turn back to attack

QUAKER
MEETING HOUSE

COPSE

CADWALADER

Mercer sights British
and intercepts

to Maidenhead
& Trenton

MERCER

STONY BROOK

WASHINGTON & SULLIVAN
WITH MAIN ARMY

palacios

through the air) and for perhaps ten minutes the outnumbered rebel infantry shot at the British. But it was slow work; many of them were
carrying rifles, which took a long time to load, and Mawhood sensed that
the moment was right for a bayonet charge. He gave the order to attack
and the long ranks of regulars suddenly surged forward on the run—a
curling ribbon of scarlet and white that boiled down the hill in a splendidly disciplined charge, bayonets gleaming in the morning sun, helmets
and breastplates sparkling with light. In a matter of seconds the redcoats
covered the forty yards that separated them from the rebels and were in
among them, yelling and cursing, breath sobbing in their throats, bayonets lunging and slashing; there was the thud of musket butts hitting
human flesh, the ugly, animal sound of hand-to-hand fighting in the swirling confusion of angry, fear-stricken men. Mercer's gray horse thrashed
on the ground among the trees, his foreleg broken by a musket ball, and
the general ran among his men, doing his best to rally them. But too few
had bayonets, the force of that awesome red tide was irresistible, and they
broke and ran, plunging downhill through the orchard toward the Clark
house with the British behind them.

Mawhood's redcoats had a real killer instinct that morning, and the
American officers who were trying to stem the retreat took the brunt of
it. One lieutenant who had broken a leg dragged himself to a wagon in
Clark's farmyard and crawled under it, but the regulars saw him, pulled
him out, and plunged their bayonets into him. Lieutenant Bartholomew
Yeates, bleeding from a wound, was clubbed and then stabbed thirteen
times. Hugh Mercer retreated to a point about fifty yards from Clark's
barn and suddenly he was alone, completely surrounded by British soldiers. Since he was wearing an overcoat that covered his insignia of rank,
the enemy troops thought that they had caught Washington, and one of
them shouted, "Surrender, you damn rebel!" But Mercer slashed at them
with his sword until they smashed his head with a musket butt, brought
him to his knees, bayoneted him, and left him for dead. Not far away,
Captain John Fleming was trying to get his Virginians into some sort of
formation and shouted for them to dress the line. "We will dress you," a
British soldier yelled and shot Fleming dead. Off on the American left the
redcoats swarmed around the two rebel cannon. Somehow, White and
Frothingham had gotten away, but Captain Neil was killed trying to defend his gun, and the British swung both cannon around and opened fire

on the retreating rebels, most of whom were now in full flight toward some woods that surrounded the Thomas Clark house, about half a mile from the apple orchard. Colonel John Haslet, who had chosen to stay with the army for one more fight, had been over near the American battery, and he fell back toward the barn there, trying to rally Mercer's men in a line along a slope. But before he could do so, he was killed by a shot through the head, his death bringing to an end the history of the proud First Delaware Regiment, which had disbanded on December 31, 1776, leaving only its commanding officer to fight at Princeton.

At the foot of the hill below the orchard there was a fence, beyond which the ground rose gradually toward a gentle, wooded ridge where the Thomas Clark house was located. The rebels had streamed up this hill and the redcoats, with about fifty light infantrymen out in front, were in close pursuit. Suddenly, from around the edge of the trees, a column of American infantry appeared. The light infantry halted and deployed in a line behind the fence to meet this new threat, while Mawhood called back his men, who were scattered all over the battlefield, to reform their battle line. Meantime the guns were brought up and placed on a knoll off to the right of the British line, where they prepared to open fire.

The reason the American reinforcements had been delayed so long was the result of the manner in which Washington had deployed his men in the line of march. Back along Stony Brook, Sullivan's division took the right-hand turn and marched along the back road while Mercer continued along the creek, eventually colliding with Mawhood. But Sullivan had kept on going and, by the time Mawhood's attack broke Mercer's line, he was well along toward Princeton. And the reason he could not turn back and come to Mercer's assistance was that he had come abreast of the British 55th Regiment, which Mawhood had sent to reinforce the garrison in town. This outfit had reached a height of land, crowned with woods, and while the redcoats were plainly visible to Sullivan, he hadn't the faintest idea how many of them there were, so he was forced to sit tight, not daring to go to Mercer's rescue and risk the possibility that the troops in the 55th Regiment would come down on his right flank when he did. It was, in other words, a standoff between Sullivan's division and the 55th—neither commander quite daring to move toward the main battlefield, while a fight in which both of them should have been engaged raged within a few hundred yards of where they stood.

Meanwhile, Cadwalader—whose militiamen were next in the line of march behind the position Mercer had vacated—had had no end of trouble getting his green troops going again, which meant that behind Sullivan's division there was a large gap of about a thousand yards. Beyond that gaping hole, Cadwalader's men were strung out along the road. followed by Hand's regiment of riflemen, with Hitchcock's veterans bringing up the rear. As Cadwalader advanced along the back road behind the screening curtain of woods and turned left to climb the hill back of the Thomas Clark house, he heard the sounds of fighting, but he had no way of knowing, until he reached the crest of the rise, that Mercer's men were in full retreat and that he was about to lead his men into a hornet's nest. Nathanael Greene was also on the back side of the hill, and as soon as he saw Captain Joseph Moulder's two four-pounders coming up he sent them to take a position on what would be the left of a new American line. Cadwalader personally pushed and shoved his men into formation—detaching a group here and sending them to the left, another bunch of men there and directing them to the right, telling them to get into line as fast as possible. Now under any circumstances this would have been a fairly difficult maneuver—sending alternate squads of soldiers from column into line while a battle was going on—but Cadwalader's problem was compounded by the fact that his men had never fought before and had next to no experience in anything but the most rudimentary military movements. Until a few weeks before they had been civilians, and their baptism of fire this morning was under the most harrowing conditions possible.

What greeted them as they marched uncertainly out from behind the woods and over the hill was the sight of those vicious redcoats bayoneting men on the ground, four cannons blazing away in their faces, grapeshot and musket balls whistling over their heads, Mercer's men in a wild panic streaming up the hill toward them, the entire panorama erupting in a scene of fire and explosion and running, terrified men. Those green troops took one look, blinked, and ran for their lives, all mixed in with Mercer's fleeing soldiers, pounding back over the brow of the hill and piling into men who were still coming up, whom Cadwalader was trying so desperately to get into line. All within the space of a few minutes the American march on Princeton had been turned into a rout, and the "bold stroke" that Washington had foreseen was about to come unstitched and end in disaster.

3. *Not a Man but Showed Joy*

Captain Joseph Moulder does not get much space in the history books, but it is just possible that without his services on January 3, 1777, the story of the American Revolution might have turned out rather differently. With the other Philadelphia Associators, Moulder had joined Washington's army in December of 1776, in command of an artillery company that boasted three guns, three officers, and eighty-two enlisted men—mostly rough and ready "alongshoremen, Ship Carpenters, Mast, Block and Sailmakers, Riggers, &c." He and his sailor-gunners had helped out with the two Delaware River crossings, they had fought at Trenton twice—first against the Hessians and later against Cornwallis's army—and when the rebels marched to Princeton Moulder was attached to Cadwalader's brigade of militia, in charge of the artillery. After getting his orders from Greene on the back side of the hill, Moulder maneuvered two guns into place on the edge of the woods near the Thomas Clark house and he did not have to wait for anyone to tell him what to do.

The British light infantry was starting forward from the fence in a wide skirmish line, with Mawhood's main body immediately behind them, supported by four fieldpieces (the abandoned American guns were being used with the two Mawhood had with him). Moulder opened fire with grapeshot on them at once, just at the moment the British colonel was about to have his men charge the retreating rebels. For a few brief minutes, Moulder was without support of any kind—just two guns banging away by themselves against the British infantry and artillery—since Cadwalader was having no success at all getting his men to form a line of defense. He rode back and forth across the brow of the hill, bringing one or two reluctant soldiers up to the front, begging them to fire at the enemy, and finally he managed to persuade an entire company to stand there long enough to get off a volley, but then they broke and ran, carrying with them a lot of other men who were coming forward. Someone ordered Thomas Rodney, who was over on the right of the American line, to bring all the men he could find to support Moulder, so he crossed the enemy line of fire from right to left with about fifteen soldiers, to join another thirty Philadelphians who were sprawled out behind some hay-stacks and the barn, but he couldn't keep any of his men there either.

"The enemy's fire was dreadful," he said, "and three balls . . . had grazed me; one passed within my elbow nicking my greatcoat and carried away the breech of Sargeant McKnatt's gun, he being close behind me, another carried away the inside edge of one of my shoesoles, another had nicked my hat and indeed they seemed as thick as hail."

Had Mawhood realized that all that faced him on top of the hill were two guns and perhaps a score of determined men he certainly would have ordered his troops to charge the position, but he had seen what looked like the makings of a large rebel force rounding the trees beyond the crest, and although they had been driven off, he had no way of knowing how many of them were still there in the woods, waiting to sweep down on him. As it turned out, Moulder and his gunners bought the rebel army just enough time. From the north, where Sullivan's division had halted to prevent the British 55th from trying anything, a tall man on a white horse could be seen galloping toward the scene of battle with half a dozen aides and orderlies strung out behind him, and behind them came the veteran Virginia Continentals and Hand's riflemen at a dead run. Grasping the situation at once, Washington left the riflemen to form up on the right of the hill and, charging over to where Cadwalader's frightened men were huddled in the lee of the slope, reined up in front of them. "Parade with us!" he shouted. "There is but a handful of the enemy, and we will have them directly!" The Pennsylvania militia started to form into little com-panies, men ran around frantically to find their own outfits, the remnants of Mercer's beaten force fell in again, and just then Daniel Hitchcock's New England Continentals came up. Washington told Hitchcock to take his men over to the right and form alongside the Virginians and Hand's troops; he was going to lead these Pennsylvanians into battle himself.

Within a few minutes a long battle line was set, and with his hat in his hand Washington waved them forward while he rode ahead on his horse. By now the British had shifted their line somewhat to the left—probably to get out of range of Moulder's murderous fire and to edge closer to the 55th Regiment that was still perched on the hillside well beyond Maw-hood's left flank—but the American line was a formidable one, stretching the whole way across the hillside, and the men now were moving forward with guns at the ready, following their commander into battle. Washington had given them orders not to fire until he gave the signal, and when they were about thirty yards from the redcoats, he reined up, turned in the saddle, and shouted "Halt!" and then "Fire!" Almost immediately there were two thundering volleys from the opposing armies and one of Washington's new staff officers, John Fitzgerald, seeing the general out there directly in the line of fire between the two battle lines, pulled his hat over his eyes so that he would not see Washington fall. After the crashing explosion, the smoke gradually cleared, and Fitzgerald looked again, to see the commander in chief still in the saddle, calm and unharmed, waving the troops forward.

Hitchock, who had only ten days of life remaining before his tubercular lungs gave out, was bringing his New Englanders into battle like the veterans they were. Two hundred yards from the enemy they formed as if on parade—Lieutenant Colonel Nixon's New Hampshiremen on the right, three Rhode Island regiments in the center, and a Massachusetts outfit under Lieutenant Colonel Henshaw on the left, next to the Pennsylvania militia—and halfway to the British lines they halted, fired a smart volley, and then advanced again. Pausing only to fire and reload, they pushed over toward the right, threatening to turn Mawhood's flank, where Hand's riflemen were already delivering a deadly fire into the redcoats. Moulder's guns were still pouring grapeshot into the British lines, mowing men down in rows, and the awful cacophony of noise rose to a crescendo—muskets going off along both lines, the wounded screaming, cannon belching flame and noise—and suddenly Hitchcock's veterans charged, sweeping up the militia in a surge of excitement when they saw the first redcoats turn and run.

These disciplined British regulars had fought courageously and well, and now, as they fell back, they tried to save their artillery, but the Pennsylvanians were on top of them before they could bring the guns off, and Mawhood gave the order to retreat. They had to cut their way out of isolated pockets with bayonets, run back to join their fellows, and reform to fire again, and they did it magnificently, but at last they broke completely, running in disorder toward the Post Road where some of them turned left and headed for the bridge over Stony Brook. After them came the Americans, with Washington shouting "It's a fine fox chase, boys!" joyously, completely unrestrained in the moment of victory. It was the first time in a military career that dated back to the French and Indian War two decades earlier that he had seen an enemy in full flight across an open field, and he could not resist the chase, leaving to the other generals the job of taking the garrison in the town. At the dooryard of the Thomas Olden house he stopped to join a crowd of soldiers who had congregated there to get a drink of water and to pry, curiously, into the knapsacks the British had stacked in the garden before Mawhood launched his attack. The old man of the house looked them all over and wrote that there was "not a man among them but showed joy in his countenance."

Some of the Americans, instead of pausing, had swarmed onto the Post Road in pursuit of the British, and Hand's relentless frontiersmen drove in from the right, nearly trapping the redcoats, but Mawhood ordered his men to charge with bayonets and they broke through the rebels, crossed the bridge, and ran up the hill on the other side. The British dragoons, who had been engaged from start to finish of the battle, made a stand at the top of the hill, giving Mawhood's infantry time to get away safely, but when the cavalrymen were beaten off, the retreating redcoats scattered in all directions—some following Mawhood toward Maidenhead, others pursued by the riflemen for four miles along Stony Brook toward Pennington. Some were shot, others were taken prisoner, and Hand's marksmen —despite their fatigue and hunger—kept after them until well after dark, finally rejoining Washington the following day. The general, who had fallen in with the Philadelphia Light Horse, was riding on their heels and found the fields littered with gear dropped by the British, which he had the men pick up. At last, satisfied that he could inflict no further damage on the enemy in that direction, he turned around and rode back to Princeton.

Near the edge of town, the men in the 55th Regiment had watched helplessly while Mawhood retreated toward the Post Road, and when they disappeared from view, the commander carried out the last order he had received from the colonel—he faced about and headed toward Princeton to join the 40th Regiment. As they crossed a brook that forms a ravine known as Frog Hollow, they found the 40th already drawn up in line on the crest of the bank on the opposite side and immediately fell in on their left. Sullivan, still moving along the back road, followed this movement warily and then came up along the south side of the ravine to face the enemy. These soldiers of the 55th and 40th regiments were some of the best the British army had, and they knew what discipline and training could accomplish even in the face of heavy odds, but they had also just seen the 17th and part of the 55th destroyed by the rebels, and the heart had gone out of them. When Sullivan sent several regiments to scale the slope and threaten the British left, the redcoats panicked, abandoned their strong position, and fled in confusion toward the town. Some didn't even stop in the village but headed to the northeast, taking a roundabout route —well away from the main road—to Brunswick. But others, pursued closely by Sullivan's division, realized they could not get away and dashed into Nassau Hall, knocked the glass out of the windows, and opened fire on the advancing Americans. There was a hurried consultation outside the big stone building and then Lieutenant Alexander Hamilton and Captain Moulder wheeled up some guns and started blasting away at the walls. One shot went through the prayer hall, decapitating the portrait of King George II inside; another bounced off the side of the building and nearly killed James Wilkinson's horse; then a handful of men led by Captain James Moore—an angry Princeton resident whose house had been looted by the enemy—rushed the front door and broke it down. From one of the windows a white flag fluttered, the Americans backed off, and out of the door came the humiliated regulars—"a haughty, crabbed set of men," as one non-com termed them—to lay down their arms. The battle of Princeton was over.

The ubiquitous Sergeant White, always one to see what he could scrounge in the wake of the fighting, slipped into the college building, caught a glimpse of something he wanted very much, and methodically locked himself into the room. On a table sat a plate of toast, a teapot, "and everything ready for breakfast," so he sat down and helped himself. "I was very hungry," he admitted, "marching all night, and fighting in the morning," but he got enough to satisfy himself and then looked around to see if there was anything else of interest. There was: a brand new, silk-lined British officer's coat, so fresh that the paper was still on the plated buttons; an elegant silk skirt, a pair of silk shoes, and a small gilt Bible—all of which he gathered up before leaving the room. Outside the hall, White learned that the troops had been instructed to throw away their dirty old blankets and replace them from British supplies, so he attended to that. Huge barrels of flour were strewn all around the place, and as many of

these as could be taken off were being loaded into wagons while the rest
were knocked open and the flour spilled onto the ground. Several women
came up and looked hungrily at the flour, and White told them to scoop
as much of it as they could hold in their aprons and take it home. The en-
terprising sergeant, wasting no time, informed a captain who was supervising the loading that he was going to a nearby house and would be back
in a few minutes. He went up to the door and asked the woman who lived
there if she would be willing to bake him a few cakes, if he paid for them
in flour. Yes, she would, she replied. Well, asked White, choosing his
words very carefully, "Do you have any daughters?"

"What do you want to know that for?" the woman asked.

"I am steady as a pious old deacon," White assured her. "How many
have you?"

The woman admitted cautiously that she had two girls, and White told
her that he had a present for each one, which he would give them when
he came back to collect the cakes. After wandering about inquisitively for
awhile, he returned and was introduced to the daughters, one of whom received the elegant silk skirt and the other the silk shoes, while White
went away happily, stuffing his precious cakes into a knapsack. But there
was still one bit of business to attend to: heading back to rejoin his outfit
he met an officer from one of the rifle regiments and sold him the British
officer's coat for eighteen dollars. It would be perfect for him, the New
England trader said; only the buttons would have to be changed.

Elsewhere in town, rebel officers wandered about, waiting for Washington to return from his pursuit of the enemy, and a few of them, like
White, were lucky enough to find meals that had been prepared for British officers. For the first time in days the troops had a chance to enjoy a
few moments of relaxation, and they walked about the village, admiring
the handsome brick houses and especially the fifty-two-room college
structure, although they found the town "ravaged and ruined by the
enemy." One sergeant got to thinking about the change in his own attitude since the day on Long Island when he went into battle for the first
time and had to fortify himself with a healthy swig of rum. Here, he realized, he had required no stimulants, and he discovered to his astonishment
that the end of one of his fingers had been shot off without his feeling it.

Although Washington minimized this aspect of the battle's aftermath
in his report to Congress (probably for fear that the members would treat

less generously his requests for provisions), the soldiers who began by walking about the town like tourists ended their stay by looting it as thoroughly as if it belonged to the enemy. A good many of Sullivan's men had somehow formed the impression that Princeton was a Tory stronghold and regarded this as a license to steal whatever they could lay their hands on. One artillery captain found a box full of silver coins, which he elected not to divide among the other men of the regiment according to established practice. Men broke into houses and went through them like a swarm of locusts, carrying off articles of value, destroying what they could not take with them, and between this and what the British did to the town when they returned later, the place looked to one observer like "a deserted village; you would think it had been desolated with the plague and an earthquake, as well as with the calamities of war; the college and church are heaps of ruin; all the inhabitants have been plundered; the whole of Mr. Stockton's furniture, apparel, and even valuable writings, have been burnt; all his cattle, horses, and dogs, sheep, grain, and forage, have been carried away." (The redcoats went so far as to pull the shoes off a local blacksmith's feet and take them away with them.) In addition to what was lifted from homes, the Americans got off with substantial quantities of blankets, guns, and other stores from the British reserves and appropriated a large number of livestock and horses.

Out on the field of battle, Dr. Benjamin Rush had arrived to perform his unhappy duties, and he observed that the ground was still wet with blood and strewn with the bodies of dead and grievously wounded men. Washington had returned to the field and gave orders that only the wounded were to be taken off; there was no time to bury the dead. So small groups of men roamed the orchard and wheatfield, following the cries of the wounded and taking the worst cases to nearby homes (the houses of Thomas and William Clark, being closest to the battlefield, were used as field hospitals), while others were loaded into wagons and hauled off to the village. By comparison with the brutality they had seen inflicted on Mercer's men, the Americans reckoned themselves merciful: "You are safe enough," some of the wounded redcoats were told, "we are after live men." Hugh Mercer's aide, Major Armstrong, found the general where he had fallen in the orchard, unconscious and bleeding from his wounds, and he and others carried him to the Thomas Clark house to be treated by a British surgeon's mate. Rush did what he could for the mortally wounded Captain William Leslie, a nephew of the British general and the son of a Scottish earl, but Leslie died the next day in Pluckemin and was buried by the Americans with full military honors. A college student who had remained in town walked over the battlefield during the afternoon and was dismayed by the "dismal prospect of a number of pale, mangled corpses." Not until the following day were 36 Americans and British buried in a common grave at the top of the field where Mawhood had launched his attack, and other bodies were interred in the village or in the neighboring countryside. When William Howe made his report on the battle to Germain he listed the British losses at 276, which did not include 10 men of the Royal Artillery who had been killed; but his estimates were deliberately low. Washington told Israel Putnam that the enemy losses were between 500 and 600—a figure that included 300 known prisoners.

Whatever the total may have been, the fact was that the crack British 4th Brigade—the flower of the army—had been shattered, at a cost to the rebels of 30 enlisted men and 14 officers killed. What hurt most, of course, was the loss of some of the finest and least replaceable American officers—particularly Mercer, who died after nine days of agony, and Haslet. It had all happened within the space of about forty-five minutes—with two little armies meeting head on in a field outside an obscure college town—but the effect was to be far beyond the numbers involved. For the moment Washington hadn't the leisure to reckon the gains or the cost; Cornwallis was on the march, and he dared not risk his utterly exhausted army in another engagement.

Two hours after the rebels occupied Princeton, scouts brought word that Cornwallis was within sight of the bridge at Worth's Mill. Washington was still harboring the hope that he could give the troops some rest and then march to Brunswick to seize the stores there, but this report put an end to that prospect; the British coming up from Trenton were fresh, Cornwallis would be out for revenge, and there was no time to lose. He had already instructed General James Potter to have his Pennsylvania militia destroy the bridge over Stony Brook and Captain Thomas Forrest's battery was there in support, but those men could not be expected to hold off the kind of determined attack that Cornwallis would throw at them.

The long roll on the drums was beaten, the tired men fell in, and the columns started moving out of town, bound northeast. (The Pennsylvania militia was still so green that the men had not known two days earlier that the long roll meant that the army was to assemble on the double whenever it was heard, day or night, and they had to be informed in special orders that "every Officer and Soldier must turn out with the greatest alacrity and form on their proper Ground." Having been through a battle now, they were behaving like veterans and knew what to do.) Some of these boys had been on their feet for forty-eight hours, during which time they had fought two battles in the dead of winter, made a forced night march across sixteen rugged miles, and been almost without food or drink. They were approaching the outer limits of human endurance and it was a real question how far they could travel; when Washington saw the way they looked marching out of the college town, he abandoned any idea he had had of moving against Brunswick or any other post. "The harassed state of our troops," he reported to Congress, "and the danger of losing the advantage we had gained by aiming at too much, induced me, by the advice of my officers, to relinquish the attempt."

In the wake of the departing army, Major John Kelly had taken personal charge of the demolition work at the bridge, and it didn't take him long to realize that he was not going to have much time for the job. On the rise beyond him, where Mawhood's troopers had first caught sight of the American army, the first British skirmishers came into view. These were men from Leslie's brigade, which had been sent on ahead of Cornwallis' own troops, and behind them, strung out along the road from Trenton, was the whole British army. Leslie's men had encountered the beaten, demoralized fugitives of Mawhood's command straggling along the road, had heard snatches of conversation about the battle up there in Princeton, and they were boiling mad and ready to take on the first rebels they saw. Several cannon were brought up to open fire on the bridge, but John Kelly was a stubborn Irishman, and he had a notion to spoil things as much as possible for the bloody lobsterbacks. He and his men kept right on with their work, hacking away at the bridge timbers and throwing them off into the stream, while Forrest's guns fired at the British. Cornwallis rode up, saw what was going on, and told Leslie he thought they should take no chances on having the army caught in the narrow defile formed by the stream under those rebel guns, so more artillery was wheeled up and put into action. The fire was really heavy now, and one cannonball hit a plank that Kelly was standing on, catapulting him into the icy river and doing nothing for his temper. He made it to shore all right, but he knew there was nothing more he could do now, and since nothing much remained of the bridge but the stringers, he believed it would be some time before the bulk of the British army—particularly their guns and ammunition wagons—would be pursuing Washington.

Cornwallis' redcoats had found a nearby ford and some of them were across the stream, hotfooting it after the rebels. Poor Kelly was the only fellow they caught—his dousing in the stream had soaked his clothes through, and the air was so cold they froze solid, making it impossible for him to run. More British waded waist-deep through the icy water, others retrieved enough planks to enable foot soldiers to cross the bridge, and they stormed up the road on the Princeton side of the creek, reached the crest of the hill, and were advancing along the main road when a cannon-ball whistled over their heads. They stopped, some officers came forward and talked things over, and they saw, up ahead, the battery of eight six-pounders which Mawhood had placed across the main thoroughfare ear-lier to prevent a rebel attack on the town. There was a good deal of scurrying about, more troops were summoned, flankers sent to right and left to turn the rebel line, and finally, after about an hour had passed, the redcoats advanced to storm the battery. They moved forward slowly, wondering why the guns were silent, and then someone in the advance perceived that the battery was not manned. The single shot that had gone over their heads had been fired by a couple of stragglers from Kelly's de-tail and the rebels had long since departed, all unaware of Cornwallis's elaborate reconnaissance in force.

An old story was repeated as the British entered the town. As at Newark and so many other points along the line of the American retreat through New Jersey, the last rebels were straggling out of one end of the village just as the British advance was entering the other. When the Eng-lish generals came in—"in a most infernal sweat—running, puffing, and blowing, and swearing at being so outwitted," as Henry Knox heard later, the only signs of the rebels were their dead and wounded, the spiked British cannon, thick columns of smoke rising from the stacks of hay and ammunition dumps they had touched off. There had not been enough horses to haul the captured cannons, so all but one had been put out of commission and abandoned; the only gun to fall into rebel hands was a brass six-pounder which Major Thomas Procter appropriated, leaving his own iron three-pounder in exchange for it. While search parties went off to locate the dead and wounded from the 17th and 55th regiments, Cornwallis dispatched the light troops and mounted dragoons to pursue the rebels.

These men were capable of moving fast, and the ragged American army was so encumbered with herds of cattle and sheep, prisoners, and wagonloads of booty that it didn't take the British long to catch up. Once again it was Joseph Moulder and his sailor-gunners who bought Washington's men some time. He was with the rear guard, and when they saw the troopers riding up behind them they loaded and opened fire. The trouble was that Moulder couldn't bring up teams of horses to haul the guns off once they had dispersed the enemy; the British light infantry had arrived to support the cavalry and the musket fire was so intense he did not dare risk exposing the horses, so the captain shouted for help, lashed a couple of long ropes to each cannon, assigned forty men to each line to pull it along the road every time he fired, and drove off the enemy. Like Sergeant White, Moulder was not the man to spike his guns and leave them (and his men were "no grass combers" either, he said proudly), even though the commander in chief had given strict orders to abandon the guns if necessary to save the men. But for all his efforts, the British were getting closer, threatening to burst in on the army's rear, when twenty or more Philadelphia cavalrymen came back and formed a line across the road. That finally discouraged the pursuers, who let the Americans go on their way. A few days later there was a curious sequel to Moulder's small but important rear-guard action; he was brought before a court of inquiry to explain why he had exposed his men in this way, and although he was exonerated, the proceedings made it clear that the commanding general was more interested in preserving experienced gunners than he was in saving their weapons.

Three miles northeast of Princeton the army crossed Millstone Creek and arrived at Kingston, where there was a fork in the road. The main highway went straight on to Brunswick, while the left-hand turn followed the winding course of the little river downstream toward Somerset Court House, and here, at this intersection, Washington had his final opportunity to change his mind about seizing those British stores in Brunswick. Major Wilkinson remembered that the commander in chief and several other general officers halted for quite awhile at that crossroads, looking wistfully in the direction of Brunswick, with everyone speculating on what they could do if only they had some fresh troops. But the moment passed and was lost for all time; it was eighteen miles to Brunswick, it had started to snow again after they left Princeton, and none of the men could be asked to do anything more after what they had been through. Henry Knox, bemoaning the fact that the troops had been without "rest, rum, or provisions for two nights and days," thought that 1,000 additional soldiers could have "struck one of the most brilliant strokes in all history," and Washington later expressed the conviction that a successful attack on Brunswick, with its stores and bulging military chest, could have put an end to the war. Had he possessed definite information about what the British had in that place he would have been even more chagrined than he already was.

The officer in command there, Brigadier General Edward Mathew, was in a first-rate state of nerves over what he was to do if the Americans descended on him and tried to make off with several treasures in his possession. Fugitives from the fighting at Princeton had been arriving since late morning, carrying confused and uncertain accounts of the battle, and a while later a British officer who had escaped brought word that the rebels had left the place and were marching up the Brunswick road. Mathew did not have much with which to stop them—only a small garrison guard and the 46th Regiment which had arrived the preceding day—but he did what he could and posted his men on the heights outside of town, determined to make a show of force that might scare Washington off. At the same time, he loaded all the stores into wagons and dispatched them—along with £70,000 in specie and his very important prisoner, Major General Charles Lee—under heavy guard to a bridge about two miles away, thinking he could get them across the Raritan and then destroy the span if the rebels came. But Mathew could breathe a sigh of relief; no American was capable of attacking his post that day.

Before leaving Kingston, Washington had its bridge demolished to impede Cornwallis' progress, and when the British general arrived with his army, he was further delayed by having to ford Millstone Creek before he decided to push on toward Brunswick. He knew how slim Mathew's resources were, and after what had happened at Trenton, he was taking no chances on Washington outwitting him again; the stores and military chest were more important to him right now than the rebel army, and although it was close to six o'clock he figured he had to keep moving. Meanwhile, he sent a strong cavalry detachment down the left bank of the Millstone to keep an eye on the Americans, and the horsemen arrived at Rocky Hill just as Washington's van approached the town on the opposite side of the stream. Strong as they were, they were not up to taking on the entire American army, and they watched until the last straggler had trudged down the road that led to Somerset Court House, some seven miles away. It was dusk when Washington got there and Thomas Rodney, who was with the van when it marched into town, said that if they had come along an hour earlier they might have captured all the supplies and baggage of the British 4th Brigade—twenty wagonloads of clothing alone—which had been left in a nearby village guarded by only 200 men. Once again, Washington's low opinion of the New Jersey militia was confirmed; it seems that 400 of the latter had surprised the British wagon train and surrounded it, but when the enemy commander, a Captain Scott, formed his men into a square behind the wagons, the militia "were afraid to fire on them and let them go off unmolested," as Rodney wrote in disgust.

By the time the last rebel regiments staggered into town it was eight o'clock at night and freezing cold, and there was no place for them to stay but outdoors. Unfortunately, the prisoners had to be locked up in the courthouse building, so the captors simply dropped in their tracks and slept on the ground; some men collected all the fence rails and loose pieces of wood they could find and built bonfires around which they clustered. The Pennsylvania militiamen were the worst off of the lot, for some stupid officer had sent all their blankets from Trenton to Burlington with the other stores the night before, probably assuming that the wagons would go wherever the troops went. (The poor fellows never did see their blankets again, and the suffering they endured on account of the loss was largely responsible for their unwillingness to stay with the army when it went into winter quarters.) "Our army was now extremely fatigued," wrote Thomas Rodney, putting it mildly, "not having any refreshment since yesterday morning," but the men were up at daybreak and on the march again to Pluckemin, which looked like paradise when they got there. As one captain rejoiced, "we got plenty of beef, pork, &c., which we had been starving for a day or two, not having time to draw and dress victuals." And the commander in chief decided that they ought to have a day of rest, since the army had to wait for the return of Hand's riflemen, who had gone off in pursuit of the fleeing British and been prevented from rejoining Washington by Cornwallis's return to Princeton. Those veterans had had a perfectly dreadful time; they were just as tired and hungry as the others and had been "obliged to encamp on the bleak mountains, whose tops were covered with snow, without even blankets to cover them." When they finally came in, the army made its way to Morristown on January 5 and 6.

A peaceful, protected village on a plateau at the foot of Thimble Mountain, Morristown could be approached by the enemy only through narrow, rugged gorges that afforded almost complete safety, and here there was wood in abundance for log huts and fires, and food in the surrounding countryside. (The gunners in Joseph Moulder's battery were elated when one of their buddies, whom they thought they had lost at Princeton, turned up unexpectedly with a cart loaded with poultry.) In addition, Morristown's geographical location was almost ideal. Only thirty miles from the enemy in New York and Staten Island, the village was protected on the east by the range of parallel ridges known as the Watchung Mountains, which stretched from the Raritan River to the northern boundary of New Jersey; behind them, Washington's lines of communication with New England and Philadelphia were secure, and he could watch for British movements out of New York and move quickly to almost any threatened point without interference. Here he would wait and watch and try to hold together what would remain of his army after the six-week-bonus men left. New recruits would arrive slowly, but when they did, it would be on Washington's own terms—a three-year enlistment. Men would come from all the states, he hoped, and he intended to discourage the strong local feeling that had prevailed in the army by substituting the term "American" for the regional designations. It was, he thought, "the greater name."

4. A Time of Shaking

At Morristown the winter set in in earnest, but sooner or later, from all parts of the state and beyond, reports filtered through from the outside world. Washington's thoughts turned more and more to spring and to assembling wagons, grain, gunpowder and shot, horses, clothing, and the other necessities for a campaign, but what he could learn about the British did nothing to diminish his satisfaction over the victories he had won. In his hurry to get to Brunswick, Cornwallis had driven his army so hard over the sloppy roads that a number of wagons broke down, and rather than wait until they were repaired, he left them by the side of the high road in charge of a quartermaster and a guard of about 200 men. Just before night fell on January 3, about twenty New Jersey cavalrymen led by Captain John Stryker caught sight of the forlorn collection of wagons and their jumpy guards and that night they moved quietly through the woods, surrounded the British, and suddenly loosed a barrage of musket fire at them.

Stryker had instructed his men to yell like fury when they opened fire, and the British guards, thinking they were attacked by a large rebel force, bolted away from their campfires and out into the night, never stopping to look back. Stryker's troopers dismounted, calmly set about repairing the wagons, and hauled them off to Washington's camp at Morristown, where it was discovered to everyone's joy that they contained large quantities of winter clothing. Nor was this the last cross Cornwallis's men had to bear that same night. They were only slightly less tired and hungry than the Americans, they had seen the grisly aftermath of the battle in Princeton (Ensign Glyn and other officers believed that Washington's army must have consisted of 15,000 men, to inflict so many casualties), and now their general was pushing remorselessly toward Brunswick in a march that did not end until the last man limped into town at nine o'clock the next morning. Some of the Hessians were so fatigued "they could barely totter," one of them wrote; their baggage was so jumbled up in the line of march that they had halted again and again, and at each stop "it was quite a job to get the men on their feet."

In the days that followed the pressure never let up. British outposts were established on all roads leading into Brunswick, guards were strengthened at the principal communication centers between there and New York, and the soldiers got orders to be at their alarm stations "half an hour before Daybreak, and to remain under arms till Sun Rise, this to be continued every Morning till further notice." They were to keep their weapons with them at all times, an emergency alarm system was instituted, and in his orders Cornwallis even went so far as to hint at the general demoralization that pervaded the army. He was thoroughly aware, he said, "of the great fatigue which the Troops have suffered, yet he flatters himself, if a glorious opportunity should happen of attacking the Enemy, they will exert themselves upon that occasion, not thinking an unexpected March a hardship." Writing to Germain a few days later, Cornwallis reported that most of the damage the rebels had done in New Jersey had been repaired and that Washington, who was at Morristown with about 7,000 men, could not "subsist long where he is. I should imagine that he means to repass the Delaware," the general added. "The season of the year will make it difficult for us to follow him, but the march alone will destroy his army."

Yet somehow the nonchalance of that letter did not quite square with the tone of Cornwallis's orders to his troops, and it was evident in other quarters that efforts were being made to paper over the facts of the calamitous week. Publicly, General Howe made no mention of the battle at Princeton beyond effusive praise of Colonel Mawhood and other officers and men of the 17th Regiment for their "Gallantry and good Conduct in the Attack made upon the Enemy," while James Rivington's newspaper described the engagement as a brilliant victory for the regulars which had cost the Americans 400 casualties. Just before the battle, Ambrose Serle was tending Lord Howe, who was indisposed with a "bilious Cholic," but he confided to his journal on Saturday, January 4, that there was "indistinct" news of an action somewhere in New Jersey. "All men were anxious to hear the Particulars," he noted, but on Sunday his anxiety vanished. It had turned out to be no more than a skirmish, he said, between 700 or 800 British and 4,000 rebels, in which the latter had lost about 300 men, while only 20 regulars were killed and 100 wounded. Several days later Serle was still assuring himself that "the Rebels have gained no Credit in the Jersies," and he was further heartened by hearing his new friend Andrew Allen compute the total American losses for the past year at no less than 25,000 men.

Most of the comment turned on Trenton and the failure of the Hessians, who were convenient whipping boys, and one of the few to mention the British defeat at Princeton was General von Heister, who had not yet learned that he was to be dismissed and who wrote to his master in Hesse that "an English brigade has shared the same fate as the Rall brigade." The only difference, he said, was that "The English regiments have no flags or cannon with them and so are saved the misfortune of losing them." Heister was mistaken about the cannon, but he knew exactly what the prince was going to say about those captured regimental colors and he was doing his best to take the sting out of the humiliation.

Howe, who had not bothered to go over to New Jersey to see what might be done after the Hessians lost Trenton, had discovered how tenuous his chain of posts really was and remedied the situation tardily by withdrawing the troops from all but Perth Amboy and Brunswick, at each of which he stationed 5,000 men, which was enough to discourage the rebels from trying anything. Meanwhile he had other more important things on his mind: he was supervising the final arrangements for his investiture as Knight Commander of the Bath on January 18, the queen's birthday—a festive affair that would be celebrated with an elaborate supper party, a ball, and various other entertainments. According to one newspaper account, the general would be invested with the order by his brother, the admiral, assisted by General von Heister in the presence of a "numerous Assembly," after which the ball would be opened by His Excellency Governor Tryon and a Miss Clark. Fireworks, skating and sleighing parties, and street dancing were all on the program, and the soldiers and sailors were to be given special liberty for the night. For all his preoccupation, however, Howe recognized the meaning of what had taken place in the icy wastes of New Jersey, and two days after the celebration he wrote to Germain, expressing concern that the enemy's successes had "thrown us further back than was at first apprehended, from the great encouragement it has given the rebels. I do not now see a prospect of terminating the war, but by a general action, and I am aware of the difficulties in our way to obtain it, as the enemy moves with so much celerity than we possibly can." To a general with no stomach for winter campaigning, the rapidity with which the Americans had moved was incomprehensible.

The effects of Trenton and Princeton were, after all, in the eye of the beholder, and Henry Knox, whose artillery had been a significant factor in both battles, was puffed up about the achievement. "The enemy were within nineteen miles of Philadelphia," he said proudly, "they are now sixty miles. We have driven them from almost the whole of West Jersey. The panic is still kept up." If that last statement was accurate, the soldiers at Morristown were in luck, for they were certainly in no condition to do anything further to the enemy. Psychologically, they were in as precarious a state as they were physically, as Washington hinted on January 8. Writing to the Pennsylvania Council of Safety, he thanked them for alerting him to an eclipse of the sun the following day. Had it come without warning, he thought, it was just the sort of thing that would adversely "affect the minds of the soldiery."

There were several thousand militiamen in camp, but the Continental Army hit rock bottom on January 19, when only 800 veterans answered roll call. Nathanael Greene described the army as "a shadow of a force," and Washington was hard put to say how they would be able to "rub along" until new recruits started coming into camp. Meanwhile, the American commander was doing his utmost to befuddle the enemy and cannily distributed his men around town so thinly that even local residents guessed that he had 40,000 on hand. Happily, there were a few encouraging omens: a report came in that the New Jersey militia had taken heart from the victories and were volunteering for duty; Nathanael Greene was convinced that the army's accomplishments would soon put "a very different face upon affairs." *

* In the light of all that befell them, it is remarkable how optimistic Washington's principal lieutenants could be. Greene's positive state of mind never entirely deserted him during the war, despite a career that must have been a maddening blend of military defeats and personal disappointments, only occasionally leavened with moments of triumph. His virtue as a soldier was that he never stopped learning, and after the fall of Fort Washington he redeemed himself at Trenton, Brandywine, Germantown, Monmouth, and Newport. But there were complaints from Congress that he was dominating the commander in chief; he had a run-in with the civilian authorities while he was serving as quartermaster general; and not until Washington sent him south in 1780 to replace Horatio Gates did he come into his own. Usually outnumbered and insufficiently supplied, he succeeded there largely because of his insight into the mind of his foe, Cornwallis, and his mastery of guerrilla warfare. In a

Beyond their mountain fastness, news of Trenton and Princeton flew through the country as if on wings, and on January 6 Nicholas Cresswell, the indefatigable English traveler who was still visiting in Virginia, first learned something about the affair at Trenton. He saw at once that "the minds of the people are much altered. Their late successes have turned the scale and now they are all liberty mad again." Recruiting parties that had been unable to get a single man a week earlier were collecting them in company lots now, and Cresswell estimated that the war might be prolonged by as much as two years because the Americans had recovered from their fright. It would be no easy matter to throw them into such confusion again. "Confound the turncoat scoundrels and the Hessians together," he stormed. "The rascals will be stronger than ever. Even the parsons, some of them, have turned out as Volunteers and Pulpit Drums or Thunder, which you please to call it, summoning all to arms in this cursed babble. D——— them all."

On the part of Hessian and British soldiers there was a growing realization that they were up against something quite different from what they had experienced earlier; as a fusilier in the Lossberg regiment perceived, "far too little was thought of the enemy who up to now had not been able to withstand us on any occasion." Lieutenant Colonel William Harcourt, the man in command of the troopers who captured Charles Lee, sensed that the situation in America had altered dramatically. Harcourt was no admirer of the rebel soldiers—had, in fact, formed a low opinion of them during the first year of fighting—but he was beginning to think that

---

land of steaming swamps and musical place names, Greene's method was swift, deadly movement; his philosophy, "We fight, get beat, rise, and fight again." Although he never won a major victory, he never lost a campaign, and even before he had pushed Cornwallis toward Yorktown and defeat, it began to dawn on Americans that Greene was, if not the best, at least the second-best field commander they had. He summed up his achievement more modestly: there were few generals, he said, who have "run oftener, or more lustily than I have done, But I have taken care not to run too far, and commonly have run as fast forward as backward, to convince our Enemy that we were like a Crab, that could run either way."

Ater the war Greene found himself saddled with debts he had contracted in order to supply his army, so he sold his Rhode Island property and moved to a plantation given him by the grateful state of Georgia. But he was not to enjoy any rest from his labors here; in 1786, after a long, hot day in the rice fields, he died of sunstroke at the age of forty-four. Half a dozen years later an inventive young man named Eli Whitney visited Greene's widow at the plantation, was struck by the need to make such unprofitable land productive, and within ten days had designed a machine called the "cotton-gin."

something was wrong with the way the government in London was conducting the war and the manner in which the generals were waging it.

Writing to his father, he blasted the Hessians for "scandalous negligence and cowardice," but went on to blame Howe for what had happened, for arranging the winter quarters so that they were too isolated for a relatively small army to maintain and protect. The war had become a new kind of conflict, somewhere along the way, and where the British army had formerly gone about its business surely and confidently, now it suffered badly from lack of intelligence about the enemy and missed one opportunity after another for a stunning blow. Whenever the redcoats did go out in force to attack the rebels, they were harried mercilessly all the way back to their base; they should never march without artillery, he concluded, since the Americans only showed respect for them when they could bring up their guns. And although the admission came hard, he had to say that whereas it was once the fashion to treat the rebels "in the most contemptible light, they are now become a formidable enemy." They had a lot to learn, Harcourt could see: they were totally ignorant of drill and didn't know the first thing about moving large groups of men about; yet they seemed to possess many of the requisites that made good troops, such as "extreme cunning, great industry in moving ground and felling of wood, activity and a spirit of enterprise upon any advantage." The young colonel would not have known the meaning of the words, but the rebels—at the instigation of their commander in chief—had discovered the enormous effectiveness of something that would come to be called guerrilla warfare. Beyond anything else, the tactics employed at Trenton and Princeton showed what a small, determined body of men could do, moving swiftly and unexpectedly against isolated units of a superior army. Coming at a time when the British people and most of the rest of the world expected the American rebellion to fall apart, they had accomplished something far more important than alleviating the panic that afflicted their countrymen; they made it plain, as John Hancock was to see, that the conquest of America was an unattainable prospect.

In London the public at large knew next to nothing about what was happening in America. They could, of course, read published reports from the British commander in chief and, by guessing what lay between the lines, discern something. They also had limited access to American newspapers and journals, but it was generally conceded that these were inflammatory and unreliable. The truth was that not many people concerned themselves with the events or the rights or wrongs of what was going on; they were much more likely to fall back on the comfortable assumption that the government, which ought to know, had told them that the rebels were contemptible antagonists and that the war would be brief and conclusive. As a foreign visitor observed caustically, this attitude was a factor of the English character. If you spoke to the average London tradesman about the British Constitution, he would tell you that it was a glorious one; but ask him what it was and you discovered he was ignorant of its first principles. The fellow had a deep reverence for the monarchy, which embodied for him the sum total of religion, politics, and trade. He was sure that London was the finest city in the world and the river Thames the largest in the universe, and it was in vain to tell him that there were many rivers in America beside which the Thames resembled a ditch, or that the newly independent states were much more extensive in breadth than the British Isles combined.

There were, to be sure, some voices beside those of the Opposition in Parliament that were questioning the government's policies. A number of newspapers began attacking Lord North's program more vehemently, condemning the tactics and behavior of William Howe and asking whether the taking of Long Island, for example, which had earned the general a knighthood, was worth one fortieth part of what it had cost to reclaim it, or what the price of occupying the entire American coastline would be at those exorbitant rates.† One Englishman calculated that the

---

† This was a mild foretaste of what was to come. Although Howe had nothing to do with planning the Canadian expedition of 1777, which ended in Burgoyne's defeat at Saratoga, he inexplicably removed his army from any possibility of co-operating with Burgoyne by sailing leisurely off to Philadelphia on July 23. By backing and filling in New Jersey and then moving his troops from Staten Island to Philadelphia by sea, he wasted the entire spring and summer (it took him a full two months to travel these 100 miles). Not surprisingly, Germain became increasingly hostile toward him, Charles James Fox and other members of the Opposition were agitating for an investigation of Howe's prosecution of the war, and the general, anticipating correctly that he would get the blame for Burgoyne's defeat, asked to resign. On May 25, 1778, three years to the day after his arrival in Boston, he sailed for England.

There followed a long, inconclusive inquiry of Howe's conduct by Parliament—an investigation punctuated by acrimonious pamphlet attacks and counterattacks from the sidelines (one of Howe's most persistent critics was Joseph Galloway, the loyalist refugee). The only discernible result of all this was a widespread suspicion that there had been something treacherous about Howe's conduct. In 1780 Sir William published his own defense of his conduct of the war and almost simultaneously lost the seat he had held in Parliament for two decades. In 1803 he retired from the army and was appointed governor of Plymouth, where he died at the ripe age of eighty-five.

expense of the war, from the time of the battle of Lexington through the
end of 1776, was no less than £30,000,000, including the losses suffered
by merchants and planters, and that 20,000 troops, at least, had been lost
through battle, sickness, and desertion. Supposing America *could* be
conquered, he asked, what advantage was to be gained from it? And if
it should be lost, what then? "The small progress made by so large an
army and fleet in a whole campaign" and the ineffectiveness of the
Howes' peace proclamations proved that "the latter alternative is but too
probable."

Some people were beginning to wonder whether the king's ministers
were right, after all, or even if they were telling the truth, and M.P.s and
peers who had supported North's policies admitted to one another that
they were uneasy about the course of events. One Londoner, after
reading the reports about Trenton and Princeton, put his finger close to
the heart of the British problem. "The small scale of our maps deceived
us," he said. An Englishman studying the globe could see that the word
"America" took up no more space than the word "Yorkshire," and might
conclude that the territories they represented were the same size. Nor did
he stop to think that Charleston was as far from Boston as London was
from Venice. "We have undertaken a war against farmers and farmhouses, scattered through a wild waste of continent," he said, "and shall
soon hear of our General being obliged to garrison woods, to scale mountains, to wait for boats and pontoons at rivers, and to have his convoys and
escorts as large as armies. These, and a thousand such difficulties, will rise
on us at the next stage of the war. I say the next stage, because we have
hitherto spent one campaign, and some millions, in losing one landing-
place at Boston; and, at the charge of seven millions and a second campaign, we have replaced it with two other landing-places at Rhode Island
and New York . . . Something more is required, than the mere mechani-
cal business of fighting, in composing revolts and bringing back things to
their former order."

A similar thought was in the back of Lord George Germain's mind
when he wrote the Howe brothers concerning the feasibility of pursuing
their peace mission. He hoped earnestly that the unexpected events at
Trenton and Princeton would not buoy up the rebels so much that they
would be prevented from seeing "the real horrors of their situation" and
ask for pardons. Frederick the Great, who had won and lost more battles

than most men could count, was wise enough not to exaggerate the importance of any one victory or defeat, but he concluded, after following Washington's vicissitudes against overpowering odds, that the former colonies would now be able to keep their independence. And in England Horace Walpole, who kept a close eye on the journals and an ear to the gossip in government circles, reported that General Washington's reputation was soaring and that his march from Trenton around Cornwallis's flank was acknowledged to be a military masterpiece.

What the British government found vastly more disturbing than any reaction at home was the marked change of attitude in the palace of Versailles. There the ambassador, Lord Stormont, met frequently with Charles Gravier, Comte de Vergennes, France's minister of foreign affairs, and their polite, civilized conversations had, until now, glossed over a situation well known to both of them—that France was secretly supplying the rebels with arms, cannon, and clothing through Caron de Beaumarchais' dummy corporation, Hortalez & Cie. (Beaumarchais was operating out of a mansion that had belonged to the Dutch embassy—"a house so beautiful that nobody could live in it," one man said—where he resided with his whole family, including his mistress, and supervised the flow of supplies and munitions to the Americans.) But in January the two diplomats had a tense, uncomfortable meeting; Stormont had learned through one of his numerous agents that the ships now loading cargoes for America in French harbors would not even be flying American colors—they would be sailing under the flag of France, manned by French crews, indicating that the government of Louis XVI was growing bolder—to the point of risking a showdown with Great Britain. And on February 25 Stormont stomped in to see Vergennes with an even more serious complaint: an American privateer, the *Reprisal*, had brought four captured English vessels into a French port, and Stormont demanded that France return the prizes to their rightful owners and take steps to prevent rebel privateers from seizing British ships off the coast of France.

As luck would have it, the news of Trenton and Princeton was received at the French court that day, and Stormont saw that the accounts were being read with unconcealed glee. In the weeks that followed he found the French attitude hardening perceptibly; there was a distinct change from the previous fall, when British victories had made the possibility of the rebels' success seem remote, if not impossible. As Stormont warned in a report to the secretary of state in London, "It is certain, My Lord, that the general animosity against us and the wild enthusiasm in favor of the rebels was never greater than it is at present . . . that M. de Vergennes is hostile in his heart and anxious for the success of the Rebels I have not a shadow of a doubt."

On the American home front, a little prosperity stretched a long way in the winter of 1777 and a lot of old, rancorous scores were being settled. Marauding bands of militia were out again all over New Jersey and the Tories, who had felt relatively secure during the British occupation, felt the hot breath of fear once more. Rebel forces seized Hackensack, Newark, and Elizabethtown, a group of local soldiers forced fifty Waldeckers to surrender in Monmouth County, New Jersey troops camped on the shore opposite Staten Island, and the countryside beyond the enclaves of the opposing armies was tight with anxiety. John Adams, confident that General Howe would "repent his mad march through the Jerseys," saw that "the people of that Commonwealth begin to raise their spirits exceedingly and to be firmer than ever. They are actuated by resentment now, and resentment coinciding with principle is a very powerful motive."

Take, for instance, the unhappy tale of the Van Cortlandt family.

Philip Van Cortlandt, after graduating from King's College in New York and having considerable success as an investor, moved in 1772 to a country estate near Hanover, New Jersey, where he farmed, bred mares, operated a pearl ash works, and contemplated a joyous future life. Van Cortlandt was an intimate of the royal governor, William Franklin, but even after the Declaration of Independence—although he refused to take up arms against the king—he continued to socialize occasionally with acquaintances on the other side, Washington, Greene, and Putnam among them. Early in December 1776, when Charles Lee's army was marching down through New Jersey, a boy came to the house to warn him that he was going to be arrested, and Van Cortlandt fled, leaving his wife, Catharine, and nine children behind. Ten minutes later a party of armed Americans appeared at the door, saying they had orders to take Van Cortlandt prisoner and deliver his favorite horse, Sampson, to General Lee; then they clumped through the house searching for the loyalist, muttering threats that terrified Catharine and the children, and finally left when they were satisfied that he wasn't there.

In the weeks that followed, Catharine was plagued by constant visits from rebel troops, who stopped by to demand something to eat or a place to spend the night. A New England company moved into the kitchen, soldiers roamed through the nursery at all hours, a French officer sent his cavalrymen over every day for feed from the granary, the woods were cut down, and no farmer would sell her food, no miller would grind the grain. One night a bunch of rebel officers held a party at the house and demanded that Catharine dance with them, in company with "some tawdry dressed females I had never seen, and among them the colonel's housekeeper, whom I did not know." The family was almost without food, and when one of the children picked up a dirty piece of bread from the floor and offered it to her mother, it was the last straw; she went to see General St. Clair and begged him to ask Washington to give her a pass into New York. For weeks she waited, and when the pass finally came through, Catharine Van Cortlandt collected her children, bid a tearful adieu to their home—which neither she nor her husband would see again—and traveled through a snowstorm to Hackensack. A woman who owned an inn there refused them admittance when she heard the family name, since it was public knowledge that Philip Van Cortlandt had accepted a lieutenant colonelcy in the New Jersey loyalist brigade, but one resident took pity and gave them lodgings for the night. The next day, riding through a sleet storm, Catharine pleaded with a farmer for some milk for her youngest, but when he discovered who she was he swore at her and said "he would not give a drop to any Tory Bitch." At last they arrived at Hoboken ferry, with all that remained of their property clutched in their hands. As she wrote her husband, when he left she had been "hearty and blooming," but she feared that he would find her "much altered now" as a result of what she had been through.

Other loyalists who had relied on the British to protect them did a rapid about-face with the change in rebel fortunes, thereby thoroughly bewildering the Hessians, who couldn't fathom what was going on. One of the Germans told the story of arriving in Trenton to find the residents all swearing allegiance to the King of England; then, when the American troops attacked the town, the very same people were seen shooting at the Hessians from their houses. Before winter ended the loyalists in Manhattan were in a desperate way for food and fuel, despite the British presence; if a family was lucky enough to own a cow, they would let the animal nurse her calf until it was ready to butcher and then slaughter both. And British soldiers going out into the New Jersey countryside for provisions and firewood were the targets of snipers wherever they went—"Not a stick of wood, a spear of grass, or a barrel of corn," Judge Thomas Jones wrote, "could the troops in New Jersey procure without fighting for them." It was increasingly difficult to tell where a man's loyalties really were these days, and for many people in New Jersey, doing their utmost to survive a time of acute scarcity, one side began to look as villainous as the other.

As the Reverend Mr. Shewkirk observed, thinking back upon a year that had been full of troubles, "these times have been a time of shaking and what had no root is dropped off."

5. *Not an Enemy in the Jersies*

The snows of 1776 were melting. Notice of it came first when icicles clinging to the eaves of soldiers' huts shrank in the sun and from every overhang water dripped, insistent, like the ticking of metronomes. The days grew longer and warmer, each one exceeding its predecessor's quota; along the fringes of newly bared brown earth the retreating snow wore a gray, unhealthy look. Where there had been ice there were now pools of water; roads were bottomless, brimming with mud. Birds flew in from the south to reclaim remembered territory, and finally the sole relics of winter were stubborn patches of white lodged in ravines or hidden beneath boulders on the north slopes of the Watchungs. Streams, swollen, dirty, and angry, plunged toward the valley to swell a torrent already racing to the sea. Sap was rising, and the fecund earth, warming to life and hope, began to stir from its long sleep. April was water and mud; May the leafing out of trees and soft winds that dried the soil. Where had the time gone, farmers wondered. Winter was over.

Somehow the army in Morristown had survived it, which was more than most people would have bet on six months earlier, and as the vanished season became a memory, even the quarters of winter were shed like an obsolete cocoon. On May 28 the commander in chief moved from Morristown to Middle Brook, on the Raritan River above Brunswick, and three days later the army followed. "We shall get languid here," Adam Stephen predicted, thinking it was too soft compared to what they had endured. The enemy, he reminded himself, "are in possession of a fine country, well supplied with green [i.e., young] lamb, veal, beef, mutton and pretty girls."

Unlike Stephen, "Joe Gourd" Weedon was delighted with what he saw in Middle Brook on his return from a long leave. Not only did the men have comfortable tents, but they were healthy, well armed, well clothed, and, from General Washington down to the privates on sentry duty, in the highest spirits imaginable. Weedon could not help thinking what a change had occurred since December. Immense quantities of muskets and ammunition had arrived from France—for most of which Portsmouth, New Hampshire, was the port of entry; not a day passed but there were new faces in the ranks, and general orders reflected the commander in chief's determination that everyone should know and be prepared to do exactly what was required of him. That even included fifers and drummers, who were expected to practice regularly while the infantry drilled. "Nothing," Washington stated, "is more agreeable and ornamental than good music."

It might be said that Washington was no better off than he was a year earlier, listening for whatever tune Howe might call, waiting to see what the British would do before he made a move. Yet there was a difference, an important one, which became evident as soon as Sir William finally launched his campaign. On the night of June 17, 27,000 British and Hessian troops crossed from Staten Island to New Jersey, to all intents and purposes poised for a march on Philadelphia. That was when it became clear that the rebels were not going to play this thing quite the way Howe expected them to and that certain things the British had taken for granted during the previous campaign no longer applied. Although Washington had neither the means nor the intention of meeting Howe head on out there in the flatlands of New Jersey, he was not retreating as he would have done the previous fall. He had learned something about the British, which was that they had no fondness for marching through open country with an enemy force menacing their rear, and he planned to capitalize on that knowledge by threatening to do what he could not, in fact, do—attack. (by not taking the fight to the British he knew he was laying himself open to criticism, especially in Congress, from those "who wish to make themselves popular at the expense of others, or who think the cause is not to be advanced otherwise than by fighting," but now even that did not worry him.)

So while Howe and his mammoth army dawdled in the vicinity of Brunswick, marching and countermarching, making a show of heading for Philadelphia while trying their best to lure Washington into the open, the latter waited at Middle Brook, watching for a chance to pounce on any unit that became separated from that ponderous host. Howe's junior officers, grumbling about the slowness and lack of purpose with which the campaign had begun, were angered by a rumor they heard, to the effect that Admiral Howe had told Joseph Galloway there was no hope of "obtaining America by arms." The charade the general was conducting made it appear to them that he had no real idea where he was going, and by the time he had actually marched nine or ten miles down the road, Howe had convinced even himself that he was going nowhere—nowhere, that is, toward bagging the fox. Worse, the threatened British advance had stirred up a mare's nest in New Jersey and it began to look as if the whole damned countryside was rising. Militiamen were out all over the place, and as Major John André noted, all approaches to the British camp "were infested by ambuscades."

What had not come to pass in 1776, in other words, was happening now. Large numbers of Pennsylvania and New Jersey militiamen were actively under arms—a phenomenon as discouraging to the enemy as it was heartening to local people, Washington believed. It was this kind of thing—and only this—that would "inspire the people themselves with a confidence in their own strength, by discovering to every individual the zeal and spirit of his neighbors." The immediate result, as Henry Knox predicted to Lucy on June 21, was that "in five days there will not be an enemy in the Jersies." Sure enough, wearying of trying to draw the rebel army into battle, Howe retired to Staten Island on the night of June 25, removing from the state of New Jersey the last British and Hessian soldiers. Since the previous November, when Cornwallis crossed the Hudson and came storming into Fort Lee, the British had controlled the area.

Now they had gone, abandoning New Jersey just as they had left Boston to the Americans a year before.

They would come again somewhere else, as mighty as ever, overrunning city and countryside, plunging rebel partisans into despair. Yet somehow the fact that they had pulled out of occupied territory for the second time in as many years put things in a slightly different light, giving rise to some speculation that whatever happened during this campaign or the next might not be the end of everything after all.

There was a long, long road ahead for the rebels, and in the spring of 1777 one would have had to be blessed with second sight to make out what was at the end of it, but in at least two respects things were distinctly different from what they had been seven or eight months earlier. For one, the army was an altogether different army. It had turned a corner of some kind, and the men who were part of it seemed to sense this instinctively. A high percentage of the veterans had gone home, but there were still enough old-timers around who had endured the worst that the enemy and the forces of nature had been able to throw at them. This hard core had had the experience of beating the Hessians and the British regulars in battle, and that was something they were not likely to forget. There was no surety of ultimate victory in this—it was simply one of those small but important considerations a man turns over in his mind on the march or while he sits in front of a campfire, looking into the flames, wondering if what has been accomplished once cannot be done again.

Equally significant was the subtle change in the army's commander. All the old problems and worries were with him, and would remain; in the months and years to come the predicament of the army and the cause alike would worsen more often than it improved. But like the veterans who marched behind him, Washington had Trenton and Princeton and all they signified under his belt, and no one was going to take that away from him. Whatever had been won there had been the result of his determination and exercise of sheer will, and he had emerged from the experience with a confidence that was not going to be easily shaken.

On December 7, 1776, the American agent in France, Silas Deane, had sent Congress a list of French officers who had volunteered to serve with General Washington's army. The names included that of the Marquis de Lafayette, a distinguished young nobleman to whom Deane promised the rank of major general in the Continental Army. One of the many things

Lafayette came to realize after he had served for a time with that army was that the cause and its commander were synonymous—that the liberties of America and the continued existence of its fighting force both depended in large measure upon one individual, who was, it could be fairly said, the rock on which they were anchored. George Washington had been candid with Congress at the time he received his appointment as commander in chief; he told them he was not sure he had the ability or the experience the task required. But a year and a half of war had altered those deficiencies. Once he realized that he could never hope to outmatch the British on their own terms, he knew he had to lure them into situations that were unfamiliar to them, where the advantage would be with him. The war should be defensive, he kept reminding Congress and his officers; avoid a general action at all costs, never put anything to the risk "unless compelled by a necessity into which we ought never to be drawn."

His best plans were relatively simple ones, because he knew no others and because, even if he had, he lacked officers and men with the experience to carry out anything but uncomplicated maneuvers. And as his remark when he decided not to go on to Brunswick after the battle of Princeton revealed, he was constantly aware of the danger of losing all by aiming too high. Patient and absolutely determined, he was capable of waiting for another opportunity to come along because he knew he had no alternative, and unlike Charles Lee, who came so close to replacing him, he was driven not by private or personal ambition, but by motives that could only be called idealistic. In an age when commanders of armies fought with their men, George Washington had all the attributes that inspired soldiers to follow: composure, dignity, presence, a deep determination, and an absolute unwillingness to accept defeat. Not many men ever saw Washington disturbed by bad news; it was much more likely to have the opposite effect on him, acting like a goad that brought out the best in his character, stiffening his resolve to win against odds that would have defeated a less resolute man before he began.

More clearly than anyone else at the time, Washington had realized that the final hours of 1776 marked off the end of the line, that the dream which Thomas Paine and Thomas Jefferson had voiced earlier in the year would vanish on the winds of winter unless he personally did something to salvage it and make his countrymen realize that it was worth fighting and dying for. So what took place along the icy Delaware River was not just the story of men enduring unbelievable hardship and winning several battles that were negligible in terms of the number of men engaged and which had almost no immediate effect upon Great Britain's resolve to continue the war. They demonstrated that the new American nation had a fighting chance to win what it had set out to achieve if people would only stick at it long enough, with the determination it would require.

Because those battles were fought, in other words, history passed a turning point. The army and the cause it represented could and would endure. The issues that had been responsible for the war in the first place would be settled at some future time and place. The King of France would decide that it was worth his while to support the Americans, setting in motion the chain of events that was to culminate in the triumphs at Saratoga and Yorktown. And since without Trenton and Princeton there would have been no army to fight at Saratoga and Yorktown, the campaign Washington had just won was the decisive one of the war. For nearly a year—ever since the British army evacuated Boston—George Washington had been seeking a victory, and by the time he reached the Pennsylvania bank of the Delaware River the sands were running out. There remained only a few days and hours in which to achieve it, and what he did was something that had to be done or the cause of independence was lost irretrievably.

The fighting would go on for five more years, in a struggle that was just as bitterly contested as anything that had gone before, with as much hardship and heartache for the Americans and as much stubborn determination on the part of George III and his ministers. It was, the Earl of Chatham would say four months before the end came at Yorktown, "a most accursed, wicked, barbarous, cruel, unnatural, unjust, and diabolical war." And where is the Englishman, he asked, "who on reading the narrative of those bloody and well-fought contests can refrain lamenting the loss of so much British blood shed in such a cause, or from weeping on whatever side victory might be declared?"

By then the conflict had developed, as so many Englishmen feared, into something far more serious than an inter-family struggle, having become a world war in which Great Britain found herself fighting alone against the French, Spanish, and Dutch, as well as the Americans, and squeezed economically by a league of armed neutrals organized by Catherine the

Great of Russia. Yet in spite of everything that conspired against him, George III never really bowed to the inevitable, never yielded an inch from the resolve that the empire must be preserved, intact and undiminished, lest the loss of the colonies set off a reaction like a set of dominoes falling, with the West Indies, Ireland, and the other possessions ultimately going their way until England was left alone, her resources utterly reduced. He never forgave nor forgot, and in his declining years, long after the war was over, confided to a friend, "I shall never rest my head on my last pillow in peace and quiet as long as I remember the loss of my American colonies."

As Lord North had foreseen, the war went on despite all the pressures public and private against it, continuing until the English people were ultimately sick to death of it and unwilling to let it drag on any longer. At no time, North said, had it been the war of the king or of the king's ministers, regardless of what men thought. It was the war of Parliament and the people, and it never ceased to have popular support "until a series of unparalleled disasters and calamities caused the people, wearied out with almost uninterrupted ill-success and misfortune, to call out as loudly for peace as they had formerly done for war."

The Americans' revolution survived—survived in some mysterious way that no one could quite fathom—in no small part because of what George Washington and his soldiers achieved against all the odds that nature and a vastly superior military force could pit against them. At the time of the battles of Trenton and Princeton the number of men serving in the Continental Army against the assembled might of Great Britain was no more than the number of students in a fair-sized modern high school. Because of their accomplishments, the waning days of 1776 were not the end of everything, but a new beginning. Washington's problems would remain with him through it all—not enough men or weapons or skilled officers, insufficient supplies, inadequate food, disease and misery in the violent heat of summer and the paralyzing cold of winter. The capital would fall to the enemy, the army would freeze and starve and mutiny, Washington's difficulties with Congress would mount, there would be a plot against his leadership, one of his trusted officers would betray the country. The obstacles were beyond all counting.

But never again, in all the long history of the war, would the dream of independence look so dim or unattainable as it had in the fading light of Christmas Day, 1776.

ACKNOWLEDGMENTS

In the course of some years of work on this book it has been my good fortune to have access to one of the great libraries of the land, the New York Public Library, where I have been given assistance, hospitality, and the privilege of doing much of my research in the Frederick Lewis Allen Room. To the staff there, I am extremely grateful.

I have also called upon the facilities of various other institutions, including The New-York Historical Society, the Yale Club and Century Association libraries, the Library of Congress, the National Maritime Museum in Greenwich, England, the Princeton University Library, and the Morristown National Historical Park. Members of the staffs at all these institutions have my deep appreciation for their courtesy and co-operation.

To Samuel Vaughan of Doubleday, who encouraged me to undertake this book and who was unfailingly helpful during every stage of the work, I am greatly indebted. My thanks are also due his colleague Lee Barker and to Orville Prescott, for their enthusiastic and patient support.

Dr. Francis Ronalds, former superintendent of the Morristown National Historical Park, whose prodigious knowledge of the American Revolution has been generously offered to hundreds of writers on the subject, gave me many leads to contemporary documents and put the facilities of the library at Washington's Headquarters at my disposal on several occasions.

Adrian C. Leiby, whose book *The Revolutionary War in the Hackensack Valley* was frequently useful, also gave me the benefit of his advice on certain aspects of the campaign in New Jersey.

My sincere thanks go to Mrs. Karen Van Westering for her attentive and cheerful assistance during production of this book and to Joseph P. Ascherl for the care he took in its design. I am indebted also to Mrs. Peggy Buckwalter for obtaining the illustrations reproduced herein.

To the Alan Williams family I am obligated for the warm memory of an evening's hospitality and suggestions that made even a tour of the Princeton battlefield during a hurricane tolerable.

Along the way I also benefited from assistance given me by Bruce Catton, Howard Peckham, James Flexner, Richard P. McCormick, Samuel Smith, and Mary Elizabeth Wise, to all of whom, many thinks.

No one but a writer who works at home appreciates the extent of his debt to a family and friends who sympathize with his lonely occupation and make it possible for him to pursue it, uninterrupted and in peace. To Millie Ann Mickens and Chester Phillips, who helped in many ways—my thanks.

For her gift of understanding, my deepest gratitude goes to my wife, Bobs.

NOTES

The years have not been kind to our Revolution. We tend nowadays to be intolerant of ancestors, both near and far, as if the relative simplicity of their day somehow exempted them from the vicissitudes of a more complex world. Because the world has altered so dramatically during the past two centuries, it is often difficult to imagine what led people to certain conclusions or persuaded them to believe and act as they did.

Wherever possible, the narrative of this book has been based upon contemporary evidence. I have tried to draw my conclusions from the testimony of individuals who were either on the scene or somehow related to it, in order to see matters through their own eyes and on their own terms. History, unfortunately, has a way of confirming what we already know, but at the time the events described here occurred the issues were by no means so clear or simple as hindsight makes them. Where I have used later material—reminiscences and memoirs written after the war—it was because a particularly vivid recollection met the test of plausibility and did not vary substantially from other known facts.

This is not intended as a book for scholars, and I have not included footnotes to document various assertions or citations. What follows are notes for the general reader who may be interested in learning more about a particular aspect of these events or who wishes to know which books I found most helpful. So, while the following notes cover most of the important elements of this account, they are not inclusive.

Nearly all references are to the complete Bibliography which follows these Notes.

CHAPTER ONE

1. A Gentleman from England with Genius in His Eyes

Leiby, in *The Revolutionary War in the Hackensack Valley*, provides some interesting sidelights on Hay. Born on the island of Jamaica in 1754, he was awarded his intriguing name in honor of a wealthy benefactress of the family, and as a young man came to New York to attend college. Hay made money, received substantial grants of land in Vermont, and was offered a commission in the British army, but despite all this he was an avid patriot who suffered heavily for his commitment to the cause. After his house and barns in Haverstraw were burned in 1777 and the remainder of his property carried off in 1779, Hay petitioned the New York legislature for relief, saying, "My farm is now almost a wilderness, having no hands to work it. My negroes have all been taken away; and the whole of my little live stock has been for some time past expended."

Lieutenant Joseph Hodgkins' comments here and elsewhere are taken from Wade and

Lively's delightful book, *This Glorious Cause*. It consists, as the prefatory remarks indicate, of "the adventures of two company officers in Washington's army"—Hodgkins, a cobbler, and Nathaniel Wade, a carpenter—both from Ipswich, Massachusetts. They saw a good deal of the war and their grandsons collected and assembled their papers, which Wade and Lively eventually edited.

Nathanael Greene's remark about his preoccupation with paper work is the first of many citations from Douglas Southall Freeman's *George Washington* (especially Volume IV, *Leader of the Revolution*). Not many contemporary documents escaped the attention of the tireless Virginia historian, and the result is a monumental piece of scholarship that is essential reading for any student of Washington and the war. Washington's own activities receive considerable attention in this book, and I have not attempted in these Notes to annotate all sources of information about them; but anyone wishing to pursue the subject further will find it all in Freeman.

Most of the material on Thomas Paine was drawn from Fast and Foner, and Bernard Bailyn has some perceptive observations about him in *Pamphlets of the American Revolution, 1750–1776*.

2. The River Is Passed, and the Bridge Cut Away

The deliberations of the citizens of Buckingham County, Virginia, appear in Force, Fourth Series, Volume VI, pages 458–61 (hereafter cited as Force, IV, 6, 458–61). Reading the records of those caucuses and the careful instructions to delegates, one gets a real feeling of the dilemma that confronted people of the time and the forthrightness with which they determined to meet it.

For the story of the Declaration of Independence, I relied on a number of sources, among them Becker, Burnett, and Malone, and Commager and Morris, *The Spirit of 'Seventy-Six*, about which a word here. Professors Commager and Morris assembled the record of the American Revolution as told by participants, selecting their material with enormous skill and contributing, as explanatory bridges between these excerpts, as clear and as informative a commentary on the war and all its aspects as it has been my privilege to read. I found myself referring again and again to these volumes, which are so full of rich commentary, personal description, historical judgments, and references to the most pertinent contemporary accounts.

The names of Samuel Webb and Alexander Graydon first appear in this chapter, and the reader will find them elsewhere throughout the book, since both men wrote highly readable, eyewitness accounts of much that is described herein. Webb was a New Englander, from a family which had made a good deal of money in the West Indian trade, and through the influence of his stepfather, Silas Deane, he was appointed aide to Israel Putnam and afterward joined Washington's official family. He left Washington to take command of a regiment at the age of twenty-three and had a brief, exciting career in the Hudson Highlands before being captured by the British and held on parole for nearly three years—"subject," as he put it, "to the whims and caprice of the British commanders and of the Continental Congress." Released in 1781, he rejoined his regiment and remained with it until the army was disbanded. Like Webb, Graydon wrote his memoirs some time after the events he describes, but one has the feeling that while he made judgments based on hindsight, he was not one to alter the facts, and his story has the strong ring of truth as told by an intelligent man.

3. *A Business of Necessity*

Much of the information on Nathanael Greene's early life and military service comes from Thayer's biography.

For George Washington's day to day activities, Freeman's fourth volume, already cited, is indispensable. James Flexner's *George Washington in the American Revolution* is a highly readable, well-balanced study of the man, which was extremely helpful.

For an insight into the complex character of the commander in chief, I can think of no better source than Marcus Cunliffe's brilliant and perceptive study, *George Washington: Man and Monument*, which comes closer to hitting the mark on this remarkable and enigmatic personality than most of the hundreds of volumes that have been written about him. Like that other great Virginia war leader, Robert E. Lee, Washington is extremely difficult to see in anything like human terms; despite his voluminous correspondence and the flood of official documents to which his name was signed, the inner man seems to be partly in shadow, screened by a shyness or reserve that nearly always kept the emotions in hand. When I began work on this book I was not certain that I would ever come to understand or even to "like" Washington, if that is the way to put it, and I deliberately let his actions and words speak for themselves whenever possible. And when it was done I was still not certain that I knew him any better as a person—only that I realized, as never before, that he *was*, as Lafayette said, the Revolution, that he was the one man without whom it could not have been won.

Cresswell's *Journal* is a lively, spontaneous report by a twenty-four-year-old Englishman who came to America in 1774 against the wishes of family and friends, to see the land, assess its opportunities, and decide whether or not he would settle here, and he recorded in some detail all he saw and heard during his travels.

Some of the material on the army in Boston owes much to Allen French's *The First Year of the American Revolution*, a superb study of the first twelve months of war which is so rich in both information and insight into the minds and mood of that generation. I have also drawn upon Freeman, IV, and my own *The Battle for Bunker Hill*.

CHAPTER TWO

1. *We Must Tax Them*

For general background on England during one of its most exciting and luminous centuries, two studies by J. H. Plumb are essential. His *England in the Eighteenth Century* and *The First Four Georges* are perceptive, splendidly written books, and his characterization of the times, the principal figures, and the complex issues that confronted them are admirable.

I also found extremely useful Professor Plumb's opening chapter in *The American Heritage Book of the Revolution* and his article "Our Last King," on George III.

Although three-quarters of a century have passed since the appearance of Trevelyan's majestic six-volume work *The American Revolution*, inevitably yielding much new scholarship and conclusions that differ with his, the work, as Richard Morris writes, "still casts its spell over the reader" as it did at the turn of the century, and few other books capture so faithfully the spirit of the generation that lost the first British Empire or convey such sympathy for the English opponents of George III and his ministers.

Another first-rate examination of the issues behind the war is Bernard Donoughue's *British Politics and the American Revolution*, which deals with the government's attitude and objectives vis-à-vis the colonies as hostilities became virtually inevitable. Piers Mackesy's *The War for America, 1775–1783* was especially helpful; I found it extremely valuable for its analysis of how the British government functioned.

Information concerning Vergennes and the French court's posture toward England and the colonies may be found in several sources, including *The American Heritage Book of the Revolution*, Boatner's *Encyclopedia*, and Pearson's *Those Damned Rebels*.

Figures on Britain's national debt come from Donoughue, where the differing points of view of Great Britain and the colonies are also discussed. On the matter of British and colonial attitudes, numerous studies are useful, among them Alden's *Pioneer America*, Miller's *Origins of the American Revolution*, Lloyd's *The King Who Lost America*, and Gipson's monumental work.

2. America Will Be Brought to Submission

An informative, well-written account of how the news of Lexington and Concord reached England will be found in Arthur Tourtellot's *William Diamond's Drum*. Tourtellot also published—in conjunction with that book—a limited edition of what is the definitive bibliography concerning the battles which began the war. Another good book on the subject is Donoughue's.

Franklin's letter to Strahan appears in Scheer and Rankin's *Rebels and Redcoats*.

For the repercussions of Bunker Hill, I have relied principally on my own book *The Battle for Bunker Hill* and on Alden's *General Gage in America*, and Mackesy.

3. Everyone Who Does Not Agree with Me Is a Traitor

For material on George III—especially the personality and family relationships of that complex, unhappy man—I drew upon several sources, principally Alan Lloyd's recently published *The King Who Lost America*. This is, as Lloyd states, a book for the general reader, and the author manages to bring his subject to life and to make him understandable. Plumb's *The First Four Georges*, already cited, and his incisive article "Our Last King," are extremely useful. Mackesy discusses the king as a war leader and Donoughue covers fully his attitude toward the colonists and his determination to employ a policy of coercion. His illness is extensively discussed in Macalpine and Hunter's *George III and the Mad-Business*.

The opinion that prevailed in England concerning the colonists' aptitude for war is treated by Mackesy, who also describes the government's assessment of the Americans' military capabilities. As already noted, I have made use of this book for information about the workings of the British government.

Descriptions of Lord North appear in numerous sources, among them Mackesy, Donoughue, and Lloyd, and the opposition's comments about the first minister may be found in several volumes of Force, particularly in IV, 6, 44–187. Lloyd and Trevelyan are good on the principal opposition leaders—Burke, Fox, Barré, and others.

The Olive Branch Petition and its reception in London are discussed at some length by French.

4. It Was the War of the People

For most of the parliamentary debates on the American question, I relied upon Force, IV, 6, where the speeches of both sides and the roll call of votes on crucial issues are recorded. There is endless fascination in reading those impassioned words and studying the tally of votes upon which so much was to depend. One of the most interesting aspects about the policy of coercion is the role played by the country gentlemen—a matter that has been rather neglected by historians until fairly recent times. These people not only gave the North administration the majority it needed; they also represented, for the duration of the war, its chief source of strength. In the record of the debates, however, few speeches by these men appear, which makes one conclude that they were for the most part silent, often unthinking accessories to what was going on, men far more concerned with preserving the status quo and punishing the colonists than they were in finding workable answers to the acute problems of empire. Lloyd, Sosin, and others make the point that a marked increase in George III's popularity followed the decision to use force against the colonists—a policy enthusiastically supported by the country gentlemen.

On the subject of British military estimates, Mackesy and Donoughue are helpful, as is French. Opinions of various Englishmen with respect to the colonists' fighting abilities can be found in Robson's *Letters from America*, French, and Commager and Morris.

5. A Full Exertion of Great Force

French's *First Year* has a good discussion of the debate on the question of employing foreign mercenaries, but I have drawn most heavily on Force, IV, 6, where the acrimonious arguments on this subject are quoted extensively. No other question that came before the Houses of Parliament stirred up more controversy or such bitter opposition, and it is a testimony to the overwhelming support enjoyed by the North administration that this touchy issue could be taken in stride. Full particulars of the treaties with the German princelings appear in Force, IV, 6, 271–87 and 356–56. By all odds the best description of those courts and the soldiers in whose lives they dealt is to be found in Lowell.

The controversial Lord George Germain is discussed most interestingly by Mackesy, in whose book he figures as the principal character. Mackesy believes that Germain is "the most traduced of all English statesmen" and goes to considerable lengths to rescue his reputation, pointing out the magnitude of the task he faced. The unsavory Sandwich receives his due from Mackesy.

The best study of the Howe brothers is Troyer Anderson's, whose thoughtful, objective treatment is remarkable when it is realized that the private papers of the Howe family were destroyed by fire and that, as Anderson notes, "never did two men keep their own counsel more carefully." These two men have often been accused of deliberately losing the war, but Anderson found little or nothing to support such a claim against the Howes, who were so intimately connected with the failures of British policy during the first three years of the Revolution. French has some valuable material on the general, and the debate in Parliament concerning their assignment is recorded in Force, IV, 6. The king's speech of May 23, 1776, summarizing Britain's policy toward the rebellious Americans is in the same volume, page 388.

CHAPTER THREE

1. A Mere Insidious Maneuvre

Much information on the able, engaging Henry Knox and his wife Lucy may be found in Drake and Brooks. The Knox papers, rich in humor and detail, and covering his wartime service and the postwar years, are in the Massachusetts Historical Society. Regrettably, there are few really first-rate modern biographies of Washington's lieutenants.

Various details of the abortive effort of the Howes to negotiate with Washington may be found in Freeman, IV, *The Spirit of 'Seventy-Six*, and in Serle's *Journal*. The latter is particularly useful since, as Lord Howe's civilian secretary, he had the admiral's ear and was privy to his private thoughts on the peace efforts.

The letter from John Morin Scott's daughter appears in Lossing, II, 599n. Before this work was published in 1850, Lossing traveled some 8,000 miles through the former colonies and Canada, visiting all the important landmarks of the war, the battlefields and houses that were related in one way or another to those heroic events which were still fresh in the nation's memory, and "communing," as he said, "with men of every social and intellectual grade." Sketch pad and notebook in hand, he talked with garrulous old men about their experiences, picked up bits and pieces of fact and hearsay, drew pictures of many now-vanished buildings, and strung all this together in a disorganized, not very scholarly, but utterly charming and often valuable work.

Daniel McCurtin's *Journal*, which ended so unhappily for my purposes with the arrival of the British fleet off New York, is quoted in Freeman, IV.

The figures on the size of the British expeditionary force come from Ward's *The War of the Revolution*, 209. This two-volume work, published posthumously, remains in my opinion the outstanding military history of the conflict. It originated in Ward's definitive study of the Delaware Line, published as *The Delaware Continentals, 1776–1783*, to which I also referred frequently, and no book I have seen surpasses its narrative skill or brings to life more successfully the heroic tale of the Continental Army. It is, as Ward stated, not a history of the American Revolution, but "a history of the war that was caused by the Revolution."

Conditions in the British camp on Staten Island were reported by a young Scotsman, James Falconer, in a letter to his mother, quoted in Force, V, 1, and the account of the Hessians burning the effigies of Washington, Witherspoon, Lee, and Putnam, is from Sir John Moore's *Diary*, quoted in Montross, 107.

Rawdon's patronizing letter about the plight of the local girls is in Commager and Morris, *The Spirit of 'Seventy-Six*, 124.

An excellent summary of the strategic importance of New York City and the Hudson River is in Mackesy, where one will also find a description of the principal land routes between New Jersey and Connecticut. Bruce Bliven, Jr., in his splendid book *Battle for Manhattan*, discusses the significance of the island to British planners. A most interesting article on the Hudson waterway is "The Hudson River Lives," by Robert H. Boyle, in the *Audubon Magazine*, March 1971. Originally the Hudson was known as the North River to the Dutch, who called the Delaware the South River and the Connecticut the Fresh River. (In those halcyon days, Boyle notes, it was not uncommon to find Gowanus oysters—which were known as the best in the country—up to a foot in length.)

Material on John Sullivan may be found in the only recent biography I am aware of, by Charles P. Whittemore.

In his autobiography, John Adams depicted the meeting with Lord Howe, and his starchy comments on Sullivan also appear there. How the admiral could have had any real optimism that this meeting would produce results is a mystery. Charles Lee aptly described the attitude prevailing among hard-core rebels in a letter to Benjamin Rush, saying that anyone who believed reconciliation with England possible "ought to be pelted at with stones by the children when he walks the streets as a common Town Fool."

2. *The Troops Were in High Spirits*

Adrian Leiby's excellent volume on the war in the Hackensack Valley was invaluable here, not only for a description of this part of New Jersey, but especially for an understanding of the incessant conflict between loyalist and rebel partisans which so divided the state. Painstakingly researched and documented, thoroughly readable, Leiby's book is an example of local history at its best.

The frigate *Pearl* and the victualing ships were not the first vessels to pass the Hudson River forts and the chevaux de frise. In July, H.M.S. *Phoenix* and *Rose*, with several smaller vessels, had sailed upriver and anchored in the Tappan Zee—an episode that gave no comfort to the Americans. On October 9 three frigates—H.M.S. *Phoenix*, *Roebuck*, and *Tartar*—along with two tenders and the schooner *Tryal* set sail from Bloomingdale in the morning to try the rebel defenses. It took over an hour for the squadron to pass the forts and by the time they drew out of range they had taken a severe pounding and had lost nine men killed and eighteen wounded, but the exploit demonstrated conclusively the vulnerability of the rebel works. This was the episode that formed the basis of Dominic

Serres' painting "Forcing the Hudson River Passage," which shows the smoke from the guns of Fort Lee (then known as Fort Constitution) atop the Palisades on the left, with Fort Washington and its batteries and Jeffrey's Hook on the right.

Washington's correspondence with the New Jersey Committee of Safety and the Continental Congress may be found in Force, V, 3. This same volume has several exchanges of letters concerning Major Charles Stewart's manservant.

Greene's letter to Washington and Magaw's note about the British surrender demand are in Force, V, 3, 699–700, and Washington's report to Congress about the battle is in the same volume, 706–08. Greene's letter to Henry Knox describing the affair (quoted in this and the next chapter) is in various sources, including Drake, 33–34.

3. *A Citadel Within Reach*

Considering the importance of the loss to the Americans, it is surprising that the battle for Fort Washington has been so neglected by modern historians. The most thorough accounts of the affair were published around the turn of the century or earlier. Much of the material in them can be found by perusing the numerous primary sources, and a number of contemporary accounts have come to light since, but these remain the best general studies of the event: Bolton's *Fort Washington*, DeLancey's *The Capture of Mount Washington*, and Johnston's *The Campaign of 1776*. Among them, they have good descriptions of the area and of the fortifications and cite rather fully the best contemporary accounts available to the authors. These works should be supplemented by reference to other primary sources, including Graydon's *Memoirs*, which are rich in detail, Mackenzie, Peebles, Kemble, Howe, Serle, Glyn, Stirke, Heath, Hart, my article, "New War Letters of Banastre Tarleton," and numerous references in Force, Fifth Series, Volume III. Good contemporary maps are absolutely essential to a study of the engagement, and the most useful one is that drawn by Claude Joseph Sauthier for Lord Percy, published in London by William Faden in 1777. It is available at the New York Public Library and at the Library of Congress' Map Division.

Although Colonel Magaw played an important role in this battle, he was pretty well lost to history after his capture, since he remained a prisoner of the British until October 25, 1780, when he was finally exchanged. Not surprisingly, he did not re-enter the army and died early in 1790.

The story of William Demont's desertion is an important piece of DeLancey's book, and most of the salient details are printed there, but it is instructive to read Christopher Ward's argument that Demont's treachery was of little importance (since Howe was planning to attack the fort anyway and probably had adequate information about its defenses from other sources). This appears as Appendix E in Ward's *The War of the Revolution*, II, 940. My own inclination is to believe, as stated, that Demont's information prompted Howe to move on the fort more quickly than he might otherwise have done. Whatever the merit of Ward's arguments, it is hard to see how Demont's information about the defenders and their works could have been anything but helpful to the attackers.

Baurmeister's letters and journal provide some information on Knyphausen, and Lossing, II, 103, has a description of him, including the fact that he spread butter on his bread with his thumb. Lowell describes the discomforts of the Hessians en route to America, but the horrors of the voyage were not confined to German soldiers; graphic comments may be found in many contemporary journals and diaries.

4. *Ye Should Never Fight Against Yer King*

The same sources cited for the previous chapter were useful here.

Information on movements and activities of British naval vessels comes from the ships' logs, which repose in the National Maritime Museum in Greenwich, England. Generally speaking, the reports are in terse naval style, but since the officers who wrote the entries were accustomed to do so with precise attention to the hour, they place accurately the time of certain occurrences and occasionally yield interesting details. In using these logs, care must be taken concerning the dates, since logs were kept according to the nautical day, which was twelve hours ahead of civil time and began at noon.

Several quotations here are from the letters of Ensign George Hart and are used by kind permission of the editors of *American Heritage*. Commissioned in August 1775, Hart came to America with the 46th Regiment of Foot, participated in the attack on Charleston and in the battles of Long Island, Brooklyn Heights, and Forts Washington and Lee. He served with Howe's army at Brandywine and Germantown, and with Clinton at Monmouth; then he was sent to the West Indies. Later, Hart was with Cornwallis in India, became a lieutenant general in 1811, and died in 1832 at the ripe age of eighty. The letters to his father, while adding little to known facts, are full of details about all he saw and experienced.

A letter from Lord Howe, dated November 23, 1776 (Force, V, 3, 817), states that the flatboats, manned by seamen from British transports, were commanded by Captain Wilkinson of the *Pearl*, assisted by Captain Molloy and three lieutenants. Wilkinson so distinguished himself in this task that his continued presence with the boats was regarded as essential, and the *Pearl* was for some little time under the command of its first lieutenant. In the subsequent attack on Fort Lee, twenty flatboats under Captain Phipps ferried the men in Cornwallis' assault force over to New Jersey.

Since Colonel Johann Rall's career ended in disgrace, few of his contemporaries had anything good to say about him, but there is little doubt of his courage and zest for battle, as demonstrated at Chatterton's Hill and at Fort Washington. Lowell has some interesting commentary on his earlier career, which included service with the Russians against the Turks.

A good description of the American riflemen and their weapon appears in Ward's *The War of the Revolution*, 106–7.

The journal of Ensign Thomas Glyn, cited here and elsewhere, is in the possession of the Princeton University Library. While it contains for the most part succinct entries about fairly well-known occurrences, occasionally Glyn took the time to record a personal observation or to comment in a way that sheds light on events.

One of the most useful and interesting diaries is that of Captain Frederick Mackenzie.

Covering his service in America from 1775 to 1781, it reflects its author's thorough professionalism. Written with soldierly precision, his reports are clear, direct, informative, and remarkably fair, for Mackenzie seems to have had no rancor toward the Americans; he relates the facts impersonally, and it is evident from the diaries that he was a keen observer who gave considerable thought to the problems confronting both his own army and that of the enemy.

The journal of John Reuber, of Rall's regiment, is quoted in Commager and Morris, 494.

A letter describing what Magaw's men did to the Hessians a week before the battle at Fort Washington is in Force, V, 3, 630.

Both Bolton and DeLancey have the story about Gooch's escapade; Hohenstein's remarks are quoted by Bolton.

Cadwalader's report to Washington is mentioned in Freeman, IV, 253n., and DeLancey and Bolton have material on the plight of the rebel prisoners.

The diary of the Reverend Mr. Shewkirk is quoted by Johnston in *The Campaign of 1776*, 120.

5. The Rebels Fled Like Scared Rabbits

Freeman, IV, 253, and Thayer, 121–25, relate much of the criticism of Greene that was so widespread in the aftermath of the Fort Washington disaster, and Washington's anguished letter to John Augustine Washington is in Freeman, IV, 266.

I am indebted to Professor Richard P. McCormick of Rutgers University for the story of Aldington's role in planning the attack on Fort Lee. While studying loyalist records in the Public Record Office in London, Professor McCormick came across an affidavit from Cornwallis testifying to Aldington's services in guiding his troops when he landed in New Jersey. Apparently Aldington served with the British throughout the war and later fled to England. The site of the British landing has been debated by Revolution buffs in New Jersey for years, and Adrian Leiby has been most helpful in pinpointing the location.

Information concerning Colonels Grayson and Harrison appears in Force, V, 3, and in Leiby's Hackensack book. The latter quotes the British officer on the state of confusion at Fort Lee and is most informative about this entire operation. Howe's own report appears in Force, V, 3, 925. The recollection of the Hackensack resident about Greene's troops is in Leiby, 72.

CHAPTER FOUR

1. These Things Raise the Heads of the Tories

Allen French's *First Year* is still the best source of information on the beginning of the war and the immense difficulties encountered by the Americans in raising and supporting an army. He discusses the problem of re-enlistments on pages 503–27. Other helpful sources are Ward's *The War of the Revolution*, Heitman (who lists the components of all regiments), and Boatner, in the entry on the Continental Army. The deputy adjutant general's Orderly Book at Fort Ticonderoga, quoted in *The Bulletin of the Fort Ticonderoga Museum*, Vol. III, No. 13, July 1933, contains the particulars of Congress' "Reward and Encouragement" for enlisting.

In addition to various comments from observers like Mackenzie and letters scattered through Force, IV and V, I have turned again and again to Bolton's *The Private Soldier Under Washington* for intimate details concerning the Continental Army, its food and other supplies, equipment, and day to day activities.

My own book *The Battle for Bunker Hill* is the source of information on the musket and its assets and liabilities, and Thacher's *Military Journal* records the story of the Massachusetts colonel and his dispute with the Pennsylvania troops.

Bolton, again, is good on the problem of finding decent officers, and the letters of Washington (in Force, IV and V, and elsewhere) and his top field commanders are full of complaints such as those quoted from Reed, Lee, Greene, and others.

The punishment for rebels is taken from Flexner's *George Washington in the American Revolution*, page 14, and Washington's appeals to Congress for cavalry and artillery are in Force, V, 3, 675, 927, 1166, and elsewhere. Drake's biography of Knox has some material on the train of artillery, but I have relied for much of the material used here on articles in the Boston *Chronicle*, Feb. 8–15, and May 30–June 6, 1768.

The desperate search for men appears again and again in letters in Force, V, 3. On the recurring problem of regional disputes, a letter from Washington to Congress, written in May of 1776, is revealing. Usually a stickler for discipline, the general confessed that he had found it expedient to "yield many points in fact, without seeming to have done it" in order to avoid discussion of political matters which "ought to be kept a little behind the curtain." Time, he thought, was the only way to eradicate these long-standing regional prejudices.

Leiby's volume on the Hackensack Valley is an excellent source of information on New Jersey's loyalists.

Peter Van Schaack's poignant letter to the New York Convention appears in Commager and Morris, *The Spirit of 'Seventy-Six*, and that volume is also the source of certain other accounts of loyalists cited herein.

Van Doren's *Benjamin Franklin* discusses the relationship between Franklin and his son, and a wealth of material on the loyalists, including William Franklin, may be found in Sabine's introductory essay as well as in specific entries.

The reaction in Parliament to Howe's proclamation appears in Force, V, 3, 1001, and elsewhere.

2. *The Times That Try Men's Souls*

An informative article on Clausewitz and his theories is in the summer 1971 issue of *Horizon* ("Clausewitz: How Not to Win a War," by Correlli Barnett).

The quotation from Judge Thomas Jones is one of many taken from his *History of New York During the Revolutionary War*. An affluent man, Jones lived at Great Neck, Long

Island, had a large estate in New York, and was related by marriage or social ties to many of the colony's most determined loyalists. In 1773 he was appointed by the royal governor to succeed his father as a justice of the New York Supreme Court; three years later he was charged with "disaffection to the American cause" and was arrested, sent to Connecticut, and then released on parole. Imprisoned again in 1779, at the end of the war he had lost everything—judicial position, property, and all respect for the blunderers who had failed to put down the rebellion, which Jones passed off as a "groundless, radical, and desperate movement." Although the judge could not have seen many of the events he describes, his book is endlessly entertaining and informative for the state of mind of a man who both hated the rebellion and was sick at heart over the way the British government and military leaders mishandled it.

Grayson's letter to Lee is in Force, V, 3, 779, and the account of the express rider is in the same volume, 795 and note.

Few characters of the Revolution are more fascinating or interesting than Charles Lee, and the best study of him is Alden's biography, which covers his career in detail. Refuting the claim of certain nineteenth-century historians that Lee was a traitor (as evidenced by the "plan" he gave his British captors for conquering the rebels), Alden makes a case for him by stating that his proposal was a subtle ruse to lead the British astray. But few of Lee's actions were as interesting as his imaginative mind and complex personality or the great gift of phrase that makes his letters such delightful and amusing reading. Joseph Reed's revealing letter to Lee about Washington is in Force, V, 3, 793, and Lee's extraordinary communication to Bowdoin in the same volume, 811–12. His reply to Reed is quoted in Freeman, IV, 269, where the entire Lee–Reed exchange and Washington's dilemma are discussed fully.

Paine's estimate of Washington is in Force, V, 3, 1292.

Samuel Webb's letter sizing up the army's state is in Freeman, IV, 263.

A discussion of Paine's pamphlet *The Crisis* appears in both Fast and Foner, and although the story of how and where it came to be written is shrouded in mystery, it seems clear that Paine wrote the first part of it—the impassioned appeal—in or near Newark, where tradition has him composing it on a drumhead during the army's short stay there. It seems likely that Paine added to this emotional message later, before he took the manuscript to Philadelphia, including an account of the retreat through New Jersey, in which he participated. Like *Common Sense*, *The Crisis* was an immediate success and it had the great virtue that it could be set in one block of type and printed on two sides of a single sheet of paper, in which form it was distributed as a handbill or tacked up as a poster. Overnight, the phrases "summer soldier" and "sunshine patriot" were on every tongue. In this and succeeding *Crisis* papers, Paine defined the issues at stake and managed to make his adopted countrymen realize that they were matters that went far beyond the present conflict in their significance for mankind. A remarkably skilled propagandist, Paine never admitted to his readers how bad things really were; he told them as much as he wanted them to know, omitting the worst. He saw much of the war personally, and from his correspondence it is evident that he saw it more clearly than most men of his time.

3. The Campaign Having Closed

General Howe's long report on the campaign is in Force, V, 3, 921–25, and his proposal for the 1777 campaign, which included a strike from Canada, is interesting in the context of discussions then being held in London that led, eventually, to Burgoyne's campaign and the British defeat at Saratoga.

Numerous contemporary descriptions of the fire in New York exist—each side claiming that the other had set it. There is some reason to suppose that it may have been the work of British camp followers, who were accomplished looters and who moved into the city like a swarm of locusts when the rebels and their partisans fled. Such conflagrations were common in cities of that day. All houses had wood-burning fireplaces that threw off sparks, most buildings were made of wood, with shingle roofs, and once a blaze got started the only way to fight it was with buckets of water. So a fire of any real size almost inevitably got out of hand.

Both Mackesy and the Wickwires are informative on this matter of the British officer corps and the command system that was so badly in need of reform. The trouble at the top was typified by a remark made by Charles Jenkinson, who succeeded Barrington as secretary at war. He was "no minister," Jenkinson admitted, and thus "could not be supposed to have a competent knowledge of the destination of the army, and how the war was to be carried on."

There is exasperatingly little contemporary information on the intriguing Mrs. Loring. I have drawn on my Bunker Hill book for this, and for some of the description of conditions in the British army. Belcher, Mackesy, the Wickwires, and Robson's *The American Revolution* are all valuable on the latter subject. Robson also discusses the tactical problems faced by the British army in the American countryside—problems so unlike any that the men or their commanders had experienced in Europe. Many letters from British officers testify to this surprisingly unexpected obstacle.

The contents of the intercepted letter from Washington to the Board of War are described in Force, V, 3, 1326. This was by no means an isolated instance; time and again one finds Washington and his officers speaking of the unreliability of messengers, the ever-present danger from spies, informers, and enemy cavalry.

The Wickwires' study of Cornwallis, covering his career in America, is a fine portrait of an able man.

My account of the Delaware regiment, Haslet, and Lieutenant Anderson owes much to Ward's *The Delaware Continentals*, which traces the history of that outfit.

Information on Witherspoon may be found in Malone, Milhollen, and Kaplan, and in Wertenbaker's *Princeton*. Solomon Clift's description of the captive Tory is in Scheer and Rankin's *Rebels and Redcoats*, 204.

Smith's *The Battle of Trenton* has the story of Benjamin Randolph coming to see Washington in Trenton, and Freeman, IV, covers the general's daily movements fully.

The advance toward Princeton and the sudden retreat to Trenton is described in Ward's *The Delaware Continentals*. Howe's orders declaring the campaign at an end are from his *Orderly Book*, for December 14, 1776; and his letter to Germain, confessing to nervousness about the New Jersey posts, is in Force, V, 3, 1316–17.

4. The Game Is Pretty Near Up

Washington's comments to Congress on the short-term enlistees is from Force, V, 3, 1081–83. Despite his continuous pleas, Congress never resolved the problem and for the duration of the war the army was short of experienced men. What the commander in chief was up against, because of Congress' determined reliance on militiamen, is suggested by a letter written in April of 1776 by a Delaware officer to the Committee of Secrecy, War, and Intelligence in Wilmington: "I am sorry to inform you that the Militia are not so ready to turn out on this important occasion as I could wish, owing, I am certain, to their being at this season engaged in the farming business."

Charles Willson Peale's failure to recognize his own brother on the banks of the Delaware is related by Flexner, *George Washington in the American Revolution*, 161–62.

Judge Jones's comments concerning Howe's failure to build boats is quoted by Partridge, 110n.

The Pennsylvania Council of Safety proclamation appears in Force, V, 3, 1033, and Ward, I, 286, is the source of the quotation describing the flight from the capital.

Ambrose Serle recorded the substance of his conversations with Joseph Galloway and the Allens in his *Journal*, from which I drew this discussion of their meetings.

Israel Putnam's letter to Washington describing the situation in Philadelphia appears in Force, V, 3, 1164. Washington's doleful remarks about the probable fate of the capital are from Freeman, IV, 282.

The voluminous Washington–Lee exchanges may be seen in Force, V, 3, under the appropriate date, and Cadwalader's letter to Morris is in the same volume, page 1231.

Although Robert Morris' activities were not directly related to my story, he is one of the truly interesting figures of the war and, like Lee (although for very different reasons), a highly controversial one. Howard Swiggett's biography covers his career, and much detail concerning the Secret Committee can be found in Boatner, under "Robert Morris" and "Secret Committee." The relationship with Silas Deane is another fascinating aspect of Morris' complex dealings; a number of Deane's letters to Congress, in Force, V, 3, testify to the exasperating nature of the task he faced in trying to represent the United States almost without instructions from home.

5. A Most Miraculous Event

The capture of Charles Lee is described in various sources, but I have relied almost entirely on Banastre Tarleton's own account, since the young cavalryman was so intimately involved in the escapade and relates the story so dramatically. The Tarleton letters quoted appear in my article, "New War Letters of Banastre Tarleton," in *The New-York Historical Society Quarterly* for January 1967.

Alden's *Lee* and Freeman, IV, contain numerous references to the Lee affair, and Webb's letter appears in the *Correspondence and Journals*.

CHAPTER FIVE

1. We Have Not Slept One Night in Peace

The fullest, most detailed, and in many respects the best account of the battles of Trenton and Princeton is Stryker's (unless otherwise noted, subsequent references to "Stryker" are to his book on the battles). Although he accepted certain old traditions without question and often failed to cite his authorities, his book has an Appendix of great value to the student, in which are reprinted in full or in part many contemporary documents that cannot easily be located elsewhere. A briefer, more recent account is Smith's *The Battle of Trenton*, in which many Hessian accounts are cited and which contains very clear, modern situation maps. I am greatly indebted to Mr. Smith for letting me make a copy of microfilms of Hessian court-martial testimony which he collected. Further information on the battle and its preliminaries may be found in Ward, I, and in Freeman, IV.

A description of the episode in Salem in which Leslie participated is in Ward, I, 21–22.

The best map I found covering the area of operations in the fall and winter of 1776–77 is "A Map Containing Part of the Provinces of New York and New Jersey, Drawn from Surveys Compiled by Thomas Millidge, Major 1st Battalion New Jersey Volunteers, 1780"—a map made for Oliver Delancey by Andrew Skinner in 1781 and available from the Map Division of the Library of Congress. It has the great virtue of showing all the hamlets, taverns, and churches of New Jersey in addition to topographical features. Since so many place names have been changed over the years, a map of this kind is essential for identifying the references to minor locations found in contemporary accounts. Another highly useful map—especially for the Delaware River crossings and the area around Trenton and Princeton—is William Faden's "Plan of the Operations of General Washington Against the King's Troops in New Jersey . . . ," published in London in 1777 and available at the Library of Congress and the New York Public Library.

Force, V, 3, 1165 and elsewhere, includes references to the flotilla commanded by Thomas Seymour, and Mayor Lawrence's efforts to spare the town of Burlington are described by Stryker. This latter source and Smith's *The Battle of Trenton* also indicate the location of British and Hessian troops and describe the various skirmishes that immediately preceded the battle.

Kemble's *Journal* contains frequent references to the Hessians and their behavior, and General Robertson's testimony before the House of Commons appears in Commager and Morris' *The Spirit of 'Seventy-Six*, 527 et seq., where the Congressional Committee's report may also be found. Bill, 33–34, describes the damage done to the college at Princeton.

I have relied on Lowell's informative work for the Hessian background in Germany. Baurmeister's *Journal* has several passages on the beauty of the American countryside. The quotation from the American concerning Hessian plundering is in Force, V, 2, 996; and Colonel von Heeringen's comments on the battle of Long Island are in Lowell, 65.

Stryker's *The Old Barracks* has some useful information on the construction of that building and its use during the French and Indian War. For the description of Trenton and its principal streets, I resorted to several maps drawn by Hessian soldiers, reproduced in Stryker, and to the *Atlas to Marshall's Life of Washington.*

Wiederhold's sarcastic observations about Rall's preoccupation with parades and band music are in Stryker, 198–99, as are various letters from Grant, Donop, and Rall about the situation in and around Trenton (pages 332–35). The quotation from the Hessian officer complaining that they had not slept one night in peace is on page 484.

Stryker, 122–125, also has the story of the Tory farmer arriving at Abraham Hunt's house on Christmas Eve with a message for Rall.

2. *The Snow Was Tinged with Blood*

While Stryker has some information on John Honeyman, the best account appears in *American Heritage*, August 1957, in Leonard Falkner's article "A Spy for Washington." The tale's veracity turns chiefly on the testimony of later authorities, notably Honeyman's daughter, but most of the pieces fit together and the account rings true. Washington had a highly effective intelligence system, and he was extremely careful to protect the cover of his agents, which explains why so little was known about Honeyman. For further information on intelligence activities during the war, the reader should consult Van Doren's *Secret History* and Bakeless, *Turncoats, Traitors and Heroes.*

Both Stryker and Freeman, IV, are good on the placement of rebel contingents prior to the attack on Trenton, and Stryker reprints on pages 340–41 Reed's letter to Washington, urging him to act. For the approaches to Trenton and the routes taken by units of Washington's army, I found the maps in Smith's *The Battle of Trenton* very helpful.

Ward has a good description of the Durham boats (I, 294), but I found it most instructive to inspect the replica of one of these boats which is on display at the Washington Crossing State Park. A plaque contains an informative legend.

Leiby, 100, has the account of the manner in which Christmas was celebrated in the Highlands, and Wilkinson's recollection of how the route to the river was marked with blood from the men's feet is in Stryker, 129. His conversation with Washington about Gates is in Freeman, IV, 309.

As noted earlier, the paucity of good officers is a constantly recurring theme in the correspondence of Washington and his lieutenants. Knox's remarks, written on September 23, 1776, appear in Brooks, 70–71, and one may find in Force, V, 3, 949 et seq., a revealing list of New York officers with comments by superiors on their qualifications. It was as close as anyone came in those days to the modern fitness report, and the list is full of comments like "bad, indifferent, middling, scoundrel," "cashiered for defrauding his men," "a very low-lived fellow," "at present under arrest," "had better be dismissed," "not so careful as might be wished," and so on. Only infrequently does one find the phrases "a good officer" or "an exceeding good officer."

A good source of information on the competent colonel from Marblehead is Billias' *General John Glover*, and Abbatt's *The Battle of Pell's Point* contains an account of one of his important but neglected battles.

Flexner, *George Washington in the American Revolution*, and Freeman, IV, have details on the river crossing, and Washington's letter to Congress, in Stryker, 217 is helpful. The general's instructions to the men to keep by their officers is in Commager and Morris, 512, and Freeman, IV, 312, recites the account of the meeting with Captain Anderson.

3. I Wanted the Victory Complete

For most of the material in this chapter I depended upon eyewitness reports, many of which appear in sources already cited—Freeman, IV, Stryker, Commager and Morris, Smith's *The Battle of Trenton*, Force, V, 3, and others. Alfred Hoyt Bill's *The Campaign of Princeton, 1776–1777* is an excellent short account of the engagements at Trenton and Princeton, and although it does not contain notes on sources, the bibliography is useful. Smith makes much use of German accounts of Trenton, gathered from various letters and from testimony brought out during the extensive court-martial proceedings after the defeat. The contemporary sources, too numerous to mention here, appear in the books listed above, with a few exceptions.

Since Sergeant White makes his appearance here for the first time, this is the place to note his delightful little book *A Narrative of Events* published in Charlestown, Massachusetts in 1833 ("at the earnest request of many young men") and available at the Library of Congress. White enlisted in Colonel Richard Gridley's regiment of artillery (of which Henry Knox was an officer) early in May 1775 and reports that he was almost immediately made an assistant to the adjutant because he "could spell most any word," a claim not substantiated by his book. His account is full of homely, humorous details (the first time he met George Washington, he says, the commander in chief remarked that he was very young to be in the service, to which White replied that he was young but growing older every day. Washington, he notes, "turned his face to his wife, and both smilled" [*sic*]). He served at Trenton and Princeton, but in February 1777, when his enlistment ran out, decided to go home. His captain urged him to stay on, telling him he would certainly be made an officer, but White "did not care about a commission" and took his leave of the army. And one can see him, in the twilight of his life, relating tales of those glorious days for the young men who finally persuaded him to set it all down on paper for posterity.

In addition to other sources cited, there is some useful material in a manuscript at the Morristown National Historic Park under the title, *Journal of the Honourable Fusilier von Alt-Lossberg: Trentown Affair.*

4. The Army Was in the Most Desperate Situation

James Ewing's communications with Washington are in Force, V, 3, 1429, 1444.

Freeman, IV, has the story about the captured Hessians, and Stryker is useful on the aftermath of the battle, including criticism of Rall's actions, the treatment of the Hessian prisoners in Philadelphia, and their ultimate disposition in the South. Freeman, IV, 325–46, covers the preliminaries to the battle of Princeton, including Washington's decision to return to New Jersey after the Trenton victory. Freeman and Flexner, in his Revolution volume, discuss the dramatic appeal to the troops by Washington and his officers, and the sergeant's recollection of Washington's words, while written long after the event, has the stamp of veracity—it is in Freeman, IV, 332. Smith, *The Battle of Princeton*, 10, has the details of Robert Morris's contribution to the war chest.

Since there is no satisfactory record of what was going on in Washington's mind at this time concerning future operations, I have surmised that he did not yet know what he was going to do, but was waiting to see what would develop. He put a close watch on the British, as Joseph Reed's foray toward Princeton indicates (an episode described by Smith, *The Battle of Princeton*, 11), but not until he received the spy's map from Cadwalader and interrogated Reed's prisoners did he have anything tangible to go on. (The map, incidentally, is reproduced in Bill, opp. page 100, and is from the Map Division, Library of Congress.)

Freeman, IV, 334, is the source of the story about Stephen Olney and the officer named Bridges.

CHAPTER SIX

1. We'll Bag Him in the Morning

For the movements of Cornwallis's forces out of Princeton and the size and subsequent division of his army, Smith's *The Battle of Princeton*, Bill, Stryker, and Ward, I, are all useful.

Colonel Edward Hand is described in Lossing, I, 247n., and his earlier experience with the riflemen at the siege of Boston is discussed by Ward, I, 106. Smith has the best coverage of Hand's delaying action between Princeton and Trenton, and there is a letter from Henry Knox in Brooks, 83–84, describing the final retreat to the bridge and the artillery action there. Sergeant White, who was with the artillery, also describes that night's events, and the mention of Grothausen's death appears in Stryker.

Bill and Stryker both mention Erskine's advocacy of a night attack on the rebel lines, and the Wickwires discuss the council of war held by Cornwallis, at which it was decided to hold off until morning.

Rodney's description of the scene on the morning of January 3 is in Freeman, IV, 349.

2. It Seemed to Strike an Awe upon Us

It is almost impossible to determine whose idea it was to move against Princeton. Several American officers, including St. Clair, later claimed credit for it, but no contemporary document sheds light on the question. As I have tried to indicate, some such move was almost certainly in Washington's mind prior to the moment of decision, and a combination of circumstances—Cadwalader's map, the intimate knowledge of the area possessed by certain officers, and the fact that he really had no appealing alternatives—persuaded him that the night march by his right flank was the only possible solution to a near-desperate problem. Having served on the frontier before the war, Washington was an improviser as this and other maneuvers indicate, he was daring, and he seems at times to have believed that his men were capable of executing a movement that a more conservative officer would have considered impossible. (His belief that Magaw's men could somehow be extricated from Fort Washington is a case in point.) And to all this must be added that strong streak of pride, which prompted him to remark that he wished to "avoid the appearance of a Retreat."

Here again, Smith's *The Battle of Princeton*, Stryker, Freeman, IV, Ward, I, and Bill contain most of the available information about the rebel army's movements, the events of the night march, and the commencement of the battle. Sergeant White has a highly personal, colorful description of the affair, continuing through the battle and its aftermath, and there is a good letter from Henry Knox in Brooks, 84.

Cadwalader's map is a key to the conduct of the battle, and I found a map drawn by E. Sandoz in January 1899—"A Plan of the Battle of Princeton"—immensely helpful in determining the route taken by various units of the rebel army after they crossed Stony Brook and headed toward the back road. This map also indicates the location of the modern highway to Trenton as well as most of the old landmarks, making it easier to place the action on a trip to the battlefield, and, although I cannot be certain of this, I suspect it was the basis of the excellent map which may be seen in the field opposite the Princeton battle monument. The series of situation maps in Wertenbaker's "The Battle of Princeton," though difficult to follow, are also valuable.

For the location of Princeton landmarks, I have relied also on Wertenbaker's article and his *Princeton*.

The remarks by the old man (traditionally, Thomas Olden) who witnessed the battle are both useful and interesting; they appear in Stryker and are also discussed in Wertenbaker's "The Battle of Princeton," 84–86.

3. Not a Man but Showed Joy

What little information I could find about Captain Moulder and the Philadelphia Associators was derived from a variety of sources—Wertenbaker's "The Battle of Princeton," Stryker, and Boatner, among others—and Ward's *The Delaware Continentals* is the source of Rodney's comments on the battle. The general works cited for the previous chapter are also helpful here.

Sergeant White told his own version of the battle and its aftermath in his *Narrative*, and Smith's *The Battle of Princeton* includes details of the damage to the town and the plundering of houses by Americans and British alike.

Here again, Knox's letter in Brooks, 85, is interesting for his view of the action, and Ensign Glyn's *Journal* has several references to the engagement, from the British vantage point.

4. A Time of Shaking

The incident involving Captain John Stryker is related by Stryker, 302.

A manuscript labeled "Boeking, Heinrich Ludwig," in possession of the Morristown National Historical Park, translated by Hans Mayer, the librarian, and given me by Dr. Francis Ronalds, is the source of the comment on the Hessians' fatigue on the road to Brunswick.

Ensign Glyn recorded Cornwallis's orders to the troops in his *Journal*, and Bill, 124, quotes Cornwallis's letter to Germain, citing his opinion that Washington could not subsist for long at Morristown.

Ambrose Serle's *Journal*, 168–71, has his remarks on the battle, including Andrew Allen's reaction.

Bill, 125–26, quotes Heister's letter and has some information on the preparations for Howe's investiture. Stryker, 482, gives Howe's comments to Germain.

Knox's pride in the American success is from the letter in Brooks, 85–86.

Cresswell's exasperation over the rebel triumph, written in Loudoun County, Virginia, where he got the news, is in his *Journal*, 179.

Harcourt's letter to his father appears in Commager and Morris, *The Spirit of 'Seventy-Six*, 524.

There is a most informative communication from a foreign visitor to London in Force, V, 3, 1048, on which I relied for the opinion about the average Englishman's state of mind. The calculation of the war's cost is in Force, V, 3, 1029. Trevelyan, 198–200, has the quotation from the Londoner criticizing British myopia when it came to maps. Stryker, 483, reprints Germain's letter to the Howes, and Trevelyan, 200, cites Frederick the Great's remarks.

Two useful sources on French plans are Pearson's *Those Damned Rebels*, in which Stormont's difficulties at the French court are described, and Whitridge's "Beaumarchais and the American Revolution." Pearson's book was published too recently to be of much aid to me, but it is a most interesting study of the war as it appeared to the English, and his accounts of Stormont's tribulations in the palace of Versailles are illuminating.

The unhappy saga of Catharine Van Cortlandt is reported fully in "A Loyalist's Wife," by Vernon-Jackson.

Belcher, II, 208, quotes Judge Jones on the difficulty of obtaining wood and food from New Jersey, and the Reverend Mr. Shewkirk's remarks are in Johnston, *The Campaign of 1776*, 124.

5. Not an Enemy in the Jersies

The observations of Stephen and Weedon are printed in Freeman, IV, 425–26.

Washington's instructions to fifers and drummers appear in Flexner's Revolution volume, 203, as does André's comment (page 205).

Knox's letter to his wife is reprinted in Brooks, 91–2.

Chatham's eloquent statement on the war, quoted briefly here, is cited fully in *Life of Pitt*, I, 61, by Earl Stanhope.

BIBLIOGRAPHY

ABBATT, WILLIAM. *The Battle of Pell's Point.* William Abbatt. Tarrytown, N.Y. New York, 1901.

ADAMS, CHARLES FRANCIS, Editor. *Familiar Letters of John Adams and His Wife Abigail Adams, During the Revolution.* With a Memoir of Mrs. Adams. Hurd & Houghton. New York, 1876.

ADAMS, JOHN. *Diary and Autobiography of John Adams.* 4 vols. L. H. Butterfield, Editor. Atheneum. New York, 1964.

ALDEN, JOHN RICHARD. *General Gage in America.* Louisiana State University Press. Baton Rouge, 1948.

———. *General Charles Lee: Traitor or Patriot?* Louisiana State University Press. Baton Rouge, 1951.

———. *A History of the American Revolution.* Alfred A. Knopf. New York, 1969.

———. *Pioneer America.* Alfred A. Knopf. New York, 1966.

ALT-LOSSBERG. Journal of the Honourable Fusilier von Alt-Lossberg. Morristown National Historical Park.

ANDERSON, TROYER STEELE. *The Command of the Howe Brothers During the American Revolution.* Oxford University Press. New York, 1936.

BAILYN, BERNARD, Editor. *Pamphlets of the American Revolution, 1750–1776.* 2 vols. Harvard University Press. Cambridge, 1965.

BAKELESS, JOHN. *Turncoats, Traitors and Heroes.* J. B. Lippincott. Philadelphia and New York, 1959.

BAURMEISTER, MAJOR. *Revolution in America: Confidential Letters and Journals 1776–1784 of Adjutant General Major Baurmeister of the Hessian Forces.* Bernhard A. Uhlendorf, Editor. Rutgers University Press. New Brunswick, 1957.

BECKER, CARL. *The Declaration of Independence: A Study in the History of Political Ideas.* Vintage Books. New York, 1942.

BELCHER, HENRY. *The First American Civil War.* 2 vols. Macmillan. London, 1911.

BERGEN COUNTY HISTORY: *1970 Annual.* Bergen County Historical Society. River Edge, N.J., 1970.

BILL, ALFRED HOYT. *The Campaign of Princeton, 1776–1777.* Princeton University Press. Princeton, 1948.

BILLIAS, GEORGE ATHAN. *General John Glover and his Marblehead Mariners.* Henry Holt. New York, 1960.

———, Editor. *George Washington's Generals.* William Morrow. New York, 1964.

BLIVEN, BRUCE, JR. *Battle for Manhattan.* Henry Holt. New York, 1955.

BOATNER, MARK MAYO, III. *Encyclopedia of the American Revolution.* David McKay. New York, 1966.

BOLTON, CHARLES KNOWLES. *The Private Soldier Under Washington*. George Newnes. London, 1902.

BOLTON, REGINALD PELHAM. "The Fighting Around New York City in 1776," in *Proceedings of the New York State Historical Association*, Vol. XXV, Quarterly Journal, Vol. VIII, 1927.

———. *Fort Washington: An Account of the Identification of the Site . . . with a History of the Defence and Reduction of Mount Washington*. The Empire State Society of the Sons of the American Revolution. New York, 1902.

BOWEN, CATHERINE DRINKER. *John Adams and the American Revolution*. Little, Brown. Boston, 1950.

BROOKS, NOAH. *Henry Knox: A Soldier of the Revolution*. G.P. Putnam. New York, 1900.

BURNETT, EDMUND CODY. *The Continental Congress*. W. W. Norton. New York, 1964.

CARRINGTON, HENRY B. *Battles of the American Revolution*. A. S. Barnes. New York, 1876.

CARY, JOHN. *Joseph Warren: Physician, Politician, Patriot*. University of Illinois Press. Urbana, 1961.

CHASTELLUX, FRANÇOIS JEAN, MARQUIS DE. *Travels in North America in the Years 1780, 1781 and 1782*. Revised translation with Introduction and Notes by Howard C. Rice, Jr. 2 vols. University of North Carolina Press. Chapel Hill, 1963.

COMMAGER, HENRY STEELE, and MORRIS, RICHARD B., Editors. *The Spirit of 'Seventy-Six*. Bobbs-Merrill. New York, 1958.

CRARY, CATHERINE SNELL. "The Tory and the Spy: The Double Life of James Rivington," in *William & Mary Quarterly*, Vol. XVI, No. 1, January 1959.

CRESSWELL, NICHOLAS. *The Journal of Nicholas Cresswell, 1774–1777*. Dial Press. New York, 1924.

CUMMING, WILLIAM P., and ELIZABETH C. "The Treasure of Alnwick Castle," in *American Heritage*, Vol. XX, No. 5, August 1969.

CUNLIFFE, MARCUS. *George Washington: Man and Monument*. New American Library. New York, 1958.

DECKER, MALCOLM. *Brink of Revolution: New York in Crisis, 1765–1776*. Argosy Antiquarian. New York, 1964.

DELANCEY, EDWARD F. *The Capture of Mount Washington—November 16th, 1776—The Result of Treason*. Reprinted from *The Magazine of History*, February, 1877.

DONOUGHUE, BERNARD. *British Politics and the American Revolution: The Path to War, 1773–75*. Macmillan. London, 1964.

DRAKE, FRANCIS S. *Life and Correspondence of Henry Knox*. Samuel G. Drake. Boston, 1873.

FALKNER, LEONARD. "A Spy for Washington," in *American Heritage*, Vol. VIII, No. 5, August 1957.

FAST, HOWARD, Editor. *The Selected Work of Tom Paine*. Duell, Sloan and Pearce. New York, 1945.

FLEXNER, JAMES THOMAS. *George Washington: The Forge of Experience*. Little, Brown. Boston, 1965.

——— *George Washington in the American Revolution*. Little, Brosn. Boston, 1967.

FONER, PHILIP S., Editor. *The Complete Writings of Thomas Paine.* 2 vols. Citadel Press. New York, 1945.

FORCE, PETER, Editor. *American Archives: Fourth Series, Containing a Documentary History of the English Colonies in North America from the King's Message to Parliament of March 7, 1774, to the Declaration of Independence by the United States.* 6 vols. M. St. Clair Clarke and Peter Force. Washington, D.C., 1837–1846.

———. *American Archives: Fifth Series, Containing a Documentary History of the United States of America from the Declaration of Independence, July 4, 1776, to the Definitive Treaty of Peace with Great Britain, September 3, 1783.* 3 vols. M. St. Clair Clarke and Peter Force. Washington, D.C., 1848–1853.

FREEMAN, DOUGLAS SOUTHALL. *George Washington.* 6 vols. Charles Scribner. New York, 1954.

FRENCH, ALLEN. *The First Year of the American Revolution.* Houghton Mifflin. Boston, 1934.

GIPSON, LAWRENCE HENRY. *The Coming of the Revolution, 1763–1775.* Harper & Row. New York, 1954.

———. *The Triumphant Empire: Britain Sails into the Storm, 1770–1776.* Alfred A. Knopf. New York, 1958.

GLYN, THOMAS. Ensign Glyn's Journal on the American Service with the Detachment of 1,000 Men of the Guards Commanded by Brigadier General Mathew in 1776. Princeton University Library.

GRAYDON, ALEXANDER. *Memoirs of His Own Time by Alexander Graydon.* J. S. Littell, Editor. Philadelphia, 1846.

GREENE, EVARTS BOUTELL. *The Revolutionary Generation, 1763–1790.* Macmillan. New York, 1956.

HALL, EDWARD HAGAMAN. *Margaret Corbin: Heroine of the Battle of Fort Washington, 16 November 1776.* American Scenic and Preservation Society. New York, 1932.

HART, GEORGE VAUGHAN. Letters of George Vaughan Hart, September 1775 to October 1777. Collection of George V. Hart.

HEATH, WILLIAM. *Heath's Memoirs of the American War.* A. Wessels. New York, 1904.

HEITMAN, FRANCIS B. *Historical Register of Officers of the Continental Army.* Rare Book Shop Publishing Company. Washington, D.C., 1914.

HOWE, SIR WILLIAM. *Orderly Books, November 15, 1775–May 23, 1778.* Collections of The New-York Historical Society for the Year 1883. New York, 1884.

JOHNSTON, HENRY P. *The Campaign of 1776 Around New York and Brooklyn.* Long Island Historical Society. Brooklyn, 1878.

———. *Observations on Judge Jones' Loyalist History of the American Revolution: How Far Is It an Authority?* D. Appleton. New York, 1880.

JONES, THOMAS. *History of New York During the Revolutionary War.* 2 vols. New-York Historical Society. New York, 1879.

KEMBLE PAPERS. 2 vols. Collections of The New-York Historical Society for the Year 1883. New York, 1884.

KETCHUM, RICHARD M., Editor. *The American Heritage Book of the Revolution.* Narrative by Bruce Lancaster and J. H. Plumb. American Heritage Publishing Co. New York, 1958.

———. *The Battle for Bunker Hill*. Doubleday. Garden City, N.Y., 1962.

———. "England's Vietnam: The American Revolution," in *American Heritage*, Vol. XXII, No. 4, June 1971.

———. "New War Letters of Banastre Tarleton," in *The New-York Historical Society Quarterly*, Vol. LI, No. 1, January 1967.

KNOLLENBERG, BERNHARD. *John Adams, Knox, and Washington*. American Antiquarian Society. Worcester, Mass., 1947.

———. *Origin of the American Revolution, 1759–1766*. Macmillan. New York, 1960.

KOKE, RICHARD J. "Forcing the Hudson River Passage: October 9, 1776," in *The New-York Historical Society Quarterly*, Vol. XXXVI, No. 4, October 1952.

LAING, ALEXANDER. *American Ships*. American Heritage Press. New York, 1971.

LEIBY, ADRIAN C., in collaboration with ALBERT T. KLYBERG, JR. and EMORIE A. LEIBY. *The Huguenot Settlement of Schraalenburgh: The History of Bergenfield, New Jersey*. Bergenfield Free Public Library. Bergenfield, 1964.

———. *The Revolutionary War in the Hackensack Valley*. Rutgers University Press. New Brunswick, N.J., 1962.

LLOYD, ALAN. *The King Who Lost America: A Portrait of the Life and Times of George III*. Doubleday. Garden City, N.Y., 1971.

LOSSING, B. J. *Pictorial Field Book of the Revolution*. 2 vols. Harper Brothers. New York, 1850.

LOWELL, EDWARD J. *The Hessians and the Other German Auxiliaries of Great Britain in the Revolutionary War*. New York, 1884. Reprint of original by University Microfilms. Ann Arbor, Mich., 1960.

MACALPINE, IDA, and HUNTER, RICHARD. *George III and the Mad-Business*. Pantheon Books, New York, 1970.

MACKENZIE, FREDERICK. *Diary*. 2 vols. Harvard University Press. Cambridge, 1930.

MACKESY, PIERS. *The War for America: 1775–1783*. Harvard University Press. Cambridge, 1964.

MAIN, JACKSON TURNER. *The Social Structure of Revolutionary America*. Princeton University Press. Princeton, 1965.

MALONE, DUMAS, MILHOLLEN, HIRST, and KAPLAN, MILTON. *The Story of the Declaration of Independence*. Oxford University Press. New York, 1954.

MARTIN, JOSEPH PLUMB. *Private Yankee Doodle*. George F. Scheer, Editor. Little, Brown. Boston, 1962.

MATTHEWS, WILLIAM, Compiler. *British Diaries: An Annotated Bibliography of British Diaries Written between 1442 and 1942*. University of California Press. Berkeley and Los Angeles, 1950.

MAUROIS, ANDRÉ. *A History of England*. Farrar, Straus & Cudahy. New York, 1958.

MEIGS, CORNELIA. *The Violent Men*. Macmillan. New York, 1949.

MERCANTILE LIBRARY ASSOCIATION. *New York City during the American Revolution*. New York, 1861.

MILLER, JOHN C. *Sam Adams: Pioneer in Propaganda*. Little, Brown. Boston, 1936.

———. *Origins of the American Revolution*. Little, Brown and Company. Boston, 1943.

MONTROSS, LYNN. *Rag, Tag, and Bobtail*. Harper & Brothers. New York, 1952.

MOORE, FRANK. *Diary of the American Revolution*. 2 vols. Charles Scribner. New York, 1858.

MORRIS, RICHARD B. *The American Revolution Reconsidered*. Harper & Row. New York, 1967.

MORSE, JEDIDIAH. *Annals of the American Revolution*. Hartford, 1824.

NATIONAL MARITIME MUSEUM, Greenwich, England: A Journal for His Majesty's Ship the Pearl, beginning the 30th of December 1775 and ending the 30th of December 1777; by Lieutenant Wm. Nicholl.

———. A Journal of the Proceedings on board His Majesty's Ship Pearl, Thomas Wilkinson Esq. Commander, Kept by William Scott, Lieutenant, 1776 & 1777.

———. A Journal of the Proceedings of His Majesty's Ship Pearl, Captain Thomas Wilkinson, Commander, between the 11th of January 1776 and the 13th of February 1777.

O'DEA, ARTHUR J. *Washington and his Army in Bergen County*. Bergen County Bar Association. Hackensack, 1957.

PAINE, THOMAS. *Common Sense and The Crisis*. Dolphin Books. Garden City, N.Y., 1960.

PARTRIDGE, BELLAMY. *Sir Billy Howe*. Longmans, Green. New York, 1932.

PATTERSON, SAMUEL WHITE. *Knight Errant of Liberty: The Triumph and Tragedy of General Charles Lee*. Lantern Press. New York, 1958.

PEARSON, MICHAEL. *Those Damned Rebels: The American Revolution as Seen Through British Eyes*. G. P. Putnam. New York, 1972.

PEEBLES, CAPTAIN JOHN. Journal. Morristown National Historical Park.

PLUMB, J. H. *England in the Eighteenth Century*. Penguin Books. Baltimore, 1966.

———. *The First Four Georges*. John Wiley & Sons, Inc. New York, 1967.

———. "Our Last King," in *American Heritage*, Vol. XI, No. 4, June 1960.

PUTNAM, ISRAEL. *Memoirs of the Life, Adventures, and Military Exploits of Israel Putnam*. Evert Duyckinck. New York, 1815.

ROBSON, ERIC. *The American Revolution in its Political and Military Aspects, 1763–1783*. Oxford University Press. New York, 1955.

———, Editor. *Letters from America*. Barnes & Noble, Inc. New York, 1950.

———. "The War of American Independence Reconsidered," in *History Today*, Vol. II, No. 5, May 1952.

SABINE, LORENZO. *The American Loyalists*. Charles C. Little & James Brown. Boston, 1847.

SCHEER, GEORGE F., and RANKIN, HUGH F. *Rebels and Redcoats*. World Publishing Company. Cleveland and New York, 1956.

SERLE, AMBROSE. *The American Journal of Ambrose Serle, Secretary to Lord Howe, 1776–1778*. Edward H. Tatum, Jr., Editor. Huntington Library, San Marino, Calif., 1940.

SHIPTON, CLIFFORD K. *New England Life in the 18th Century.* Harvard University Press. Cambridge, 1963.

SHY, JOHN. *Toward Lexington: The Role of the British Army in the Coming of the American Revolution.* Princeton University Press. Princeton, 1965.

SINGLETON, ESTHER. *Social New York Under the Georges, 1714–1776.* D. Appleton. New York, 1902.

SMITH, PAUL H. *Loyalists and Redcoats: A Study in British Revolutionary Policy.* University of North Carolina Press. Chapel Hill, 1964.

SMITH, SAMUEL STELLE. *The Battle of Princeton.* Philip Freneau Press. Monmouth Beach, N.J., 1967.

———. *The Battle of Trenton.* Philip Freneau Press. Monmouth Beach, N.J., 1965.

SOSIN, JACK M. *Agents and Merchants: British Colonial Policy and the Origins of the American Revolution, 1763–1775.* University of Nebraska Press. Lincoln, 1965.

STIRKE, LIEUTENANT HENRY. "A British Officer's Revolutionary War Journal, 1776–1778," S. Sydney Bradford, Editor, in *Maryland Historical Magazine,* Vol. 56, No. 1, June 1961.

STRYKER, WILLIAM S. *The Old Barracks at Trenton, New Jersey.* Trenton, 1885.

———. *The Battles of Trenton and Princeton.* Houghton, Mifflin. Boston, 1898.

SWIGGETT, HOWARD. *The Extraordinary Mr. Morris.* Doubleday. Garden City, N.Y., 1952.

SYRETT, HAROLD C., Editor. *The Papers of Alexander Hamilton,* Vol. I. Columbia University Press. New York, 1961.

THACHER, JAMES. *Military Journal During the American Revolutionary War.* Silas Andrus. Hartford, Conn., 1854.

THAYER, THEODORE. *Nathanael Greene: Strategist of the American Revolution.* Twayne Publishers. New York, 1960.

TOURTELLOT, ARTHUR BERNON. *William Diamond's Drum.* Doubleday. Garden City, N.Y., 1959.

———. *A Bibliography of the Battles of Concord and Lexington.* Privately published. New York, 1959.

TREVELYAN, GEORGE OTTO. *The American Revolution.* One-volume condensation edited by Richard B. Morris. David McKay. New York, 1964.

TRUMBULL, JOHN. *The Autobiography of Colonel John Trumbull.* Theodore Sizer, Editor. Yale University Press. New Haven, 1953.

VAN DOREN, CARL. *Benjamin Franklin.* Viking Press. New York, 1938.

———. *Secret History of the American Revolution.* Viking Press. New York, 1941.

VERNON-JACKSON, H. O. H. "A Loyalist's Wife: Letters of Mrs. Philip Van Cortlandt, December 1776 to February 1777," in *History Today,* August 1964.

WADE, HERBERT T., and LIVELY, ROBERT A. *This Glorious Cause* . . . Princeton University Press. Princeton, 1958.

WALPOLE, HORACE. *The Letters of Horace Walpole,* Vol. VI. John Grant. Edinburgh, 1906.

WARD, CHRISTOPHER L. *The Delaware Continentals, 1776–1783.* Historical Society of Delaware. Wilmington, 1941.

———. *The War of the Revolution.* 2 vols. Macmillan. New York, 1952.

WEBB, SAMUEL BLACHLEY. *Correspondence and Journals*. Collected and edited by Worthington Chauncey Ford. Vol. I. New York, 1893.

WERTENBAKER, THOMAS JEFFERSON. "The Battle of Princeton," in *The Princeton Battle Monument*. Princeton University Press. Princeton, 1922.

————. *The Founding of American Civilization: The Middle Colonies*. Charles Scribner. New York, 1949.

————. *Princeton, 1746–1896*. Princeton University Press. Princeton, 1946.

WHITE, J. *A Narrative of Events as they Occurred from Time to Time in the Revolutionary War* . . . Charlestown, Mass. 1833.

WHITRIDGE, ARNOLD. "Beaumarchais and the American Revolution," in *History Today*, February 1967.

WHITTEMORE, CHARLES P. *A General of the Revolution: John Sullivan of New Hampshire*. Columbia University Press. New York, 1961.

WICKWIRE, FRANKLIN and MARY. *Cornwallis: The American Adventure*. Houghton Mifflin. Boston, 1970.

INDEX